God's Word Alone is both a fitting t[...] sake and a constructive contributio[...] own right. *Sola Scriptura* has becon[...] in contemporary theology, but Barrett's book goes a long way to correcting modern and postmodern caricatures of the doctrine. I particularly appreciated the chapters on the Reformers' own understanding of Scripture as the supreme and final authority for the church and how this is rooted in its being the only wholly reliable authority, a consequence of its nature as divinely authored and inspired. Barrett here covers all the theological bases—biblical, historical, and systematic—as one might expect of a home run.

KEVIN J. VANHOOZER, Research Professor of Systematic
Theology, Trinity Evangelical Divinity School

Perhaps the greatest crisis in the evangelical world today is the loss of any meaningful commitment to the functional authority of Scripture. While lip service is paid to biblical "inspiration" and perhaps even some sense of the Bible's "infallibility," the final, functional authority of inerrant Scripture to govern both our beliefs and behavior has gradually disappeared. This alone makes Matthew Barrett's book on *sola Scriptura* so essential to the church in our day. If the Bible, and the Bible alone, isn't our final and determinative authority, the church will have lost its bearings and be cast hopelessly adrift on the sea of personal subjectivity. It is a massive understatement to say this book is much needed today. I cannot recommend it too highly.

SAM STORMS, Lead Pastor for Preaching and Vision,
Bridgeway Church, Oklahoma City, OK

The 500th anniversary of Luther's nailing the ninety-five theses to the door of the chapel of the Wittenberg Castle provides an eminently suitable occasion to remind ourselves of one of the five *solas* of the Reformation: *sola Scriptura*, "Scripture alone." Matthew Barrett takes his readers through some of the controversies surrounding the Bible that have arisen across this last half millennium and competently demonstrates the relevance of the doctrine of Scripture in our day. In the final analysis, the issue is revelation: What is the locus of God's gracious self-disclosure—God generously giving up his privacy, as Carl Henry used to say?

D. A. CARSON, Research Professor of New Testament,
Trinity Evangelical Divinity School

Matthew Barrett's *God's Word Alone* is a comprehensive discussion of the nature and role of Scripture. He deals with the church's historical controversies, especially during the Reformation period, with the place of God's speech during the history of redemption, and with all the topics of current discussion including inerrancy, clarity, and sufficiency. Barrett's knowledge is very broad and his position thoroughly biblical. I pray that God will give it a wide distribution.

JOHN M. FRAME, J. D. Trimble Professor
of Systematic Theology and Philosophy,
Reformed Theological Seminary Orlando

The Reformation doctrine of *sola Scriptura* teaches that the Bible is the only infallible and sufficient rule for Christian faith and practice. Matthew Barrett's new study provides persuasive evidence that this doctrine is firmly rooted not only in the Reformation but in the early church and in Scripture itself. In very readable prose, Barrett graciously provides thoughtful and nuanced responses to the objections of critics of this doctrine. Moreover, he demonstrates that the doctrine of biblical inerrancy has resided as a central teaching of the Western churches since the patristic era. This is a welcomed and much-needed resource for Christians in a day in which much confusion exists regarding the doctrines of *sola Scriptura* and biblical inerrancy. For this reason, the volume belongs in the libraries not only of teachers, seminary students, and pastors but laypersons as well. Highly recommended.

JOHN D. WOODBRIDGE, Research Professor of
Church History and Christian Thought, Trinity
Evangelical Divinity School, Deerfield, Illinois

This book—what a feast! Appetizing opening chapters recount how the Bible's authority came to be trashed in the modern West, even in many church circles. Then comes the main course: how God's saving work and presence have always intertwined with his written Word. Lastly, dessert: tasty slices of Scripture's truth, clarity, and sufficiency. A world awash in error and self-destruction cries out for meaning and direction. This book shows why skepticism of Scripture is a bad idea, and why devoting ourselves to studying, living, and spreading the Word of God written—inspired, inerrant, and authoritative—holds such promise, for this world and the next.

ROBERT W. YARBROUGH, Professor of New Testament,
Covenant Theological Seminary, St. Louis, Missouri

Matthew Barrett's book on the authority of Scripture is a welcome addition to the growing number of recent books on Scripture. I loved the richly theological texture of the book. From beginning to end we are treated to a deep and careful reflection on what is entailed in the recognition of Scripture as the Word of God written. The Bible's own teaching rightly has a prominent place. The teaching of the Reformers is appropriately a particular interest, given the series in which this volume appears. Modern and postmodern challenges, and the detailed, informed responses that have been made to them, are given due attention. Yet Barrett keeps drawing the lines of connection to the person and character of the God whose word Scripture is. Assaults on the Word of God go back to the garden of Eden. Ultimately they each involve an assault upon the person, character, and purpose of God even when this is not the conscious intent of those involved. Here is an articulate, informed, edifying, and persuasive account of why the Reformation doctrine of *sola Scriptura* should be taught, celebrated, and defended—not only against those who would deny it but also against those who claim to hold it while perhaps defining it in a way that unwittingly exalts the individual ("Scripture alone" doesn't mean "me alone"). I expect to be recommending this book often.

MARK D THOMPSON, Principal, Moore Theological College, Sydney

Without belief in Scripture alone as our supreme and trustworthy authority, the very faith of the church must totter. Dr. Barrett has mounted an impressive defence of the key Reformation doctrine of Scripture, demonstrating just how vital it remains today. This book will do great good in grounding the faith of a new generation.

MICHAEL REEVES, President and Professor of Theology,
Union School of Theology, Oxford, England

Sometimes the doctrine of Scripture is treated as separate from the other doctrines of Christianity—as a sort of preamble to the faith. Helpfully, Barrett draws in the Bible's own Trinitarian, covenantal, and salvation-historical themes to offer a persuasive alternative to various attempts to evade scriptural authority. It's an argument, to be sure, but also an edifying essay that helps us to understand what we're doing when we submit our reason to God's judging and saving speech.

MICHAEL HORTON, J. G. Machen Professor of Systematic Theology and Apologetics, Westminster Seminary California; author of *The Christian Faith: A Systematic Theology for Pilgrims on the Way*

I welcome this fresh study of the formal principle of the Reformation—the belief that God's written Word is the inspired norm by which all other religious authorities and traditions must be judged. Evangelicals are gospel people and Bible people, and this book shows why adherence to the latter is crucial for the advance of the former.

TIMOTHY GEORGE, founding dean, Beeson Divinity School of Samford University; general editor of the *Reformation Commentary on Scripture*

On the foundation of a careful examination of the confession of biblical authority and challenges to that confession from the Reformation through postmodern debates within evangelical circles, Barrett's work sets for a nuanced proposal for the utterly reliable, error-free Scriptures which center on God's coming to earth as Jesus Christ. Barrett's Trinitarian presentation of the metanarrative from creation in Genesis to the last day in Revelation offers readers useful patterns for presenting and applying the Bible and its message within the twenty-first-century context.

ROBERT KOLB, Professor Emeritus of Systematic Theology, Concordia Seminary, St. Louis, Missouri

Every generation must think afresh what the foundations of its faith are. The Bible is the unchanging Word of God, but our perceptions of its role and relevance deepen as we confront new challenges that our mission to the world throws up. In this clearly presented and closely argued book, Dr. Barrett takes us through the main issues of our time, showing how and why they have arisen and offering ways and means by which they may be addressed. This is a key work and a valuable resource for pastors, teachers, and students alike.

GERALD BRAY, Research Professor of Divinity, Beeson Divinity School, Samford University

God's Word ALONE

THE AUTHORITY OF SCRIPTURE

The Five Solas Series

Edited by Matthew Barrett

THE **5 SOLAS** SERIES

God's Word

ALONE

THE AUTHORITY OF
SCRIPTURE

What the Reformers Taught . . .
and Why It Still Matters

MATTHEW BARRETT

FOREWORD BY R. ALBERT MOHLER JR.

ZONDERVAN

God's Word Alone—The Authority of Scripture
Copyright © 2016 by Matthew M. Barrett

This title is also available as a Zondervan ebook.

Requests for information should be addressed to:
Zondervan, *3900 Sparks Dr. SE, Grand Rapids, Michigan 49546*

Library of Congress Cataloging-in-Publication Data

Names: Barrett, Matthew, 1982- author.
Title: God's word alone— the authority of scripture: what the reformers taught . . . and
    why it still matters / Matthew Barrett.
Description: Grand Rapids: Zondervan, 2016. | Series: The five Solas series | Includes
    bibliographical references and index.
Identifiers: LCCN 2016012911 | ISBN 9780310515722 (softcover)
Subjects: LCSH: Bible—Evidences, authority, etc. | Reformed Church—Doctrines.
Classification: LCC BS480 .B3545 2016 | DDC 220.1/3—dc23 LC record available at
    https://lccn.loc.gov/2016012911

Cover design: Christopher Tobias/Outerwear for Books
Interior design: Kait Lamphere

Printed in the United States of America

HB 01.06.2022

To my mother,
for giving me the sacred Scriptures.
"Jesus loves me this I know,
for the Bible tells me so."

Verbum Domini Manet in Aeternum
"The Word of the Lord endures forever"

Contents

Part 1: God's Word under Fire, Yesterday and Today

Part 2: God's Word in Redemptive History

Part 3: The Character of God's Word and Contemporary Challenges

A Note from the Series Editor

What doctrines could be more foundational to what it means to be an evangelical Protestant than the five *solas* (or *solae*) of the Reformation? In my experience, however, many in evangelical churches today have never heard of *sola Scriptura* (Scripture alone), *sola gratia* (grace alone), *sola fide* (faith alone), *solus Christus* (Christ alone), and *soli Deo gloria* (glory to God alone).

Now it could be that they have never heard the labels but would recognize the doctrines once told what each *sola* means. At least I pray so. But my suspicion is that for many churchgoers, even the content of these five *solas* is foreign, or worse, offensive. We live in a day when Scripture's authority is questioned, the exclusivity of Christ as mediator as well as the necessity of saving faith are offensive to pluralistic ears, and the glory of God in vocation is diminished by cultural accommodation as well as by individual and ecclesiastical narcissism. The temptation is to think that these five *solas* are museum pieces of a bygone era with little relevance for today's church. We disagree. We need these *solas* just as much today as the Reformers needed them in the sixteenth century.

The year 2017 will mark the 500th anniversary of the Reformation. These five volumes, written by some of the best theologians today, celebrate that anniversary. Our aim is not merely to look to the past but to the present, demonstrating that we must drink deeply from the wells of the five *solas* in order to recover our theological bearings and find spiritual refreshment.

Post tenebras lux

Matthew Barrett, series editor

Foreword

As we approach the 500th anniversary of the Reformation, I am tremendously grateful for the literature that faithful Protestant and evangelical scholars are producing that advances the great truths recovered by Luther, Calvin, and the other Reformers. We must always remember that what was at stake in the Reformation was nothing less than the authority of Scripture and the gospel of Jesus Christ.

Many historians note that two driving principles served as the engine to Reformation theology. The material principle of the Reformation was *sola fide*—the doctrine of justification by faith alone. This central emphasis in Luther's theology was not only the truth of the gospel that liberated him from perpetual guilt and "swung open the gates of heaven" but it was also the public rally point for the Reformation. The truth that sinful man could be justified by faith alone, apart from works of the law and apart from the sacramental system of Rome, ignited the firestorm of the Reformation in sixteenth-century Europe.

Yet behind this "material principle" of the Reformation was a deeper and perhaps even more fundamental commitment—*sola Scriptura*, or the affirmation that the Bible alone is the ultimate authority for life and doctrine. Historians refer to *sola Scriptura* as the formal principle of the Reformation, the doctrine that shaped the contours of Reformation conviction. It was this commitment to the ultimate authority of Scripture that gave the Reformers the courage to separate with Rome in their proclamation of the gospel.

True Christianity and true gospel preaching depend on a firm commitment to the authority of Scripture. That is why, since the time of the Reformation, the inspiration, inerrancy, and authority of Scripture have been under constant attack. In the Enlightenment, modernist philosophers like Descartes, Locke, and Kant confronted Western culture with a series of questions that ultimately transformed the notion of truth in the Western mind. The result was a totalitarian imposition of the scientific model of rationality upon all truth, the claim that only scientific data can be objectively understood, objectively defined, and objectively defended. In other words, the modernist worldview did not allow for the notion of special revelation and openly attacked the possibility of supernatural intervention in world history. Modernity thus presented the church of the Lord Jesus Christ with a significant intellectual crisis.

In the United States, there was a quintessentially American philosophy that developed, known as pragmatism, that also challenged the ultimate authority and truthfulness of Scripture. Pragmatism was the idea that truth is a matter of social negotiation and that ideas are merely instrumental tools whose truthfulness will be determined by whether they meet the particular needs of the present time. In the eyes of the pragmatists, ideas were nothing but provisional responses to actual challenges, and truth, by definition, was relative to the time, place, need, and person.

As most of us are aware, modernity has given way to postmodernity, which is simply modernity in its latest guise. Postmodernism is nothing more than the logical extension of modernism in a new mood. Claiming that all notions of truth are socially constructed, postmodernists are committed to total war on truth itself, a deconstructionist project bent on the casting down of all religious, philosophical, political, and cultural authorities. A postmodernist ahead of his times, Karl Marx warned that in the light of modernity, "all that is solid melts into air."

The only way to escape the rationalist claims of modernism or the hermeneutical nihilism of postmodernism is the doctrine of revelation—a return to the doctrine of *sola Scriptura*. Christians must remember that in the doctrine of the inspiration and authority of Scripture bequeathed to us by the Reformers, we can have confidence in God's Word in spite of the philosophical and theological problems of the age. God has spoken to us in a reasonable way, in language we can understand, and has given us the gift of revelation, which is his willful disclosure of himself. As Carl F. H. Henry stated, special revelation is nothing less than God's own forfeiture of his personal privacy so that we might know him.

Indeed, the war against the authority and truth of Scripture has been raging since the Reformation and has continued into our own generation. Back in 1990, theologian J. I. Packer recounted what he called a "Thirty Years' War" over the inerrancy and authority of the Bible. He traced his involvement in this war in its American context back to a conference held in Wenham, Massachusetts in 1966, when he confronted some professors from evangelical institutions who "now declined to affirm the full truth of Scripture." That was fifty years ago, and the war over the truthfulness of the Bible is still not over—not by a long shot.

As Evangelicals, we must recognize that as the theological heirs of the Reformers, we cannot capitulate to revisionist models of the doctrine of Scripture. An affirmation of the divine inspiration and authority of the Bible has stood at the center of the Reformed faith since the sixteenth century. We are those who confess along with the Reformers that when Scripture speaks, God speaks. Scripture alone is the ultimate authority for life and doctrine. In a sense, Reformed theology hangs on the accuracy of that singular proposition.

The theology of the Reformation cannot long survive without the church's explicit commitment to the authority of Scripture above all else. Without the authority of Scripture, our theological convictions are merely conjectures and our preaching becomes nothing more than a display of human folly. As the Reformers understood and taught, *sola Scriptura* is vital for the life of the church. Scripture is the fount from which flows all faithful preaching, discipleship, and worship.

Matthew Barrett's *God's Word Alone* is a faithful restatement of the Reformation doctrine of *sola Scriptura*. Barrett carefully and compellingly argues for the divine inspiration and ultimate authority of Scripture. Barrett also shows that Scripture claims for itself the attributes of inerrancy, clarity, and sufficiency. He does all of this with careful attention to the modern theological challenges that have attempted to overthrow a biblical doctrine of Scripture. This is the type of book of which the Reformers would have been proud. This is the type of book the church needs today.

As we approach the 500th anniversary of the Reformation, my hope is that the theology of the Reformers finds new life in the modern church. The health of the church is directly connected to the strength of our commitment to the authority and truthfulness of Scripture. Let this book fuel that commitment, strengthen your confidence in God's Word, and compel you to be faithful to the gospel.

R. Albert Mohler Jr.

President, The Southern Baptist Theological Seminary

Acknowledgments

This book is not longer than other books I have written. However, it has been the most difficult book I have written so far. The reason is simple: the enormous importance of the doctrine of Scripture was a heavy weight on my shoulders as I wrote.

Much hangs in the balance today when it comes to the doctrine of Scripture. Few doctrines have come under such severe attack in the modern era. The twenty-first century is no exception. Yet few doctrines could be more important to the evangelical faith. So in writing this volume, I felt an incredible duty to get it right. As much as I hope the reader will benefit from this book, ultimately it was not the reader I was most concerned about, but God himself. After all, I am dealing with his holy, sacred Word, and I tremble lest I fail to take God seriously (Isa 66:2). Therefore, I have an audience of one, and it is his opinion I care about above any other.

That said, in my labor over this manuscript, I had the support of so many people. I cannot name them all here, but a few deserve mention. First, I would like to begin by thanking Ryan Pazdur, who invited me to edit this series and has improved each book by his editorial pen. Ryan has guided this series from start to finish. Without his vision for this series, as well as his editorial skills, there wouldn't be one! I am also thankful to the Zondervan staff, particularly Jesse Hillman, who has worked hard to make sure the end product is superb and that it gets into the hands of readers.

I am also indebted to many friends and colleagues who spent time offering feedback, especially Fred Zaspel, Thomas Schreiner, J. V. Fesko, Michael Haykin, Chris Castaldo, Korey Maas, and Robert Kolb, who read the manuscript early on and improved it in countless ways with their insights. My gratitude also extends to James Grant, who devoted time to improving the work.

But perhaps the person I am most indebted to is my wife, Elizabeth. She has been so generous. Her patience with me while I finish a thought and am late to dinner, her flexibility in allowing hundreds of books to flood our house all in the name of "research," and her constant dialogue with me on the topic of this book demonstrate her love and care not only for me but for the Word of God. Seeing a mother of four rise early each morning so that she can read her Bible is a visual reminder to me why I ventured to write this book in the first place.

Last, I want to dedicate this book to my mother, for she first gave me the Scriptures. The mothers of Timothy, Augustine, and so many others had irreplaceable roles in the conversions of their sons. I can say the same. Thank you, Mom, for telling me about Jesus at a young age. God used your gospel words to shine light into my darkness. And your support ever since has been invaluable. This book is for you.

Semper Reformanda

Matthew Barrett

London, 2015

Abbreviations

ANF	*Ante-Nicene Fathers*
ApOTC	Apollos Old Testament Commentary
BCOTWP	Baker Commentary on the Old Testament Wisdom and Psalms
BECNT	Baker Exegetical Commentary on the New Testament
BSac	*Bibliotheca Sacra*
CD	*Church Dogmatics*
CWMS	*The Complete Writings of Menno Simons.* Edited by John C. Wenger. Scottdale, PA: Herald Press, 1956.
DLGTT	Richard A. Muller. *Dictionary of Latin and Greek Theological Terms: Drawn Principally from Protestant Scholastic Theology.* Grand Rapids: Baker, 1985.
EBC	Expositor's Bible Commentary
JETS	*Journal of the Evangelical Theological Society*
LCC	Library of Christian Classics. Edited by J. Baillie et al. 26 vols. Philadelphia: Westminster, 1953–66.
LW	*Luther's Works.* Edited by J. Pelikan and H. Lehmann. 55 vols. American edition. St. Louis and Philadelphia: Concordia, 1955–86.
NAC	New American Commentary
NICNT	New International Commentary on the New Testament
NICOT	New International Commentary on the Old Testament
NIGTC	New International Greek Testament Commentary
NIVAC	NIV Application Commentary
NPNF[1]	*Nicene and Post-Nicene Fathers*, Series 1
NPNF[2]	*Nicene and Post-Nicene Fathers*, Series 2
OTL	Old Testament Library
PNTC	Pillar New Testament Commentaries

PRRD   Richard A. Muller. *Post-Reformation Reformed Dogmatics.* 4 vols. 2nd ed. Grand Rapids: Baker Academic, 2003.

PS   *Patrologia Syriaca.* Rev. ed. Ignatio Ortiz de Urbina. Rome: Pontifical Biblical Institute, 1965.

TJ   *Trinity Journal*

TNTC   Tyndale New Testament Commentaries

TOTC   Tyndale Old Testament Commentaries

WA   *D. Martin Luthers Werke: Kritische Gesamtausgabe.* 66 vols. Weimar: Hermann Böhlaus Nachfolger, 1883–1987.

Z   *Huldreich Zwinglis Sämtliche Werke.* Edited by Emil Egli, George Finsler, et al. Corpus Reformatorum. Vols. 88–101. Berlin, Leipzig, Zürich, 1905–56.

ZECNT   Zondervan Exegetical Commentary on the New Testament

Introduction

Sola Scriptura

> Scripture alone is the true lord and master of all
> writings and doctrine on earth. If that is not granted,
> what is Scripture good for? The more we reject it,
> the more we become satisfied with men's books and
> human teachers. —*Martin Luther*
>
> I approve only of those human institutions which are
> founded upon the authority of God and derived from
> Scripture. —*John Calvin*
>
> *Sola Scriptura* "is the corner-stone of universal
> Protestantism; and on it Protestantism stands, or else
> it falls." —*B. B. Warfield*

"So what if everything in the Bible isn't true and reliable or from God? That doesn't really matter, does it? The Bible still remains an authority in my life." Though it has been years now, I remember hearing these words as if it were yesterday. I had no idea what to say in response.

I was shocked because I was hearing these words from a churchgoing, Bible-carrying, evangelical Christian. This person saw no relation between the truthfulness of Scripture and the authority of Scripture, as if one had nothing to do with the other.

In that moment I realized two things: First, the Reformation doctrine of *sola Scriptura* is just as important today as it was in the sixteenth century. In the sixteenth century the Reformers faced off against Rome because the Roman church had elevated tradition and its magisterium to the level of Scripture. Nevertheless, Rome still believed Scripture itself was inspired by God and therefore inerrant, that is, trustworthy, true, and without error.[1]

---

1. Rome did not use the term *inerrant*, but the concept itself was affirmed.

21

Since the sixteenth century, Protestantism (and its view of the Bible) has undergone an evolution in its identity. Movements such as the Enlightenment, Liberalism, and, more recently, postmodernism have elevated other voices to the level of Scripture or even above Scripture, and the inspiration and inerrancy of Scripture have been abandoned, something Rome never would have done in the sixteenth century. Today, many people reject that the Bible is God-breathed and truthful in all it asserts.

As Carl Henry pointed out in his magnum opus, *God, Revelation, and Authority,* the church throughout history has faced repeated attacks on the Bible from skeptics, but only in the nineteenth and twentieth centuries have the truthfulness and trustworthiness of God's Word been questioned, criticized, and abandoned by those within the body of Christ.[2] To the Reformers, this would have been unthinkable, yet this is the day we live in. Not only do Bible critics pervade the culture but now they have mounted the pulpit and sit comfortably in the pews.

If Carl Henry is right, then there is legitimate cause for alarm. Repeated attacks on Scripture's own character reveal the enmity and hostility toward the God of the Bible within our own souls.[3] One of the most significant needs in the twenty-first century is a call back to the Bible to a posture that encourages reverence, acceptance, and adherence to its authority and message.

Along with the realization that *sola Scriptura* is just as applicable today as it was in the sixteenth century, I also saw that many Christians in the church have no idea what *sola Scriptura* is or what it entails. What is the relationship of the authority of the Bible to attributes such as inspiration, inerrancy, clarity, and sufficiency? Even if we accept that the Bible alone is our final authority, we may have no idea *why* this is true. Is it because the Bible is the best guidebook we can find?

These questions led me to carefully study the massive shifts in authority that have taken place since the Reformation. I wanted to better understand the relationship between biblical authority and the nature of Scripture, namely, its own inspiration, inerrancy, clarity, and sufficiency. In this book, we will begin by exploring the past

---

2. Carl F. H. Henry, *God Who Speaks and Shows: Fifteen Theses, Part Three,* vol. 4, *God, Revelation, and Authority* (repr. Wheaton, IL: Crossway, 1999), 17, 374.

3. J. van Genderen and W. H. Velema, *Concise Reformed Dogmatics,* trans. Gerrit Bilkes and ed. M. van der Maas (Phillipsburg, NJ: P&R, 2008), 73.

so that we better understand the present, and we will address each of these key attributes to retrieve this indispensable doctrine for the church today.

What is *Sola Scriptura*?

The title of this book is *God's Word Alone: The Authority of Scripture*, which is another way of saying *sola Scriptura*. But what is *sola Scriptura*? *Sola Scriptura* means that *only Scripture, because it is God's inspired Word, is our inerrant, sufficient, and final authority for the church.*

First, this means that Scripture alone is our *final* authority. *Authority* is a bad word in our day of rugged individualism. But the Bible is all about authority. In fact, *sola Scriptura* means that the Bible is our chief, supreme, and ultimate authority. Notice, however, that I didn't say the Bible is our *only* authority. As chapter 10 will explain more thoroughly, *sola Scriptura* is too easily confused today with *nuda Scriptura,* the view that we should have "no creed but the Bible!" Those who sing this mantra believe that creeds, confessions, the voices of tradition, and those who hold ecclesiastical offices carry no authority in the church. But this was not the Reformers' position, nor should it be equated with *sola Scriptura.*

Sola Scriptura acknowledges that there are other important authorities for the Christian, authorities who should be listened to and followed. But Scripture alone is our *final* authority. It is the authority that rules over and governs all other authorities. It is the authority that has the final say. We could say that while church tradition and church officials play a *ministerial* role, Scripture alone plays a *magisterial* role. This means that all other authorities are to be followed only inasmuch as they align with Scripture, submit to Scripture, and are seen as subservient to Scripture, which alone is our supreme authority.

Second, *sola Scriptura* also means that Scripture alone is our *sufficient* authority. Not only is the Bible our supreme authority, but it is the authority that provides believers with all the truth they need for salvation and for following after Christ. The Bible, therefore, is sufficient for faith and practice. This notion of the Bible's sufficiency has been powerfully articulated by Reformation and Reformed confessions. The Belgic Confession (1561) states: "We believe that those Holy Scriptures fully contain the will of God, and that whatsoever man ought to believe unto salvation is sufficiently taught therein."[4] And the Westminster Confession of Faith (1646) says: "The whole counsel of God concerning all things necessary for His own glory, man's salvation, faith and life, is either expressly set down in Scripture, or by good and necessary consequence may be deduced from Scripture: unto which nothing at any time is to be added, whether by new revelations of the Spirit, or traditions of men [Gal 1:8–9; 2 Thess 2:2; 2 Tim 3:15–17]."[5] In short, the Bible is enough for us.

Third, *sola Scriptura* means that only Scripture, because it is God's *inspired* Word, is our *inerrant* authority.[6] Notice that the basis of biblical authority—the very reason why Scripture is authoritative—is that God is its divine author. The ground for biblical authority is divine inspiration. As the Westminster Confession of Faith says, "The *authority* of the Holy Scripture, for which it ought to be believed, and obeyed, dependeth not upon the testimony of any man, or Church, but wholly *upon God* (who is truth itself) *the author thereof*; and therefore it is to be received, *because it is the Word of God* [1 Thess 2:13; 2 Tim 3:16; 2 Pet 1:19, 21; 1 John 5:9]."[7] Scripture is the church's final and sufficient authority because Scripture *is* the Word of God. One of the most important chapters in this book for applying *sola Scriptura* is chapter

---

4.   "The Belgic Confession (1561)," in *Reformed Confessions of the 16th and 17th Centuries in English Translation, Volume 2, 1552–1566*, ed. James T. Dennison Jr. (Grand Rapids: Reformation Heritage, 2010), 427 (article VII). Also consider two other confessions: The French Confession (1559) says that Scripture is the "rule of all truth, containing all matters necessarily required for the worship of God and our salvation," and therefore it is not right to "add unto or to take from" it ("The French Confession [1559]," in Dennison, *Reformed Confessions, Volume 2*, 142 [article V]). And The Thirty-Nine Articles (1563) says, "Holy Scripture containeth all things necessary to salvation: so that whatsoever is not read therein, nor may be proved thereby, is not to be required of any man, that it should be believed as an article of Faith, or be thought requisite or necessary to salvation" ("The Thirty-Nine Articles [1562/63]," in Dennison, *Reformed Confessions, Volume 2*, 755 [article VI]).

5.   In chapter 10 we will address the complex issue of how we make sense of sufficiency in light of general revelation, the role of the Holy Spirit, and extrabiblical sources.

6.   Some will prefer to use the word *infallible* instead (which does have historical precedent). I am fine with using the word *as long as* one means, by infallible, that Scripture (in total) is not capable of erring. However, I would reject those who use the word to say that Scripture is true only in its saving message but not in its specifics (e.g., historical details). As I will explain in chapter 8, *infallible* and *inerrant* are complementary and compatible concepts, *infallible* (Scripture *cannot* err) being an even stronger word than *inerrant* (Scripture *does not* err). Therefore, I think it is historically and biblically erroneous to use the word *infallible* to convey something less than inerrancy.

7.   "The Westminster Confession of Faith (1646)," in *Reformed Confessions of the 16th and 17th Centuries in English Translation, Volume 4, 1600–1693*, ed. James T. Dennison Jr. (Grand Rapids: Reformation Heritage, 2014), 235 (I.IV), emphasis added.

7, where we see why Scripture and Scripture alone (not Scripture *and* Tradition) is God-breathed and, on this basis, stands unshakable as the church's final, flawless authority.[8] What Scripture says, God says.

To get a full picture of *sola Scriptura*, we need to go beyond saying that the Bible is inspired or God-breathed. Inspiration should lead to an understanding that the Bible is perfect, flawless, and inerrant. In other words, inerrancy is the necessary corollary of inspiration. They are two sides of the same coin, and it is impossible to divorce one from the other. Because it is God speaking—and he is a God of truth, not error—his Word must be true and trustworthy in all that it addresses.

Because inerrancy is a biblical corollary and consequence of divine inspiration—inseparably connected and intertwined—it is a necessary component to *sola Scriptura*.[9] The God of truth has breathed out his Word of truth, and the result is nothing less than a *flawless* authority for the church. In saying this, I am aware that my inclusion of inerrancy in our definition of *sola Scriptura* (and in this book) will prove to be controversial, given the mixed identity of evangelicalism today. However, were we to divorce the truthfulness and trustworthiness of Scripture from its authority, disconnecting the two as if one was unrelated to the other, then we would be left with no doctrine of *sola Scriptura* at all. Should Scripture contain errors, it is unclear why we should trust Scripture as our supreme and final authority.[10] And should we limit, modify, or abandon the total inerrancy of Scripture, we set in motion tremendous doubt and uncertainty regarding the Bible's competence as our final authority. The ground for the believer's confidence that all of Scripture is the Word of God is shaken.[11]

---

8. In chapter 1 we will see how Rome differs in its elevation of Tradition as a second infallible source of divine revelation.

9. The Chicago Statement on Inerrancy nicely captures the relationship between inspiration and inerrancy: "Being wholly and verbally God-given, Scripture is without error or fault in all its teaching" ("The Chicago Statement on Biblical Inerrancy," in *Inerrancy*, ed. Norman L. Geisler [Grand Rapids: Zondervan, 1980], 494 [point 4 of "A Short Statement"]). Again: "We affirm that the doctrine of inerrancy is grounded in the teaching of the Bible about inspiration," Geisler, *Inerrancy*, 497 (article XV). Also consider "The Bible alone, and the Bible in its entirety, is the Word of God written and *is therefore* inerrant in the autographs" (the Evangelical Theological Society, http://www.etsjets.org/about/constitution#A3; emphasis added).

10. John Frame, *The Doctrine of the Word of God* (Phillipsburg, NJ: P&R, 2010), 547; J. I. Packer, *Beyond the Battle for the Bible* (Westchester, IL: Cornerstone, 1980), 17.

11. Clark H. Pinnock, "Limited Inerrancy: A Critical Appraisal and Constructive Alternative," in *God's Inerrant Word*, ed. John Warwick Montgomery (Minneapolis: Bethany, 1973), 145, 150, 156.

The Chicago Statement on Inerrancy makes this point as well: "The *authority* of Scripture is inescapably impaired if this total divine *inerrancy* is in any way limited or disregarded."[12] In other words, to reject inerrancy is to undermine confidence in the Bible's authority, and what could have more relevance to *sola Scriptura* than biblical authority? As Roger Nicole once exclaimed, "What is supremely at stake in this whole discussion [of *inerrancy*] is the recognition of the *authority* of God in the sacred oracles."[13] It should not surprise us to find that in the recent history of evangelicalism, leaders have rallied around statements such as the Cambridge Declaration (1996), affirming inerrancy's inseparability from *sola Scriptura* in stating, "Scripture alone is the *inerrant* rule of the church's life," and they "reaffirm the *inerrant* Scripture to be the sole source of written divine revelation, which alone can *bind* the conscience."[14]

As we will explore more thoroughly in the first chapter, what is often missed in retellings of Luther's progress to the Diet of Worms is the question of *why* Luther's stance on Scripture was so detested by Rome. After all, Rome *also* affirmed Scripture's authority and inspiration. So what made Luther's stance on biblical authority so different and so offensive to the Roman church? The answer is that Luther had the audacity to say that *only* Scripture is the *inerrant* authority.[15] While

---

12.   "The Chicago Statement on Biblical Inerrancy," in Geisler, *Inerrancy*, 494 (point 5 of "A Short Statement"), emphasis added.

13.   "Are we going to submit unconditionally to the voice of God who has spoken? Or, are we going to insist on screening the message of the Bible, accepting only what appears palatable and remaining free to reject what does not conform to our preconceived criteria?" Quoted in Robert Saucy, *Scripture: Its Power, Authority, and Relevance* (Nashville: Nelson, 2001), 160, emphasis added.

14.   "The Cambridge Declaration," http://www.alliancenet.org/cambridge-declaration; emphasis added. The declaration was affirmed by the Alliance of Confessing Evangelicals and signed by council members such as John Armstrong, Alistair Begg, James M. Boice, W. Robert Godfrey, John D. Hannah, Michael S. Horton, R. Albert Mohler Jr., R. C. Sproul, and David Wells, among others.

15.   Some will object that Luther and the Reformers did not use the label *inerrancy*, so it is anachronistic and unjustified to use this term in relation to our definition of *sola Scriptura*. Yes, it is true that the Reformers never used the term *inerrancy*. However, such an objection fails to realize that though the *term* was not used, the *concept* was affirmed. The Reformers may not have fleshed out a concept of inerrancy as meticulous as we have today (after all, inerrancy was not their main battle with Rome). However, this does not mean that the basic concept of inerrancy and its most fundamental components are not present in their writings. For the sake of simplicity, I will use the words *inerrant* or *inerrancy* whenever I am referring to the Bible as a book that does not err. For Luther's affirmation of Scripture's inerrancy, see *LW* 1:121; 4:14; 12:242; 22:254, 259; 31:11, 282; 32:11, 98; 35:128, 150; 36:136–37; 39:165. For defenses of the Reformers' affirmation of inerrancy, see Robert D. Preus, "Luther

popes and councils err, Scripture alone does not! For Rome, Scripture *and* Tradition were *inerrant* authorities. For Luther, Scripture *alone* is our *inerrant* authority.

What distinguished Luther and the rest of the Reformers from church leaders in Rome was their claim that as important as tradition is (and they thought it was extremely important), tradition is not without error. That honor goes to Scripture *alone*. In fact, it is because Scripture alone is inspired by God and consequently inerrant that the Reformers believed Scripture alone is the church's *final* authority, sufficient for faith and practice.[16]

Moving Forward

So where do we go from here? Together, we will take three steps to better understand the origins, development, and contemporary relevance of the doctrine of *sola Scriptura*.

First, this book will travel back in time to demonstrate that a shift in authority has taken place since the Reformation, one that has massive

---

and Biblical Infallibility," in *Inerrancy and the Church*, ed. John D. Hannah (Chicago: Moody, 1984), 99–142; J. Theodore Mueller, "Luther and the Bible," in *Inspiration and Interpretation*, ed. John F. Walvoord (Grand Rapids: Eerdmans, 1947), 87–114; Mark D. Thompson, *A Sure Ground on Which to Stand: The Relation of Authority and Interpretive Method in Luther's Approach to Scripture* (Eugene, OR: Wipf & Stock, 2004); James I. Packer, "John Calvin and the Inerrancy of Holy Scripture," in Hannah, *Inerrancy and the Church*, 143–88; Kenneth Kantzer, "Calvin and the Holy Scriptures," in Walvoord, *Inspiration and Interpretation*, 115–55; W. Robert Godfrey, "Biblical Authority in the Sixteenth and Seventeenth Centuries: A Question of Transition," in *Scripture and Truth*, ed. D. A. Carson and John Woodbridge (Grand Rapids: Baker, 1992), 225–43, 391–97; Roger R. Nicole, "John Calvin and Inerrancy," *JETS* 25 (1982): 425–42; Eugene F. Klung, "Word and Spirit in Luther Studies Since World War II," *TJ* 5 (1984): 3–46; John D. Woodbridge, *Biblical Authority: A Critique of the Rogers/McKim Proposal* (Grand Rapids: Zondervan, 1982), 49–100; Richard A. Muller, *Post-Reformation Reformed Dogmatics*, 4 vols. 2nd ed. (Grand Rapids: Baker Academic, 2003), 2:289–90.

16. See R. C. Sproul, *Scripture Alone: The Evangelical Doctrine* (Phillipsburg, NJ: P&R, 2005), 18. To clarify, I am not saying that inerrancy is *the* basis on which we believe that the Bible is authoritative. Rather, as mentioned already, the Bible is authoritative because it is inspired by God. So inspiration is the *basis* of biblical authority. However, we should be careful that we do not then conclude that inerrancy has nothing to do with authority. Actually, the relation between inerrancy and authority is crucial. While inerrancy may not be the *ground* of authority, nevertheless, inerrancy is the necessary consequence of inspiration and therefore inseparably connected to inspiration (e.g., the Bible is truthful because the God who breathed it out is a God of truth). Therefore, to abandon the inerrancy of Scripture is to do untold harm to Scripture's authority, creating distrust and suspicion within the reader toward divine authorship. If the Bible contains errors, one naturally begins to question whether it is truly authoritative as well. All that is to say, while inerrancy may not be the all-sufficient basis or ground of *sola Scriptura*, it is a necessary and essential component due to its inseparable tie to inspiration.

implications for today. Part 1 begins with the Reformation and its heroic adherence to *sola Scriptura* in the face of insurmountable opposition from Rome. We will also examine the massive crisis in authority that erupted shortly after the Reformers passed from the scene, beginning with the Enlightenment, progressing through theological Liberalism, and climaxing today with postmodernism. As we shall see, a seismic, earthquaking shift in biblical authority has occurred, reorienting our ecclesiastical landscape.

While I seek to fairly and accurately represent the diverse voices of the past, I also provide critiques along the way. My aim is to show that abandonment of biblical authority has been under way since the Enlightenment, and the church is worse off because of it. What is the solution? We must retrieve and apply *sola Scriptura* to our contemporary challenges.

You will want to pay special attention to the section entitled "How Shall We Then Proceed?" at the end of chapter 3. There I explain how we can approach Scripture in contrast to many of the modern and postmodern approaches represented. I argue that we must begin by listening to what Scripture has to say about itself, rather than imposing a modern or postmodern agenda on the text. We must have an open ear to the biblical categories that Scripture itself provides as the Holy Spirit guides us in its interpretation. We must allow Scripture's own voice to affirm *and* correct our pre-understanding of what Scripture is and how it should be read. Such an approach pays heed to the self-authenticating nature of Scripture, the internal testimony of the Holy Spirit, as well as the humility fostered by faith seeking understanding, a motto the Reformers retrieved from the church fathers.[17]

Second, we will incorporate a biblical theology of God's Word, and in doing so trace the redemptive-historical context for the doctrine of Scripture to show that the triune God has made himself known covenantally and his covenantal word always proves true.[18] By understanding the nature of God's oral and written Word in the story line of redemptive history, we are better equipped to see to how Scripture describes itself and to grasp the inherent attributes of Scripture.[19] In this, I make two assumptions:

---

17. Also note our treatment in chapter 1 of the self-authenticating nature of Scripture in our discussion of John Calvin.

18. I will use "word" to refer to God's diverse forms of speech throughout redemptive history and "Word" to specifically refer to either Scripture or Jesus Christ.

19. While we do not treat the attributes of Scripture until part 3, these attributes are

First, that God's Word is inherently and invariably *Trinitarian* in nature. Throughout redemptive history, each person of the Trinity participates in the delivery of divine revelation (see chapter 4), yet it is the Holy Spirit in particular who takes on a central role, carrying along the biblical authors so that they speak from God (2 Pet 1:21). In addition, I assume that God's Word, though communicated in a variety of ways, is undeniably *covenantal* in character. Not only does God communicate who he is and what he will do within the context of divinely initiated covenants, but Scripture itself *is* a covenantal document. As we will learn in chapters 4 and 5, Scripture is the constitution of the covenant between God and his people.[20] Therefore, to reject God's Word is to reject his covenant as well.[21] Redemptive history demonstrates that the covenantal Word of the triune God proves true. His covenantal promises, both spoken and written, will not fail, and nowhere is this more evident than in the incarnation of Christ, the Word made flesh.

Third, rather than limiting ourselves to the attribute of sufficiency (as treatments of sola Scriptura *sometimes do), we will systematically explore the range of scriptural attributes in order to defend biblical authority against the many challenges it faces today.* Once we see that Scripture is God-breathed, we will look to inspiration's natural corollary, the inerrancy of Scripture. As with inspiration, we will discover that the Bible affirms its own truthfulness and trustworthiness. Furthermore, as we address both inspiration and inerrancy, we will give special focus to Jesus, demonstrating that our Lord himself believed Scripture to be both God-breathed and without error. Our discussion will take us back to the doctrine of God, and we will learn that Scripture is fundamentally truthful because its divine author is a God of truth.

Last, we will turn to the attributes of clarity and sufficiency. In the wake of Rome's muddy Tiber and postmodernism's murky waters, few doctrines have been so quickly dismantled as the clarity of Scripture. Nevertheless, we will argue that when God speaks, he intends to be heard and understood. Not only is our God not silent (as Francis Schaeffer so famously put it) but the silence is broken by his clear and effective speech. Lack of clarity is not a quality to be attached to the

---

inseparably connected to the story line of Scripture and show themselves throughout this story as we move from the first Adam to the last Adam, Jesus Christ.

20. Meredith G. Kline, *The Structure of Biblical Authority* (Grand Rapids: Eerdmans, 1972).

21. See Frame, *Doctrine of the Word*, 356.

work of the divine architect of language. Finally, sufficiency will close our study. Few attributes have such warm and practical implications for life, putting real flesh on the skeleton of *sola Scriptura*. Having established Scripture's own testimony to its sufficiency, we will answer contemporary challenges to sufficiency from traditionalism (with a particular focus on Rome and her view of the canon) to science and reason, and finally experience and culture.

With our course mapped out, *tolle lege*!

PART 1

God's Word under Fire, Yesterday and Today

CHAPTER 1

The Road to Reformation: Biblical Authority in the Sixteenth Century

> While I slept, or drank Wittenberg beer . . . the Word
> so greatly weakened the Papacy that never a Prince or
> Emperor inflicted such damage upon it. I did nothing.
> The Word did it all. —*Martin Luther*

> The foundation of our religion is the written word, the
> Scriptures of God. —*Huldrych Zwingli*

> The Reformation of the sixteenth century was founded
> upon the authority of the Bible, yet it set the world
> aflame. —*J. Gresham Machen*

There they sat. Relics. Lots of them. There was a cut of fabric from the swaddling cloth of baby Jesus, thirteen pieces from his crib, a strand of straw from the manger, a piece of gold from a wise man, three pieces of myrrh, a morsel of bread from the Last Supper, a thorn from the crown Jesus wore when crucified, and, to top it all off, a genuine piece of stone that Jesus stood on to ascend to the Father's right hand. And in good Catholic fashion, the blessed Mary was not left out. There sat three pieces of cloth from her cloak, "four from her girdle," four hairs from her head, and, better yet, seven pieces from "the veil that was sprinkled with the blood of Christ."[1] These relics and countless others (nineteen-thousand bones from the saints!) stood ready to be viewed by pious pilgrims. The relics were the proud collection of Frederick the Wise, elector of Saxony, Martin Luther's prince. And they sat in the

---

1. All these details come from Roland H. Bainton, *Here I Stand: A Life of Martin Luther* (Peabody, MA: Hendrickson, 1950), 53.

Castle Church at Wittenberg, prepared for showing on All Saints' Day, November 1, 1516.[2]

In the midst of all this fanfare was also one essential ingredient—the procurement of indulgences. Veneration of the relics was accompanied by the issuance of an indulgence, a certificate guaranteeing the buyer that time in purgatory would be reduced and remitted by up to 1,902,202 years and 270 days.[3] An indulgence was the full or partial remission of temporal punishment for sins. It was drawn from the Treasury of Merit, a storehouse of grace which was accumulated by the meritorious work of Christ and by the superabundant merit of the saints.[4]

The Coin in the Coffer Rings

Indulgences were the bingo games of the sixteenth century. In a complicated set of political affairs involving Albert of Brandenburg, Pope Leo X utilized the selling of indulgences to fund the completion of St. Peter's Basilica, but not just any indulgence would do.[5] Pope Leo issued a plenary indulgence, one that would apparently return the sinner to the state of innocence first received at baptism.[6]

There was no one so experienced as the Dominican Johann Tetzel in

---

2.   Gordon Rupp, *Luther's Progress to the Diet of Worms* (New York: Harper & Row, 1964), 51–54; Martin Brecht, *Martin Luther: His Road to Reformation, 1484–1521* (Philadelphia: Fortress, 1985), 175–83; Bainton, *Here I Stand*, 53.

3.   Rupp, *Luther's Progress*, 51–54; Brecht, *Luther: His Road*, 175–83; Bainton, *Here I Stand*, 28–29, 53.

4.   "Indulgences had to do with the sacrament of penance, and only with one part of that: the works of satisfaction which the penitent sinner was required to perform in order to pay the penalty of sin. Medieval theologians distinguished between the guilt incurred by sin and the penalty that had to be paid, since no sin could go unpunished. When the guilt was forgiven by God through the absolution of the priest, the penalty of eternal condemnation was commuted into works of satisfaction which the priest then imposed upon the repentant sinner according to the seriousness of the sin committed. An indulgence was the additional prerogative of the church to release penitents from these works of satisfaction. Since the thirteenth century, the power to permit such a relaxation or 'indulgence' of the penitential obligation was derived from the 'treasury of the church.' This treasure contained the accumulated merits of Christ and the saints which, since they were superfluous for those who had originally acquired them, stood available for ordinary sinners in the church. An indulgence applied these merits to the penitent sinner and canceled the debt he would otherwise be obliged to pay off with works of satisfaction" (Scott H. Hendrix, *Luther and the Papacy: Stages in a Reformation Conflict* [Philadelphia: Fortress, 1981], 24).

5.   Brecht, *Luther: His Road*, 175–83; Hendrix, *Luther and the Papacy*, 25; Bainton, *Here I Stand*, 54–63.

6.   *Instructio Summaria*, in *Dokumente zum Ablasstreit*, ed. W. Köhler (Tübingen, 1934), 104–16; "Summary Instruction for Indulgence Preachers," in *Protestant Reformation*, ed. Hans J. Hillerbrand, rev. ed. (New York: Harper Perennial, 2009), 15; Brecht, *Luther: His Road*, 175–238.

marketing this once-in-a-lifetime opportunity. What exactly did the sinner receive in buying this indulgence? According to unscrupulous sellers like Tetzel, the impression was given that the indulgence would result in the total forgiveness of all sins.[7] Not even the sin of raping the mother of God could outweigh the efficacy of these indulgences![8] Even the horrors of years in purgatory could now be removed. And if this was not good enough, one also had the opportunity to buy an indulgence slip for one's loved ones in purgatory (and one need not be penitent himself for such an indulgence to be effective).[9] With the appropriate amount of money, repentance was now for sale, and any sin could be covered.

Going from town to town with all the pomp of Rome, Tetzel flamboyantly laid a heavy guilt trip on his hearers: "Listen to the voices of your dear dead relatives and friends, beseeching you and saying, 'Pity us, pity us. We are in dire torment from which you can redeem us for a pittance. . . . Will you let us lie here in flames? Will you delay our promised glory?'" And then came Tetzel's catchy jingle: "As soon as the coin in the coffer rings, the soul from purgatory springs." With just a quarter of a florin, you could liberate your loved one from the flames of purgatory and into the "fatherland of paradise."[10]

By the end of 1517, Martin Luther had had enough. One year prior, Luther had preached against the corruption of indulgences.[11] This time, he would put his objections in writing for academic debate. Luther drew up ninety-five theses exposing the abuse of indulgences, denying the power and authority of the pope over purgatory, and testing whether the pope truly had the welfare of the sinner in mind.[12]

---

7. In "Summary Instruction for Indulgence Preachers" (Hillerbrand, *Protestant Reformation*, 15–18), a manual Albert prepared, this plenary indulgence is said to result in the full remission of all sins not only on this earth but in purgatory. And one need not show evidence of contrition or even go to confession. See Hendrix, *Luther and the Papacy*, 25–26, 31. Luther, however, became frustrated, given the misunderstanding this cultivated among common people. Brecht captures Luther's discontent: "The indulgence agents only demand that people pay, but they do not explain what indulgences are and what use they serve. Thus the misunderstanding arises that people are immediately saved after obtaining indulgences. But through indulgences as such one does not obtain the grace which makes one righteous or more righteous, but only the removal of penitential punishments and satisfactions. The people, though, expect indulgences to give them complete remission of sins and the kingdom of heaven, and so, by neglecting genuine repentance, they sin" (Brecht, *Martin Luther: His Road*, 188–89).

8. Hendrix, *Luther and the Papacy*, 25–26; Bainton, *Here I Stand*, 59.

9. See "Summary Instruction for Indulgence Preachers," in Hillerbrand, *Protestant Reformation*, 18; Hendrix, *Luther and the Papacy*, 26; Bainton, *Here I Stand*, 59.

10. John Tetzel, "A Sermon [1517]," in Hillerbrand, *Protestant Reformation*, 19–21.

11. Brecht, *Luther: His Road*, 185–86.

12. Martin Luther, *Ninety-Five Theses, 1517*, in *LW* 31:17–34; cf. Luther, *Explanations*

When they were finished, his theses were posted to the Castle Church door on October 31, 1517.

Despite his disagreements with the pope, Luther was just trying to be a good Catholic, reforming the Church from the clear abuses he had witnessed. At this point, Luther wasn't trying to position the authority of Scripture over the pope—at least not explicitly. Nevertheless, the seeds of confrontation had been planted. Luther was arguing that the pope did not have power over purgatory for the remission of sin or its penalty—clearly questioning the pope's authority on this matter.[13]

"The Scriptures Cannot Err"

Though Luther's theses were written in Latin for academic debate, others translated them and spread them throughout Germany. Soon everyone was talking about Luther's theses.

Interpreting Luther's theses as an affront to papal authority, Tetzel called for Luther to be burned at the stake as a heretic.[14] Then, in a second set of theses, Tetzel defended papal authority and infallibility.[15] Luther's *Explanations of the Ninety-Five Theses* would confirm Tetzel's suspicions, arguing that the pope's primacy and supremacy were not ordained by God at the genesis of the church but had evolved over time.[16]

Luther also traded fighting words with Sylvester Prierias, a Dominican theologian appointed by Leo X to respond to Luther's theses. It became clear to Prierias that authority was the issue at stake in all of Luther's arguments. Prierias wrote in his *Dialogue concerning the Power of the Pope*, "He who does not accept the doctrine of the Church of Rome and pontiff of Rome as an infallible rule of faith, from which the Holy Scriptures, too, draw their strength and authority, is a heretic."[17] Luther responded by pointing out that Prierias cited no Scripture to prove his case and wrote to Prierias, "Like an insidious devil you pervert the Scriptures."[18] Luther exposed the contradictions

---

of the Ninety-Five Theses, 1518, in *LW* 31:77–252. See also Brecht, *Luther: His Road,* 183–90; Rupp, *Luther's Progress,* 52–53; Hendrix, *Luther and the Papacy,* 30–31; Bainton, *Here I Stand,* 62–63.

13. Hendrix, *Luther and the Papacy,* 29–30; Brecht, *Luther: His Road,* 183–90; Bainton, *Here I Stand,* 63–65.

14. Brecht, *Luther: His Road,* 199, 206–7; Rupp, *Luther's Progress,* 54–55.

15. Brecht, *Luther: His Road,* 209; Hendrix, *Luther and the Papacy,* 35–36.

16. See Luther, *Explanations,* in *LW* 31:77–252. Cf. Bainton, *Here I Stand,* 72.

17. Quoted in Heiko A. Oberman, *Luther: Man between God and the Devil* (New Haven: Yale University Press, 1982), 193. See also Hendrix, *Luther and the Papacy,* 44–52.

18. Quoted in Bainton, *Here I Stand,* 73.

and corruptions of the papacy by pointing to the examples of Julius II and his "ghastly shedding of blood," as well as the "outrageous tyranny of Boniface VIII." Luther then asked Prierias, "If the Church consists representatively in the cardinals, what do you make of a general council of the whole Church?"[19]

It's important to remember that papal infallibility would not be declared official dogma until the First Vatican Council in 1870.[20] However, Prierias's response to Luther shows how many already believed the pope was infallible and inerrant whenever he spoke *ex cathedra* ("from the seat" as the vicar of Christ on earth).[21] As Martin Brecht explains, not only were the Roman church and pope considered infallible, but "the authority of the church stood explicitly above that of the Scriptures," even authorizing the Scriptures.[22] On this point too Luther disagreed with Prierias, not only appealing to Scripture's authority but also to Augustine's letter to Jerome where Augustine elevates Scripture's authority, emphasizing that the Bible alone is inspired by God and without error.[23] The "radicalism" of Luther's reply to Prierias "lies not in its invective but in its affirmation that the pope might err and a council might err and that only Scripture is the final authority."[24]

Following his dispute with Prierias, Luther faced off against the Dominican cardinal Cajetan, perhaps the most impressive theologian of the Roman Curia. They met in October of 1518 in Augsburg, and an argument between the two lasted for several days.[25] Luther was commanded to recant, which he would not do. When Cajetan confronted Luther with Pope Clement VI's bull *Unigenitus* (1343)—a bull that, according to Cajetan, affirmed that "the merits of Christ are a treasure

---

19. Ibid.

20. Tierney argues that there "is no convincing evidence that papal infallibility formed any part of the theological or canonical tradition of the church before the thirteenth century; the doctrine was invented in the first place by a few dissident Franciscans because it suited their convenience to invent it; eventually, but only after much initial reluctance, it was accepted by the papacy because it suited the convenience of the popes to accept it." Brian Tierney, *Origins of Papal Infallibility, 1150–1350: A Study on the Concepts of Infallibility, Sovereignty and Tradition in the Middle Ages*, ed. Heiko A. Oberman, Studies in the History of Christian Thought 6 (Leiden: Brill, 1972), 281.

21. To clarify, Rome did not believe the pope was infallible and inerrant by virtue of his own righteousness, but only by speaking *ex cathedra*. See Timothy George, *Reading Scripture with the Reformers* (Downers Grove, IL: IVP Academic, 2011), 110.

22. Brecht, *Luther: His Road*, 243.

23. George, *Reading Scripture*, 111.

24. Bainton, *Here I Stand*, 74.

25. See Martin Luther, *Proceedings at Augsburg 1518*, in *LW* 31:253–92.

of indulgences"—Luther rejected it along with Pope Clement's author-ity. "I am not so audacious," said Luther, "that for the sake of a single obscure and ambiguous decretal of a human pope I would recede from so many and such clear testimonies of divine Scripture. For, as one of the canon lawyers has said, 'in a matter of faith not only is a council above a pope but any one of the faithful, if armed with better authority and reason.'" When Cajetan responded that Scripture must be inter-preted by the pope who is above not only councils but Scripture itself, Luther replied, "His Holiness abuses Scripture. I deny that he is above Scripture."[26] Harold Grimm summarizes the conflict this way: "The more Cajetan insisted upon the infallibility of the papacy the more Luther relied upon the authority of Scripture."[27]

Luther's greatest challenge would come the following year at the Leipzig debate with the Catholic disputant Johannes von Eck.[28] Though the debate would formally be an engagement between Eck and Andreas Karlstadt, Luther anticipated that he would have an oppor-tunity to participate. After all, Eck's real target was Luther himself.[29] In the months leading up to the debate, Luther rigorously prepared himself, knowing that papal supremacy was the critical point under debate. In his research Luther had to address two key passages Rome relied on: (1) In Matthew 16:18–19 Jesus calls Peter the "rock" that he will build his church on, conferring upon Peter the "keys of the kingdom." According to Rome, here Jesus teaches that Peter is the first pope, giving to Peter (and his successors by default) the foundational position in the erection of his church. Since Peter (and by implication all future popes) is given the "keys of the kingdom," the pope possesses supreme authority and control over the church and infallibly exercises that authority as the supreme ruler when he teaches as the vicar of Christ on earth. (2) In John 21:15–19 Jesus tells Peter to "feed my lambs." Again, Rome saw Jesus as conferring on Peter the exclusive right to exercise power over the church.

Luther, however, rejected these interpretations. He believed that

---

26. As quoted in Bainton, *Here I Stand*, 80. For the debate over the Bull *Unigenitus*, see Rupp, *Luther's Progress*, 61; Hendrix, *Luther and the Papacy*, 59–61; Brecht, *Luther: His Road*, 252–55.

27. Luther, *Proceedings at Augsburg*, in *LW* 31:256 (cf. 262, 284–85). See also Brecht, *Luther: His Road*, 263–65.

28. See Martin Luther, *The Leipzig Debate*, in *LW* 31:307–325.

29. Brecht, *Luther: His Road*, 299–322.

Rome was reading the papacy and its claims to power back into the Bible. In interpreting Matthew 16:18–19, Luther followed the interpretive tradition that applies this promise either to Christ's disciples or to the very faith confessing Jesus as the Christ.[30] As Brecht observes, for Luther the "rock is not any particular church, but the invincible church is wherever the Word of God is heard and believed." It is faith which "possesses the keys, the sacraments, and the authority in the church."[31] And in interpreting Jesus's command to feed his sheep, Luther argued that this has nothing to do with the exclusive power of the pope, but refers instead to preaching. Luther concluded that neither one of these passages supports papal supremacy. Luther rejected papal infallibility as well as the belief that the pope exclusively possessed the correct interpretation of the Bible.[32] Rome's twisting of Scripture to bolster its ecclesial power only demonstrated to Luther that a Babylonian captivity had indeed come upon the church.[33]

When it was time for the debate, Eck brought the central issue to the table: Who has final authority, God's Word or the pope? For Eck, Scripture received its authority from the pope. Luther strongly disagreed, arguing instead that Scripture has authority over popes, church fathers, and even church councils, all of which have erred in the past.[34] Moreover, said Luther, not only is Scripture our only infallible authority, but a schoolboy with Scripture in his hand is better fortified than the pope![35]

Lest we miss the obvious, it is important to note that for Luther, *sola Scriptura* was directly connected to the *inerrancy* of Scripture. Luther did not use the term *inerrancy* in his writings or in debate, yet the *concept* is present throughout his thinking on the matter.[36] If

---

30. Brecht, *Luther: His Road*, 308.
31. Ibid.
32. Ibid.
33. Ibid.
34. Rupp, *Luther's Progress*, 114.
35. For a more extensive overview of the entire debate, see Brecht, *Luther: His Road*, 309–22.
36. For Luther's affirmation of Scripture's inerrancy, see LW 1:121; 4:14; 12:242; 22:254, 259; 31:11, 282; 32:11, 98; 35:128, 150; 36:136–37; 39:165. For defenses of the Reformers' affirmation of inerrancy, see Preus, "Luther and Biblical Infallibility," 99–142; Mueller, "Luther and the Bible," 87–114; Thompson, *Sure Ground on Which to Stand*; Packer, "John Calvin and the Inerrancy of Holy Scripture," 143–88; Kantzer, "Calvin and the Holy Scriptures," 115–55; Godfrey, "Biblical Authority," 225–43; 391–97; Nicole, "John Calvin and Inerrancy," 425–42; Klung, "Word and Spirit," 3–46; Muller, *PRRD*, 2:289–90; Woodbridge, *Biblical Authority*, 49–100; contra Paul Avis, *In Search of Authority: Anglican*

```
```

Scripture is not inerrant, then *sola Scriptura* is without a foundation. For Luther, what made the Bible alone the supreme authority was that not only was it inspired by God, but as a result of being God-breathed, the Scriptures, *and the Scriptures alone, could not and do not err.* On the other hand, church councils and popes can and do err. So while Rome believed Scripture *and* Tradition were inerrant authorities, Luther argued that Scripture *alone* is our inerrant authority from God.[37] As Luther would state in his 1521 treatise *The Misuse of the Mass:*

> Since the Fathers have often erred, as you yourself confess, who will make us certain as to where they have not erred, assuming their own reputation is sufficient and should not be weighed and judged according to the Scriptures? . . . What if they erred in their interpretation, as well as in their life and writings? In that way you make gods of all that is human in us, and of men themselves; *and the word of men you make equal to the Word of God. . . . The saints could err in their writings and the sin in their lives, but the Scriptures cannot err.*[38]

Elsewhere Luther would argue that the fathers "have erred, as men will; therefore I am ready to trust them only when they give me evidence for their opinions from Scripture, *which has never erred.*" Luther quotes Augustine in support of this point: "I have learned to do only those books that are called the holy Scriptures the honor of believing firmly that *none of their writers has ever erred.*" Therefore, concludes Luther, "Scripture alone is the true lord and master of all writings and doctrine on earth."[39] Luther believed inerrancy was a necessary corollary to *sola Scriptura* and a key component of biblical authority and sufficiency.[40] Contrary to Rome, Luther protested that God's

Theological Method from the Reformation to the Enlightenment (London: Bloomsbury, 2014), 27.

37. For Rome's definition of "Tradition," see *Catechism of the Catholic Church*, 2nd ed. (New York: Doubleday, 1995), sections 80–82, 120, 891. We will interact more thoroughly with this definition in chapter 10 since defining tradition and its role is a dividing line between Protestants and Roman Catholics. I will use "Tradition" to refer to Rome's view and "tradition" to refer to the Protestant view.

38. Martin Luther, *The Misuse of the Mass*, in *LW* 36:136–37, emphasis added.

39. "If that is not granted, what is Scripture good for? The more we reject it, the more we become satisfied with men's books and human teachers" (Martin Luther, *Defense and Explanation of All the Articles*, in *LW* 32:11–12, emphasis added).

40. Paul Althaus, *The Theology of Martin Luther*, trans. Robert C. Schultz (Philadelphia: Fortress, 1966), 6–7; R. C. Sproul, "*Sola Scriptura*: Crucial to Evangelicalism," in *The Foundation of Biblical Authority*, ed. James Montgomery Boice (Grand Rapids: Zondervan, 1978), 105.

Word *alone* was the church's *flawless* authority. To deny this, Luther believed, was to reject the *sola* of *sola Scriptura*. It was to make the teachings of men equal to the Word of God, as if they too were not only God-breathed but without error.

At Leipzig, Luther was quickly classified as a heretic, joining the ranks of his forerunners John Wycliffe and Jan Hus. "I see that you are following the damned and pestiferous errors of John Wycliffe, who said, 'It is not necessary for salvation to believe that the Roman Church is above all others.' And you are espousing the pestilent errors of John Hus, who claimed that Peter neither was nor is the head of the Holy Catholic Church."[41] At first Luther denied such an association with Hus, who was condemned by the Council of Constance and burned at the stake in 1415 as a heretic. But during a break in the debate, Luther realized that Hus had taught exactly what he believed about the authority of the church. When he returned to the debate, he boldly declared:

> It is not in the power of the Roman pontiff or of the Inquisition to construct new articles of faith. No believing Christian can be coerced beyond holy writ. By divine law we are forbidden to believe anything which is not established by divine Scripture or manifest revelation. One of the canon lawyers has said that the opinion of a single private man has more weight than that of the Roman pontiff or an ecclesiastical council if grounded on a better authority or reason.[42]

When Eck responded that Luther was "heretical, erroneous, blasphemous, presumptuous, seditious, and offensive to pious ears" should he defend Hus, Luther then made himself abundantly clear about the fallibility of councils:

> I assert that a council has sometimes erred and may sometimes err. Nor has a council authority to establish new articles of faith. A council cannot make divine right out of that which by nature is not divine right. Councils have contradicted each other, for the recent Lateran Council has reversed the claim of the councils of Constance and Basel that a council is above a pope. A simple layman armed with Scripture is to be believed above a pope or a council without it. As for the pope's decretal on indulgences I

---

41. As cited in Bainton, *Here I Stand*, 101. See also Rupp, *Luther's Progress*, 69; Hendrix, *Luther and the Papacy*, 87–88.

42. Cited in Bainton, *Here I Stand*, 102.

say that neither the Church nor the pope can establish articles of faith. These must come from Scripture. For the sake of Scripture we should reject pope and councils.[43]

Luther's stance was further solidified when the debate moved to the topic of purgatory. Eck defended purgatory by appealing to 2 Maccabees 12:45, but Luther retorted that the Apocrypha was not canonical and therefore was not authoritative.

After the debate, Eck returned to Rome reporting this "Bohemian virus" to the Pope, and Luther left the debate only to become further convinced that Scripture, not the pope, was the Christian's final authority.[44] In the end, Luther realized that if the pope was to have authority over Scripture, then reform from within was impossible. As Reeves observes, "The pope's word would always trump God's. In that case, the reign of the antichrist there was sealed, and it was no longer the church of God but the synagogue of Satan."[45]

The Leipzig debate is one of the most pivotal events of the Reformation. Eck's name in German means "corner," and playing off of Eck's name, many at the time believed that Eck had "cornered" Luther, showing from church history that Luther was aligned with the heretic Hus.[46] Yet while Eck may have cornered the reformer, Luther's appeal to Scripture over popes and councils removed the rug of Rome's authority right out from under Eck's feet. Eck appealed to councils, but Luther went to the fountain itself: Scripture and Scripture alone.

Captive to the Word of God: Luther at the Diet of Worms

Tensions escalated, and in 1520 Luther produced several tracts and essays, writing like a madman. In August came *To the Christian Nobility of the German Nation*, calling into question the authority of the pope, specifically the pope's exclusive right to interpret Scripture and call a council.[47] Luther also denied that the church held a monopoly on the proper interpretation of Scripture. Luther rejected papal infallibility and claimed that the pope must answer to Scripture.

---

43. Ibid., 103.
44. Ibid.
45. Michael Reeves, *The Unquenchable Flame: Discovering the Heart of the Reformation* (Nashville: B&H Academic, 2010), 45.
46. Timothy George, *Theology of the Reformers*, rev. ed. (Nashville: B&H Academic, 2013), 81.
47. Martin Luther, *To the Christian Nobility of the German Nation*, in *LW* 44:115–219.

In October came *The Babylonian Captivity of the Church* where Luther argued that God's gift of righteousness is received by faith alone (*sola fide*), and therefore Rome is in error to claim that divine grace comes only through the priest's distribution of the sacraments (which Luther argued were limited to two rather than seven). Here again Luther gave clear hints of his belief in *sola Scriptura*. "What is asserted without the Scriptures or proven revelation," Luther protested, "may be held as an opinion, but need not be believed."[48]

The last of the three treatises came in November. In *The Freedom of a Christian*, dedicated to Pope Leo X, Luther positively put forth the idea of an exchange, that our sin is imputed to Christ while Christ's righteousness is credited to us.[49] Luther made it clear that good works do not merit righteousness but are the fruit that comes from being declared righteous.

Prior to any of these three works being published and disseminated, Pope Leo X had issued a papal bull. The decree, made on June 15, 1520, called Luther's teaching a "poisonous virus" and demanded that Luther recant in sixty days or be excommunicated. The bull, entitled *Exsurge, Domine*, had four summons: "Rise up, Lord," "Rise up, Peter," "Rise up, Paul," and "Rise up, all saints." Leo X declared that Luther was a wild boar, ravaging God's vineyard, a pestiferous virus, as well as a serpent creeping through the Lord's field, and he must be stopped. His books were to be burned, and should he not recant in sixty days after receiving the bull, he would be declared anathema!

How did Luther respond? After receiving the bull on October 10 of that year, Luther waited sixty days before publicly burning it on December 10, exclaiming, "Because you have confounded the truth of God, today the Lord confounds you. Into the fire with you!"[50] Luther had declared war. There was no going back now. The break with Rome was inevitable. On January 3, 1521, Luther was excommunicated by Leo X in the bull *Decet Romanum Pontificem*.[51]

In 1521 Luther was summoned to Worms for an Imperial Diet before Charles V, ruler of the Holy Roman Empire and a committed Roman Catholic. On April 17, a great crowd gathered for the event. To

---

48. Martin Luther, *The Babylonian Captivity of the Church*, in *LW* 36:29.
49. Martin Luther, *The Freedom of a Christian*, in *LW* 31:327–78.
50. For Luther's rationale, see *Why the Books of the Pope and His Disciples Were Burned*, in *LW* 31:279–395.
51. Oberman, *Luther*, 22–23; Hendrix, *Luther and the Papacy*, 117.

keep Luther safe, he was escorted like a thief through alleys, likely to the rear entrance of the bishop's residence.[52] Wearing the garb of the Augustinian order, Luther appeared before Charles V, who supposedly said upon seeing Luther, "He will not make a heretic out of me."[53]

Luther's publications were set out on a table, and he was asked whether he would stand by what he had written or recant. Luther did not take this moment lightly. He feared speaking rashly, not wanting to do harm to God's Word and put his own soul in jeopardy.[54] So Luther asked for time to think about his answer. After thinking the matter through, Luther returned the next day and spoke with boldness, stating that his writings fell into three categories. First, there were books on piety, which were so evangelical that even his enemies acknowledged their usefulness. Second were his books against the papacy, but neither could he recant these since they only spoke against the pope's laws that were contrary to the true gospel. To recant these would be to approve the pope's tyranny! "Good God, what sort of tool of evil and tyranny I then would be!"[55] Third, and last, were his books against specific persons who defended this popish tyranny. But again, he could not recant these for the same reasons. Instead, Luther asked that he be refuted with real proofs of his wrongdoing. The Scriptures, said Luther, should be determinative in this matter. Should he be shown his errors *from the Scriptures*, he would gladly recant, and not only recant but he would be the first in line to burn his books.[56] By the end of his reply, Luther was sweating profusely due to the hot, overcrowded room.

Johann von der Eck was the official responsible for responding to Luther, and he was not pleased with Luther's reply. He disagreed with the distinctions Luther had made and demanded that Luther recant the heresies taught in these books. Von der Eck was clear that the Tradition of the church and its councils could not be questioned by a single individual like Luther.[57] So he demanded that Luther give him a clear answer. Would he recant or not? At that, Luther spoke these famous words:

52. Brecht, *Luther: His Road*, 452.
53. Ibid., 453.
54. Ibid.
55. Ibid., 458.
56. Ibid.
57. Ibid., 460.

Unless I am convinced by the testimony of the Scriptures or by clear reason (for I do not trust either in the pope or in councils alone, since it is well known that they often err and contradict themselves), I am bound by the Scriptures I have quoted and my conscience is captive to the Word of God. I cannot and I will not retract anything, since it is neither safe nor right to go against conscience. I cannot do otherwise, here I stand, may God help me, Amen.[58]

While popes and councils contradict each other, and therefore err, Scripture alone does not err.[59] Scripture, Luther believed, is the *norma normans* (the norming norm), rather than the *norma normata* (the determined, ruled, or normed norm).[60] With his speech now finished, Luther left and returned to his quarters, only to lift up his hands and shout, "I've come through, I've come through."[61]

Background to the Debate: Tradition or Tradition?

Luther and the Reformers believed that for the early church fathers, Scripture *alone* (as opposed to Scripture *and* Tradition) was inspired by God, perfect and flawless as a source of divine revelation, and therefore the final and ultimate authority in all matters of faith and practice.[62] Tradition was a tool meant to assist the believer in understanding Scripture's meaning. While Scripture possesses *magisterial* authority, tradition's authority was always *ministerial*, a handmaiden to the biblical witness, rather than an authoritative voice governing Scripture. Tradition is subject to Scripture because only Scripture is the inerrant and infallible written source of God's revelation to his people. Heiko Oberman has called such a view of tradition and Scripture "Tradition 1" (T1).[63] Against Rome's accusation that the Reformers had departed

---

58. "Luther at the Diet of Worms, 1521," in *LW* 32:112.
59. Brecht, *Luther: His Road*, 460–61.
60. See Luther, *Babylonian Captivity*, in *LW* 36:107.
61. Brecht, *Luther: His Road*, 461.
62. Keith Mathison has demonstrated at length that the early church fathers affirmed Tradition 1 (on which, see above). Keith A. Mathison, *The Shape of Sola Scriptura* (Moscow, ID: Canon, 2001), 19–48.
63. Heiko Augustinus Oberman, *The Harvest of Medieval Theology: Gabriel Biel and Late Medieval Nominalism*, rev. ed. (Cambridge: Harvard University Press, 1963), 361–93; Heiko Oberman, *The Dawn of the Reformation* (Edinburgh: T&T Clark, 1986; repr., Grand Rapids: Eerdmans, 1996), 276; Heiko Oberman, *Forerunners of the Reformation: The Shape of Late Medieval Thought Illustrated by Key Documents* (Philadelphia: Fortress Press, 1981), 54–55. Oberman sees two basic views of Scripture and tradition: "Tradition 1," or "T1," and

from the tradition of the church fathers, the Reformers argued that their stance (T1) was actually the view of the fathers.[64]

While many of the fathers were characterized by Tradition 1, in the late medieval period we begin to see signs of another view, what we can call "Tradition 2" (T2). Tradition 2 is the view that divine revelation has not one but two sources: Scripture *and* ecclesiastical Tradition, the latter of which includes the pope and the magisterium.[65] This view holds that Scripture is *not* sufficient in and of itself, nor the *sole infallible* authority and source of divine revelation. Scripture must now share that stage with church Tradition, its equal in many respects. This means that ecclesiastical Tradition is not a subordinate authority to Scripture, but an equally infallible and inerrant authority.[66] Tradition 2 gained prominence between the years 1100 and 1400, and by the time of the Reformation, it was the position taught by the Roman Church, as Luther and Calvin attest to in their early years of education.[67]

During the medieval years we see a widening of the gap between Scripture and tradition. While Scripture and tradition were closely aligned in the early church, in the late Middle Ages the two were severed from each other, so that tradition became something *in addition to* Scripture. For many late-medieval fathers, this was not problematic since they believed God had provided *two* sources of divine, infallible revelation, one being Tradition. Where Scripture was ambiguous, silent, or even deficient, the second source of revelation (Tradition) spoke with clarity and authority even though it was an unwritten tradition that was in view.[68]

"Tradition 2," or "T2," as having been the principal competitors through most of church history. By contrast, Anthony Lane argues for a total of four highly influential views and later expanded the number to six: See A. N. S. Lane, "Scripture, Tradition, and Church: An Historical Survey," *Vox Evangelica* 9 (1975): 37–55; Anthony Lane, "Tradition," in *Dictionary for Theological Interpretation of the Bible*, ed. Kevin J. Vanhoozer (Grand Rapids: Baker, 2005), 810–11. However, Mathison disagrees, arguing that historical data rules out such a multiview classification (*The Shape of Sola Scriptura*, 86n.13).

64. Oberman, *Dawn of the Reformation*, 270.

65. See Oberman, *Forerunners of the Reformation*, 54–55.

66. Moreover, in T2 the Church is credited with creating Scripture, not the other way around. If Scripture is not sufficient, neither is it absolutely necessary. The church is not dependent upon Scripture for its existence. While Scripture may be important for the church's ongoing health, the church is not derivative of Scripture. Of course, this would differ significantly from the early church fathers and the Reformers, whom we have yet to consider.

67. There is debate among scholars, however, as to exactly who was first responsible for T2. Compare Heiko Oberman's *Forerunners of the Reformation* with Alister McGrath's *The Intellectual Origins of the European Reformation* (Oxford: Basil Blackwell, 1987), 140–51.

68. Alister E. McGrath, *Reformation Thought*, 4th ed. (Oxford: Wiley-Blackwell, 2012), 93.

Though we can characterize pockets of the late-medieval period as a shift toward T2, this does not mean that the church unanimously agreed on the authority of that Tradition. While advocates of T2 agreed there were two sources of revelation, they were not all unified in how they should understand Tradition. The central question in the debate became: Who has final authority in matters of doctrine, the pope or church councils? Those who chose the pope became known as *curialists*, while those who chose church councils were called *conciliarists*.

Curialism's argument for papal control and dominion traced a line from the medieval period all the way back to Constantine. Constantine's Christianization of the Roman Empire, says Timothy George, "coupled with the barbarian onslaughts of the fifth century, left the bishop of Rome in a politically strategic position," as would become evident in Pope Gelasius I at the end of the fifth century when he wrote that the bishop of the see was to be considered "pre-eminent over all priests" and deserved the church's greatest honor.[69] Pope Gregory VII followed in Gelasius's trail, and in 1075 he wrote *Dictatus Papae* declaring that the Roman Church "had never erred, nor ever, by the witness of Scripture, shall err to all eternity."[70] This statement, a straightforward affirmation of ecclesiastical supremacy and infallibility, would be followed by the arguments of Innocent III (1198–1216), who claimed that the pope was the mediator between God and man, having superior authority even over the emperor. And in his papal bull in 1302, *Unam Sanctam*, Pope Boniface VIII topped them all by stating that only God has the right to judge the pope, for the pope has authority over all: "We declare, state, define and pronounce that it is altogether necessary to salvation for every human creature to be subject to the Roman Pontiff."[71]

The Great Western Schism (1378–1417) would raise some problems with these claims as the office of pope was brought into serious question. By 1409, three different popes were each claiming equal rights to the papal throne. Who was right? Perhaps even more importantly, "Who gets to decide who is right?" Pope or council? Even here, however, the debate was not straightforward. Those arguing that the pope decided had to determine which pope had the authority to make that

---

69. George, *Theology of the Reformers*, 31. For what follows in this section I am indebted to George.

70. Cited in Brian Tierney, *The Crisis of Church and State, 1050–1300* (Englewood Cliffs, NJ: Prentice Hall, 1964), 49–50.

71. Ibid., 189.

decision. Each of the three vying for papal territory thought he was the God-ordained choice, condemning the others with vehemence. In fact, each pope excommunicated the others!

The conciliarists took a very different stance, believing authority and power resided not in one individual but in ecclesiastical councils.[72] They believed the entire affair served to prove their position. As George explains:

> At the heart of the conciliar theory was the fundamental distinction between the universal church (representatively embodied in a general council) and the Roman Church (consisting of pope and cardinals). Already in canon law a loophole to the doctrine that the pope was above human judgment had been provided in the clause— *nisi deprehendatur a fide devius*, "unless he deviates from the faith." Such deviation was interpreted to mean not only manifest heresy but also such acts as threatened the integrity of the church.[73]

To the relief of many, the Council of Constance (1414–1418)— which condemned Jan Hus to be burned at the stake—convened in order to address these issues and resolve the problem of the three popes. Yet rather than choosing one of the three candidates—Gregory XII, Benedict XIII, John XXIII—they selected a fourth, Martin V. They issued a decree, *Sacrosancta* (1415), which declared the primacy and superiority of *conciliarism*. You would assume that the conciliarists had won the day, since a church council and not a pope had finally put the issue to rest. Yet ironically the pope they chose, Martin V, would disagree with the council, declaring the council's decision void. And so the debate continued.

With the Reformation just around the corner, curialism was gaining the upper hand. In *Execrabilis* (1460), the bull of Pope Pius II, the pope threatened excommunication to anyone who supposes he "can appeal from the Pope . . . to a future council."[74] *Execrabilis* "struck

---

72. For example, consider Pierre d' Ailly (d. 1420), Jean Gerson (d. 1429), and Dietrich of Niem (d. 1418). George qualifies, however, that the conciliarists did not seek to "abolish the papacy but to relegate it to its proper role within the church." He explains: "They claimed that the *plenitude potestatis*, 'fulness of power,' resided only in God, not in any individual man, not even in the pope. The conciliarists advocated one pope, one undivided church, and a program of moral reform modeled on the example of the early church" (George, *Theology of the Reformers*, 33).

73. Ibid. George is building off of the expertise of Brian Tierney.

74. Quoted in ibid.

at the heart of conciliarism . . . [and] thus declared—with more vigor than Pope Martin V before—null and void the two famous decrees of Constance: *Sacrosancta* (the superiority of the council over the pope—April 6, 1415) and *Frequens* (at least once every ten years a council as highest court of appeal—October 9, 1417)."[75]

On the eve of the Reformation, papal primacy was further buttressed by Pope Julius II (1503–13), who stacked the Fifth Lateran Council (1512–17) with cardinals in his favor, including Cajetan, who heralded papal supremacy. For the Reformers, this entire debate between the pope and the councils simply demonstrated the inconsistency and self-destructive nature of the T2 view. Rome was claiming that Tradition was on an equal level with Scripture, but which Tradition, that of papal superiority or the Tradition affirmed by the councils? How could Rome claim to have a unified, infallible Tradition when those within that Tradition disagreed with one another, even anathematizing other popes?[76]

An Obstinate Schismatic and Manifest Heretic

Knowing the background leading up to his appearance at Worms, we see that Luther rejected the two-source theory (T2), which viewed oral Tradition as a second, extrabiblical, and inerrant source of divine revelation passed down from the apostles to the magisterium. While Luther greatly valued the fathers and councils that defended orthodoxy, he still argued that Scripture alone is our infallible source of divine revelation (T1).

And while it may still be a matter of debate whether Luther actually said the exact words "Here I stand," the words are consistent with his position. The following year Luther replied to Henry VIII, whom he called "King Heinz," saying:

> For me it is enough that King Heinz cannot quote a single
> Scripture. . . . I place against the sayings of all Fathers, and every

---

75. Oberman, *Forerunners of the Reformation*, 213–14.
76. Commenting on the Great Western Schism, Joseph Ratzinger (later to become Pope Benedict XVI) highlights this weakness (ironically): "For nearly half a century, the Church was split into two or three obediences that excommunicated one another, so that every Catholic lived under excommunication by one pope or another, and, in the last analysis, no one could say with certainty which of the contenders had right on his side. The Church no longer offered certainty of salvation; she had become questionable in her whole objective form—the true Church, the true pledge of salvation, had to be sought outside the institution" (Joseph Ratzinger, *Principles of Catholic Theology* [San Francisco: Ignatius, 1987], 196).

artifice and word of angels, men and devils, the Scripture and the gospel. Here I stand, here I bid defiance, here I strut about and say, God's Word for me is above everything. I will not give a hair though a thousand Augustines, a thousand Heinz-churches were all against me, and I am certain that the true church with me holds fast to the Word of God.[77]

In this letter to King Henry, we see how Luther was able to hold *sola Scriptura* and church tradition in proper balance. For Luther, Scripture is the sole infallible authority to such an extent that it would not matter if a thousand Augustines or Henrys were against him.[78] At the same time, Luther does not go as far as some radical reformers would, disregarding tradition altogether. Luther ends his statement by saying, "I am certain that the true church with me holds fast to the Word of God." He cares about the tradition so much that he is confident that the "true church" is in his corner. Luther believed that the church throughout the ages would serve as a witness to *sola Scriptura* in a ministerial role, subordinate to the infallible authority of Scripture itself.

One final word must be said about Luther's defense at the Diet of Worms. Luther said, "Unless I am convinced by the testimony of the Scriptures *or by clear reason*." By clear or evident reason (*ratione evidente*), Luther has in mind logical inferences the exegete draws from the biblical text and its principles.[79] His statement here is not an affirmation of autonomous reason. Following Augustine's doctrine of pervasive depravity, Luther despised the belief that sinful man, living after the fall of Genesis 3, could somehow use his rational capabilities as a source of Christian truth *independent* of Scripture. Luther did not believe that by his own reason a man could draw theological conclusions sufficient for the Christian life.[80] To the contrary, Luther believed that reason, like tradition, held a *ministerial* rather than a magisterial role.[81] Contemporary attempts to blame Luther for the Enlightenment's elevation of reason, therefore, are out of line and misguided.

---

77. WA 10.II.256.

78. J. I. Packer, "'Sola Scriptura' in History and Today," in *God's Inerrant Word*, ed. John Warwick Montgomery (Minneapolis: Bethany, 1973), 61n.3.

79. Brecht, *Luther: His Road*, 452.

80. Packer, "'Sola Scriptura,'" 44.

81. For an excellent treatment of Luther's use of reason in light of *sola Scriptura*, see Thompson, *Sure Ground on Which to Stand*, 265–71.

A Bible for Every German

Shortly after Luther's stance at Worms, the verdict was clear: Luther was indeed "an obstinate schismatic and manifest heretic." On his trip home, Luther was kidnapped by men with swords and bows. Had he been murdered? Some feared the worst, including the German painter Albrecht Dürer, who grieved, "O God, if Luther be dead who will proclaim the holy gospel so clearly to us?"[82] But Luther had not been killed. He had been kidnapped by allies, not enemies. Friedrich the Wise had orchestrated his safe escape to Wartburg Castle.

What did Luther do while in hiding? He wrote sermons for the German churches and labored diligently in translating the Greek New Testament into German, completing it in under four months. Though he finished his first translation in 1522, he would return to the work of translating the New Testament again and again with ongoing revisions.

After his exile, Luther formed a committee to begin translating the Old Testament as well. Supervising the project, Luther personally translated large sections of the Old Testament and oversaw everybody else's translations. In 1534 the German translation of the Bible, including both the Old and New Testaments, was ready for the public. Even after its publication, Luther and his committee would continue with further revisions. So influential was Luther's work that some have estimated that by the time of his death in 1546 more than a half million copies of his Bible were in the hands of the people![83]

Why do we note Luther's German translation of the Scriptures? His work in this area demonstrates that Luther not only affirmed *sola Scriptura* but practiced it as well. At the time, the work of Bible translation was far from innocent. Luther knew that it could be a cannonball blowing a hole right through the wall of the infallible authority of the pope.[84] Luther was committed, even in the face of persecution, to seeing the Word of God translated into the vernacular so that the people of God could read it for themselves and see the gospel truths that had so transformed his own life. The Bible became a jewel in the hands of the Reformers not because it was a "handbook for happy living" or a "primer of metaphysics about God," but because in it the

---

82. Bainton, *Here I Stand*, 188.

83. George, *Theology of the Reformers*, 331.

84. Richard Lints, *The Fabric of Theology: A Prolegomenon to Evangelical Theology* (Grand Rapids: Eerdmans, 1993), 147.

Christian possessed the "the swaddling clothes in which Christ lies."[85] By devoting himself to Bible translation, Luther was sending a loud message to the German people that the Bible holds supremacy over all human traditions.

Sola Scriptura and Huldrych Zwingli

Luther was not the only Reformer to affirm Scripture's infallibility and authority. A priest in Switzerland, Huldrych Zwingli (1484–1531), who was ministering high in the Alps, came to many of the same conclusions that Luther did. Zwingli's turn to Reformation theology came less suddenly and more progressively, and he claimed to have arrived at his conclusions independently of the German Reformer.[86] Zwingli was influenced by humanist scholar Desiderius Erasmus and was especially indebted to his 1516 edition of the Greek New Testament. Zwingli feasted upon the biblical text, memorizing all of Paul's epistles in Greek. By turning to God's Word, Zwingli saw his great need to be "led by the Word and Spirit of God" and to "set aside all these [human teachings] and to learn the doctrine of God direct from his own Word."[87]

Zwingli was called as priest to the Minster church in Zurich, and on January 1, 1519, Zwingli surprised his congregation by abandoning the lectionary.[88] Instead, Zwingli began preaching through the Gospel of Matthew, chapter by chapter, verse by verse, since the "text was to be treated as a whole," every word dispensed from God's own mouth.[89] Zwingli was done with what he called "canned" sermons; it was time to lead the people through the Word of God![90] Zwingli's method (*lectio continua*) was greatly inspired by John Chrysostom. After Zwingli finished Matthew, he continued preaching through Acts, 1–2 Timothy, Galatians, and 1–2 Peter. By 1525 Zwingli had preached through most of the New Testament, so he started preaching the Old Testament.[91]

---

85. George, *Reading Scripture with the Reformers*, 256.

86. *Z* 2:149; *Huldrych Zwingli: Writings*, ed. and trans. E. J. Furcha and H. W. Pipkin (Allison Park, PA: Pickwick, 1984), 1:119. For a much more in-depth discussion of Zwingli than I can provide here, see George, *Theology of the Reformers*, 113–70.

87. *Z* 1:379. See also *Of the Clarity and Certainty of the Word of God*, in *Zwingli and Bullinger*, ed. G. W. Bromiley, LCC (Louisville: Westminster John Knox, 1953), 90–91.

88. George, *Theology of the Reformers*, 117. The lectionary prescribed what was to be read and which biblical texts were to be assigned for each week.

89. Bruce Gordon, *The Swiss Reformation* (New York: Manchester University Press, 2002), 51; G. R. Potter, *Zwingli* (New York: Cambridge University Press, 1976), 60.

90. George, *Theology of the Reformers*, 117.

91. Ibid.

The seeds of the Reformation in Zurich, however, almost died before they had a chance to take root. Between August 1519 and February 1520, a plague stormed through Zurich, taking the lives of more than two-thousand people. Barely escaping death, Zwingli found his heart struck by God's grace, and he was convinced that he could depend upon Christ alone for his justification. On October 10, 1522, Zwingli resigned as priest of Zurich. However, the city council hired him as preacher, which gave Zwingli the opportunity and leverage needed to begin implementing Protestant reform, which would begin at the grassroots level.[92]

Tensions continued to rise in the city, however, and on January 29, 1523, more than six hundred people gathered in Zurich's town hall for the First Zurich Disputation, where Zwingli put forth his *Sixty-Seven Articles*.[93] Zwingli was ready for a debate with Johannes Fabri, bringing with him his Hebrew Old Testament, Greek New Testament, and Latin Vulgate. In the debate with Fabri, the issue of biblical authority became the focal point. When Rome's doctrine of the intercession of the saints and Mary was raised, Zwingli placed the burden of proof on Fabri, asking him to tell the council exactly where in Scripture such a doctrine is found. Fabri appealed to the history and traditions of the church, while Zwingli appealed to Scripture, for unlike tradition he believed that Scripture alone is inspired by God, is without error, and is our final authority. While Fabri claimed that the church assembled as a council cannot err, Zwingli argued that the church, as represented by popes, cardinals, and bishops, as well as various councils, *had* erred and the different representatives had even contradicted each other. Scripture alone, exclaimed Zwingli, is free from error. Every common person, argued Zwingli, should have a copy of the Greek New Testament. No longer could bishops and priests claim special authority and privilege to the Bible as the only ones who can and should interpret its meaning, as if the common Christian did not also have the Holy Spirit. The clergy were no longer to have a monopoly on Scripture.[94]

Toward the end of the meeting, a priest in the meeting spoke up, asking whether one should refrain from reading Gregory or Ambrose

---

92. Z 3:446; Gordon, *Swiss Reformation*, 56; George, *Theology of the Reformers*, 119.

93. For the points that follow, consult Ulrich Zwingli, *Ulrich Zwingli (1484–1531): Selected Works*, trans. Lawrence A. McLouth (1901; repr., Philadelphia: University of Pennsylvania Press, 1972), 38–110; Ulrich Zwingli, "The Sixty-Seven Articles of Zwingli," in *Zwingli: Selected Works*, 111–17.

94. George, *Theology of the Reformers*, 121; Gordon, *Swiss Reformation*, 58.

and instead read only Scripture.[95] In his response, Zwingli carefully avoided what we have called *nuda Scriptura*. He answered that it is just fine to read the fathers and benefit from them. However, should something be discovered that runs contrary to the Scriptures, one must let the Scriptures correct the fathers. Zwingli reminded his audience that this was not merely his opinion, it was the opinion of Gregory and Ambrose themselves, for they appealed to the Scriptures to support their writings, showing where ultimate authority rests. At that moment, Hans von Schlieren, a priest, asked how he could accomplish such reading when he was too poor to buy books. Zwingli insisted that no one should be without a copy of the Bible, and he appealed to the citizenry to make sure that they helped their priests purchase a copy of the Scriptures. Zwingli's point was clear: even if you could afford nothing else, you must have the Scriptures. They *alone* are the final authority. They *alone* are the words of God.

That day in January 1523, the council, having heard both sides, reached its decision: Zwingli was to continue proclaiming the Scriptures.[96] This declaration formally assumed the Protestant principle of *sola Scriptura*. This *sola* had already been acknowledged by the council back in 1520 when the council said that all preaching was to be based on and consistent with the Bible.[97] When Zwingli was retained as a city employee after he resigned in 1522 as people's priest, it was yet another indicator that the cause of *sola Scriptura* and "Bibliocracy" was advancing.[98] This First Disputation recognized the Scriptures as the "infallible judges" that could arbitrate the debate between Protestantism and Rome.[99] *Sola Scriptura* became the formal principle of Zwingli's Swiss reformation, and Zwingli labored doggedly to see every aspect of the church wholly reformed according to God's Word.[100]

Radicalizing the Bible: *Nuda Scriptura*

To this point we have seen that an affirmation and defense of *sola Scriptura* lay at the nucleus of the sixteenth-century Reformation. This

---

95. This dialogue appears to have occurred after the council had declared its decision.
96. Bernd Moeller, *Imperial Cities and the Reformation*, trans. Erik Midelfort and Mark U. Edwards (Philadelphia: Fortress, 1972), 54n.1.
97. George, *Theology of the Reformers*, 121.
98. Ibid.
99. Ibid., 131.
100. G. W. Bromiley, "General Introduction," in Bromiley, *Zwingli and Bullinger*, 29–31.

did not mean that Reformers like Luther, Zwingli, and Calvin were posing a strict either/or dilemma: Scripture *or* tradition. While the Reformers rejected Rome's understanding of tradition (as an additional extrabiblical and infallible source of revelation alongside Scripture) and upheld the supremacy and final authority of Scripture *over* tradition, it would be a mistake to think the Reformers did not value tradition or see it in some sense as a subordinate authority. The Reformers believed tradition was on their side. As far as the fathers and councils were consistent with Scripture, Luther said, they were to be listened to and obeyed.[101] In fact, the Reformers became very frustrated when certain radicals sought to discard tradition altogether. For the Reformers, *sola Scriptura* meant the Bible is our final authority, but it did not mean the Bible is our only authority. The more radical elements of the Reformation were not defending and practicing *sola Scriptura*; they were turning to *nuda Scriptura*.[102]

Though countless radical reformers could be mentioned here, we can broadly group them into three types.[103] The Anabaptists saw the Bible as their foundation and favored the New Testament over the Old Testament. They strove to return the church to the golden days of the apostles. The second group, the Spiritualists, looked to the Holy Spirit in their own experience as a superior witness and authority over the external ecclesiastical rituals and ceremonies.[104] For some of the

---

101. Martin Luther, "Sermons on the Second Epistle of St. Peter," in *LW* 30:166.

102. Why did the radicals take such a skeptical stance toward tradition? The radicals believed that the true church had been lost after Constantine came into power in the fourth century (some went back further and argued it was lost right after the apostles!), and the church was not recovered until the sixteenth century when the radicals started their own renewal movement. The radicals believed there was no point in depending on and paying regard to a tradition that was corrupt. To them, church tradition was fruit from the poisonous tree. More often than not, this resulted in an extreme emphasis on the individual, especially that individual who was more blessed with the Spirit than others. Each person could interpret the Bible however he or she pleased, with no regard for the community of believers in ages past. See Jaroslav Pelikan, *Obedient Rebels* (London: SCM, 1964), 36–38; Meic Pearse, *The Great Restoration: The Religious Radicals of the 16th and 17th Centuries* (Carlisle, UK: Paternoster, 1998), 37–38, 146–47; McGrath, *Reformation Thought*, 95–96, 100–102.

103. These three categories come from George H. Williams and Angel Mergal, eds., *Spiritual and Anabaptist Writers* (Philadelphia: Westminster, 1957), 19–38. See also George H. Williams, *The Radical Reformation* (Kirksville, MO: Sixteenth Century Journal, 1992). These categories do not deny overlap or similarities between groups, nor do these labels exhaustively cover every radical reformer. But they do capture the main differences between many of the radical reformers.

104. The insistence on the individual's right to interpret Scripture however he sees best and the disregard for the exegetical consensus of the past too often resulted in the exaltation

Spiritualists, baptism and the Lord's Supper were to be abandoned in favor of the inner testimony of the Spirit.[105] The third group, the Evangelical Rationalists, held that it was not the Bible or the Spirit but rather reason that captivated their allegiance. Granted, this emphasis on reason was to be accompanied by the Spirit and guided by the Bible, but in the end the emphasis was on human reason. As a result, some rejected doctrines of the faith that appeared *unreasonable*, such as the Trinity or the deity of Christ. What united all three of these groups was the belief that for all their reform, the Reformers had not gone far enough.

Consider two examples. The Spiritualist Thomas Müntzer (c. 1489–1525) set the Spirit against the Bible, elevating new revelations from the Spirit over the old written text. Scripture, he protested, is nothing more than ink on paper. "Bible, Babel, buble!"[106] Müntzer believed that what we need in our own day is for God to speak afresh with new revelation, just as he did to the biblical authors in their day. We need a new Daniel, one who is led not by Scripture but by the Spirit. Müntzer confidently proclaimed that he was this new Daniel.[107]

Müntzer, however, was not all that different from Rome in his position, for they both agreed that the Bible was not enough and needed an infallible, inspired interpreter. The difference was that while Rome said infallible Tradition was the remedy, Müntzer believed that a prophet from the Spirit was the answer. What we need today, he said, is the "new Elijah, the new Daniel, to whom is given the key of David to open the book sealed with seven seals."[108]

How did Luther respond to Müntzer? Luther originally had recommended him for ministry, but as time passed, he would come to call him the "Satan of Allstedt." Roland Bainton accurately captures Luther's frustration and disgust:

---

of the individual especially blessed with the Spirit. Pelikan, *Obedient Rebels*, 36–38; Pearse, *Great Restoration*, 37–38, 146–47.

105. One example would be Caspar Schwenckfeld.

106. Quoted in Bainton, *Here I Stand*, 263.

107. Thomas Müntzer, "Sermon before Princes," in Williams and Mergal, *Spiritual and Anabaptist Writers*, 47–70.

108. Bainton, *Here I Stand*, 263. See Thomas Müntzer, "Auslegung des zweiten Kapitels Daniels," in Franz Lau, *Der Linke Flügel der Reformation, Klassiker des Protestantantismus*, ed. Heinold Fast (Bremen: Carl Schünemann, 1962), 292; Heinold Fast, *Schriften und Briefe, Kritische Gesamtausgabe*, ed. Günther Franz, Quelle und Forschungen zur Reformationsgeschichte 33 (Gütersloh: Gütersloher Verlaghaus, 1968), 504–11.

Müntzer was readily able to find support for his view of the spirit in the Scripture itself, where it is said that "the letter killeth, but the spirit giveth life" (II Cor. 3:6). Luther replied that of course the letter without the spirit is dead, but the two are no more to be divorced than the soul is to be separated from the body. The real menace of Müntzer in Luther's eyes was that he destroyed the uniqueness of Christian revelation in the past by his elevation of revelation in the present.[109]

Müntzer elevated the Spirit over the historic written Word, leading Luther to conclude that Müntzer "had swallowed the Holy Ghost, feathers and all."[110] Internal, inward, subjective spiritual experience had taken the place of the historic, objective Scriptures. Müntzer was advocating not *sola Scriptura* but *sola experientia*!

The second example of a radical reformer is the Dutch Anabaptist Menno Simons (1496–1561), from whose name comes the group we know today as the Mennonites. Unlike those at Münster who resorted to violence, Menno would become a pacifist, believing that nonviolence was one of the true marks of the church. He would spend his life as a hunted heretic, moving from place to place baptizing new followers. While Menno liked the Reformers' rejection of many of Rome's doctrines, he did not side with the Reformers on everything, including Chalcedonian Christology, predestination, the bondage of the will, and infant baptism. And while Menno may have shared the Reformers' affirmation of Scripture's infallibility and authority, he was far more critical when it came to tradition. "Luther and Melanchthon," he said, "have correctly expressed themselves according to the Scripture" but "did not follow their own advice!"[111] In an effort to be consistent, Menno refused to appeal to Nicaea, Constantinople, or the fathers in his *Confession of the Triune God* (1550). To do so, he believed, was to go beyond the Bible. Menno's lack of consultation with the fathers becomes painfully obvious when he departed from Nicene and Chalcedonian Christology by arguing that Jesus assumed a celestial humanity.[112] If Menno would have paid attention to the history of

---

109. Bainton, *Here I Stand*, 264.
110. Ibid.
111. *CWMS*, 312.
112. This meant that Jesus passed through Mary like water passes through a pipe. On Menno's struggle to be consistent with his radicalization of *sola Scriptura*, see George, *Theology of the Reformers*, 289–90.

doctrine, he would have avoided this heresy. Instead, his ignorance of the past cursed him to repeat it.

Menno did not go in the direction of other radicals, such as the Spiritualists, who elevated the Spirit above the Word. He came into direct conflict with David Joris, who claimed to be the "true" Third David and favored the unwritten, internal "word" of the Spirit. Joris's words are as shocking today as they were in the sixteenth century: "Faith is revealed in the power of the Spirit and in the power of truth, not in the telling of the Biblical story, nor in the story of the miracles of the apostles and prophets, nor in the corporeal proof of the outer cross of Christ, nor in his incarnation, his death or his resurrection, nor in his second coming."[113]

The radicals mentioned here give us a small taste of their views.[114] Summarizing the beliefs of the radical reformers is difficult since there was such an array of diversity among them. Nevertheless, we can fairly conclude that if Rome adhered to T2 and the Reformers to T1, the radicals affirmed Tradition O. They were typically characterized by an attitude of skepticism and even outright disregard for anything that smelled like tradition. Their disregard was captured with much bombast by Sebastian Franck (1499–1542) when he remarked: "Foolish Ambrose, Augustine, Jerome, Gregory—of whom not one even knew the Lord, so help me God, nor was sent by God to teach. Rather, they were all apostles of Antichrist."[115] The radical reformers, living up to their name, radicalized *sola Scriptura*.[116]

Sola Scriptura in the Vernacular: William Tyndale

Luther's German New Testament was printed in Wittenberg in 1522, and it would have an enormous impact for the Protestant cause. But Luther was not the only one to translate the Scriptures into the common language of the people. William Tyndale's translation of the Bible into English was printed only a few years later in 1525 at Cologne by a printer named Peter Quentell.

Tyndale was educated at Oxford and lived in Cambridge when

---

113. Quoted in ibid., 293.

114. For a more in-depth treatment of the radicals, see Pearse, *Great Restoration*.

115. McGrath, *Reformation Thought*, 102. Also consider the Schleitheim Confession, drafted by Michael Sattler in 1527.

116. Ibid., 10. Unfortunately, some evangelicals radicalize *sola Scriptura* in our own day, a problem we will address more thoroughly in chapter 10.

Luther's writings were burned in 1521 at both London and Cambridge. Tyndale was breathing in the air of Erasmus, who had resided at Queen's College, where he worked studiously on his Greek New Testament. With Luther's revolutionary ideas swimming around in the heads of young theologians and Erasmus's groundbreaking work in the Greek text freshly printed, the atmosphere was ripe for further advances. The people were hungry to read the Bible, even if the legal authorities said otherwise. Tyndale felt a deep-rooted conviction that he was called to make God's Word available to God's people. John Foxe recounts a telling encounter with Tyndale that reveals his single-minded passion:

> Master Tyndale happened to be in the company of a learned man and in the communing and disputing with him, drove him to that issue that the learned man said, "We would be better off without God's law than the pope's." Master Tyndale hearing that, answered him, "I defy the pope and all his laws," and said, "if God spare my life, ere many years, I will cause a boy that driveth a plow shall know more of the Scripture than thou doest."[117]

Tyndale, as hinted earlier, was influenced by Erasmus, and in another place we see a similar statement spoken by Erasmus:

> I would that even the lowliest women read the Gospels and the Pauline epistles. And I would that they were translated into all languages so that they could be read and understood not only by Scots and Irish, but also by Turks and Saracens. . . . Would that, as a result, the farmer sings some portion of them at the plow, the weaver hums some parts of them to the movement of his shuttle, the traveler lightens the weariness of the journey with stories of this kind![118]

Note a key difference between these two men. While Erasmus said "I would" (*utinam*), Tyndale said "I will"! This difference in verb tense, however slight it might seem, serves to characterize the two men. Where Erasmus wished and speculated, Tyndale was resolved

---

117. John Foxe, *The Unabridged Acts and Monuments Online*, 1563 ed. (HRI Online, Sheffield, 2011), 570, http://www.johnfoxe.org. For an excellent overview of Tyndale that I rely on, see George, *Theology of the Reformers*, 327–76.

118. Quoted in John C. Olin, ed., *Christian Humanism and the Reformation* (New York: Fordham University Press, 1987), 101. Erasmus quips, "Do you think that the Scriptures are fit only for the perfumed?" Quoted in Roland H. Bainton, *Erasmus of Christendom* (New York: Scribner, 1969), 141.

and determined.[119] As monumental as Erasmus's critical edition of the Greek New Testament was when it was published in 1516—indeed, Erasmus had provided Luther and Tyndale with a Greek text—nevertheless, Erasmus himself never translated the Bible into the vernacular.[120] Tyndale's translation, in this regard, would be revolutionary. While John Wycliffe (or perhaps his disciples) had translated into English from the Latin Vulgate, Tyndale would translate directly from the Hebrew and Greek.

To do this, Tyndale had to find a safe haven to complete the work since it was illegal, punishable by death. At thirty years old, Tyndale left his homeland and traveled to the continent. As he worked, he was constantly in hiding, seeking to avoid Cardinal Thomas Wolsey and Sir Thomas More. Both of these men were vicious enemies, unrelenting in their drive to see him captured.

Some believe Tyndale traveled to Wittenberg. Why Wittenberg? To see Luther, of course! Perhaps Tyndale sat under Luther as he lectured and preached, and took advantage of the opportunity to read and study Luther's German New Testament.[121] In 1525 Tyndale's own translation into English was finished and ready to print, but he met great opposition in his first attempt to print. Even as the pages were rolling off the press, the facilities of the printer at Cologne (Peter Quentell) were raided.[122] Tyndale grabbed what he could and picked up the project again at Worms under the printer Peter Schoeffer.[123] This time he was successful, and copies of his New Testament were distributed by the thousands. By 1526 plans were made to import Tyndale's translation into England where Christians waited eagerly to smuggle the Bible in and distribute copies. Soon, Tyndale's New Testament began

---

119. George, *Theology of the Reformers*, 334; Anne Richardson, "Tyndale's Quarrel with Erasmus: A Chapter in the History of the English Reformation," *Fides et Historia* 25 (Fall 1993): 53.

120. Erasmus's second edition was published in 1519.

121. To clarify, Tyndale did not go to Wittenberg because he was looking for a gracious God, but because translating the Bible into the vernacular was not granted by the English church. Up to this point, Tyndale's reform was closer to Erasmus than it was to Luther. See Carl R. Trueman, "Pathway to Reformation: William Tyndale and the Importance of the Scriptures," in *A Pathway into the Holy Scripture*, ed. P. E. Satterthwaite and D. F. Wright (Grand Rapids: Eerdmans, 1994), 13–15.

122. David Daniell, *William Tyndale: A Biography* (New Haven: Yale University Press, 1994), 108–10. As to why Tyndale's translation was illegal, see McGrath, *Reformation Thought*, 112.

123. George, *Theology of the Reformers*, 336.

to infiltrate the homes of believers willing to do anything to read the Bible in their native tongue.

The English king, Henry VIII, responded by banning the Bible. Cuthbert Tunstall preached against it in his sermons and even had copies burned in the churchyard of St. Paul. But Tyndale, who was constantly seeking refuge, continued his work, starting a translation of the Old Testament from Hebrew and having his translation of the Pentateuch published in Antwerp in 1530.[124] Tyndale's work on the Old Testament would be left unfinished, however, since he was finally caught in Antwerp, kidnapped, imprisoned, and then, on October 6, 1536, strangled to death at the stake where his body was burned. He was only forty-two. His final prayer before being put to death was: "Lord, open the King of England's eyes."[125]

Why is Tyndale's story so important to our understanding of *sola Scriptura*? Tyndale believed Scripture possessed the words of eternal life. By bringing the Bible to the common person in the common language, the Word of God was, often for the very first time, piercing the hearts of the people, igniting gospel reformation that the church had for so long been without.[126] Underneath all of his efforts and work was a grand assumption—that holy Scripture is its own interpreter—*sacra scriptura sui ipsius interpres.*[127] This Reformation slogan, which goes back to Augustine, does not simply mean that the clearer passages of Scripture are to interpret the less clear texts. It means that Scripture interprets us, the reader. As we have seen, the Reformers constantly appealed to tradition to support their understanding of the text. This slogan, however, conveys the idea that correct interpretation requires that we must submit ourselves to the Bible's interpretation of us. "The Bible does not lend itself to being analyzed and mastered as a mere literary artifact from antiquity," warns Timothy George. Instead, to "read the Bible is to encounter a numinous other." For Tyndale, the "Bible is its own interpreter in the sense that it does its own interpreting: it interprets its readers."[128] Naturally, then, Scripture stands over against

---

124. David Daniell, ed., *Tyndale's Old Testament* (New Haven, CT: Yale University Press, 1992).

125. Foxe, *Unabridged Acts*, 1076.

126. See Tyndale's epistle "To the Reader" in W. R. Cooper, ed., *The New Testament: The Text of the Worms Edition of 1526 in Original Spelling*, with a preface by David Daniell (London: British Library, 2000), 553. Also consult Daniell, *Tyndale's Old Testament*, 4.

127. For Luther's use of this phrase, see *WA* 7.97; Packer, "'Sola Scriptura,'" 45.

128. George, *Theology of the Reformers*, 341.

human authorities, even correcting them when in error. What is *new* about the Reformers' position is not that the Bible speaks with God's authority, nor that the Bible nourishes God's people, but their belief that the "Scripture interprets Scripture" principle precludes Rome's position that an infallible pope or council must give us the infallible interpretation. Reformers like Tyndale argued that the Scriptures can challenge declarations by popes and councils, even moving God's people to dissent from them if they are found to be contrary to Scripture.[129]

Such a *forte* in the Reformers' thought is best illustrated in Tyndale's disciple John Rogers and his encounter with Bishop Stephen Gardiner. Gardiner asserted with great confidence, "You can prove nothing by the Scripture. The Scripture is dead; it must have a living expositor." Rogers replied to the contrary, "No, the Scripture is alive!"[130] Like his mentor Tyndale, Rogers was also burned at the stake. But the point he argued was one worth dying for: Scripture is no dead document, but a living, breathing Word because through it the Spirit convicts the sinner and opens his eyes to the gospel of Jesus Christ. In this sense, it is appropriate to say that the formal principle of the Reformation, *sola Scriptura*, naturally gives birth to the material principle, *sola fide*.[131]

Tyndale's commitment to Bible translation, which ultimately cost him his life, was grounded in his belief in *sola Scriptura*. Tyndale knew the fathers well, even quoting them from time to time. However, in contrast to Thomas More, his Catholic opponent, Tyndale refused to place the fathers or church councils on equal standing with Scripture. He writes, "What is the cause that we damn some of Origen's works, and allow some? How know we that some is heresy and some not? By the Scripture, I trow. How know we that St. Augustine (which is the best, or one of the best, that ever wrote upon the Scripture) wrote many things amiss at the beginning, as many other doctors do? Verily, by the Scriptures."[132] According to Tyndale, Scripture is the only infallible source of divine revelation, and therefore it sits in judgment of even the best church fathers, who can err.[133]

---

129. Packer, "'Sola Scriptura,'" 44.
130. Foxe, *Unabridged Acts*, 1094.
131. George, *Theology of the Reformers*, 341.
132. *PS* 1:154.
133. We have limited ourselves to Tyndale, but to see how *sola Scriptura* was defended in the English Reformation, see Philip E. Hughes, *Theology of the English Reformers* (London: Hodder and Stoughton, 1965), 11–44.

Sola Scriptura in Geneva: Calvin versus Sadoleto

John Calvin is the last Reformer we will discuss in the context of *sola Scriptura*, but he is by no means the least! Calvin was a second-generation Reformer, yet some consider him to be one of the greatest voices of the Reformation due to his ability to synthesize the Christian religion. Like Luther before him, Calvin was a strong and persistent defender of *sola Scriptura*. And while Calvin was a theologian of many controversies, the controversy that brings *sola Scriptura* to the fore-front was his written debate with Cardinal Jacopo Sadoleto, bishop of Carpentras in southern France.[134]

On March 18, 1539, Cardinal Jacopo Sadoleto wrote a letter to the magistrates and citizens of Geneva. He adopted an aggressive tone, writing to the Genevans to persuade them to return to Rome. Sadoleto's letter was timely, because in April of the previous year John Calvin and his colleague Guillaume Farel had been banished from the city and exiled from the pulpit due to conflict with the civil rulers. Sadoleto saw this as the perfect opportunity to write to the Genevans, urging them to return to the Catholic fold.

The council that received Sadoleto's letter, committed as they were to the Protestant Reformation, struggled to find a worthy theologian who could respond to Sadoleto. The letter was sent on to authorities in Bern, who assured the Genevan magistrates that an appropriate responder would be recruited. Ironically, Calvin was chosen. The letter was sent to Calvin in Strasbourg, and he responded in a mere six days.

Sadoleto argued that the Genevans had departed from the one true church, which "errs not, and even cannot err, since the Holy Spirit constantly guides her public and universal decrees and Councils."[135]

---

134. Just prior to Calvin's tract, Luther had written his own work on the same topic, making similar arguments. *On the Councils and the Church* (*LW* 41) was prompted by Pope Paul III's decision to convoke a general council in 1537. Luther's argument is broken down into three sections: (1) Luther argues that the fathers and councils contradicted themselves and therefore it is mistaken to think that there is infallible doctrinal agreement. (2) The purpose of the early councils was not to establish new doctrine beyond the scope of Scripture. Furthermore, the authority of a council does not reside in the office itself but in its agreement with Scripture. Where a council disagrees with or contradicts Scripture, it has no authority. Where it does agree with Scripture, it is authoritative. But it is not authoritative simply because its decisions have been declared so by certain individuals. (3) The most essential mark of the church is whether it adheres to God's Word. For God's people to be God's people, they must possess God's Word. On these points, and their similarity to Calvin's argument, see David C. Steinmetz, *Luther in Context*, 2nd ed. (Grand Rapids: Baker Academic, 2002), 88–90.

135. *Letter by James Sadolet, a Roman Cardinal to the Senate and People of Geneva; in*

This meant that the dilemma for the Genevans was straightforward but serious:

> Whether is it more expedient for your salvation . . . by believing and following what the Catholic Church throughout the whole world, now for more than fifteen hundred years . . . approves with general consent; or innovations introduced within these twenty-five years, by crafty, or, as they think themselves, acute men; but men certainly who are not themselves the Catholic Church?[136]

According to Sadoleto, Calvin and the Reformers "tear the spouse of Christ in pieces," but now the Genevans, with Calvin banished, have the opportunity of a lifetime: they can return to the one, true faith of the one, true church, which is infallible.[137]

Given the threat, Calvin's reply to Sadoleto had to be hard-hitting. Calvin begins by accusing Sadoleto of misconstruing the proper relationship and order between the Spirit, the Word, and the church. The Spirit, says Calvin, "goes before the Church, to enlighten her in understanding the Word, while the Word itself is like the Lydian Stone, by which she tests all doctrines."[138] The church did not create the Word, but rather the Word, by the power of the Spirit, created the church. Therefore, the church is to test all doctrines by the inerrant standard and authority of the Word. The heart of the matter is the question of authority. For Sadoleto, it is the church that carries equal authority to (if not greater authority than) Scripture. For Calvin, Scripture alone is inspired by God and, as a result, without error. Therefore, Scripture alone is the ultimate and final authority.[139]

Calvin unravels Sadoleto's argument by exposing the corruption of the church. The "purity of the gospel" has been compromised through seeds of superstition, sown by "monsters of impiety."[140] Calvin's tone is indignant: the church has been robbed and devoured by its own leaders. The "sacred Supper" has been replaced by "a sacrifice, by which

---

which he endeavours to bring them back to the allegiance of the Roman Pontiff, in *John Calvin: Tracts and Letters,* ed. and trans. Henry Beveridge (Edinburgh: Banner of Truth, 2009), 1:18–19.

136. Ibid., 14.

137. Ibid., 18.

138. *Reply by John Calvin to Letter by Cardinal Sadolet to the Senate and People of Geneva,* in Beveridge, *John Calvin: Tracts and Letters,* 1:37.

139. Ibid., 66.

140. Ibid., 48.

the death of Christ is emptied of its virtues."[141] Indulgences have
"crept in with fearful dishonour to the cross of Christ."[142] And the
church is now characterized by "the accursed worship of images."[143]
For the sake of human traditions, "Christian liberty has been crushed
and destroyed."[144] All in all, the light of divine truth has "been extin-
guished, the word of God buried, the virtue of Christ left in profound
oblivion, and the pastoral office subverted."[145] In Calvin's estimation,
the situation could not be worse.

This is why the Reformers have "been careful to purge the churches
which the Lord has committed to us."[146] While Sadoleto viewed the
Reformers as declaring war against the church, the Reformers contended
against such evils to assist the church in "her extreme distress."[147] Like
Luther, Calvin believed that it was Rome, not the Reformers, who were
the real theological innovators. True unity would occur only when the
church returned to Scripture and submitted to its supreme authority—
the Word of God.

Sola Scriptura in Calvin's Institutes

Calvin's debate with Sadoleto gives us a taste of his underlying conviction of *sola Scriptura*. But this engagement is much like the appetizer
before the meal, which we find in Calvin's *Institutes of the Christian
Religion*. Four points in particular deserve our attention.

First, Calvin says that Scripture *is* the Word of God. Calvin was a
firm believer in the inspiration of Scripture (i.e., Scripture is breathed
out by God; 2 Tim 3:16).[148] In various ways, God put into the minds
of his patriarchs "what they should then hand down to their posterity."
A "firm certainty of doctrine was engraved in their hearts, so that they
were convinced and understood that what they had learned proceeded
from God." By his Word, says Calvin, "God rendered faith unambigu-
ous forever, a faith that should be superior to all opinion." At the proper
time, and in order for his Word to continue from generation to gen-

141. Ibid., 48–49.
142. Ibid., 49.
143. Ibid.
144. Ibid.
145. Ibid.
146. Ibid.
147. Ibid.
148. See especially John Calvin, *Institutes of the Christian Religion*, ed. John T. McNeill,
trans. Ford Lewis Battles (Philadelphia: Westminster, 1960), 1.8.1–9.

eration, God recorded his Law on "public tablets" and the "prophets afterward added as its interpreters."[149] God not only set forth his law, but Christ, the Mediator between God and man, is the only one who can accomplish true reconciliation and redemption. Therefore, since we are born in darkness and blind to the things of God, as glorious as the theater of creation is in revealing God as Creator, it is insufficient to save.[150] We need God to reveal himself not only as Creator but as Redeemer, and such a revelation comes in and through Scripture.[151] As Calvin explains, "In order that true religion may shine upon us, we ought to hold that it must take its beginning from heavenly doctrine and that no one can get even the slightest taste of right and sound doctrine unless he be a pupil of Scripture." It is in Scripture that God bears witness to himself and is "truly and vividly described to us from his works," works not appraised by our "depraved judgment but by the rule of eternal truth."[152] Hence, Scripture speaks with authority, for it is from God and it is God's message to needy sinners. For Calvin, what Scripture says, God says.

Second, Scripture receives its authority not from the church but *from God*. It pleased God to "hallow his truth to everlasting remembrance in the Scriptures alone [cf. John 5:39]." Hence, believers are to view the Scriptures as the "living words of God" and therefore fully authoritative because they have "sprung from heaven."[153] It is no surprise, then, that Calvin rejects Rome's "pernicious error" that "Scripture has only so much weight as is conceded to it by the consent of the church," as if the "eternal and inviolable truth of God depended upon the decision of men!"[154] Calvin believes Rome mocks the Holy Spirit when she asks, "Who can assure us that Scripture has come down whole and intact even to our very day? Who can persuade us to receive one book in reverence but to exclude another, unless the church prescribe a sure rule for all these matters? What reverence is due Scripture and what books ought to be reckoned within its canon depend, they say, upon the determination of the church."[155] Calvin believes that such a view

---

149. Ibid., 1.6.2.
150. On the insufficiency of generation revelation, see ibid., 1.6.3–4.
151. Ibid., 1.6.1–3.
152. Ibid., 1.6.3.
153. Ibid., 1.7.1.
154. Ibid.
155. Ibid.

is refuted by these words from the apostle Paul in Ephesians 2:20: the church is "built on the foundation of the apostles and prophets." If the "teaching of the prophets and apostles is the foundation, this must have had authority before the church began to exist."[156]

Let's consider this in more detail. Did Rome have a valid point here? Are not the writings of the prophets and apostles in doubt until the church declares them authoritative? No, responds Calvin, for "if the Christian church was from the beginning founded upon the writings of the prophets and the preaching of the apostles, wherever this doctrine is found, the acceptance of it—without which the church itself would never have existed—must certainly have preceded the church."[157] Calvin is clear that the church does not give Scripture its authority. Instead, the church receives that which God has already put in place, bearing witness to that which God has declared in his Word. Therefore, the question (or objection), "How can we be assured that this has sprung from God unless we have recourse to the decree of the church?" is as silly as asking, "Whence will we learn to distinguish light from darkness, white from black, sweet from bitter?" Just as white and black objects testify to their own color, or sweet and bitter foods to their own taste, so does Scripture fully exhibit "clear evidence of its own truth."[158]

Third, Calvin was clear that Scripture's credibility does not depend on man's reason but on the testimony of the Holy Spirit. Calvin explains that we will never be persuaded of the trustworthiness and authority of Scripture's doctrine until we are "persuaded beyond doubt that God is its Author." Therefore, the "highest proof of Scripture derives in general from the fact that God in person speaks in it." In that light, we must look to a "higher place than human reasons, judgments, or conjectures" and turn instead to the "secret testimony of the Spirit." The "Word will not find acceptance in men's hearts before it is sealed by the inward testimony of the Spirit." The same Spirit who spoke through the prophets will penetrate "into our hearts to persuade us that they faithfully proclaimed what had been divinely commanded."[159] For Calvin, Word and Spirit are inseparable, as the two go hand in

---

156. Ibid., 1.7.2.
157. Ibid.
158. Ibid. Calvin will also appeal to the witness of the Holy Spirit to the truthfulness of Scripture. See 1.7.4.
159. Ibid., 1.7.4.

hand, never contradicting each other, but validating and confirming each other.[160]

Fourth, only Scripture is our *infallible* and *inerrant* authority. Like Luther, Calvin's stance on the supremacy of Scripture over tradition reveals his belief in what we today refer to as the inerrancy of Scripture. Calvin did not explicitly articulate a doctrine of inerrancy with all of the nuancing used today in response to modern and postmodern challenges. But we would be misrepresenting Calvin to say that the basic *concept* of inerrancy is not present throughout his writings.[161] Calvin's affirmation of Scripture's perfection is crucial to his defense of *sola Scriptura* in his polemic against Rome. For Calvin, God's perfect and flawless revelation of himself grounds Scripture's supremacy and authority over any and every human authority. If Scripture contained errors and imperfections, Calvin could not exalt Scripture above tradition as the determining norm. But because Scripture is inerrant, Calvin can confidently affirm, in opposition to Rome, that only the Bible is our infallible and inerrant source of divine revelation. Armed with such a conviction concerning Scripture's authority, Calvin can say that the "power of the church, therefore, is not infinite but subject to the Lord's Word and, as it were, enclosed within it."[162]

The inerrancy of Scripture is what sets Calvin's *sola Scriptura* doctrine apart from Rome. Calvin writes, "What could come forth from the defiled mouth of Isaiah and the foolish mouth of Jeremiah but filth and folly, if they spoke their own word? But they had holy and pure lips when they began to be instruments of the Holy Spirit."[163] Calvin has more in mind here than the way every believer is led by the Spirit. Calvin also has in mind that unique act of inspiration in redemptive history. When the Spirit came upon God's chosen servants to pen Scripture, what they wrote was pure and holy. Calvin says the same of the apostles in the New Testament. This is the fundamental difference between the apostles and their successors. While the apostles are "sure and genuine scribes of the Holy Spirit, and their writings are therefore to be considered oracles of God," all those who

---

160. Ibid., 1.8.13; 1.9.2–3.

161. For Calvin's affirmation of inerrancy, see Packer, "John Calvin and the Inerrancy of Holy Scripture," 143–88; Kantzer, "Calvin and the Holy Scriptures," 115–55; Nicole, "John Calvin and Inerrancy," 425–42; Woodbridge, *Biblical Authority*, 49–100.

162. Calvin, *Institutes*, 4.8.4.

163. Ibid., 4.8.3.

came after taught what was already sealed in Scripture. Those who followed "are now not permitted to coin any new doctrine," but are simply "to cleave to that doctrine which God has subjected all men without exception."[164] Such a truth applies to the whole church, even those in the highest ecclesiastical positions. They too are subject to the inerrant authority and judgment of Scripture. And lest we think Calvin disconnects biblical authority from biblical inerrancy and the truthfulness of God, he concludes that "God deprives men of the capacity to put forth new doctrine in order that he alone may be our schoolmaster in spiritual doctrine as he alone is true [Rom 3:4] who can neither lie nor deceive. This rule pertains as much to the whole church as to individual believers."[165] In short, it is because God, the divine author, is a God of truth that his Word is also a Word of truth with no error mixed in it. Anything less would compromise the very character of God.

Calvin's argument here directly opposes Rome. Calvin protests Rome's teaching that "councils are governed directly by the Holy Spirit, and therefore cannot err," as well as Rome's claim to "coin dogmas" since the "church has the power to frame new articles of faith."[166] To the contrary, unlike Scripture, the church is not infallible or inerrant. It is true, says Calvin, that the church has been "sanctified by Christ," but "only the beginning of its sanctification is visible here."[167] The "end and perfect completion will appear when Christ, the Holy of Holies [cf. Heb., chs. 9, 10], truly and perfectly fills the church with his holiness."[168]

Rome's affirmation of ecclesial infallibility is again shown to be erroneous, says Calvin, when we understand the proper role between Word and Spirit. For Calvin, Word and Spirit are integral, and Rome goes wrong in bifurcating one from the other. Her belief that mother church cannot err is based upon her assumption that the "church is governed by the Spirit of God" and therefore "can proceed safely without the Word." No matter "where it may go, it can think or speak only what is true." Should the church "ordain anything beyond or apart from God's Word, this must be taken as nothing but a sure oracle of

---

164. Ibid., 4.8.9.
165. Ibid.
166. Ibid., 4.8.10.
167. Calvin is commenting on Eph 5:26–27.
168. Ibid., 4.8.12.

God."[169] Yet such a view clearly differs from the Protestant view: "Our opponents locate the authority of the church outside God's Word; but we insist that it be attached to the Word, and do not allow it to be separated from it."[170]

Calvin goes on to demonstrate the fallibility of the church, showing how councils and popes in the past have seriously disagreed with one another, even condemned one another, and at times taught heresy.[171] As we saw with Luther, we would err to conclude that Calvin was against the statements of church councils. In fact, Calvin believed that councils could serve a very important purpose, presenting an authoritative voice for orthodoxy that was far more powerful than any one individual on his own.[172] Yet councils are authoritative only as far as they are consistent with Scripture. Again we see this Reformation principle at work: the authority of councils is *ministerial*, subordinate to the *magisterial* authority of the Bible. Where a council departs from Scripture—and several councils have—that council's authority is not to be heeded, but Scripture is to be followed instead, for it alone is without error.[173]

The Council of Trent and Calvin's *Antidote*

So how did Rome respond to the Reformers' defense of *sola Scriptura*? At the Council of Trent in 1546, in its Fourth Session on April 8, Trent had this to say:

> The council clearly perceives that this truth and rule are contained in written books and in unwritten traditions which were received by the apostles from the mouth of Christ himself, or else have come down to us, handed on as it were from the apostles themselves at the inspiration of the Holy Spirit. Following the example of the orthodox fathers, the council accepts and venerates with a like feeling of piety and reverence all the books of both the Old and the New Testament, since the one God is the author of both, as well as the traditions concerning both faith and conduct, as either directly spoken by Christ or dictated by the Holy Spirit, which have been preserved in unbroken sequence in the Catholic Church.[174]

169. Ibid., 4.8.13.
170. Ibid.
171. Ibid., 4.9.1–14.
172. Ibid., 4.9.13.
173. Ibid., 4.9.14.
174. Session 4 of "Dogmatic Decrees of the Council of Trent, 1545–63," in *Creeds and*

Was Trent affirming two sources of infallible divine revelation (Scripture *and* unwritten Tradition)? This is a question that is hotly debated today. Some argue that the "unwritten traditions" spoken of by Trent do not add anything new but merely serve to interpret Scripture. In other words, it is not that two separate sources are in view, but merely that the content is conveyed through two different mediums.[175] Others, like medieval scholar Heiko Oberman, reject such a reading of Trent, believing the council to have affirmed the T2 position.[176] Weighing the historical evidence, the latter view seems far more likely.[177]

When we look at the circumstances that led to the fourth session of Trent, we find a serious debate about these issues. In the preliminary drafts of the council, the authors wrote that the truths "are contained partly [*partim*] in Scripture and partly [*partim*] in the unwritten traditions." Two Roman Catholic theologians—Nacchianti and Bonnucio—stood against this wording, arguing that the sufficiency and authority of Scripture was being undermined.[178]

As with many events in history, timing is everything. War erupted and the session ended. The records from the council simply come to an end. No clue is given as to what happened next.[179] Beyond the irritation

Confessions of Faith in Christian Tradition, vol. 2, *Part Four: Creeds and Confessions of the Reformation Era*, ed. Jaroslav Pelikan and Valerie Hotchkiss (New Haven: Yale University Press, 2003), 822.

175. For example, Josef Rupert Geiselmann, "*Das Konzil von Trient ueber das Verhaeltnis der Heiligen Schrift und der nicht geschriebenen Traditionen*," in *Die Muendliche Ueberlieferung* (Munich, 1957), 125–206; Rupert Geiselmann, *Die Heilige Schrift und die Tradition* (Freiburg: Herder, 1962), 270; Rupert Geiselmann, "Scripture, Tradition, and the Church: An Ecumenical Problem," in *Christianity Divided*, ed. D. J. Callahan, H. A. Obermann, and D. J. O'Hanlon (London: Sheed and Ward, 1962), 39–72; George H. Tavard, *Holy Writ or Holy Church: The Crisis of the Protestant Reformation* (London: Burns & Oates, 1959), 242–45. This view also seems to be held by Evangelicals and Catholics Together; see Charles Colson and Richard John Neuhaus, eds., *Your Word Is Truth: A Project of Evangelicals and Catholics Together* (Grand Rapids: Eerdmans, 2002), 5, 9–58, 79–101.

176. Oberman, *Harvest of Medieval Theology*, 407; Oberman, *Forerunners of the Reformation*, 53–65; Oberman, *Dawn of the Reformation*, 286–87 (esp. 287n.67). Also consult G. C. Berkouwer, *The Second Vatican Council and the New Catholicism*, trans. L. B. Smedes (Grand Rapids: Eerdmans, 1965), 89–111.

177. Alister E. McGrath, "Faith and Tradition," in *The Oxford Handbook of Evangelical Theology*, ed. Gerald R. McDermott (New York: Oxford University Press, 2010), 87–88.

178. For their views and further exchanges, see Hubert Jedin, *A History of the Council of Trent* (New York: Nelson, 1961), 2:75–79.

179. R. C. Sproul, "*Sola Scriptura*: Crucial to Evangelicalism," in Boice, *Foundation of Biblical Authority*, 108–9; Timothy George, "An Evangelical Reflection on Scripture and Tradition," in Colson and Neuhaus, *Your Word Is Truth*, 23–24.

of these two priests, we do not have further details leading up to the final draft, which took out the word "partly." The final product of the council reads: "These truths and rules are contained in the written books *and* in the unwritten traditions." Whether *partim* was deleted due to the protest of these priests or for some other reason, we cannot say.

What is clear is that many in Rome *did* affirm a two-source view when interpreting Trent. On April 6, 1546, the cardinal legate Cervini announced that the final version is "in substance" the same. Oberman concludes, "This would hardly seem compatible with the idea that the Council changes its mind."[180] Additionally, the famous Roman Catholic apologist of the sixteenth and seventeenth centuries, Robert Bellarmine, as well as the *Catechismus Romanus* (1566), interpreted Trent in this way. Likewise, Vatican I (1869–70), the papal encyclical *Humani Generis*, and Pope John XXIII's *Ad Petri Cathedram* all argued for two sources of revelation.[181] Furthermore, the ultimate step was taken in 1870 when Vatican Council I declared papal infallibility an official Roman Catholic doctrine. When the pope speaks *ex cathedra* from his throne on behalf of the whole church, addressing issues on faith and morals, his speech for the church is infallible.[182]

Though more nuance is added, Vatican II (1962–65) unquestionably reaffirmed papal infallibility as well as Tradition as a second conduit, or mode, of divine revelation. In all these statements, the Roman Catholic Church continued to reject *sola Scriptura*.[183] And when we examine the 1995 *Catechism of the Catholic Church*, there can be no doubt that Rome affirms Tradition as an equal second source of divine revelation and authority with Scripture, strongly reaffirming papal infallibility as dogma as well.[184] The Catechism, echoing Vatican

180. Oberman, *Dawn of the Reformation*, 288.
181. For example, Session 3 of "First Vatican Council," in *Creeds and Confessions of Faith in Christian Tradition*, vol. 3, *Part Five: Statements of Faith in Modern Christianity*, ed. Jaroslav Pelikan and Valerie Hotchkiss (New Haven: Yale University Press, 2003), 346; Oberman, *Dawn of the Reformation*, 290; Sproul, "*Sola Scriptura*," 108–9.
182. See Session 4 of "First Vatican Council," in Pelikan and Hotchkiss, *Creeds and Confessions*, 3:356–58. For a brief history, see A. B. Hasler, *How the Pope Became Infallible: Pius IX and the Politics of Persuasion* (New York: Doubleday, 1981). For two critiques, see R. C. Sproul, *Are We Together?* (Orlando, FL: Reformation Trust, 2012), 85–100; Hans Küng, *Infallible? An Inquiry* (New York: Doubleday, 1983).
183. See *Dei verbum* in "Doctrinal Decrees of the Second Vatican Council, 1962–65," in Pelikan and Hotchkiss, *Creeds and Confessions*, 3:650–62.
184. *Catechism of the Catholic Church*, 2nd ed. (New York: Doubleday, 1995), sections

II, unapologetically rejects *sola Scriptura*: "The Church does not derive her certainty about all revealed truths from the holy Scriptures alone. Both Scripture and Tradition must be accepted and honored with equal sentiments of devotion and reverence."[185]

If we return to Trent for a moment, we find that not only did Trent reject the Reformers' doctrine of *sola Scriptura*, they went further, including the Apocrypha in the canon as well. The Reformers believed that the Apocrypha was not written under the inspiration of the Spirit for many reasons, one being that it taught doctrines (e.g., purgatory) that contradicted the Old and New Testaments. Trent also defended the Latin Vulgate as the only authentic version of the Scriptures, which Calvin argued was loaded with "innumerable errors." Trent denied the right to interpret Scripture contrary to "mother Church," who alone possesses the authority to judge the right interpretation of the Bible.[186]

Calvin issued a formidable response to Trent in his *Acts of the Council of Trent: with the Antidote*.[187] In this treatise, Calvin acknowledges that "Scripture came not by the private will of man (2 Pet 1. 21)."[188] And he advises that in cases of obscure passages, it is wise to consult the wisdom of others to arrive at the true meaning. In other words, Calvin is not advocating unbounded individualism when interpreting the Bible. His position was nuanced, rejecting what he saw among the radical reformers. The church should be a source of guidance and counsel. Yet Rome goes too far in restricting the right of interpretation to herself, thereby elevating herself to the seat of supreme judge of Scripture

---

80–82, 120, 891. It should be qualified, however, that there have been recent Roman Catholics seeking to move Rome in the direction of a "living tradition," what Oberman calls T3. See Oberman, *Dawn of the Reformation*, 290–96.

185. *Catechism of the Catholic Church*, 82. Even ecumenical attempts have recognized that the divide over *sola Scriptura* remains. See Colson and Neuhaus, *Your Word Is Truth*; Mark A. Noll and Carolyn Nystrom, *Is the Reformation Over? An Evangelical Assessment of Contemporary Roman Catholicism* (Grand Rapids: Baker Academic, 2005). Space does not allow me to explore Catholic dialogue since Vatican II, but see Robert Strimple, "The Relationship between Scripture and Tradition in Contemporary Roman Catholic Theology," *Westminster Theological Journal* 40, no. 1 (1977): 22–38.

186. John Calvin, *Acts of the Council of Trent: with the Antidote*, vol. 3, *John Calvin: Tracts and Letters*, ed. and trans. Henry Beveridge (repr., Edinburgh: Banner of Truth Trust, 2009), 66, 71–72.

187. One should also consult Martin Chemnitz's response to Trent, which was considered by Protestants to be the definitive reply. Martin Chemnitz, *Examination of the Council of Trent*, trans. Fred Kramer, 4 vols. (St. Louis: Concordia, 1971). Also consult William Whitaker's 1588 *A Disputation on Holy Scripture against the Papists Especially Bellarmine and Stapleton* (Morgan, PA: Soli Deo Gloria, 2000).

188. Calvin, *Council of Trent*, 74.

interpretation, as if she alone possesses the true and right interpretation which must be followed by every Christian without question. To Calvin, when the Council of Trent refers to Scripture and Tradition, it really means that Scripture must be interpreted by Tradition. And to this Calvin responds, "They wish, by their tyrannical edict, to deprive the Church of all liberty . . . for, by the meaning which they affix to Scripture what it may, it must be immediately embraced." Calvin continues, "Except themselves, moreover, no man will be permitted to prove anything out of Scripture."[189]

Rome had limited scriptural interpretation to the clergy. Everyone else had to trust that what Rome says Scripture says. And why would anyone doubt Rome's interpretation? After all, Rome's exposition of Scripture is flawless, for she carries equal authority as a second source of divine revelation. Here we see the nucleus of Rome's thinking: Scripture is *not* enough. It is dark and mysterious. What is needed is the church, which carries with her the official, infallible interpretation. Her legacy and her Tradition are needed as a second source of divine revelation to tell the individual Christian what Scripture says.

Calvin, as we might guess, was not persuaded by Rome's huffing and puffing: "Just stand and let the smoke clear away."[190] The ancient writers never intended to carry our "faith beyond the Scriptures." Indeed, our faith is always confined to the Scriptures as our final authority. And while there were certain customs the fathers received from the apostles, other customs are clearly not from the apostles. This is precisely where Rome leads so many astray. She persuades others that all of her traditions are directly from the apostles, and therefore binding, when many of them are not. How do we know? We know because they are in conflict with Scripture. Therefore, doctrine depends not on unwritten Tradition but on the Scriptures. As Augustine said, "Faith is conceived from the Scriptures."[191]

Conclusion

Initially, we might be tempted to think that the Reformers were inventing something new in the doctrine of *sola Scriptura*. Yet understood correctly, the Reformers were seeking to return to the position

---

189. Ibid.
190. Ibid., 69.
191. Ibid., 70.

of the fathers, a single-source theory of divine revelation.[192] One cannot read Luther or Calvin very long without encountering quotations from the fathers.[193] For example, some of Luther's favorites included Augustine, Cyprian, and Chrysostom, and Luther saw himself in this great tradition of "Abel." By contrast, those who opposed him stood in the tradition of "Cain"; they were "sophists" who appealed to Aristotle, Scotus, Occam, and Biel.[194] The Reformers were on a mission to demonstrate that they were retrievers of right doctrine practiced by the true tradition of the fathers (bona partum pars). So we would be mistaken to think that the Reformers were anti-tradition and anti-authority. They recognized the authority of the traditions passed on from century to century, and saw them (especially the church creeds of Nicaea and Chalcedon) as valuable guides to biblical interpretation.[195]

Where the Reformers drew the line was in thinking, as their Catholic counterparts did, that ecclesiastical tradition, conveyed by either the pope or magisterium, was on an equal pedestal with Scripture. So while the Reformers generally adhered to the traditional interpretation of Scripture, they were not afraid to correct the fathers where they felt they had ventured into unbiblical territory and could no longer justify their interpretation with Scripture itself.[196]

In the next chapter, we'll move to the modern age and see how the fires ignited by the Reformation would flicker and die in some places. Bold new minds were on the horizon, questioning sola Scriptura in a radically new way, seeking to put out its light.

---

192. To be fair, Rome did too. Hence, it has been pointed out that the Reformation was a battle of two traditions.

193. George, Reading Scripture with the Reformers, 81.

194. See Oberman, Forerunners of the Reformation, 28–29.

195. McGrath, Reformation Thought, 101; Michael Allen and Scott R. Swain, Reformed Catholicity: The Promise of Retrieval for Theology and Biblical Interpretation (Grand Rapids: Baker Academic, 2015), 49–94. Contra Brad S. Gregory, The Unintended Reformation: How a Religious Revolution Secularized Society (Harvard: Belknap, 2012), 77–123; A. N. Williams, "Tradition," in The Oxford Handbook of Systematic Theology, ed. John Webster, Kathryn Tanner, and Iain Torrance (New York: Oxford University Press, 2007), 364.

196. McGrath, Reformation Thought, 102; Thompson, Sure Ground on Which to Stand, 252–65.

CHAPTER 2

The Modern Shift in Authority: The Enlightenment, Liberalism, and Liberalism's Nemeses

> They shall wander from sea to sea, and from north to east; they shall run to and fro, to seek the word of the LORD, but they shall not find it. —Amos 8:12 ESV

> The Bible has emerged from these fires, as out of all others, without so much the smell of smoke upon its garments. —B. B. Warfield

> Christianity is founded upon the Bible. It bases upon the Bible both its thinking and its life. Liberalism on the other hand is founded upon the shifting emotions of sinful men. —J. Gresham Machen

> They claim to see fern-seed and can't see an elephant ten yards away in broad daylight. —C. S. Lewis

We might assume that with the Reformation's recovery of *sola Scriptura*, Protestantism had overcome the objections of the Roman church and forever sailed smoothly into the sunset. History, however, tells a very different story! While Luther and Calvin may have succeeded in addressing Rome's papalism in the sixteenth century, with the advent of modernism, rationalistic biblical criticism produced a "new papalism": the infallibility of the biblical scholar.[1]

The "new papalism" of critical biblical scholarship planted seeds of doubt throughout the biblical text, leading many to wonder if the Bible

---

1. J. I. Packer, *God Has Spoken: Revelation and the Bible*, 3rd ed. (Grand Rapids: Baker, 1993), 26–27.

was truly divine revelation. Where the Reformers urged interpreters to approach the text with reverence and hermeneutical humility, the reader was now encouraged to approach the text as its lord and judge. Consequently, there arose a spiritual deafness as rationalistic criticism separated man's witness to God's Word from revelation itself. "God's Word was one thing, Holy Scripture was another."[2] The Bible was now viewed as a collection of fallible books, and the Augustinian heritage of the past—which believed that what Scripture says, God says—was discarded. It was now the scholar's obligation to save the Bible by ridding it of any theological beliefs or assumptions that were out of line with modern scientific methods.[3] Such a critical approach to the Bible continues today, arguing that until inspiration and inerrancy are disposed of, the Bible will never be truly understood.

Undoubtedly, Luther and Calvin would have been shocked to encounter this new papalism. While Rome set its Tradition and magisterium up as an equal authority to Scripture, in the days of the Reformers, Rome still viewed Scripture as God's inspired and inerrant Word.[4] In the centuries that followed, the challenge to *sola Scriptura* was no longer limited to Scripture's sufficiency. It now extended its tentacles to Scripture's infallibility and purity as well.

In this chapter and the next we will trace the decline of biblical authority from the start of the modern era up to the present day. Since space is limited, we will be painting with a broad brush, looking at some of the major players in this card game. One thing will become crystal clear: there has been, and continues to be, a growing crisis of biblical authority.

The Reign of Autonomous Reason: The Enlightenment

In the sixteenth century, Reformation theology—including *sola Scriptura*—took root in Western Europe. This is evident in the

2. Ibid.
3. Ibid.
4. It should be qualified, however, that post-Vatican II, inerrancy among Roman Catholics became a matter of dispute. For example, compare the first draft of Vatican II on inerrancy with its fifth draft. See Walter M. Abbott, ed., *The Documents of Vatican II* (New York: Guild, 1966), 119. For a critique, see D. A. Carson, *Collected Writings on Scripture* (Wheaton, IL: Crossway, 2010), 59–61; Robert L. Saucy, "Recent Roman Catholic Theology," in *Challenges to Inerrancy: A Theological Response*, ed. Gordon Lewis and Bruce Demarest (Chicago: Moody, 1984), 215–46; Anthony N. S. Lane, "Roman Catholic Views of Biblical Authority from the Late Nineteenth Century to the Present," in *The Enduring Authority of the Christian Scriptures*, ed. D. A. Carson (Grand Rapids: Eerdmans, 2016), 292–320.

numerous Lutheran and Reformed confessions, each of which either assumed or explicitly affirmed *sola Scriptura*, the formal principle of the Reformation.[5] By the seventeenth century, new theological winds had begun to blow. Major doctrines affirmed by the Reformers and the Protestant scholastics were now questioned, including the authority of Scripture. And by the eighteenth century, an entirely different understanding of the Scripture was widely accepted. Germany and Switzerland, previously territories devoted to Lutheran and Reformed theologies, fell under the sway of Enlightenment philosophy.[6]

It is difficult to precisely define the Enlightenment, since it refers to a broad movement over a number of years.[7] Immanuel Kant (1724–1804) attempted to describe this mind-set in an article he wrote on the topic, using the German word *Aufklärung* to describe the Enlightenment approach:

> Enlightenment is man's release from his self-incurred tutelage. Tutelage is man's inability to make use of his understanding without direction from another. Self-incurred is this tutelage when its cause lies not in lack of reason but in lack of resolution and courage to use it without direction from another. *Sapere aude!* "Have courage to use your own reason!"—that is the motto of enlightenment.[8]

This "Age of Reason," as Kant and others would describe the Enlightenment era, was not unique in emphasizing reason. Every age up to the eighteenth century had utilized and valued reason to some extent. What distinguished the Enlightenment was *how* it viewed reason. The Enlightenment individual believed he could have access to

---

5. Muller, *PRRD*, 2:63–441; W. Robert Godfrey, "Biblical Authority in the Sixteenth and Seventeenth Centuries: A Question of Transition," in *Scripture and Truth*, ed. D. A. Carson and John Woodbridge (Grand Rapids: Baker, 1992), 225–50.

6. Alister E. McGrath, *The Making of Modern German Christology: 1750–1990*, 2nd ed. (Eugene, OR: Wipf & Stock, 2005), 14.

7. I will acknowledge the diversity of Enlightenment thought later. However, it should be qualified at the start that I am not committed to "paradigmatic" history when I use the word "Enlightenment" as if to summarize a universal way people thought about Scripture in the eighteenth century. Dale Van Kley has demonstrated that Kant's definition of Enlightenment did not represent all individuals, particularly Christians who did affirm inspiration and inerrancy (Lutherans, Pietists, Wesleyans, Edwards, etc.). See Dale K. Van Kley, *French Revolution: From Calvin to the Civil Constitution, 1560–1791* (New Haven: Yale University Press, 1996).

8. Immanuel Kant, "What Is Enlightenment?" in *The Enlightenment: A Sourcebook and Reader*, ed. Paul Hyland (London: Routledge, 2003), 54.

pure human reason, which would allow him to tear down traditional ecclesiastical myths that only served to oppress societies of ages past.[9] The Enlightenment man confidently declared to the world that he had come of age intellectually, and it was now time to liberate himself from the assumptions he had previously inherited from mother Christendom. By means of pure reason, he was now capable of discovering truth for himself, and in doing so he would pioneer a new path to enlightenment.[10] Reason was the golden ticket to a life of total objectivity, free from bias.[11]

With the elevation of reason as a sufficient source for human knowledge and achievement, there was a corresponding rejection of the Bible's necessity and sufficiency. After all, if we are able through the use of human reason to investigate and analyze God and determine his purpose and will, why do we need a historical revelation, let alone an incarnation of the Son of God? This criticism of special revelation stemmed from an optimistic view of man's abilities. For the Reformers, man possessed general revelation through the created order, and yet this was tempered by an understanding that man was pervasively corrupt in his nature and spiritually blind, suppressing the truth (Rom 1:18–32). Because of this, special revelation was seen as essential, necessary for salvation. The Enlightenment led to a rejection of this Augustinian anthropology and its doctrine of original sin. Man was now seen as inherently good. Such "anthropocentrism" is the "overriding" and "underlying acid of modernity," the *sine qua non* of the Enlightenment.[12] This optimistic view of man (what Karl Barth later criticized and labeled the "absolute man") led many to question the necessity of special revelation.[13] This is a helpful reminder to us today that one's view of the Bible is significantly impacted by one's

---

9.   McGrath, *Modern German Christology*, 15. However, McGrath qualifies that there were Enlightenment individuals who were anti-rationalists.

10.   Bruce Demarest, "The Bible in the Enlightenment Era," in Lewis and Demarest, *Challenges to Inerrancy*, 11. See also Roger E. Olson, *The Journey of Modern Theology: From Reconstruction to Deconstruction* (Downers Grove, IL: InterVarsity Press, 2013), 24; James M. Byrne, *Religion and the Enlightenment: From Descartes to Kant* (Louisville: Westminster John Knox, 1996), 5–10.

11.   Alister E. McGrath, *Science and Religion: An Introduction* (Oxford: Blackwell, 1999), 58.

12.   Olson, *Modern Theology*, 26. Olson does qualify that not all thinkers took modernity to such an extreme or viewed modernity and Christianity as incompatible.

13.   Demarest, "The Bible in the Enlightenment Era," 14.

anthropology and soteriology.[14] Those who think much of themselves will be less inclined to believe they need a word from God.

The Enlightenment project finds its seed in the thought of René Descartes (1596–1650). Descartes constructed a system that sought absolute certainty by relying upon human reason. Descartes would doubt anything and everything (including Scripture and church tradition) in hopes of discovering that which he could not doubt. At last he arrived at that most basic statement: *Cogito ergo sum*—I think, therefore I am.[15] Whether he meant to or not, Descartes had severed reason from revelation, turning man into an autonomous rational subject.[16] The result was an Enlightenment project that assumed man could achieve total intellectual certainty by means of his own reason.

The omnipotence of reason posed a serious challenge to orthodox Christianity, and few doctrines were left unaltered in its wake. Alister McGrath helpfully identifies three diverse stages or developments in the Enlightenment's reappraisal and criticism of traditional Christianity. In the first stage, the "beliefs of Christianity" were considered to be "rational," which meant they were able to stand any test of reason. In other words, because Christianity was considered a rational religion, it could endure the most severe examination. Such an approach is seen in John Locke's *The Reasonableness of Christianity* (1695). Locke considered Christianity to be a "reasonable supplement to natural religion."[17] In his view, divine revelation was not something that we should entirely abandon.

The second stage of development went a step further. Since the fundamentals of Christianity are rational, it was believed that they could be "derived from reason itself." The consequences of this shift were quite radical. Some concluded that there was no need "to invoke the idea of divine revelation." Christianity was nothing more than the "republication of the religion of nature" and so-called revealed religion was "nothing other than the reconfirmation of what can be

---

14. Roy A. Harrisville and Walter Sundberg, *The Bible in Modern Culture: Baruch Spinoza to Brevard Childs*, 2nd ed. (Grand Rapids: Eerdmans, 2002).

15. René Descartes, *Discourse on the Method*, part 4, trans. Laurence J. Lafleur (Indianapolis: Bobbs-Merrill, 1960), 24.

16. Mark S. Gignilliat, *Old Testament Criticism: From Benedict Spinoza to Brevard Childs* (Grand Rapids: Zondervan, 2012), 22; Stanley J. Grenz, *A Primer on Postmodernism* (Grand Rapids: Eerdmans, 1996), 3; Colin Brown, *Christianity and Western Thought*, vol. 1, *From the Ancient World to the Age of Enlightenment* (Downers Grove, IL: InterVarsity Press, 1990), 184.

17. McGrath, *Modern German Christology*, 20.

known through rational reflection on nature."[18] This train of thought can be found in much of English deism (e.g., John Toland, Matthew Tindal).

In the third stage, reason was exalted above divine revelation, sitting as its judge. "As human reason was omnicompetent, it was argued that it was supremely qualified to judge Christian beliefs and practices, with a view to eliminating any irrational or superstitious elements."[19] At this point, the Bible was thought to be full of errors, and reason's job was to sift through them in order to find truth.[20] Such an approach can be seen in figures such as H. S. Reimarus.

These three stages of development are helpful to note, but we must acknowledge that the Enlightenment period was very diverse, and not all Enlightenment thinkers were created equal. The spirit of the age swept many thinkers off their feet, and while some of them were outright skeptics, others sought to wed rationalism to Christianity. The spectrum ranged from skeptics to deists to traditional theists, and it varied from country to country.[21] Fragmentation was inevitable, since some rationalists sought compatibility between revelation and reason, while others—whom we might call *pure rationalists*—denied supernatural revelation altogether, assuming belief in the miraculous to be irrational.[22] In the latter case, since the truth claims of Scripture rested upon the validity of the miraculous, it followed that the Bible could not be trusted. And, since Jesus's own claims to divinity depended upon miraculous accounts, Christian orthodoxy was untenable.[23]

What made this so *avant-garde* was that pure rationalism planted seeds of doubt. Many of its proponents labored to show that Scripture no longer was trustworthy, and given how much the supernatural

---

18. Ibid. See also Brown, *Ancient World to the Age of Enlightenment*, 197–214; Demarest, "The Bible in the Enlightenment Era," 19–24; Edward G. Waring, *Deism and Natural Religion: A Source Book* (New York: F. Ungar, 1967); Gerald Cragg, *Reason and Authority in the Eighteenth Century* (Cambridge: Cambridge University Press, 1964); John Redwood, *Reason, Ridicule, and Religion* (Cambridge: Harvard University Press, 1976).

19. McGrath, *Modern German Christology*, 21.

20. John D. Woodbridge and Frank A. James III, *Church History*, vol. 2, *From Pre-Reformation to the Present Day* (Grand Rapids: Zondervan, 2013), 419.

21. Brown, *Ancient World to the Age of Enlightenment*, 288; Woodbridge and James, *Church History*, 356–60.

22. Gerald Bray, *Biblical Interpretation: Past and Present* (Downers Grove, IL: IVP Academic, 1996), 228; Olson, *Journey of Modern Theology*, 70–72.

23. Bray, *Biblical Interpretation*, 228.

pervades its pages, readers who assumed an anti-supernatural world-view were compelled to reappraise and reconstruct its message.[24]

The God Who Is Silent: Deism

Deism (from the Latin *deus*, "god") is often traced back to Lord Herbert of Cherbury (1583–1648), sometimes called the "father of deism." Deism is the belief that God created the world to run on its own, apart from his supernatural intervention or providential involvement.[25] Deists were critical of special revelation since it involved God's supernatural intervention into history. Lord Herbert also attacked religion because it rested on divine revelation, instead arguing that human reason is our judge, even over Scripture. Should anything in Scripture be found inconsistent with man's reason, it must be rejected. For many deists, doctrines like the Trinity, the incarnation, the atonement, the resurrection, original sin, hell, or the belief in miracles were seen as unreasonable and irrational.[26]

John Toland (1670–1722) was an influential deist, and his book title says it all: *Christianity Not Mysterious: A Treatise Showing That There Is Nothing in the Gospel contrary to Reason, but Also Nothing above Reason* (1696). For Toland, revelation was the maidservant of reason, not vice versa. Anything and everything in the Bible that proves incompatible with reason must be disposed of due to its irrationality.[27] Matthew Tindal (1655–1733), who wrote what many called the "Deist Bible," a work titled *Christianity as Old as the Creation, or the Gospel a Republication of the Religious Nature* (1730), argued that God's original revelation in creation was sufficient and perfect for all mankind for all time, making no further revelation needed.[28] The Bible, argued Tindal, is simply a republication of God's revelation at creation, nothing more. Like Toland, Tindal believed that everything found in the Bible must be held up to the almighty judge of human reason. "I cannot have

---

24. Ibid., 253.
25. This is a very broad definition. Some deists did try to incorporate a doctrine of divine providence.
26. Brown, *Ancient World to the Age of Enlightenment*, 204.
27. John Toland, *Christianity Not Mysterious*, in *John Toland's Christianity Not Mysterious: Text, Associated Works, and Critical Essays*, ed. Philip McGuiness et al. (Dublin: Lilliput, 1997); Peter Gay, ed., *Deism: An Anthology* (Princeton, NJ: Van Nostrand, 1968), 55–117.
28. Matthew Tindal, *Christianity as Old as the Creation* (London: Routledge/Thames, 1995).

any faith," said Tindal, "which will not bear the test of reason." This meant that orthodox doctrines had to go, including the historicity of Adam and his fall, the atonement, and eternal punishment. In short, anything in Scripture that went beyond God's revelation at creation was believed to be a superstitious addition, a corruption that crept in over time. In Tindal's opinion, the "Bible *has* perverted the original natural religion by spurious accretions, hence Scripture constitutes a lie."[29]

Many other deists took a similar approach with Scripture and its record of the supernatural, including Anthony Collins and Thomas Woolston. And while interest in deism in England dissipated by the 1750s, their ideas carried on. Some have suggested that deism was the pioneer of biblical criticism and the quests for the historical Jesus.[30] We certainly see deism take root in America with figures like Thomas Jefferson (1743–1826), who wrote what became known as *The Jefferson Bible*, using his scissors to decide what portions of the Bible were acceptable. Anything miraculous was cut out until all that remained were moral principles.[31] Or consider Thomas Paine (1737–1809), whose work *The Age of Reason* was a ruthless attack on Scripture. Paine called the study of theology the "study of nothing" for it is "founded on nothing" and can "demonstrate nothing." Rather than making the Bible the foundation for theology, he wrote, one should instead turn to the created order.[32] From Europe to the shores of America, deism undermined biblical authority in the name of reason. Some have called deism the bud that resulted in the flowering of Enlightenment rationalism.[33]

Colder Than Ice Itself: Baruch Spinoza

While the Reformers and their Puritan heirs believed the Bible to be inspired, inerrant, authoritative, clear, sufficient, and necessary, such a stance toward the Bible was rejected with the rise of what has been termed "rationalist biblical criticism" (RBC)—an approach that elevated reason above Scripture as its judge and critic.[34] This approach to the Bible presupposed anti-supernaturalism, eliminating from the

29. Demarest, "The Bible in the Enlightenment Era," 21.

30. Brown, *Ancient World to the Age of Enlightenment*, 203, 212.

31. Frank Lambert, *The Founding Fathers and the Place of Religion in America* (Princeton, NJ: Princeton University Press, 2003), 177.

32. Philip S. Foner, ed., *The Complete Writings of Thomas Paine*, 2 vols. (New York: Citadel, 1947), 1:601.

33. McGrath, *Science and Religion*, 19; Olson, *Journey of Modern Theology*, 72.

34. Harrisville and Sundberg, *Bible in Modern Culture*, 24.

start any thought that the biblical text possessed a divine origin. RBC was more than a mere method; it was an entire worldview.[35]

The emergence of RBC can be illustrated by looking at the life and thought of Baruch Spinoza (1632–77), who cleared the way for much of eighteenth-century Enlightenment thought.[36] Some have argued that Spinoza's thinking, or at least the seed of it, can be traced back to Desiderius Erasmus (1466–1536), Martin Luther's nemesis over the bondage of the will. Debates over doctrine were bitter and sour for Erasmus. He considered them pointless, divisive, unnecessary, and speculative because Scripture is not clear and can have diverse meanings. According to Erasmus, if one is being persecuted for his or her beliefs and is forced to decide between dogma and death, dogma must be compromised every time.[37] While Luther may have been excommunicated for his defense of *sola Scriptura*, Erasmus's posthumous condemnation by the church in 1559 was due to his far more radical approach to Scripture, namely, the later tradition of rationalist biblical criticism.[38] Ironically, Rome would have agreed with Luther when he wrote of Erasmus's approach to Scripture: "These words of yours, devoid of Christ, devoid of the Spirit, are colder than ice itself."[39]

Yet this same spirit—a critical eye toward dogma and the Bible as received by the church—lived on with Spinoza. Carrying on the rationalist legacy, Spinoza was the first to turn historical criticism of the Bible into a science.[40] For Spinoza, Christianity, as defined by the church, and religion in general were one giant system of superstition. His solution? Christianity must be subjected to reason.[41] Natural light from autonomous, universal human reason, he writes, will be our captain, sailing us to the island of *true* religion.[42]

---

35. Daniel J. Treier, "Scripture and Hermeneutics," in *Mapping Modern Theology: A Thematic and Historical Introduction*, ed. Kelly M. Kapic and Bruce L. McCormack (Grand Rapids: Baker Academic, 2012), 69. For a more extensive history than what is provided here, see Andrew L. Drummon, *German Protestantism since Luther* (London: Epworth, 1951); Peter Gay, *The Enlightenment: An Interpretation* (New York: Knopf, 1967).

36. See Jonathan I. Israel, *Radical Enlightenment: Philosophy and the Making of Modernity 1650–1750* (New York: Oxford University Press, 2001).

37. Harrisville and Sundberg, *Bible in Modern Culture*, 31.

38. Ibid.

39. Martin Luther, *The Bondage of the Will*, in *LW* 33:31.

40. Harrisville and Sundberg, *Bible in Modern Culture*, 33. See also Lewis Samuel Feuer, *Spinoza and the Rise of Liberalism* (Boston: Beacon, 1958).

41. Harrisville and Sundberg, *Bible in Modern Culture*, 37.

42. Gignilliat, *Old Testament Criticism*, 26.

In *Tractatus Theologico-Politicus* (1670), Spinoza aims to persuade readers that while faith and piety belong to the realm of theology, rational truth is gripped by philosophy.[43] And the Bible? For Spinoza, the Bible itself must come under the scrutiny of our reason. While Scripture may provide general ethical direction for life (e.g., piety), only philosophy can provide rational knowledge of God and creation.[44]

Spinoza was disgusted by how men "parade their own ideas as God's Word," extorting "from Holy Scripture their own arbitrarily invented ideas, from which they claim divine authority."[45] Biblical interpretation, he believed, was one giant, reeking dunghill. Men must be set free from the stench and bondage by drawing conclusions that are consistent with what we know from universal human reason. For Spinoza, truth and meaning are *not* the same thing. Truth has to do with issues of universal significance. In such a realm, reason is the way forward, for it is able to decipher matters of universal magnitude. He believed that not even time or space stand in reason's way. Not so with meaning, he argued. Meaning has to do with a culture's "expressions and artifacts." Meaning, unlike reason, is restricted and conditioned by "time and space."[46] Therefore, when we read the Bible and come across miracles and revelations (prophecies), these cannot refer to truth, he said, but only meaning. They are wrapped up in the culture of the biblical era.

For example, consider the Jewish culture of the Bible. The Hebrew authors constantly attribute what happens to God. But today, Spinoza would argue, we know better. These are cultural expressions, not universal truths for all time or something that actually happened in history. The consequence of Spinoza's approach was devastating. No longer was Scripture viewed as a divine revelation.[47] Where the biblical authors attributed their revelations to God, we should attribute them to their cultural context. The Bible is to be read and analyzed, even

---

43. Roy A. Harrisville, *Pandora's Box Opened: An Examination and Defense of Historical-Critical Method and Its Master Practitioners* (Grand Rapids: Eerdmans, 2014), 50–51.

44. Richard A. Muller, *PRRD*, 2:138.

45. Baruch Spinoza, *Tractatus Theologico-Politicus*, trans. Samuel Shirley (Leiden: Brill, 1989), 141.

46. Harrisville and Sundberg, *Bible in Modern Culture*, 38.

47. Ibid., 39; Robert M. Grant and David Tracy, *A Short History of the Interpretation of the Bible*, 2nd ed. (Philadelphia: Fortress, 1984), 106. For a more extensive treatment of Spinoza, see Gignilliat, *Old Testament Criticism*, 15–36.

criticized, just like any other book. The Word of God, he said, "is faulty, mutilated, adulterated and inconsistent," and we "possess it only in fragmentary form."[48] Spinoza demanded that the Bible be deprived of its "halo of infallibility and subjected to the same critical scrutiny due any ancient book."[49]

In assessing Spinoza's legacy, it is paramount to recognize that Spinoza completely changed how divine accommodation was understood. To understand why, we must draw our attention to Faustus Socinus (1539–1604), well known for his anti-trinitarian rationalism and the movement he birthed known as Socinianism. Up until Socinus and the rise of early modern rationalism, the church affirmed accommodation as a way of reconciling biblical passages that appeared erroneous. Correctly interpreted, these passages were cases where God accommodated biblical language to the everyday language of people. God in Scripture stooped down to convey his Word in a way that was understandable to the cultures of the day, though without forfeiting the perfection and purity of his Word.[50] Whether Chrysostom or Calvin, this view was standard.

Yet Socinus changed the definition of accommodation in a radical way.[51] For the first time, accommodation assumed an errant text. As Socinus read through the Gospels and the Epistles, for example, he felt that certain teachings from Jesus and the apostles were simply irrational. So he concluded that such teachings must be false, an intentional accommodation on their part to the erroneous beliefs of their audience.[52] Notice how this new understanding of accommodation is different from the old view. "Up to this point," observes Glenn Sunshine, "accommodation had been used to eliminate apparent errors in the text, in essence arguing that the text is true because it

---

48. Baruch Spinoza, *Theological-Political Treatise*, trans. Samuel Shirley (Indianapolis: Hackett, 2001), 145.

49. J. Samuel Preus, *Spinoza and the Irrelevance of Biblical Authority* (New York: Cambridge University Press, 2001), 22.

50. See Glenn S. Sunshine, "Accommodation Historically Considered," in Carson, *Enduring Authority of the Christian Scriptures*, 264.

51. See *An Argument for the Authority of Holy Scripture; from the Latin of Socinus, after the Steinfurt Copy. To Which Is Prefixed a Short Account of His Life*, trans. Edward Combe (London: W. Meadows, 1731).

52. "Epitome of a Colloquium Held in Racow in the Year 1601," in *The Polish Brethren: Documentation of the History and Thought of Unitarianism in the Polish-Lithuanian Commonwealth and in the Diaspora, 1601–1685*, ed. and trans. George Huntston Williams (Missoula, MT: Scholars Press, 1980), 121–22.

was accommodated to the people's needs. With Socinus, we see the opposite: the text is false because it was accommodated to the people's erroneous beliefs."[53]

Spinoza, however, took accommodation to a whole new level. Socinus's belief in an errant text was driven by his rationalism; nevertheless, he still tried to affirm biblical authority, even if it be subservient to the authority of reason.[54] Not so with Spinoza. Divine accommodation now became the means by which to abandon biblical authority completely. In the name of *sola Scriptura*, Spinoza argued that Scripture was a "closed system" (only Scripture can interpret Scripture) and therefore was totally separate from philosophy. Divine accommodation meant that Scripture had no objective, authoritative voice anymore. Rather, each person could decide for himself how to accommodate the text to his own reason.[55]

This new understanding of divine accommodation that began with Socinus only to be radicalized by Spinoza would be carried on in the centuries to come with the rise of Liberalism.[56] While Spinoza's views did not create a massive following in his lifetime, they were picked up by later thinkers such as Gotthold Lessing and Friedrich Schleiermacher. In fact, D. F. Strauss has said that Schleiermacher's *Christian Faith*, if translated into Latin, would be a clear summary of the ideas of Spinoza![57] Strauss was right, but here is the deeper problem. Unlike Spinoza, Schleiermacher was a Christian theologian. He shocked the church when he decided to incorporate Spinoza's secular ideas into the official doctrines of the Christian faith.

The Bible a Weaving of Sheer Stupidities: H. S. Reimarus

Spinoza's thought mirrors that of the radical reformers who exchanged *sola Scriptura* for *nuda Scriptura*.[58] He dispensed with

---

53. Sunshine, "Accommodation Historically Considered," 258.
54. Ibid., 259.
55. Ibid. Also see Arnold Huijgen, *Divine Accommodation in John Calvin's Theology: Analysis and Assessment*, ed. Herman J. Selderhuis, Reformed Historical Theology 16 (Göttingen: Vandenhoeck & Ruprecht, 2011), 31–33.
56. Sunshine notes how Liberals typically went for Socinus's view rather than Spinoza's view since they still wanted to maintain biblical authority to some degree. They accomplished this goal by modifying the traditional definition of divine inspiration ("Accommodation Historically Considered," 259).
57. Brown, *Ancient World to the Age of Enlightenment*, 188.
58. Gignilliat, *Old Testament Criticism*, 26.

ecclesiastical authority and tradition, believing them to be oppressive and warped by superstitious dogma.[59] The Bible had to be interpreted apart from the church and only by the elite, a principle that ran counter to the Reformers' affirmation of the priesthood of every believer. *Sola Scriptura* was perverted and used against Protestant theology to argue for an entirely different worldview.

Spinoza's legacy was imbibed by German scholar H. S. Reimarus (1694–1768), who defended "the rights of rational religion against churchly faith."[60] "One by one," said Reimarus, "I will examine the persons, deeds, teachings and writings of the Old and of the New Testament, indicating what and why each appears to contradict the pretense that through just such means a supernatural, divine revelation has been given us for our eternal bliss." The Scriptures, concluded Reimarus, are full of "downright contradiction," making them "impossible for us to believe."[61] Consider his disappointment and disgust with the Old Testament:

> It is certain . . . no book, no history in the world were so full of contradictions, and therein the name of God so often and shamefully misused: Since all the persons who are cited here as men of God, their sum total, give sheer offense, annoyance and aversion to a soul which loves honor and virtue. In the whole series of this history one finds neither patriarchs, judges and kings, nor priests and prophets, whose real and earnest purpose had been to disseminate a true knowledge of God, virtue and piety among men; to say nothing of the fact that one could encounter in it one single great, noble act useful to all. It consists of a weaving of sheer stupidities, shameful deeds, deceptions, and horrors, for which clearly selfishness and lust for power were the stimuli.[62]

"A weaving of sheer stupidities"—that was Reimarus's view of the Old Testament, and the New Testament did not fare much better. He

---

59. Harrisville and Sundberg, *Bible in Modern Culture*, 41.

60. Albert Schweitzer, *The Quest of the Historical Jesus*, trans. W. Montgomery (London: A. & C. Black, 1922), 14. Besides Reimarus, one should also consult the thought of G. W. Leibnitz (d. 1716) and Christian Wolff (d. 1754).

61. Quoted in Carl Moenckeberg, *Hermann Samuel Reimarus und Johann Christian Edelmann* (Hamburg: Gustav Eduard Nolte, 1867), 120.

62. Hermann Samuel Reimarus, *Apologie oder Schutzschrift für die vernünftigen Verehrer Gottes* (Frankfurt: Joachim-Jungius-Gesellschaft der Wissenschaften Hamburg, 1972), 671 (cf. 678–79).

believed that the Gospels were cluttered with misrepresentations of Jesus, as seen in the attestations to his deity. After all, Jesus was just one of many messianic figures in Judaism who came before him. Reimarus believed Jesus's kingdom was on earth, and ultimately he failed to usher in his messianic reign when he was crucified. What we see in the historical Jesus is not orthodox Christianity, but rather the Judaism of a failed political and apocalyptic Jewish visionary.[63] His apostles had to significantly alter Jesus's identity and message, which explains why we have so many contradictions in the Gospels. Perhaps the biggest hoax of all is the resurrection itself, which cannot be substantiated. Such a hoax only reveals a much deeper deception, namely, the misleading nature of the New Testament.[64]

Reimarus also presupposed the impossibility of miracles. Instead, he said the miracles of Jesus should be explained within a naturalistic worldview. For example, the story of Jesus miraculously feeding five thousand can be attributed to the generosity of the wealthy in the crowd. After witnessing Jesus's kindness in distributing the fish and loaves of the boy's lunch, the well-off people in the crowd decided to share their lunches with everyone else. Or consider Jesus walking on water. What *really* happened, Reimarus explained, was that Jesus was walking very close to the shore and it only appeared as if he was walking on water. Reimarus and others came to such conclusions because they approached Scripture just as they would any other ancient manuscript. Nothing was to be assumed when opening the Bible, especially presuppositions that it was true and inspired by God.[65]

Since the New Testament was assumed by Reimarus and others to be inaccurate, the apostles *had* to make up a new system, one they completely fabricated. In light of the corruption of the Scriptures, they said, one must pull off the dirty husk in order to find the pure and clean kernel of moral truth within. They believed the Bible is a book like any other book, one that must be analyzed, scrutinized, and criticized, beaten until it coughs up the little truth it possesses. In this, Reimarus went well beyond *Scripture alone* to the *historical-critical method alone*.[66] As a result, historical criticism was set against divine

---

63. McGrath, *Modern German Christology*, 34–35.
64. Ibid., 35.
65. Craig L. Blomberg, *Jesus and the Gospels* (Nashville: B&H, 1997), 80.
66. Harrisville and Sundberg, *Bible in Modern Culture*, 61.

revelation, and man became the authoritative arbitrator of biblical truth in his quest to discover the historical Jesus.[67]

Falling into the Ugly Broad Ditch: G. E. Lessing

To this point, we have seen that one of the main pillars of the Enlightenment was its total trust in reason. Reason was believed to be omnicompetent. However, a second pillar can be identified as well, namely, the Enlightenment's skepticism toward history.[68] To be more precise, it was the Enlightenment's complete reliance upon reason which made it distrustful of history. This is exemplified in German philosopher G. E. Lessing (1729–81), famous (or infamous!) for his "ugly broad ditch." Lessing argued that there is *absolute* truth and *contingent* truth. Absolute truth is rooted in human reason and therefore is trustworthy. Reason provides us with universal truth. Contingent truth, he reasoned, is based on historical events and therefore is arbitrary.[69] If "no historical truth can be demonstrated," concluded Lessing, "then nothing can be demonstrated by means of historical truths." The "accidental truths of history can never become the proof of necessary truths of reason."[70] Lessing was quite honest with the problem this presented: "That, then, is the ugly broad ditch which I cannot get across, however often and however earnestly I have tried to make the leap."[71]

Lessing's divide between the necessary truths of reason and the accidental truths of history left him open and ready to embrace the shocking conclusions of Reimarus: that Christianity revolves around a bewildering, distorted, and misleading narrative.[72] Even though the historical details of the Bible have drowned in a cesspool of problems, the moral truths of Jesus's teaching have floated to the top and are still worth fetching out. Practically, this means that the ethical instruction of Jesus can be labeled as absolute truth, for it rises to the surface,

---

67. Gerhard Maier, *The End of the Historical-Critical Method*, trans. Edwin W. Leverenz and Rudolph F. Norden (St. Louis: Concordia: 1977), 25; Harrisville and Sundberg, *Bible in Modern Culture*, 61; McGrath, *Modern German Christology*, 34.

68. McGrath, *Modern German Christology*, 28.

69. See Harrisville and Sundberg, *Bible in Modern Culture*, 63.

70. G. E. Lessing, "On the Proof of the Spirit and Power," in *Lessing's Theological Writings*, ed. and trans. Henry Chadwick (Stanford: Stanford University Press, 1956), 53–55. For a thorough study, see Gordon E. Michalson, *Lessing's Ugly Ditch: A Study of Theology and History* (University Park: Pennsylvania State University Press, 1985).

71. Lessing, "On the Proof of the Spirit and Power," 53–55.

72. Harrisville and Sundberg, *Bible in Modern Culture*, 63.

overcoming the particulars of the biblical text below.[73] For the Bible, this means that the only things in the Bible worth retaining are those truths that mankind can ascertain on his own.[74] There is nothing in the Bible that could not have been discovered by human reason alone.[75]

Inevitably, all of this leads to doubts about the reliability of the Bible. If we carefully consider the resurrection accounts in the Gospels, Lessing argues, since we were not there, we are dependent on the reports of the biblical authors. But why should we trust them concerning something we have not experienced and witnessed ourselves?

The central issue for Lessing (and for the entire Enlightenment period) is *human autonomy*. We do not embrace and submit to truth because an authority outside of ourselves says so, he argued. To the contrary, truth must pass the test we set for it, the test of the autonomous intellectual. Weighing the claims in front of him with what he knows to be true, the rational thinker can verify the facts, determining whether such claims are reasonable or not.[76] While Luther and Calvin made the individual captive to the Word, the Enlightenment made the Word captive to the individual.

Liberalism's Theology from Below: Friedrich Schleiermacher

If the Enlightenment's hot day in the sun was the eighteenth century, Liberalism's was the nineteenth century, bleeding into the twentieth century as well. But what is theological Liberalism? Protestant Liberalism was an intentional renovation of Christian orthodoxy to accommodate Enlightenment thought. This did not mean that Liberalism accepted the rationalism of the Enlightenment uncritically. But it did believe in the necessity of recasting Christianity to meet the concerns raised by the Enlightenment.[77]

By adopting the Enlightenment's anthropocentric optimism, Liberalism advocated a "theology from below." A "theology from *above*" sees special revelation as the Christian's norm (i.e., *sola*

---

73. Ibid.
74. Ibid.
75. Lessing, "On the Proof of the Spirit and Power," 53 (cf. 51–56). See also Lessing, "The Education of the Human Race," in Chadwick, *Lessing's Theological Writings*, 82–98.
76. McGrath, *Modern German Christology*, 30.
77. Olson, *Journey of Modern Theology*, 126–28; Claude Welch, *Protestant Thought in the Nineteenth Century, Volume 1: 1799–1870* (New Haven: Yale University Press, 1972), 142.

Scriptura). A "theology from *below*" looks first to human experience as one's norm. In liberal theology one acquires knowledge about God from universal human experience. Revelation may still play a role in the liberal theologian's system, but such revelation must be evaluated and assessed by human experience, which sits as the ultimate judge and jury.[78] Gary Dorrien, a leading contemporary authority on Protestant Liberalism, says it this way: Liberalism sought to be "genuinely Christian without being based upon external authority." It was an effort to make Christianity "modern and progressive," and the Scriptures were now "interpreted from the standpoint of modern knowledge and experience."[79] In short, religious knowledge and experience, not Scripture, became the determining norm.

A theology from below approaches the Bible critically. Scripture may be a classic of human literature, but we can never conclude that it is supernaturally given, inspired by God and without error.[80] Liberalism was committed to a certain form of the historical-critical method so that stress fell on the Bible as a *human* book. The supernatural in the Bible could be explained by ordinary causes.[81] Large portions of the Old Testament, it was argued, were simply fictional. Numerous biblical persons and places never actually existed, and many biblical events never really happened. The New Testament fared only slightly better, since its portrait of Christ was historically inaccurate.[82] We should not miss the connection here between inerrancy and *sola Scriptura*. For Protestant Liberals, the rejection of the former resulted in the rejection of the latter. Scripture lacked supreme authority and was insufficient in part, they believed, because it was full of inaccuracies, both historical and theological.

Liberalism also held a largely negative view of *dogma*.[83] Doctrine must necessarily be subjugated to religious experience and intuition. The Bible itself was merely a human reflection on religious experience, not revelation from God, a record of human experience that could evolve from generation to generation, much like poetic idiom.[84] To

---

78. Olson, *Journey of Modern Theology*, 129.
79. Gary Dorrien, *The Making of American Liberal Theology: Imagining Progressive Religion 1805–1900*, 1:1.
80. Olson, *Journey of Modern Theology*, 129.
81. Woodbridge and James, *Church History*, 793.
82. Bray, *Biblical Interpretation*, 272–73.
83. Ibid.
84. J. I. Packer, *"Fundamentalism" and the Word of God* (Grand Rapids: Eerdmans, 1958), 25–26.

believe that first-century dogma or creeds are normative for us today, they said, was preposterous.[85]

At the risk of simplifying a complex historical development, it seems fair to say that the individual who best bridges the Enlightenment and the more mature expressions of modern Liberalism is Friedrich Schleiermacher (1768–1834), often called the father of modern theology.[86] Schleiermacher created a Copernican revolution in theology because *he took special revelation off the throne of authority and replaced it with man's experience.* Theology was no longer about right dogma or infallible truths (which he denied), but about *man's* spiritual experience of the divine—man's *Gefühl,* or feeling of absolute dependence upon God ("feeling" referring to an internal, profound awareness and intuition, or God consciousness).[87] Religion, he explained, is not something you receive from outside of yourself (e.g., from divine revelation). It is something you can find within. Jesus enters this picture not as the divine Savior but as the example of what God consciousness looks like.

The ingenuity of Schleiermacher can be seen in the middle way he pioneered. On the one hand, Schleiermacher embraced the Enlightenment's focus on man and his experience as the center. We must begin with man and work from there to God, not the other way around. Following Immanuel Kant, Schleiermacher circumscribed knowledge of God to experience. However, he did not agree with Kant's restriction of "religion to the limits of reason alone," but instead wanted to restrict religion "to the limits of piety alone."[88] Schleiermacher incorporated elements of Romanticism, a movement that emphasized feelings and intuition, where he believed the rationalism of the Enlightenment had failed. Olson writes that Schleiermacher "broke decisively with the Enlightenment by insisting on the uniqueness of religion as an irreducible element of human experience."[89]

---

85. Ibid.

86. Karl Barth, *Protestant Thought: From Rousseau to Ritchl,* trans. Brian Cozens (New York: Harper, 1959); Karl Barth, *The Theology of Schleiermacher: Lectures at Göttingen,* ed. Dietrich Ritschl, trans. Geoffrey W. Bromiley (Grand Rapids: Eerdmans, 1982); Brown, *Ancient World to the Age of Enlightenment,* 51.

87. Friedrich Schleiermacher, *The Christian Faith,* trans. H. R. Mackintosh and J. S. Stewart, 2 vols. (New York: Harper & Row, 1963), 1:12. See also Friedrich Schleiermacher, *On Religion: Addresses in Response to Its Cultured Critics,* trans. Terrence N. Tice (Richmond, VA: John Knox, 1969). For a more in-depth treatment, see Olson, *Journey of Modern Theology,* 134–40.

88. Olson, *Journey of Modern Theology,* 139.

89. Ibid.

What was the effect of Schleiermacher's approach on his under-standing of the Bible? He saw the Bible as valuable *not* as an inspired, inerrant, and sufficient Word *from* God (indeed, it is full of contra-dictions), but only as that which points us to the God-consciousness of Jesus.[90] The Bible, he argued, is not the determining norm or our supreme source for theological formulation; that role belongs to man's religious experience.[91] Man's experience, he believed, is where we begin, and experience, not Scripture, is our primary foundation and source for theology. Scripture is merely a record of what the earliest Christ-followers experienced.[92] For Schleiermacher, revelation is not external, objective, and propositional, but internal and subjective in nature.

German Bible Critics Abound

The second half of the eighteenth century and the nineteenth century witnessed the proliferation of biblical criticism. Historians estimate that between 1763 and 1817 there were at least thirty-one volumes on the doctrine of Scripture published in Germany alone.[93] Many of these advocated a Socinian (as opposed to Augustinian) view of divine accommodation, meaning that they believed the biblical authors accommodated what they wrote to the myths, fallacies, and primordial understanding of the cosmos held by many in the culture of their day.[94] Many scholars believed that those parts of the Bible, owing to a primitive worldview, could not be authentic.[95]

Not everyone agreed with Schleiermacher, of course. Some were unsympathetic because they did not share his love for Romanticism and believed that Schleiermacher had traded biblical authority for religious consciousness. Many favored the approach of Johann Semler (1725–91) instead.[96] Semler advocated the methods of historical criticism, meth-ods he believed would guarantee not only a revolution of free inquiry but the discovery of a canon within a canon.[97] Semler, known today as

---

90. Harrisville, *Pandora's Box Opened*, 120–21.

91. Olson, *Journey of Modern Theology*, 140; Alan G. Padgett and Steve Wilkens, *Christianity and Western Thought: A History of Philosophers, Ideas, and Movements*, vol. 2, *Faith and Reason in the 19th Century* (Downers Grove, IL: InterVarsity Press, 2000), 27, 39.

92. Padgett and Wilkens, *Christianity and Western Thought*, 2:60–61.

93. Woodbridge and James, *Church History*, 548.

94. Ibid.

95. Ibid.

96. See Harrisville, *Pandora's Box Opened*, 105–12.

97. Woodbridge and James, *Church History*, 548.

the father of German higher criticism, distinguished between Scripture and the Word of God, which meant that many parts of the Bible should not be considered divinely inspired or infallible. Semler sought to find the canon (Word of God) within the canon (Scripture), separating the historical from the mythical.[98]

Though we cannot explore the legions of critics here, it should be noted that many of them, though diverse in their own emphases, approached Scripture similarly. Some of the most notable included Johann Gottfried Eichhorn (1752–1827), Christian Gottlob Heyne (1729–1812), and Johann Philipp Gabler (1753–1826). Gabler, for instance, alleged that the biblical authors incorporated myth, and that while these myths might prove insightful or valuable in some sense, they must be identified and cleared out. If the scholar is to obtain a biblical theology, he must cut into the biblical text, carving out the erroneous human aspects of the Bible from its flawless, universal truths.[99]

Reconstructing Jesus (and the Bible): Strauss, Baur, and the Tübingen School

Given the emphasis these scholars placed on "myth," it is not surprising that this approach also took aim at the Christ of the Gospels. Jesus, being the central "myth," sits at the very center of the Bible's story and the Christian faith. Consider two examples.

David F. Strauss (1808–74), a student of F. C. Baur at Tübingen, categorized the acts and claims of Jesus as "myth" in his 1835 book, *Life of Jesus, Critically Examined*, a book that some believed was the most important work since Luther's Ninety-Five Theses![100]

For Strauss, myth meant that while the Bible is filled with spiritually oriented narratives and assertions, the accounts are fictional, having evolved over time into legendary status, producing the Christian

---

98. Ibid., 463; Harrisville, *Pandora's Box Opened*, 105–13. E.g., Johan Salomo Semler, *Von Freier Untersuchung des Canons*, ed. Heinz Scheible (Gütersloh: Mohn, 1967). Semler would carry on the Socinian view of accommodation referenced earlier, believing that Jesus "deliberately misapplied to himself Old Testament prophecies that were not actually messianic in order to accommodate his teachings to the misunderstandings of the Jewish people of his day" (Sunshine, "Accommodation Historically Considered," 260).

99. Woodbridge and James, *Church History*, 465.

100. David Strauss, *The Life of Jesus Critically Examined*, ed. Peter C. Hodgson, trans. George Eliot, 4th ed. (Philadelphia: Fortress, 1972); David Strauss, *The Christ of Faith and the Jesus of History: A Critique of Schleiermacher's The Life of Jesus*, trans. Leander E. Keck (Philadelphia: Fortress, 1977). See William Baird, *History of New Testament Research* (Minneapolis: Fortress, 1992), 1:246.

beliefs we have today.[101] He believed that history is insignificant (and therefore so is the "historical" Jesus) because what truly matters are the spiritualized myths that have colored the figure of Jesus, since these are what have inspired and will inspire transformation.[102] There are differences between Reimarus and Strauss (the former saw Jesus as a failed political revolutionary, while the latter saw him as a suffering Messiah who wrongly thought his crucifixion would ignite the earthly kingdom of God), but both the rationalists and the mythologizers agreed that the Jesus of history was nothing more than a man, a human being. The testimony of Scripture to his supernatural works and his divine nature, they argued, must be seen as implausible.[103] For Strauss, miracles are impossible; therefore, the resurrection accounts are mythical, not historical.[104] He writes, "What the Evangelists tell us we can no longer take to be true in the way they tell it; what the apostles believed and the way they believed it we can no longer hold necessary for salvation. . . . Also Christ can no longer be for us who he was for them. To admit this is the duty of truthfulness; to want to deny or cover it up leads to nothing other than lies, distortion of the Scriptures, and hypocrisy with regard to faith."[105]

Strauss's teacher, F. C. Baur (1792–1860), was committed to G. W. F. Hegel's dialectical philosophy, which argued that conflict between a thesis and antithesis creates a new phenomenon: synthesis.[106] Applying this philosophy to New Testament studies, Baur believed that there was a conflict between two groups in the first century: conservative Christ-following Jews who followed Peter and liberal-minded Christ-following Gentiles who followed Paul. This conflict produced a new synthesis: early Catholicism.[107] By setting Peter and Paul against each other as competing sources, Baur concluded that the New Testament we have today actually tells us very little about the historical Jesus, but instead

---

101. Blomberg, *Jesus and the Gospels*, 78.
102. Bray, *Biblical Interpretation*, 330.
103. Blomberg, *Jesus and the Gospels*, 179.
104. Padgett and Wilkens, *Christianity and Western Thought*, 2:92.
105. Strauss, *Christ of Faith and the Jesus of History*, 162.
106. See F. C. Baur, "Die Christuspartei in der korintischen Gemeinde, der Gegensatz des petrinischen und paulinischen Christenthums in der ältesten Kirche, der Apostel Paulus in Rom," *Tübingen Zeitschrift für Theologie* 3.4 (1831): 61–206; reprinted in *Ausgewählte Werke in Einzelusgaben*, 5 vols. (Stuttgart: Bad Cannstatt, 1963–75), 1:1–146; F. C. Baur, *Paul, the Apostle of Jesus Christ: His Life and Work, His Epistles and His Doctrine*, trans. A. Menzies, 2 vols. (London: Williams and Norgate, 1876).
107. Bray, *Biblical Interpretation*, 356; Blomberg, *Jesus and the Gospels*, 78.

reflects these competing theologies (and Christologies). In that light, digging up the historical Jesus became all the more difficult because he was hidden somewhere beneath these layers of competing traditions. Bauer believed that excavating the real Jesus was not impossible if the right methods were utilized.[108] This meant that the New Testament was often seen as an obstacle to recovering the historical Jesus, for it was considered the product of those in the early church who were deeply influenced by Greek philosophy. The scholar's job, he believed, was to reconstruct Jesus by reconstructing the New Testament, figuring out which Gospels and Epistles were more reliable than others. Bauer's goal was to liberate Jesus from the myths (e.g., Jesus is God) that orthodox Christians had turned into history, twisting and distorting the truth about him.

Baur's entire project presupposed philosophical naturalism when approaching the Bible. When this naturalism was combined with a reconstruction of the history of the early church, it was concluded that the New Testament could not have been inspired by God.[109] Neither could Christian doctrine as a unified system originate from the biblical text and therefore be authoritative. For Baur, the biblical text reveals an evolution of diverse, even contradictory, theologies that cannot doctrinally bind the Christian's conscience or the church's practice.[110]

In his 1906 book, *The Quest of the Historical Jesus*, Albert Schweitzer keenly observed that many of these nineteenth-century Jesus scholars simply refashioned Jesus to look the part of their own social or theological agenda.[111] According to the Jesus experts, the Gospels combined fact and fiction, so it was necessary to rid the text of late interpretations from the early church, especially those driven by theological motives, in order to find the historical Jesus.[112] Ironically, the Jesus who was excavated typically reflected the agenda of each nineteenth-century Jesus scholar. The result? There were as many "Jesuses" as scholars. Indeed, as contemporary Jesus scholar Craig Blomberg observes, even Schweitzer's Jesus "proved equally truncated: an apocalyptic prophet

---

108. Bray, *Biblical Interpretation*, 322 (cf. 323).

109. D. A. Carson and Douglas J. Moo, *An Introduction to the New Testament*, 2nd ed. (Grand Rapids: Zondervan, 2005), 49.

110. Ibid.

111. Schweitzer, *Quest of the Historical Jesus*.

112. Blomberg, *Jesus and the Gospels*, 78–79.

who believed the kingdom would come in all its fullness during his lifetime but who was sadly mistaken."[113]

The developments of nineteeth-century scholarship and the quest to reinterpret Jesus provide us with good test cases for gauging how the Bible itself has been treated and received, and for clearly identifying the types of presuppositions critics brought to the biblical text. The clear takeaway from studying this period is that many scholars ruled out much of the biblical material because they came to the Bible with an antisupernaturalist worldview, and they started from a position of methodological doubt.[114] Is it any wonder that when they came to the supernatural events of Scripture, especially events in the life of Jesus, they threw them out without a second thought?

Rethinking the Old Testament: Wellhausen

While criticism of the New Testament was developing during the nineteenth century, the Old Testament was not exempt from such criticism either. A long history of critics could be considered, but we'll consider just one, Julius Wellhausen (1844–1918). Wellhausen created waves with the publication of his book *Prolegomena to the History of Israel*.[115] He proposed a documentary hypothesis of the Pentateuch that denied Mosaic authorship and instead attributed its composition to four sources—the Yahwist/Jehovist (J), Elohistic (E), Deuteronomistic (D), and Priestly (P). These sources were spread out over long periods of time long after Moses had died.[116] Wellhausen also reconstructed Israel's history in the process. For example, the Priestly "material of the Pentateuch does not come from the Mosaic legislations established in Moses' time" but is "retrofitted to the time of Moses in its canonical presentation, though, in fact, it is from the postexilic period."[117]

Wellhausen concluded that Israelite history, as recorded in the biblical account, is plagued with inaccuracies. He argued that the Bible's history cannot be trusted, but instead needs reinterpretation if it is to align with secular history.[118] Furthermore, Wellhausen's theory

---

113. Ibid.

114. Ibid., 185 (cf. 80).

115. Julius Wellhausen, *Prolegomena to the History of Israel* (Edinburgh: Black, 1885). Also consult Wellhausen's *The Composition of the Hexateuch and the Historical Books of the Old Testament*. See Gignilliat, *Old Testament Criticism*, 62–63.

116. Bray, *Biblical Interpretation*, 304.

117. Gignilliat, *Old Testament Criticism*, 69.

118. Bray, *Biblical Interpretation*, 298.

presupposed an anti-supernatural worldview, assuming that a supernaturally revealed religion (as the Old Princetonian Benjamin Warfield liked to call it) was simply an impossibility. Israel's religion, therefore, was the same as any other religion, having a purely human origin and genesis, continually evolving up to the present age.[119] Wellhausen's theory commanded the attention of scholars everywhere, though today it is rejected by conservatives and even some liberal scholars.[120]

Liberalism's Heartbeat: Ritschl, Harnack, and Herrmann

Though they would have their own differences with Schleiermacher, the spirit of Schleiermacher lived on in figures such as Albrecht Ritschl (1822–89), Adolf von Harnack (1851–1930), and Wilhelm Herrmann (1846–1922).[121] Adolf von Harnack celebrated the abandonment of *sola Scriptura*.[122] He argued that Christian doctrine had evolved over time, and the more it evolved the more it drifted from the historical Jesus and his teachings. Our task, he advocated, is to slice through the NT to dispense with everything added by Paul and the Gnostics.[123] In the end, Jesus was not the Son of God, nor God incarnate, but a mere man who had a unique God-consciousness. Jesus was the original liberal—indeed, its poster boy—promoting the universal brotherhood of man and the fatherhood of God. George Tyrrell concludes, "The Christ that Harnack sees, looking back through nineteen centuries of Catholic darkness, is only the reflection of a Liberal Protestant face, seen at the bottom of a deep well."[124]

Or consider Wilhelm Herrmann at the University of Marburg.[125]

---

119. Gleason L. Archer, *A Survey of Old Testament Introduction* (Chicago: Moody Press, 1994), 113, 115.

120. Duane Garrett, *Rethinking Genesis: The Sources and Authorship of the First Book of the Pentateuch* (Grand Rapids: Baker, 1991), 13; Archer, *Survey of Old Testament Introduction*, 96 (see 89–126 for Archer's overview and critique); T. Desmond Alexander, *From Paradise to the Promised Land: An Introduction to the Pentateuch*, 3rd ed. (Grand Rapids: Baker Academic, 2012), 7–63.

121. For example, Albrecht Ritschl, *The Christian Doctrine of Justification and Reconciliation*, trans. H. R. Mackintosh and A. B. Macaulay (Edinburgh: T&T Clark, 1902).

122. Adolf von Harnack, *What Is Christianity?* trans. Thomas Bailey Saunders (Philadelphia: Fortress, 1986); Adolf von Harnack, *Outlines of the History of Dogma*, trans. Edwin Knox Mitchell (Boston: Beacon, 1957); Adolf von Harnack, *History of Dogma*, trans. Neil Buchanan, 7 vols., 3rd ed. (New York: Dover, 1961); Adolf von Harnack, *The Origin of the New Testament*, trans. J. R. Wilkinson (New York: Macmillan, 1925).

123. Woodbridge and James, *Church History*, 552–54.

124. George Tyrrell, *Christianity at the Cross-Roads* (London: Allen & Unwin, 1963), 49. See also Padgett and Wilkens, *Christianity and Western Thought*, 2:280.

125. See Wilhelm Hermann, *The Communion of the Christian with God: Described on the*

Herrman rejected the Bible's infallibility outright.[126] He wrote, "Luther lived in an age when the authority of Holy Scripture as the Infallible Word of God and the authority of the dogma of the ancient Church enjoyed unquestioning recognition." That day, he argued, is long gone. Scripture is no longer the "infallible law," and Protestants cannot operate under this "sure, unassailable assumption."[127]

While far more could be said, historian of Liberalism Gary Dorrien pinpoints the hinge on which Liberalism turned: "The essential idea of liberal theology is that all claims to truth, in theology as in other disciplines, must be made on the basis of reason and experience, not by appeal to external authority. Christian scripture may be recognized as spiritually authoritative within Christian experience, but its word does not settle or establish truth claims about matters of fact."[128]

Liberalism's Neo-Orthodox Nemesis: Karl Barth

In the context of the widespread Liberalism in the nineteenth and early-twentieth centuries, Karl Barth's (1886–1968) entrance to the discussion was like a breath of fresh air. Barth initiated twentieth-century theology with his commentary on Romans. While much of esteemed scholarship approached the Bible from below, seeking to humanize Scripture, Barth argued that rather than starting with man, we must begin with God.[129] No longer can we begin by imposing our own agenda onto the God of Scripture. Instead, we must allow God to have the first and final word; we are simply to listen.

Barth did not come to his views all at once, having started out under the tutelage of Liberalism. While a student at the University

---

Basis of Luther's Statements, ed. Robert T. Voelkel (Philadelphia: Fortress, 1971); Wilhelm Hermann, *Faith and Morals*, trans. Donald Matheson and Robert W. Stewart (New York: Putnam, 1904); Wilhelm Hermann, *Systematic Theology*, trans. Nathaniel Micklem and Kenneth A. Saunders (New York: Macmillan, 1927).

126. Hermann, *Communion of the Christian*, 52, 69–70.

127. Quotation from Woodbridge and James, *Church History*, 557.

128. Dorrien's focus is on American Liberalism. Nevertheless, Liberalism stretched internationally, and Dorrien's description is fitting. Dorrien, *American Liberal Theology*, 1.

129. Space is limited, so I have chosen Barth as my focus. However, one should also consider Reinhold Niebuhr (1892–1971) and Paul Tillich (1886–1965), who were on the American stage at the time. See also Emil Brunner (1889–1966) and Rudolf Bultmann (1884–1976), who were influenced by Barth but created a theology of their own, disagreeing with Barth in certain ways. For an overview of their thought on Scripture, see Alan G. Padgett and Steve Wilkens, *Christianity and Western Thought: A History of Philosophers, Ideas, and Movements*, vol. 3, *Journey to Postmodernity in the 20th Century* (Downers Grove, IL: InterVarsity Press, 2009), 146–66; Harrisville, *Pandora's Box Opened*, 182–98.

of Berlin, Barth became enamored with Harnack, and then, at the University of Marburg, with Herrmann, who himself was a pupil of Schleiermacher. Herrmann's theology, Barth confessed, had seeped "through all my pores."[130] Barth's infatuation with Liberalism would fade after ninety-six scholars, many of whom were liberal theologians and Barth's mentors, signed their names in support of Kaiser Wilhelm going to war in 1914. Barth felt that Liberalism had led these scholars to "sell out" Christianity to nationalism.[131] World War I (1914–18) exposed the hollowness of Liberalism's optimistic anthropology, revealing the horror of war and showing that Liberalism's claim that man was inherently and fundamentally good did not hold water.[132] Liberalism, argued Barth, had dispensed with God's transcendence and had overemphasized divine immanence. Theology had become anthropology. Liberals, like Schleiermacher, spoke of God merely by talking about man in a very loud voice. Barth was hungry for a theology from above, and he was convinced that the theology of Schleiermacher, Hermann, and others would only result in the destruction of the Protestant Church.[133]

Barth embarked on a mission to retrieve God's transcendence, a mission that began with his commentary on Romans, which has been said to have fallen like a bomb on the theological playground.[134] Barth wrote that the "Bible tells us not how we should talk with God but what he says to us; not how we find the way to him, but how he has sought and found the way to us. . . . It is this which is within the Bible. The word of God is within the Bible."[135] For Barth, this discovery meant entering into the strange new world of the Bible. Only God can

---

130. Eberhard Busch, *Karl Barth: His Life from Letters and Autobiographical Texts* (London: SCM, 1976), 45.

131. Padgett and Wilkens, *Christianity and Western Thought*, 3:136.

132. It needs to be qualified, however, that while Barth's theology came out of this context and was influenced by it, nevertheless his own contemporaries recognized that his theology was ultimately due to a fresh reading of Scripture itself. See Andreas Pangritz, *Karl Barth in the Theology of Dietrich Bonhoeffer* (Grand Rapids: Eerdmans, 2000), 36. Barth himself would say the same. See Karl Barth, "A Thank-You and a Bow—Kierkegaard's Reveille: Speech on Being Awarded the Sonning Prize (1963)," in *Fragments Grave and Gray*, ed. Martin Rumscheidt (London: Collins, 1971), 97.

133. Harrisville, *Pandora's Box Opened*, 175.

134. Karl Barth, *The Epistle to the Romans*, trans. Edwyn C. Hoskyns (London: Oxford University Press, 1933).

135. Karl Barth, *The Word of God and the Word of Man* (New York: Harper & Row, 1957), 43.

reveal himself to us; therefore we are utterly dependent upon a revelation outside of ourselves (*extra nos*).

The Word, or *Logos*, for Barth takes on three forms: Christ, Scripture, and the proclamation of the gospel.[136] Out of these three, Barth believed, it is in Christ that God has given us the greatest revelation of all, speaking directly through the condescension of his own Son. Scripture and the proclamation of the gospel are important too, but they are mere instruments of God's speech and cannot be called the Word of God, at least not in the same sense that Jesus is the Word of God. As Barth said, "That the Bible is the Word of God cannot mean that with other attributes the Bible has the attribute of being the Word of God." Certainly, in his mind, this would violate the freedom and sovereignty of God. The Word of God, he maintained, is not "tied to the Bible."[137] "The Bible," Barth said, "is God's Word to the extent that God causes it to be His Word, to the extent that He speaks through it."[138] Yet he maintained that Scripture remains important in the sense that it is a *witness* to Christ, who is the Word of God, the revelation.[139] Scripture is not actually revelation in and of itself, he believed, but rather *becomes* revelation when the Spirit uses it to make Christ known.[140]

Barth rejected any view that saw Scripture as God's deposited truth in propositional form. He believed that such a view constrains divine freedom and enslaves Scripture to man's control.[141] He said divine revelation cannot be chained down to Scripture because revelation is an event. For Barth, to call Scripture itself revelation is to commit the unthinkable sin of bibliolatry!

Barth may have had a higher view of Scripture when compared to Liberalism, but he did not affirm the traditional view of verbal, plenary inspiration and inerrancy. As historians have observed, Barth "did not completely turn his back on modernity," but "accepted a chastened use of biblical criticism and believed that Scripture could

---

136. Karl Barth, *Church Dogmatics* 1.1 (Edinburgh: T&T Clark, 1975; repr., Peabody, MA: Hendrickson, 2010), 120–21 (hereafter *CD*). See also Geoffrey W. Bromiley, *Introduction to the Theology of Karl Barth* (Grand Rapids: Eerdmans, 1979).

137. Barth, *CD*, 1.2, 513.

138. Ibid., 1.1, 109.

139. Ibid., 1.2, 457–63.

140. Ibid., 1.1, 109–20.

141. Ibid., 1.2, 513.

contain 'errors.'"[142] For Barth, the errancy of Scripture followed
naturally from the fact that the biblical authors were not only human
but sinners as well, prone to make mistakes in what they wrote, just as
anyone would. "The men whom we hear as witnesses speak as fallible,
erring men like ourselves," Barth asserted.[143] In fact, not only did
fallibility apply to the historical and scientific elements, but to the
spiritual aspects as well. Barth observed, "We can read and try to assess
their word as a purely human word. It can be subjected to all kinds of
immanent criticism, not only in respect of its philosophical, historical
and ethical content, but even of its religious and theological."[144] He
believed that even though the human authors embarrassed themselves
by their errors, limited and bound to the culture of their day as they
were, God used fallible Scripture to advance his will and proclaim the
name of Christ.[145]

For Barth, the division between Scripture and the Word of God
remained. He maintained that Christ *is* the Word of God, but we cannot say the same of Scripture. Instead, the Bible may *become* the Word
of God as God himself uses it (as a vehicle) in the world, but it is not the
case that the Bible *is* the Word of God. As Barth claimed, "The Bible
is God's Word to the extent that God causes it to be His Word, to the
extent that He speaks through it."

> We recollect that we have heard in this book the word of God. . . .
> Yet the presence of the word of God itself, the real and present
> speaking and hearing of it, is not identical with the existence of
> the book as such. But in this presence something takes place in
> and with the book, for which the book as such does indeed give
> the possibility, but the reality of which cannot be anticipated or
> replaced by the existence of the book.[146]

How does this compare to verbal inspiration and infallibility, key
elements of *sola Scriptura*? "Verbal inspiration," Barth explained, "does
not mean the infallibility of the biblical word in its linguistic, historical
and theological character as a human word. It means that the fallible

---

142. Woodbridge and James, *Church History*, 561. See also Olson, *Journey of Modern Theology*, 301.
143. Barth, *CD*, 1.2, 507; see also 1.2, 529–31.
144. Ibid., 1.2, 507 (cf. 509).
145. Ibid., 1.2, 531, 533.
146. Ibid., 1.2, 530.

and faulty human word is as such used by God and has to be received and heard in spite of its human fallibility."[147] In the end, Barth criticized fundamentalism for its biblicism, which turned Scripture into a paper pope.

The Evangelical Response to Barth

Barth's neo-orthodoxy (a phrase that captures Barth's attempt to get beyond modernity and recover the faith) was severely critiqued in his day. Liberals like Rudolph Bultmann believed Barth's position was far too orthodox. Others, like Richard R. Niebuhr, Paul Tillich, and Jürgen Moltmann, were not convinced Barth had really abandoned Liberalism in the end.[148]

Conservative and Reformed evangelicals did not respond favorably either. Cornelius Van Til and Carl F. H. Henry believed Barth compromised biblical authority and inerrancy in critical ways.[149] Still, Barth's views generated a significant following, and they are gaining increasing popularity today.[150] Yet many contemporary evangelicals continue to find Barth's position problematic for several reasons.[151]

First, Barth seems to rely upon the very doctrines he denies. For example, when Barth interprets Scripture, he does so *as if* the biblical text is truthful and trustworthy, communicating the very words of God.[152] Yet Barth will deny the inerrancy of the biblical witness, which means he is basing his doctrinal formulations upon a text he does not and cannot totally trust. This seems contradictory. If we cannot trust the text, how can we trust Barth's doctrine that he

---

147. Ibid., 1.2, 533.

148. See John Frame, *A History of Western Philosophy and Theology* (Phillipsburg, NJ: P&R, 2015), 366.

149. Cornelius Van Til, *The New Modernism* (1946; repr., Nutley, NJ: Presbyterian and Reformed, 1973); Cornelius Van Til, *Christianity and Barthianism* (Grand Rapids: Baker, 1962); Carl F. H. Henry, *God, Revelation, and Authority*, vol. 4, *God Who Speaks and Shows, Fifteen Theses, Part Three* (repr., Wheaton, IL: Crossway, 1999), esp. 196–200. Though not in the same evangelical camp as Van Til and Henry, G. C. Berkouwer also responded very critically to Barth in *Karl Barth* (Kampen: Kok, 1936); G. C. Berkouwer, *The Triumph of Grace in the Theology of Karl Barth* (Grand Rapids: Eerdmans, 1956).

150. Most notable are the plethora of publications by Geoffrey W. Bromiley, John Webster, George Hunsinger, Bruce L. McCormack, and others.

151. On Barth's reception in evangelical circles, see Michael S. Horton, "A Stony Jar: The Legacy of Karl Barth for Evangelical Theology," in *Engaging with Barth: Contemporary Evangelical Critiques*, ed. David Gibson and Daniel Strange (Nottingham: Inter-Varsity Press, 2008), 346–48.

152. James I. Packer, "Encountering Present Day Views of Scripture," in Boice, *Foundation of Biblical Authority*, 73.

derives from the text? We are left with an arbitrary hermeneutic, or what Carl Henry has called a "theological schizophrenia."[153] Barth's view, unfortunately, does not escape the "built-in arbitrariness" of Liberalism.[154]

Second, Barth's view of Scripture is also driven by a mistaken view of God's free will. In his misguided view of divine freedom, God is Lord, free to speak or remain silent, but should he decide to speak, we cannot conclude that he is then free *not* to stand by the words he has spoken.[155] For God not to stand by what he has said would be a denial of his own character, a betrayal of the truthfulness of his very own freedom. Therefore, while God may be free to initiate a promise or to refrain from making a promise in the first place, once God has chosen to declare a promise, his own character—indeed, his own freedom!—binds him and compels him to keep his promise.[156] Otherwise, we cannot make sense of the story line of Scripture, which is grounded in the fact that this God not only reveals his promises but makes good on his promises (see chapters 5 and 6). He is the God whose fame rests upon his reputation to be faithful and true to his word. Scripture's trustworthiness is rooted in the very trustworthiness (the character) of God himself.[157] This is not a violation of divine freedom, but the truest and most faithful expression of divine freedom to be found.

At this point, we should ask why Barth sees inscripturation as a hindrance to God's free will. After all, isn't this the God who became incarnate? If God can (and desires to) bind himself to human flesh, why can he not do this for human speech as well?[158] Some wonder whether Barth fell prey to the adoptionist heresy. Vanhoozer puts it this way: "To say that Scripture only becomes God's word when God in his freedom makes use of it is, to return to the Christological heresies, what *adoptionists* said about the Logos taking on humanity."[159]

Barth would have us believe that the finite (human words in

---

153. Henry, *God, Revelation, and Authority*, 4:14.

154. Packer, "Encountering Present Day Views of Scripture," 73.

155. Kevin J. Vanhoozer, "Triune Discourse: Theological Reflections on the Claim That God Speaks (Part 1)," in *Trinitarian Theology for the Church*, ed. Daniel J. Treier and David Lauber (Downers Grove, IL: IVP Academic, 2009), 45.

156. Ibid.

157. We will explore this important point further in chapters 7 and 8.

158. Vanhoozer, "Triune Discourse," 45n.79.

159. Ibid.

Scripture) is not capable of the infinite (Word of God)—*finitum non capax infiniti*. But the incarnation undermines such an assumption. When the eternal, divine Son adds to himself human nature in order to be not only fully God but fully man, we have conclusive proof that the finite can receive the infinite.[160] Indubitably, the incarnation of Christ drives the nail into the Barthian coffin and warns us against the danger of pitting divine transcendence against human language.[161]

If Jesus, God in the flesh, has spoken via human words (and he has), then we have an undeniable case of divine speech. Telford Work concludes, "When Jesus opens his mouth and speaks Scripture, [Barth's] distinction evaporates."[162] No longer can we distinguish between Scripture and God's Word, as if to say the former merely *becomes* the latter. Rather, we must say that Scripture *is* God's Word. "The line between divine and discourse is breached: the infinite intones."[163]

Third, while Barth is often praised for formulating his doctrine of Scripture *christologically*, evangelicals question whether Barth is truly and fully christological since his view of Scripture fails to match Jesus's own view of Scripture, let alone that of his inspired disciples (see chapter 8).[164] To put it simply, one might say that Barth doesn't get Scripture right because he doesn't get Jesus right.

Barth fails to recognize that God speaks not only through Scripture but *in* Scripture as well. It is insufficient merely to say that the Bible is a vehicle for God's Word to reach his people. We must say far more: the Bible is the ordained, supreme, and most glorious expression and proclamation of God's authoritative speech in written form.[165] It is precisely because God himself has spoken in the Scriptures, breathing out the Scriptures, that these same Scriptures possess an intrinsic and inherent authority when the gospel is announced for the salvation of the world.[166] Barth's position for many contemporary evangelicals is

---

160. Ibid., 54.

161. Ibid.

162. Telford Work, *Living and Active: Scripture in the Economy of Salvation* (Grand Rapids: Eerdmans, 2002), 85.

163. Vanhoozer, "Triune Discourse," 54.

164. Mark Thompson, "Barth's Doctrine of Scripture," in Gibson and Strange, *Engaging with Barth*, 185; Work, *Living and Active*, 79; Vanhoozer, "Triune Discourse," 45n.79.

165. Scott R. Swain, *Trinity, Revelation, and Reading: A Theological Introduction to the Bible and Its Interpretation* (New York: T&T Clark, 2011), 72–73.

166. Ibid. Also see David Gibson, "The Answering Speech of Men: Karl Barth on Holy Scripture," in Carson, *Enduring Authority of the Christian Scriptures*, 277, 284, 287–91. It is due to this third reason that McCormack's proposal, I believe, will not work (Bruce L.

in error because it fails to see that what Scripture says, God says, and God's speech does not falter or fall short.[167]

To this point, we have traced the development of the Reformation understanding of Scripture through the historical movements of the Englightenment, Liberalism, and neo-orthodoxy. Yet none of them retain the clear emphasis on *sola Scriptura* that we saw in the Reformation. This raises the question: What heritage are evangelicals indebted to if it was neither Liberalism nor neo-orthodoxy? The answer comes to us in the advent of Old Princeton.

Old Princeton's Bulwark

The nineteenth century brought with it a clear division between liberals and conservatives. Enlightenment philosophy, which elevated man's reason, downplayed man's sin, and presupposed an anti-supernatural worldview, proved critical for the advent of Liberalism in nineteenth-century Europe and early twentieth-century America.[168] Conservatives were characterized by those commitments that Liberalism rejected. Approaching theology from above, conservatives affirmed the inspiration of the Bible as the very Word of God. While they may have disagreed on exactly how inspiration occurred, they had no hesitation believing that Scripture was God-breathed. They were convinced that without this doctrine, Christianity itself could not stand.[169] And when conservatives evaluated Liberalism, they concluded that Liberalism was not based on the biblical data but rather on certain preconceived theological prejudices.[170] These beliefs, they argued, were inherently antithetical to Christianity, for they presupposed an anti-supernatural worldview from the start.[171]

Princeton Theological Seminary had become the bulwark for biblical authority, building off of the Reformed tradition, specifically the

McCormack, "The Being of Holy Scripture Is in Becoming," in *Evangelicals and Scripture: Tradition, Authority and Hermeneutics*, ed. Vincent E. Bacote, Laura C. Miguelez, and Dennis L. Okholm [Downers Grove, IL: InterVarsity Press, 2004], 55–75).

167. For other critiques, see Horton, "Stony Jar," 364; Roger Nicole, "The Neo-Orthodox Reduction," in Lewis and Demarest, *Challenges to Inerrancy*, 128–36; Carson, *Collected Writings on Scripture*, 35; Peter Jensen, *The Revelation of God* (Downers Grove, IL: InterVarsity Press, 2002), 88–93; Frame, *Western Philosophy and Theology*, 366–83.

168. David S. Dockery, *Christian Scripture* (Nashville: B&H, 1995; repr., Eugene, OR: Wipf & Stock, 1995), 51.

169. Bray, *Biblical Interpretation*, 273.

170. Ibid.

171. Ibid., 274.

Westminster Confession of Faith and the theology of Francis Turretin (1623–87). Archibald Alexander (1772–1851), Charles Hodge (1797–1878), A. A. Hodge (1823–86), and Benjamin B. Warfield (1851–1921) all defended the Bible's truthfulness and trustworthiness, seeing themselves as faithfully holding the line of biblical authority that the Reformers and Puritans strove so hard to maintain.[172] While some have seen inerrancy as an invention of Old Princeton, it has been persuasively demonstrated that these Princetonians were actually defending an age-old doctrine, going all the way back to the Reformers and even the church fathers. This is not to deny that the Princetonians developed their own views and responses in light of new and unique challenges.[173]

Warfield, the "lion of Princeton," is especially notable, and we will interact with his work regularly throughout this book. He defended biblical authority and inerrancy, but did so by appealing to the supernatural nature of the Christian worldview and its God. In 1881 Warfield teamed up with A. A. Hodge to write an article called "Inspiration" for the *Presbyterian Review*, an article that was much in line with the views of Charles Hodge, who had previously defended inspiration.[174] However, the two authors were facing new and pressing challenges from higher criticism. "From the perspective of higher criticism, authors of biblical books function more like editors who cleverly and creatively weave the strands, coming from a variety of sources, together. Advocates of higher criticism see their task as teasing the strands apart."[175] The assumption Warfield and Hodge were addressing was that the Bible was fundamentally and primarily a *human* book, not a divine one.

Reactions to their view of inerrancy were fierce. Charles A. Briggs, professor at Union Theological Seminary (New York), called Warfield's

---

172. E.g., Charles Hodge, *Systematic Theology*, 3 vols. (Grand Rapids: Eerdmans, 1946), 1:163. For a helpful overview of Old Princeton and biblical authority, see Bradley N. Seeman, "The 'Old Princetonians' on Biblical Authority," in Carson, *Enduring Authority of the Christian Scriptures*, 195–237.

173. John D. Woodbridge, *Biblical Authority: A Critique of the Rogers/McKim Proposal* (Grand Rapids: Zondervan, 1982), 119–40. Contra Jack Rogers and Donald McKim, *The Authority and Interpretation of the Bible: An Historical Approach* (San Francisco: Harper & Row, 1979). We will address this issue more in chapter 3.

174. A. A. Hodge and Benjamin B. Warfield, "Inspiration," *Presbyterian Review* 2, no. 6 (1881): 225–60.

175. Stephen J. Nichols and Eric T. Brandt, *Ancient Word, Changing Worlds: The Doctrine of Scripture in a Modern Age* (Wheaton, IL: Crossway, 2009), 27.

and Princeton's position on inspiration "idolatrous" in his 1889 book *Whither?*[176] Briggs also published articles in the *Presbyterian Review* and delivered an inaugural address (1891) that showed his strong sympathies for higher criticism. Briggs rejected *verbal* inspiration and inerrancy, arguing that the Bible never speaks of itself in this way. Inspiration, he believed, should be limited to the spiritual message of the Bible. He argued that the historic creeds of the church never teach such a doctrine. Verbal inerrant inspiration, said Briggs, is an invention of modern scholasticism, an argument (as we will see in chapter 3) that would be utilized in the twentieth century by Ernest Sandeen, Jack Rogers, and Donald McKim. Warfield responded to this charge by demonstrating that "verbal inerrant inspiration" not only was affirmed by the Westminster Assembly but is a doctrine that goes all the way back to Calvin and even Augustine.[177]

The wider reaction to Briggs was explosive. Union Theological Seminary defended him, but the Presbyterian Church USA refused to have Briggs appointed to the Robinson chair. Briggs was eventually found guilty and defrocked.[178] The entire affair split Union and the Presbyterian Church USA. This case, occurring near the end of the nineteenth century, was an early tremor of the volcanic eruption over inerrancy to come in the twentieth century.[179]

Pushback against Warfield and Hodge also came in 1891 from Harvard professor Joseph Henry Thayer, who delivered a lecture called "The Change of Attitude towards the Bible." In the lecture Thayer targeted the Princetonians' doctrine of inspiration, which he said may have been "comparatively harmless in bygone days" but had now "become a yoke." Such a view no longer fits with the advanced knowledge we now

176. Charles A. Briggs, *Whither?* (New York: Scribner's Sons, 1889), 64–73. See also Charles A. Briggs, "Critical Theories of the Sacred Scriptures in Relation to Their Inspiration," *Presbyterian Review* 2, no. 7 (1881): 554.

177. Warfield shows that Briggs took quotations out of context and twisted them to suit his own bias. See Benjamin B. Warfield, *Calvin and Calvinism*, in *The Works of Benjamin Breckinridge Warfield*, 10 vols. (New York: Oxford University Press, 1927–32; repr., Grand Rapids: Baker, 2003), 5:29–130; idem, *The Westminster Assembly and Its Work*, in *The Works*, 6:155–257, 261–333; idem, *Selected Shorter Writings*, 2 vols., ed. John Meeter (Nutley, NJ: Presbyterian and Reformed, 1970, 1973), 2:560–94.

178. For an extensive investigation into the Briggs case, see Ronald F. Satta, *The Sacred Text: Biblical Authority in Nineteenth-Century America*, Princeton Theological Monograph Series (Eugene, OR: Pickwick, 2007), 75–95.

179. For an overview of how controversy struck the Northern Baptist Convention, the Lutheran Church–Missouri Synod, and the Southern Baptist Convention, see Nichols and Brandt, *Ancient Word, Changing Worlds*, 65–68.

have, he said, due to "improved methods of philological study" (i.e., higher criticism) and "progress in science."[180] When Thayer mentions the "progress in science," he is referring to the scientific worldview of moderns, which he believed surpassed the primitive, mythological worldview of ancient civilizations.[181]

Thayer was correct in one sense. There was indeed a changing attitude toward the Bible, and the battle lines would be drawn between those who maintained Scripture's inspiration and inerrancy and those who adopted a form of Liberalism. The presupposition of the modernists was that our understanding of Christianity and biblical authority must be reconstructed and reconfigured due to the findings of modern thought and higher criticism. They insisted that we rid Christianity and the Bible of its many cultural and theological trappings that keep us from deciphering those parts of Scripture that should be retained. The cultural husk of Scripture (i.e., the beliefs of traditional Christianity) must be thrown away in order to save the kernel beneath it.[182]

The response to these modernist presuppositions led to the development of fundamentalism in America.[183] Between 1910 and 1915, conservatives published twelve volumes called *The Fundamentals* to counter the modernist attacks. While a number of the contributors to these volumes defended the inerrancy of Scripture, some did not. Scottish theologian James Orr, for example, was committed to the inspiration of Scripture but argued that inerrancy is "a most suicidal position" as it destroys the "whole edifice of belief in revealed religion."[184]

In the midst of these divisive and tumultuous times in the church, two varieties of fundamentalism eventually evolved: *intellectual* fundamentalism and *populist* fundamentalism. Populist fundamentalism boasted figureheads like C. I. Scofield, the dispensationalist who is best known for his Scofield Reference Bible (1909), as well as revivalist preachers like Billy Sunday.[185] Intellectual fundamentalists included men like J. Gresham Machen (1881–1937), who represented Calvinist doctrine at Princeton Seminary.

---

180. Quotations are from ibid., 25–26.
181. Ibid.
182. Woodbridge and James, *Church History*, 796.
183. Nichols and Brandt, *Ancient Word, Changing Worlds*, 26.
184. Quotation is from Woodbridge and James, *Church History*, 797.
185. Also consider D. L. Moody, whom we might call a *forerunner* to fundamentalism.

Liberalism's Reformed Nemesis: J. Gresham Machen

Liberalism was no longer limited to the classroom. It had successfully made its way into the pulpit. In 1910 the General Assembly of the Presbyterian Church USA required an affirmation of the Five Point Deliverance in order to be ordained.[186] Previously, candidates would say they agreed to the Westminster Standards only to then turn around once they obtained a pulpit and teach against the very doctrines taught therein. The Five Point Declaration, however, sought to remedy this problem by insisting that candidates adhere to specific doctrines prior to being ordained, doctrines the conservatives knew liberal candidates would deny. The five points were:

1. The inspiration and inerrancy of Scripture
2. The virgin birth of Christ
3. The substitutionary atonement of Christ
4. The bodily (historical) resurrection of Christ
5. The miracles of Christ[187]

In 1922 Harry Emerson Fosdick delivered his famous sermon, "Shall the Fundamentalists Win?"[188] The sermon erupted like a volcano in the Presbyterian Church, igniting a series of controversies for years to come.[189] Fosdick's sermon not only advocated tolerance of Liberalism but also demonstrated his sympathies with Liberalism as opposed to doctrines like those in the Five Point Deliverance. Possessing tremendous rhetorical abilities, Fosdick sought to persuade the masses throughout his preaching career that no longer could we be slaves to an old literalism.[190] Thanks to the methods of Liberalism, he said, the gospel could be liberated from its entanglements, and one of those entanglements is the Bible itself! Fosdick said we must dig through the Bible, pushing parts of it aside in order to excavate the truth that has been muddied.[191]

---

186. Bradley J. Longfield, *The Presbyterian Controversy: Fundamentalists, Modernists, and Moderates* (New York and Oxford: Oxford University Press, 1991), 25.

187. One should note that these points would later be opposed by many Presbyterians who stood behind the *Auburn Affirmation* in 1924.

188. Harry Emerson Fosdick, "Shall the Fundamentalists Win?," in *American Sermons: The Pilgrims to Martin Luther King Jr.* (New York: Library of America, 1999), 775–86.

189. Longfield, *Presbyterian Controversy*, 9. See also George Marsden, *Fundamentalism and American Culture*, 2nd ed. (New York: Oxford University Press, 2006), 117, 171; Robert M. Miller, *Harry Emerson Fosdick: Preacher, Pastor, Prophet* (New York: Oxford University Press, 1985), 112–17.

190. Nichols and Brandt, *Ancient Word, Changing Worlds*, 35.

191. Harry Emerson Fosdick, *The Modern Use of the Bible* (New York: Macmillan, 1924).

With the liberal worldview pressing in, J. Gresham Machen, firmly planted in the Princetonian heritage of Alexander, Hodge, and Warfield, would take center stage as one of the chief opponents of Liberalism. Machen, who himself had studied under liberals like Wilhelm Herrmann, published *Christianity and Liberalism* in 1923, and it has become the classic response to Liberalism to this day.[192] Machen's argument against Liberalism was quite simple: Protestant Liberalism, he argued, is not a different type of Christianity, but another religion altogether. Machen showed that Liberalism was in no way neutral but was driven by naturalistic presuppositions that greatly altered how one viewed the biblical text as well as the person and work of Christ. In consequence, Liberalism had created not only another Jesus, but another Bible.

Machen's defense of the Bible was multifaceted. First of all, he acknowledged that "Christian experience" is "useful as confirming the gospel message," but said Liberalism had gone wrong in saying that it did not matter whether the biblical accounts were historical (e.g., the resurrection of Christ), as if all that mattered was whether they fostered a positive and productive experience within the believer. In this liberal view, the findings of "biblical criticism" could be separated from one's existential encounter with the divine. And if that were the case, then it would matter little who the Jesus of history was. Our experience of his presence in our souls would be unaffected. Machen responded that this Liberalism may be "religious experience," but it surely is not "Christian experience." Christian experience, he insisted, "depends absolutely upon an event."[193] Machen echoes Paul's argument in 1 Corinthians 15 when he says that if the resurrection of Christ was not a historical event, then "I am of all men most miserable, for I am still in my sins." Machen concludes, "My Christian life, then, depends altogether upon the truth of the New Testament record."[194]

Moreover, Machen's defense of Scripture holds plenary inspiration and inerrancy hand in hand. Indeed, they are two sides of the same

---

In response, see "Review of Fosdick's *Modern Use of the Bible*," in *J. Gresham Machen: Selected Shorter Writings*, ed. D. G. Hart (Phillipsburg, NJ: P&R, 2004), 455–68.

192. To see how Machen was at first influenced by liberals like Herrmann, see Machen's own testimony in Ned Bernard Stonehouse, *J. Gresham Machen: A Biographical Memoir* (Edinburgh: Banner of Truth, 1987), 106–7.

193. J. Gresham Machen, *Christianity and Liberalism* (Grand Rapids: Eerdmans, 1923), 71.
194. Ibid., 73.

coin. The one flows out of the other. The "Bible not only is an account of important things," says Machen, "but that account itself is true, the writers having been so preserved from error, despite a full maintenance of their habits of thought and expression, that the resulting Book is the 'infallible rule of faith and practice.'"[195] Machen is careful to reject a mechanical dictation theory of inspiration, and instead argues that "plenary inspiration does not deny the individuality of the Biblical writers." Nor does it "ignore their use of ordinary means for acquiring information." It does not "involve any lack of interest in the historical situations which gave rise to Biblical books." However, it does deny "the presence of error in the Bible." Machen explains, "It supposes that the Holy Spirit so informed the minds of the Biblical writers that they were kept from falling into the errors that mar all other books."[196] Machen connects inspiration and inerrancy to *sola Scriptura*. Since the Bible is God-breathed and its account is a "true account," the Bible is the "infallible rule of faith and practice."[197] Contrary to Liberalism's belief, the Bible cannot be a book just like any other book.

Machen reminds us that the reliability of God's Word is based upon the trustworthiness of God himself. The "God whom the Christian worships is a God of truth." For that reason, his Word is a Word of truth.[198] If we are Christians in the true sense of the term, then we cannot ignore Christ's own view of the Scriptures. Machen observed that the "Lord Himself seems to have held the high view of the Bible."[199] Ultimately, Machen placed the burden of proof back onto Liberalism. Liberalism viewed the confessional affirmation of the Bible as the Word of God as a weak and pathetic "dependence upon a book" that "is a dead" and "artificial thing." In one of his most memorable statements, Machen counters with an appeal to the Reformers:

> The Reformation of the sixteenth century was founded upon the authority of the Bible, yet it set the world aflame. Dependence upon a word of man would be slavish, but dependence upon God's word is life. Dark and gloomy would be the world, if we were left to our own devices, and had no blessed Word of God. The Bible, to

---

195. Ibid.
196. Ibid., 74.
197. Ibid.
198. Ibid., 75.
199. Ibid.

the Christian is not a burdensome law, but the very Magna Charta of Christian liberty.[200]

Machen forcefully concludes, "It is no wonder, then, that Liberalism is totally different from Christianity, for the foundation is different. Christianity is founded upon the Bible. It bases upon the Bible both its thinking and its life. Liberalism on the other hand is founded upon the shifting emotions of sinful men."[201]

Conclusion

Evangelicals in the twentieth century would owe an enormous debt to Machen. As we will see in the next chapter, the changing attitudes toward the Bible and its authority and trustworthiness would lead evangelicals to return to the old paths of Hodge, Warfield, and Machen to combat challenges not only from without but from within.

---

200. Ibid., 78–79.
201. Ibid., 79.

CHAPTER 3

Today's Crisis over Biblical Authority: Evangelicalism's Apologetic and the Postmodern Turn

> Here then is the difference. They place the authority
> of the Church without [outside] the word of God; we
> annex it to the word, and allow it not to be separated
> from it.
>
> —*John Calvin*

> No fact of contemporary Western life is more
> evident than its growing distrust of final truth and its
> implacable questioning of any sure word.
>
> —*Carl F. H. Henry*

> Recognition of the total truth and trustworthiness of
> Holy Scripture is essential to a full grasp and adequate
> confession of its authority.
>
> —*Chicago Statement on Biblical Inerrancy*

There is a very good chance that you, as a reader of this book, attend an "evangelical" church. Perhaps you have wondered why the word *evangelical* is attached as a label to your particular church body or theological perspective. The term *evangelical* finds its heritage in the Protestant Reformation, where it was used interchangeably at times with the word *Protestant*. The word *evangelical* conveyed that the Reformers, in contrast to Rome, were defending and recovering the *euangelium* ("gospel").[1] Today, after two Great Awakenings,

---

1. John D. Woodbridge and Frank A. James III, *Church History*, vol. 2, *From*

the term has become far more complicated in its use and definition. Nevertheless, historian David Bebbington has tried to give the label precision by identifying four key components of evangelicalism. Evangelicals are those who affirm biblicism, cruci-centricism, conversionism, and activism.[2] Woodbridge and James have argued that out of these four, biblicism (an affirmation of the authority and sufficiency of Scripture) "is the first principle that provides the foundation for all the others."[3] And yet, in the twentieth century it is biblicism that has been under austere debate. For many evangelicals in America, biblicism is inseparable from the doctrine of inerrancy, though the same can be said of many British evangelicals as demonstrated by J. I. Packer's landmark book, *"Fundamentalism" and the Word of God*.[4] Evangelicals of the past saw themselves as heirs of the Reformation and naturally trumpeted *sola Scriptura* as one of their distinguishing doctrines, setting themselves apart from Roman Catholics. Today, this defining doctrine has come under fire and with it the Bible's truthfulness.

Fundamentalism and Neo-Evangelicalism

In order to understand evangelicalism today, we must return to the first half of the twentieth century, specifically fundamentalism's clash with modernist approaches to the Bible. George Marsden observes that between the 1890s and 1930s "many leaders of major Protestant denominations attempted to tone down the offenses to modern sensibilities of a Bible filled with miracles and a gospel that proclaimed human salvation from eternal damnation only through Christ's atoning work on the cross." Battle lines were drawn. "Fundamentalism was the response of traditionalist evangelicals who declared war on these modernizing trends," Marsden explains. While the war that ensued was fought over a variety of fronts, its struggle over the Bible was chief among them. "Modernists, influenced by higher criticism, emphasized

---

Pre-Reformation to the Present Day (Grand Rapids: Zondervan, 2013), 789.

2.   David W. Bebbington, *Evangelicalism in Modern Britain: A History from the 1730s to the 1980s* (London: Unwin Hymnal, 1989), 3.

3.   Woodbridge and James, *Church History*, 792.

4.   In 1957 Gabriel Hebert published *Fundamentalism and the Church of God* (London: SCM, 1957), where he attacked British evangelicals for affirming inerrancy. In response, J. I. Packer wrote one of the most famous books defending biblical authority and inerrancy: *"Fundamentalism" and the Word of God* (Leicester: Inter-Varsity Press, 1958). Packer provided a basis for British evangelicalism's belief in the Bible's inerrancy.

the Bible's human origins; fundamentalists countered by affirming its inerrancy in history and science as well as in faith and doctrine."[5]

By the 1920s fundamentalists began to realize they were losing the battle in their denominations and schools. Reform from within seemed hopeless. Many separated, choosing not to cooperate with those they believed had compromised theologically. But what distinguished some fundamentalists was not merely their separation—this had been done before—but that they made separation an article of faith. Others, Marsden notes, "did not insist on total ecclesiastical separation from modernism as a test of purity."[6] The seeds for conflict within fundamentalism had been planted.

Those fundamentalists who saw separating as absolutely essential, a mark of orthodoxy, became characterized by their disengagement with the culture.[7] Others grew dissatisfied with this approach. These individuals became known as Neo-Evangelicals, or New Evangelicals, at first seeking to reform fundamentalism from within but eventually making a permanent break with their fundamentalist brethren.[8] While they shared a common commitment to inerrancy, what set them apart was a proactive choice to be culturally engaged. Men like Harold John Ockenga (1905–85) and Carl F. H. Henry (1913–2003) sat in the driver's seat of this Neo-Evangelical locomotive, though others had a formative role as well.[9] They would not settle for the anti-intellectualism that had characterized some of the fundamentalists who came before them, but were resolved to be socially minded. And yet they were determined not to compromise theologically but to stand firm in defense of biblical authority and doctrinal orthodoxy.[10]

Fuller Seminary and Inerrancy

Harold Ockenga is particularly important not only because of his role in the National Association of Evangelicals but because he became

---

5. George Marsden, *Reforming Fundamentalism: Fuller Seminary and the New Evangelicalism* (Grand Rapids: Eerdmans, 1987), 4.

6. Ibid., 7.

7. Ibid., 76.

8. On the complex history of how these labels, which were not so clear-cut early on, evolved, see ibid., 3, 10, 146–47; George Marsden, *Fundamentalism and American Culture*, 2nd ed. (New York: Oxford University Press, 2006), 233–36.

9. For a recent study, see Owen Strachan, *Awakening the Evangelical Mind: An Intellectual History of the Neo-Evangelical Movement* (Grand Rapids: Zondervan, 2015).

10. Marsden, *Reforming Fundamentalism*, 167–70, 172.

the first president of Fuller Theological Seminary (1947), a pioneering institution at the start of the Neo-Evangelical movement. At the seminary's start, many were optimistic that the school would pave a middle way between modernists on the left and separatist fundamentalists on the right.[11] Ockenga recruited standout professors: Carl F. H. Henry, Everett Harrison, Wilbur Smith, and Harold Lindsell made up the first faculty and drew in students. Fuller Seminary stood out for many reasons, but at the core was its commitment to biblical inerrancy and confessional evangelical doctrine, coupled with its energetic engagement with the most pressing issues in Western culture.[12] Yet soon new winds would blow into Fuller, moving the school away from its original belief in an inerrant Bible.

Fuller's founding statement on Scripture read: "The books which form the canon of the Old and New Testaments as originally given are plenarily inspired and free from all error in the whole and in the part. These books constitute the written Word of God, the only infallible rule of faith and practice."[13] Here we read a very strong affirmation of *sola Scriptura* and inerrancy. The phrase "in whole and in part" rules out any view that would argue that inerrancy applies only to the salvific message and not to the historical and scientific details of the text. Moreover, for Ockenga infallibility and total inerrancy were not opposed to each other in any way, but similar and complementary concepts, both of which were to be embraced.[14]

But a change in attitude toward the Bible would develop at Fuller in the 1960s, eventually resulting in the seminary rejecting "inerrancy," viewing it as an "inadequate expression of biblical inspiration while still holding to the authority of the Bible."[15] The seminary's search for a new president revealed that two opposing camps had evolved: conservative Neo-Evangelicals and progressive Neo-Evangelicals. On what has become known as "Black Saturday" (1962), the progressives argued that the seminary needed a new statement of faith. When Ockenga asked why, Daniel P. Fuller, professor of hermeneutics and son of Fuller Seminary cofounder and evangelist Charles Fuller, responded that the statement on inerrancy needed to be changed. "Dr. Ockenga, there

---

11. Ibid., 67–68.
12. Ibid., 61–63, 72–82.
13. Ibid., 113.
14. Ibid.
15. Woodbridge and James, *Church History*, 809.

are errors which cannot be explained by the original autographs. It is simply not historically feasible to say that these errors would disappear if we had the autographs."[16] Fuller argued that inerrancy can only refer to the salvific message of the Bible. When it came to cosmology or history, God had accommodated himself to the incorrect, mistaken assumptions of the ancient time period and its people. Fuller held that these errors do not hurt the message of the Bible. Fuller believed he was simply applying the historical method, basing his examination of Scripture upon empirical evidence, and this had led him to the conclusion that there were indeed errors in the text, though they occurred in non-revelational portions.[17]

Edward J. Carnell and Wilbur Smith answered back. Carnell believed that a strictly inductive approach to the Bible was philosophically harmful and dangerous. But what was the alternative? One "should come to the Bible with the hypothesis that it was indeed the word of God. Only then do we frankly admit that we have some unsolved problems."[18] Carnell finally said to Fuller, "My list of discrepancies is longer than yours, Dan Fuller. But that did not matter, because if we come to the Bible as the verbally inspired word of God we find that we have fewer major problems with our system than with any competing systems."[19] In his analysis, Marsden brilliantly pinpoints exactly why the conservatives could not agree with the progressives on this matter:

> In their view, inerrancy was the logical implication of the statement in 2 Timothy that "all Scripture is inspired by God" (3:16). God would not inspire an error, small or large. Furthermore, Jesus's use of the Old Testament implied that he regarded it as historically accurate in detail. In the end, if one said that parts of the Bible were inerrant and other parts had error, who was to decide which was which? What standard higher than the Bible itself was to be used? Christians would be left in a morass of subjectivism and fallible human opinion.[20]

---

16. Marsden, *Reforming Fundamentalism*, 211.
17. At the same time, Fuller was persistent that his view should not be equated with Barth's neo-orthodoxy.
18. Marsden, *Reforming Fundamentalism*, 212.
19. Ibid.
20. Ibid., 213–14.

Marsden's description is telling. For the conservatives, inerrancy and *sola Scriptura* were inseparable. To reject inerrancy meant one was now looking to a standard higher than the Bible itself. While for Catholics this standard is Tradition, for the progressives, argued the conservatives, this standard became their own human reason and methods of historical criticism. Conservative Neo-Evangelicals believed history was on their side, as it had repeatedly demonstrated the dangers of rejecting inerrancy. Countless schools, like Harvard and Princeton, began in the conservative camp only to transition out, some adopting Liberalism, others going so far as Unitarianism. As a result, a "vast empire lay in ruins." Rejecting inerrancy, it was argued, would lead down this slippery slope with no return.[21]

The events that followed "Black Saturday" were critical for the progressives. Daniel Fuller became dean and David Hubbard, president. Resignations followed. Wilbur Smith joined Kenneth Kantzer at Trinity Evangelical Divinity School, as did Gleason Archer, who was known for his defense of an Old Princeton view of inerrancy, a view no longer welcome at Fuller.[22] Harold Lindsell left and went to *Christianity Today*. Lindsell did not hide his reason for leaving. It was due to the seminary's "failure to maintain Article II of the Statement of Faith either in letter or in spirit."[23]

With inerrantists transitioning out, Fuller removed from its 1964–65 catalog the sentence stating that faculty had to sign the statement of faith "without mental reservation, and any member who cannot assent agrees to withdraw from the institution."[24] This meant that while in the 1950s the majority of graduates at Fuller affirmed inerrancy, by the 1960s the majority of students now held a limited inerrancy position. Hubbard was moving the faculty and institution in a different direction. No longer did the public see Fuller Seminary as carrying on the legacy of Old Princeton for the twentieth century.[25]

In 1972 Fuller changed its confessional statement (and stance) on Scripture. The new statement read:

> Scripture is an essential part and trustworthy record of this divine self-disclosure. All the books of the Old and New Testaments, given

---

21. Ibid., 214.
22. Ibid., 224.
23. Quoted in ibid., 223.
24. Quoted in ibid., 224.
25. Ibid., 245.

by divine inspiration, are the written word of God, the only infallible rule of faith and practice. They are to be interpreted according to their context and purpose and in reverent obedience to the Lord who speaks through them in living power.[26]

Notice that while the statement refers to the written word of God as the "only infallible rule of faith and practice," it makes no mention of inerrancy. No longer was an affirmation of inerrancy required to teach at Fuller.

The tug-of-war between inerrantists and limited inerrantists did not end there. In 1976, Harold Lindsell published *The Battle for the Bible*, including a chapter called "The Strange Case of Fuller Theological Seminary." The book was dedicated to Archer, Carnell, Henry, and Smith. Harold Ockenga, then president of Gordon-Conwell Divinity School, wrote the foreword, and Billy Graham wrote a commendation. Lindsell stressed that belief in inerrancy was fundamental to being an evangelical. And he did not hold back in calling to account Daniel Fuller, Paul Jewett, and George Ladd. Lindsell put the spotlight on Daniel Fuller in particular because he believed Fuller and others had been dishonest in signing a creed they did not believe in, eventually rejecting it publicly.[27]

Hubbard and company "deplored Lindsell's 'unbiblical view of Scripture'" and "defended the seminary's right to be called 'evangelical.'"[28] Others also prepared responses. Jack Rogers, a Fuller professor, edited *Biblical Authority* (1977) and later wrote *The Authority and Interpretation of the Bible: A Historical Approach* (1979) with Donald K. McKim.[29] Rogers and McKim argued that inerrancy was the invention of rationalistic Protestant scholasticism in the seventeenth century (e.g., Francis Turretin), and in the nineteenth century Old Princeton mistakenly equated inerrancy with orthodoxy.[30] In their view, inerrancy

---

26. Fuller Theological Seminary, "Statement of Faith" (www.fuller.edu/about/mission-and-values/statement-of-faith/).

27. Not all inerrantists agreed with Lindsell's approach. For example, see Carl Henry's opinion of Lindsell's work in Marsden, *Reforming Fundamentalism*, 288; Gregory Alan Thornbury, *Recovering Classic Evangelicalism: Applying the Wisdom and Vision of Carl F. H. Henry* (Wheaton, IL: Crossway, 2014), 117.

28. Marsden, *Reforming Fundamentalism*, 282–83.

29. Jack B. Rogers, ed., *Biblical Authority* (Waco, TX: Word, 1977); Jack B. Rogers and Donald K. McKim, *The Authority and Interpretation of the Bible: An Historical Approach* (San Francisco: Harper & Row, 1979).

30. Rogers and McKim were dependent on the work of Ernest Sandeen, *The Origins of*

is a doctrine that is absent from the time of Augustine to Calvin. According to Rogers and McKim, the church during this time believed that the Bible is authoritative in spiritual matters (i.e., infallible in faith and practice), but the notion of inerrancy in *all* that Scripture addresses is a foreign idea, a late invention.

John Woodbridge responded by publishing *Biblical Authority: A Critique of the Rogers/McKim Proposal* (1982).[31] Woodbridge, the historian from Trinity Evangelical Divinity School, argued that Rogers and McKim had seriously misread and misinterpreted not only the Protestant Scholastics and Old Princeton but the entire history of the church. The *concept* of inerrancy has a long and enduring pedigree that goes all the way back to the patristic period. Woodbridge argued that it was not the conservatives who had read Warfield back into the fathers and Reformers, but Rogers and McKim who had read Karl Barth back into the fathers and the Reformers![32]

Ever since this debate, conservative evangelicals have argued that one cannot make a historical case that the phrase "faith and practice" should limit what we understand by *sola Scriptura*. To say that the Bible is our final and infallible authority in faith and practice has been used by some to say that biblical authority and inerrancy do not apply to matters in Scripture such as history and science.[33] The opposing argument goes something like this: The Bible is authoritative and true *only* when it is talking about faith and practice (i.e., spiritual matters), and this is what the church has always meant by *sola Scriptura* and infallibility.[34] But such a move misrepresents *sola Scriptura* and the history of the Reformation. The phrase "faith and practice" was never

---

Fundamentalism: Toward a Historical Interpretation (Philadelphia: Fortress, 1968); Ernest Sandeen, *The Roots of Fundamentalism: British and American Millenarianism 1800–1930* (Chicago: University of Chicago Press, 1970). See also Stephen T. Davis, *The Debate about the Bible: Inerrancy versus Infallibility* (Philadelphia: Westminster, 1977).

31. John D. Woodbridge, *Biblical Authority: A Critique of the Rogers/McKim Proposal* (Grand Rapids: Zondervan, 1982).

32. On this point, besides Woodbridge, see also Richard A. Muller, *PRRD*, 2:155; D. A. Carson, "Recent Developments in the Doctrine of Scripture," in *Hermeneutics, Authority, and Canon*, ed. D. A. Carson and John D. Woodbridge (Eugene, OR: Wipf & Stock, 2005), 10–14.

33. This is a faulty assumption. It assumes that if we say the Bible is infallible in its main message, we are simultaneously precluding its infallibility in other areas. Again, this is an illegitimate jump in logic. There is no reason why the Bible cannot be both infallible in its main message and in other details as well. For a refutation of this type of logic in Rogers/McKim, see Woodbridge, *Biblical Authority*. We will explore this issue in depth in chapter 8.

34. Besides Rogers and McKim, for an example of this type of argument, see Bruce Vawter, *Biblical Inspiration* (Philadelphia: Westminster, 1972).

used in a limiting way by the Reformers, but was designed to be an "all-embracing rubric."[35] The polemic the Reformers wielded was meant to dismantle Rome's elevation of tradition and papal authority. It was not meant to limit, restrict, or shrink the scope of biblical authority in the spheres of religion, history, and nature. As Woodbridge has demonstrated so thoroughly, it never would have crossed the mind of Protestants to "use this expression as a phrase circumscribing the extent of biblical infallibility."[36] No, such a "modern disjunction" would have been alien to them.[37]

Setting the Record Straight: Faith and Science

Woodbridge's point becomes all the more apparent when we consider the infamous controversy over science in the sixteenth and seventeenth centuries, a controversy Woodbridge himself interacts with in his debate with Rogers and McKim. Too often Christians today buy into the "conflict myth," the popular belief that Christianity and science are inherently antithetical to one another.[38] They also buy into what I would call the "faith and practice myth." According to this myth, the church has always believed that the Bible's authority and its inerrancy extend only to spiritual matters, not to matters of history and science.

No story has been so appealed to in order to sustain these myths than that of Galileo. In 1616 the Roman Catholic Church officially rejected the Copernican theory, a new and novel theory advocating heliocentrism.[39] Then, in 1633 Galileo was put on trial by the Inquisition for heresy since he advocated this theory, which resulted in time in prison.

On the surface, this appears to be a conflict between faith and science. Though that may be a popular interpretation, it is a mistaken one.

---

35. Carson, "Recent Developments in the Doctrine of Scripture," 5.

36. Woodbridge, *Biblical Authority*, 73 (see especially 72–80).

37. Carson, "Recent Developments in the Doctrine of Scripture," 5.

38. This phrase is used by Ard Louis, professor of theoretical physics at Oxford University, in an interview conducted by Eric Metaxas for Socrates in the City. See http://www.socratesinthecity.com/video/ard-louis-science-and-faith.

39. For a retelling of the story in fuller detail, see Alister E. McGrath, *Science and Religion: An Introduction* (Oxford: Blackwell, 1999), 12–13; Kirsten Birkett, "Science and Scripture," in *The Enduring Authority of the Christian Scriptures*, ed. D. A. Carson (Grand Rapids: Eerdmans, 2016), 949–56; William R. Shea, *Galileo's Intellectual Revolution* (London and Basingstoke: Macmillan, 1972); Giorgio de Santillana, *The Crime of Galileo* (Melbourne: Heinemann, 1958).

If we dig deeper, we discover that this is actually a conflict between old science and new science. In fact, some have gone so far as to call the church "pro-science." Kirsten Birkett writes, "This was not a battle between an anti-science church and a pro-science individual. On the contrary, it could be better characterized as a pro-science church, led by the academy that taught and embraced that science, against an eccentric maverick."[40] That Galileo's theory proved right in the end does not "change the true story: this is a case study in what happens when old science is threatened by new data, and the institutions that have endorsed that science are too slow to change."[41]

What we are calling "old science" is geocentrism, the belief that the Earth is at the center of the universe and the sun and planets revolve around the Earth. The "new science" is heliocentrism, the belief that the sun is at the center and the Earth revolves around the sun. This new science can be traced back to the year 1543 when Polish astronomer Nicholas Copernicus argued that the sun, not the Earth, was at the center.[42] Since the theory had very little scientific proof, it proved to be a minority view, as many other astronomers remained unpersuaded.[43] We must recognize that the received view was well established, relying upon Aristotle's impressive explanation of the laws of the universe. So the conflict that developed proved to be one between the long-held position of Aristotelian physics (i.e., the old science) and an entirely new system that lacked proper support thus far from the realm of physics.[44] With that in mind, the church's decision in regard to Galileo seemed the responsible one, especially given her loyalty to Thomas Aquinas who was very much reliant upon Aristotelian philosophy for his theology.[45] In the end, the conflict was

40. Birkett, "Science and Scripture," 950.

41. Ibid.

42. He made this argument in his work *De revolutionibus orbium coelestium* ("The revolution of the heavenly spheres"). His theory still suffered some inaccuracy, for he thought that the planets moved in a *circle* around the center.

43. Lacking later knowledge concerning the laws of motion and the theory of gravity, Copernicus could not explain how or why the Earth moved. See Birkett, "Science and Scripture," 951.

44. On Aristotelian physics, see Stephen Toulmin and June Goodfield, *The Fabric of the Heavens* (Harmondsworth, UK: Penguin, 1961); Thomas S. Kuhn, *The Copernican Revolution: Planetary Astronomy in the Development of Western Thought* (Cambridge: Harvard University Press, 1957).

45. See Birkett, "Science and Scripture," 951–52; Jerzy Dobrzycki, ed., *The Reception of Copernicus' Heliocentric Theory* (Dordrecht: D. Reidel, 1972).

not about the church opposing science, but about the church defending Aristotelian science.[46]

Now, what does all this have to do with the extent of biblical infallibility? Long story short, in a tragic yet complicated scheme to alarm the ecclesiastical authorities, Galileo's enemies accused him of contradicting the Bible, which they assumed supported Aristotelian science in its descriptions of the universe. In 1613 and 1615 Galileo wrote two letters, a *Letter to Castelli* and then a *Letter to the Grand Duchess Christina*, explaining how the Bible should be properly interpreted. In his *Letter to Castelli* Galileo addresses the issue of biblical infallibility. He writes, "[It was properly propounded to you by Madam Christina] and conceded and established by you, that Holy Scripture could never lie or err, but that its decrees are of absolute and inviolable truth." Galileo then adds, "I should only have added that although Scripture can indeed not err, nevertheless some of its interpreters and expositors may sometimes err in various ways, one of which may be very serious and quite frequent [that is] when they would base themselves always on the literal meanings of the words."[47] Notice, Galileo affirmed the *total* inerrancy of Scripture, even in regard to how the Bible spoke about the universe. The issue, for Galileo, was not inerrancy but biblical interpretation. The real question was how the Bible's genres were to be read, not whether the Bible's authority extended to its description of the universe.[48]

This becomes all the more apparent when we consider Galileo's contemporary, Johannes Kepler (1571–1630). Kepler argued for divine

46. Birkett, "Science and Scripture," 954.

47. Cited in Stillman Drake, *Galileo at Work* (Chicago: University of Chicago Press, 1978), 224. There is debate as to whether Galileo really believed Scripture's voice should extend beyond spiritual matters. At first, in his *Letter to Castelli*, he seems to answer in the negative. However, later on in 1615 he actually answers in the affirmative, saying, "Yet even in those propositions which are not matters of faith, this authority [of the Bible] ought to be preferred over that of all human writings which are supported only by bare assertions or probable arguments, and not set forth in a demonstrative way." He goes on to argue that "in the books of the sages of this world there are contained some physical truths which are soundly demonstrated, and others that are merely stated; as to the former, it is the office of wise divines to show that they do not contradict the Holy Scriptures. And as to the propositions which are stated but not rigorously demonstrated, anything contrary to the Bible involved by them must be held undoubtably false and should be proved so by every possible means" (Stillman Drake, ed., *Discoveries and Opinions of Galileo* [New York: Doubleday, 1957], 183, 194). Some have argued that Galileo only changed his view due to pressure from the authorities. Others disagree. On this debate, see Woodbridge, *Biblical Authority*, 91.

48. Alister E. McGrath, *Science and Religion: An Introduction* (Oxford: Blackwell, 1999), 12–13; Woodbridge, *Biblical Authority*, 90–99.

accommodation, asserting that the Bible describes the world as it appears to us. The Bible should not be read like a scientific textbook. Yet its statements about the natural world truthfully depict the universe *as it appears*.[49] Kepler was not trying to disprove the Bible; on the contrary he sought to show that the theory of Copernicus was consistent with the Scriptures. Had it been proven that the theory contradicted the Bible, he gladly would have dispensed with the theory.[50]

It was not until later, in the seventeenth century, that the Bible was barred from speaking to matters of science. It is not accidental that those who advocated separation of the Bible and science were also those who rejected total infallibility, but we should not conclude that this was the historic approach. As Carson warns, "Those who now wish to affirm the Bible's infallibility in the spheres of 'faith and practice' but not in all areas on which it speaks are doubly removed from the mainstream of historical antecedents."[51] Contrary to Rogers and McKim, the science debates in the sixteenth and seventeenth centuries demonstrate that neither side believed Scripture was limited to merely spiritual matters. If it was assumed that the Bible did not address scientific issues, then the debate never would have ensued in the first place. So it is critical to explode the myth that one had to choose between a "completely infallible Bible" and a Bible "whose infallibility was limited to faith and practice."[52] The real issue, according to thinkers like Kepler and Galileo, was not whether the Bible was totally infallible, but how one should interpret this totally infallible Bible on such topics as the universe.

The Chicago Statement on Biblical Inerrancy

The debate over inerrancy did not end in the 1960s and 1970s. In 1978 a group of evangelicals came together to draft a statement defending the inerrancy of Scripture in light of the many challenges it was facing. The International Council on Biblical Inerrancy (ICBI) consisted of more than three hundred of some of the most notable representatives in evangelicalism. The executive council included individuals such as Gleason L. Archer, James M. Boice, Edmund P. Clowney, John H.

---

49. Woodbridge and James, *Church History*, 340. It is important to note, as Woodbridge and James do, that this appeal to divine accommodation is very similar to Augustine and Calvin.

50. John D. Woodbridge, "Does the Bible Teach 'Science'?," *BSac* 142 (1985): 199.

51. Carson, "Recent Developments in the Doctrine of Scripture," 15.

52. Woodbridge, "Does the Bible Teach 'Science'?," 202.

Gerstner, Kenneth S. Kantzer, James I. Packer, Francis A. Schaeffer, and R. C. Sproul. The advisory board brought together figureheads such as Greg L. Bahnsen, Henri A. G. Blocher, W. A. Criswell, Gordon R. Lewis, Harold Lindsell, John F. MacArthur, Roger R. Nicole, Harold J. Ockenga, and John F. Walvoord, among others.[53]

What is commendable is that the signatories of the Chicago Statement on Biblical Inerrancy (CSBI) came together across denominational lines.[54] The product was a bold statement affirming Scripture's truthfulness and reliability, one that still remains relevant today. Its effect was visibly seen as these men went back to their denominations (e.g., Southern Baptist Convention; Lutheran Church–Missouri Synod) to bring about reformation.[55]

The preamble of the CSBI reads: "Recognition of the total truth and trustworthiness of Holy Scripture is essential to a full grasp and adequate confession of its authority." *Sola Scriptura* and inerrancy go hand in hand. Very much in the vein of the Reformers, those who signed the statement prayed that it would be "used to the glory of our God toward a new reformation of the church in its faith, life and mission."[56]

So what does the statement say about inerrancy? The CSBI begins with a short statement that connects Scripture to the character of God: "God, who is Himself truth and speaks truth only, has inspired Holy Scripture in order thereby to reveal Himself to lost mankind through Jesus Christ as Creator and Lord, Redeemer and Judge. Holy Scripture is God's witness to Himself." Furthermore, those human authors who wrote Scripture were "prepared and superintended by His Spirit." Therefore, God's Word is "of infallible divine authority in all matters upon which it touches." Since it is "wholly and verbally God-given, Scripture is without error or fault in all its teaching, no less in what it states about God's acts in creation, about the events of world history, and about its own literary origins under God, than in its witness to God's saving grace in individual lives."[57] The point is clear: *all* of Scripture is God-breathed and inerrant.

---

53. James M. Boice, ed., *The Foundation of Biblical Authority* (Grand Rapids: Zondervan, 1978), 12.

54. Stephen J. Nichols and Eric T. Brandt, *Ancient Word, Changing Worlds: The Doctrine of Scripture in a Modern Age* (Wheaton, IL: Crossway, 2009), 71–72.

55. Note the host of publications that were birthed after ICBI met. See edited works in bibliography by Boice, Hannah, Lewis and Demarest, and Nicole and Michaels.

56. "The Chicago Statement on Biblical Inerrancy," in Geisler, *Inerrancy*, 493.

57. Ibid., 494.

The articles of the CSBI begin with *sola Scriptura*. Sounding much like the Protestant Reformers, it states that Scripture is the authoritative Word of God and it does not receive its authority from the church or from tradition. In contrast to Rome, the church is subordinate to Scripture, as are church creeds and councils.[58] The CSBI stands in contrast not only to Rome but to neo-orthodoxy as well. It states: "We affirm that the written Word in its entirety is revelation given by God. We deny that the Bible is merely a witness to revelation, or only becomes revelation in encounter, or depends on the responses of men for its validity."[59]

Additionally, the CSBI affirmed verbal, plenary inspiration: "The whole of Scripture and all its parts, down to the very words of the original, were given by divine inspiration." Much in contrast to, say, Fuller Seminary, it denied that "the inspiration of Scripture can rightly be affirmed of the whole without the parts, or of some parts but not of the whole."[60] And in Articles 11 and 12 the CSBI rejected the false dichotomy many have made between *infallibility* and *inerrancy*, whereby these two terms are set over against each other. While the two may be distinguished, they cannot be set in opposition, for both affirm Scripture's truthfulness and reliability in everything it addresses. Both attest to the fact that Scripture is free from any "falsehood, fraud, or deceit."[61] Article 12 states: "We deny that Biblical infallibility and inerrancy are limited to spiritual, religious, or redemptive themes, exclusive of assertions in the fields of history and science."[62] Therefore, it will not do to say that Scripture is infallible and inerrant in its spiritual message but not in its scientific and historical claims.[63]

The CSBI was also attuned to the objection that the human aspect of Scripture made inerrancy impossible. To the contrary, it states that God "utilized the distinctive personalities and literary styles of the writers" without overriding their personalities.[64] At the same time, the Spirit's superintendence of these human writers "guaranteed true and trustworthy utterance on all matters of which the Biblical authors were

---

58. Ibid., 494 (articles 1, 2).
59. Ibid., 494–95 (article 3).
60. Ibid., 496 (article 6).
61. Ibid., 496 (article 12).
62. Ibid., 496 (articles 11, 12).
63. Ibid., 496 (article 12): "We further deny that scientific hypotheses about earth history may properly be used to overturn the teaching of Scripture on creation and the flood."
64. Ibid., 495 (article 8).

moved to speak and write." By no means, therefore, did the "finitude or fallenness" of the biblical authors introduce "distortion or falsehood into God's Word."[65]

While the CSBI says far more, it is legitimate to say that its argument for inerrancy is not to be taken lightly. The authors believed that rejecting the doctrine would have serious consequences. Biblical authority, they wrote, is "inescapably impaired if this total divine inerrancy is in any way limited or disregarded, or made relative to a view of truth contrary to the Bible's own; and such lapses bring serious loss to both the individual and the Church."[66] CSBI, therefore, inseparably connects inerrancy to authority, so that to reject the former is to do much harm to the latter.

For evangelicals today, the CSBI is still taken with utmost seriousness, in some cases even serving as the focal point in evangelical debates.[67] While some argue that the CSBI should be rejected, other evangelicals and institutions today believe it is biblically rooted and doctrinally faithful in describing what Scripture says concerning itself. For these evangelicals, inerrancy is part of the very DNA of evangelicalism. Without it, evangelicalism is no longer evangelicalism. R. Albert Mohler's confession is refreshingly honest and on target: "I am quite certain that without inerrancy evangelicalism will cease to be evangelical in any real sense. For, at the end of the day, inerrancy is the single issue that truly distinguishes evangelicalism from liberal Protestantism."[68]

The Postmodern Turn: Dancing on the Tomb of God

What can we say about the present state of biblical authority? While several movements could be highlighted, the trend that has taken prominence over the past several decades has been postmodernism. Postmodernism exploded in influence at the end of the twentieth century, and while some argue that we are now a post-postmodern culture, that claim is contested. Still, as is typical, what takes off in the academy sometimes takes decades to catch on in the church. Many

---

65. Ibid., 495–96 (article 9).
66. See point 5 of "A Short Statement," in ibid., 494.
67. The CSBI is the document under debate in *Five Views on Biblical Inerrancy*, ed. J. Merrick and Stephen M. Garrett (Grand Rapids: Zondervan, 2013). Contributors include R. Albert Mohler Jr., Peter Enns, Michael F. Bird, Kevin J. Vanhoozer, and John R. Franke.
68. R. Albert Mohler Jr., "Response to Peter Enns," in Merrick and Garrett, *Five Views*, 120.

churches today are now suffering the collateral damage of the post-modern bombs that were dropped on the Bible in the late twentieth century.[69]

To understand postmodernism, we must return to the Age of Reason. Some have argued that the Enlightenment's elevation of the individual (and reason) can be traced back to René Descartes (1596–1650), who doubted everything until he came to the one thing he could not doubt, the thinking self. Hence his famous dictum: *Cogito ergo sum*—I think, therefore I am.[70] In his search for methodological certainty, Descartes "cut the cord of reason from faith and revelation."[71] Descartes, whether he meant to or not, turned the human person into an autonomous rational subject.[72] Consequently, the Enlightenment project that followed assumed man could obtain cognitive certainty due to the objective nature of knowledge itself. All reality was subordinated to the test of reason. The world, it was thought, could be observed and analyzed from a standpoint of total neutrality. Accompanied by the methods of science, nothing stood in the way of the autonomous rational thinker.[73] This Enlightenment method demonstrates how highly reason was elevated and how much confidence man placed in his rational abilities.[74]

Many of those captivated by modernity assumed a *realist* or *objectivist* concept of knowledge, truth, and the world. Such a view continues today, for most people believe that the world in front of them is objectively real.[75] In other words, the world, by nature, possesses structure and order, apart from mankind's involvement. When it comes

---

69. To illustrate my point, my first teaching post was at a liberal arts university, and many times I encountered postmodernism in the college classroom from lay-level students who were usually no older than forty years old. Some of these individuals planned to lead churches. Even if they didn't know all the labels, postmodern presuppositions were ingrained in their thinking and were brought to the biblical text. I am convinced we will feel postmodernism's effects for years to come, even after the philosophy of postmodernism is out of vogue.

70. René Descartes, *Discourse on the Method*, part 4, trans. Laurence J. Lafleur (Indianapolis: Bobbs-Merrill, 1960), 24.

71. Mark S. Gignilliat, *Old Testament Criticism: From Benedict Spinoza to Brevard Childs* (Grand Rapids: Zondervan, 2012), 22.

72. Stanley J. Grenz, *A Primer on Postmodernism* (Grand Rapids: Eerdmans, 1996), 3; Colin Brown, *Christianity and Western Thought*, vol. 1, *From the Ancient World to the Age of Enlightenment* (Downers Grove, IL: InterVarsity Press, 1990), 184.

73. Grenz, *Postmodernism*, 4.

74. Ibid.

75. Ibid., 40–41.

to man, his intellect can precisely image reality around him, and his use of language can accurately describe reality as it is.[76] The realist-objectivist view is grounded upon the *correspondence theory of truth*, which believes that when someone makes an assertion, it must be true or false. Furthermore, we are able to decide whether such an assertion is true or false simply by comparing and contrasting the assertion with the world around us.[77] Enlightenment thinkers believed that with such an understanding of knowledge and truth, man can acquire objective, certain, and reliable knowledge of the world.

Where many Enlightenment thinkers departed from Christianity was in thinking that this quest for objective, universal truth and knowledge of the world can be done, and should be done, apart from God's Word. They turned Augustine's and Anselm's motto upside down so that it read, "I understand in order to believe," rather than "I believe in order to understand."[78] As we have seen in the previous chapter, man's reason became autonomous; God's Word became unnecessary.

Postmodernism's Nucleus

Though modernity would come under severe criticism with the rise of postmodernism, it is important to recognize that these two movements still have much in common. Both affirmed the autonomy of human reason, albeit in distinct ways. Nevertheless, postmodernism significantly differentiated itself from modernity. For our purposes, we will limit ourselves to just two characteristics that summarize the postmodern turn.

First, postmodernism is characterized by *relativism*. For the postmodernist, there is no such thing as *objective* truth. No longer can one believe that there is truth that corresponds to reality. Richard Rorty says, "Truth is established neither by the correspondence of an assertion with objective reality nor by the internal coherence of the assertions themselves."[79] Stanley Grenz notes how Jacques Derrida, the father of "deconstruction," as well as Michel Foucault and Richard Rorty,

---

76. Ibid.

77. Ibid., 41.

78. Stephen J. Wellum, "Postconservatism, Biblical Authority, and Recent Proposals for Re-Doing Evangelical Theology: A Critical Analysis," in *Reclaiming the Center: Confronting Evangelical Accommodation in Postmodern Times*, ed. Millard J. Erickson, Paul Kjoss Helseth, and Justin Taylor (Wheaton, IL: Crossway, 2004), 162.

79. Grenz is describing Richard Rorty. Grenz, *Postmodernism*, 6.

rejected the Enlightenment project when they abandoned "the quest for a unified grasp of objective reality." Their view asserts that "the world has no center, only differing viewpoints and perspectives."[80] No one text (including the Bible) gives us *the* worldview that interprets reality. Instead, postmodernity offers only "dueling texts."[81] We are left, then, with a multitude of interpretations, each being equally valid. Truth is relative and subjective. Each person's "truth" is merely the product of the community he was birthed from.[82] To claim to know *the* truth, or to possess the *only* truth, is the deadliest, most arrogant sin in the postmodern universe. In regard to religion, such epistemological relativism leads to religious pluralism in which every religious text is equally as true as any other, regardless of how incompatible they may be with one another. Such pluralism lends itself to a relativistic pragmatism. As the popular expressions go, "What is right for us might not be right for you," and "What is wrong in our context might in your context be acceptable or even preferable."[83]

Second, postmodernism is characterized by *deconstructionism*. Structuralism is the belief that "language is a social construct and that people develop literary documents—texts—in an attempt to provide structures of meaning that will help them make sense out of the meaningless of their experience." Such a view assumes that a society has a "common, invariant structure."[84] However, for the *poststructuralist* or *deconstructionist*, meaning "is not inherent in a text itself," but "emerges only as the interpreter enters into dialogue with the text."[85] And "because the meaning of a text is dependent on the perspective of the one who enters into dialogue with it, it has as many meanings as it has readers (or readings)."[86] Poststructuralists like Derrida see structuralism as "just another attempt, like that of Descartes, to stave off

---

80. Ibid., 7.
81. Ibid.
82. Ibid., 8.
83. Ibid., 15.
84. Ibid., 5.
85. Ibid., 6.
86. Ibid. Vanhoozer defines deconstruction as a "painstaking taking-apart, a peeling away of the various layers—historical, rhetorical, ideological—of distinctions, concepts, texts, and whole philosophies, whose aim is to expose the arbitrary linguistic nature of their original construction. . . . Deconstruction is thus best understood as a kind of *undoing*" (Kevin J. Vanhoozer, *Is There a Meaning in This Text? The Bible, the Reader, and the Morality of Literary Knowledge* [Grand Rapids: Zondervan, 1998], 52).

the threat of relativism by finding some stable ground for meaning."[87] The poststructuralists respond with a startling news flash: There is *no* stable ground for meaning anymore!

What happens when deconstructionism is applied to one's view of the universe? Answer: there is "no one meaning of the world, no transcendent center to reality as a whole."[88] Most fundamentally, therefore, postmodernism is an *"incredulity toward metanarratives,"* as Jean-Francois Lyotard famously concluded.[89] Or as Terry Eagleton has put it, postmodernism "signals the death" of metanarratives.[90] No worldview can give us *the* objective interpretation of reality. There may be many interpretations of reality, but no one interpretation can claim to have the God's-eye point of view.

Language plays a key role in deconstructionism. For the Enlightenment man, truth corresponds to the objective reality that we perceive and analyze. For the postmodernist, we do not approach an objective reality, but construct a reality of our own making, and we do this through language. Grenz explains:

> The Enlightenment realist view also assumes that a simple, one-to-one relationship exists between the bits of language we use to describe the world and the bits of the world we seek to know. Twentieth-century linguists argue that this is a faulty assumption. We do not simply match bits of language to bits of the world, they say, nor does any given language provide an accurate "map" of the world. Languages are human social conventions that map the world in a variety of ways, depending on the context in which we are speaking.[91]

Ludwig Wittgenstein's "language games," says Grenz, have taught us that the way we use words determines how we conceive the world around us. Postmodernists, therefore, have adopted a *nonrealist, constructivist* understanding of knowledge and truth. Language, they argue, actually creates and constructs reality, and since society is

---

87. Vanhoozer, *Is There a Meaning*, 52.
88. Grenz, *Postmodernism*, 6.
89. Jean-Francois Lyotard, *The Postmodern Condition: A Report on Knowledge*, trans. Geoff Bennington and Brian Massumi (Minneapolis: University of Minnesota Press, 1984), iv.
90. Terry Eagleton, "Awakening from Modernity," *Times Literary Supplement* (February 20, 1987): 194.
91. Grenz, *Postmodernism*, 42.

always in flux, "meanings—and, as a consequence, the world as we see it through language—are constantly shifting as well."[92] In this light, two key presuppositions of postmodernism can be identified:

1. Postmoderns view all explanations of reality as constructions that are useful but not objectively true.
2. Postmoderns deny that we have the ability to step outside our constructions of reality.[93]

"Useful" is the key word. Since each one of us is trapped by our own constructions of reality, and since these constructions are not objectively true, their value is not in their veracity but in their pragmatic benefit. The question is not whether our construction is true, but whether it is useful. As Stanley Fish argues, there is no truth in the world just waiting to be discovered. Instead, truth is determined by the community, and the community decides what is true for them based on what seems good to them.[94] And when it comes to reading a text, meaning's origin is not to be found in the author of the text, but in the reader who invents the meaning.[95] Our mission, therefore, is to deconstruct meaning. "If language really does construct meaning (as opposed to revealing an objective meaning already present in the world), then the work of the scholar is to take apart ('deconstruct') this meaning-constructing process. By deconstructing influential concepts, perhaps we can break their control over our thoughts and actions."[96]

What happens when a nonrealist view is applied to a written text, like the Bible? We end up with *hermeneutical nonrealism*. As Kevin Vanhoozer explains, for the *hermeneutical realist* "there is something prior to interpretation, something 'there' in the text, which can be known and to which the interpreter is accountable."[97] Meaning, he adds, is "prior to and independent of the process of interpretation."[98]

---

92. Ibid.

93. Ibid., 43: "Because we cannot view the world apart from the structures we bring to it, the argument goes, we cannot measure our theories and propositions in comparison to an objective, external world. To the contrary, the theories we devise create the different worlds we inhabit."

94. Stanley Fish, *Is There a Text in This Class? The Authority of Interpretive Communities* (Cambridge: Harvard University Press, 1980), 13. Vanhoozer calls Fish (and Richard Rorty) "The Users" who hold to "Neo-pragmatism." Vanhoozer, *Is There a Meaning*, 55–56.

95. Vanhoozer, *Is There a Meaning*, 56.

96. Grenz, *Postmodernism*, 43.

97. Vanhoozer, *Is There a Meaning*, 26.

98. Ibid., 48.

Not so for hermeneutical nonrealists, such as Derrida or Fish. They deny "that meaning precedes interpretive activity; the truth of an interpretation depends on the response of the reader."[99] As a result, biblical authority is done away with. In fact, authority in any text is done away with. It has to be since it is not the text but the reader (or community) who now governs and creates meaning. "The text, again, becomes only a mirror or an echo chamber in which we see ourselves and hear our own voices."[100] Or as Nietzsche said, "There are no facts, only interpretations."[101] Some have concluded that postmoderns like Derrida celebrate "the arbitrariness of meaning and truth by dancing on the tomb of God."[102]

Finally, we see that hermeneutical nonrealism is *anti-authority*. To believe that meaning comes from the author of a text or from the text itself is to succumb to hermeneutical slavery. For postmodernists, the "age of the author" is "the age of oppression."[103] "The 'real'—the stable order of things defined by words with stable meanings—hinders human freedom."[104] If one's interpretation of a text must align with the authorial intent, then the reader is servant to the author, who is master of his text. A postmodernist believes we must escape such bondage. No longer can nor should the author be the "lord of textual meaning," but the "author must die if the text is to live and the reader is to be liberated."[105] Vanhoozer explains, "The death of the author becomes a necessary step in refusing to assign a 'real' meaning to the text. . . . No longer reduced to a single message with a single correct interpretation, the text is opened to a pluralism of readings; meaning is effectively destabilized, and authority withers on the textual vine."[106]

Naturally, postmodernism is a self-professing enemy to *biblical* authority, which not only asserts that the reader is subservient to the

---

99. Ibid., 26 (cf. 48–49).

100. Ibid., 24.

101. Friedrich Nietzsche, *The Will to Power*, trans. Walter Kaufmann (New York: Vintage, 1967), 481. See Vanhoozer, *Is There a Meaning*, 58.

102. Vanhoozer, *Is There a Meaning*, 50. Vanhoozer has in mind critiques such as Brian D. Ingraffia, *Postmodern Theory and Biblical Theology* (Cambridge: Cambridge University Press, 1995), 224. But note the many divergent interpretations of Derrida described by Vanhoozer, *Is There a Meaning*, 51–52.

103. Vanhoozer, *Is There a Meaning*, 72.

104. Ibid.

105. Ibid., 69.

106. Ibid., 70.

author, to God as the divine author, but also holds that meaning and truth are determined by God, not by us, the readers. Postmodernism denies that there is an authoritative presence behind the biblical text and instead chooses *nihilism*—"the denial of meaning, authority, and truth."[107] God will not deconstruct us, cries the postmodernist, but we shall deconstruct God! What is left after deconstruction? A dead author, and in the Bible's case, a God who is dead.[108] The consequences could not be more devastating for a doctrine like *sola Scriptura*. With biblical authority undone, postmodernists

> effectively strip the Bible of any stable meaning so that it cannot state a fact, issue a command, or make a promise. Furthermore, without the author to serve as touchstone of the distinction between meaning and significance, every interpretation becomes just as authorized a version as another. A text that cannot be set over against its commentary is no authority at all. Finally, biblical authority is undermined by the instability of meaning because, if nothing specific is said, the text cannot call for any specific response. Interpreters can give neither obedience nor belief to texts that lack specificity. If there is no meaning in the text, then there is nothing to which the reader can be held accountable.[109]

The Postconservative Reconstruction of *Sola Scriptura*

The critiques raised by postmodernism have resulted in some positive (and necessary) outcomes, and it is fair to say that there is some truth in postmodernism's epistemology. If postmodernism has taught us anything, it is that we cannot retreat back to modernism. Postmodernism rightfully exposed modernism's dependence on the myth of neutrality as well as modernism's overreliance on reason, that reason is autonomous, supreme, and omnicompetent. Postmodernism has demonstrated that each person comes to a text with set presuppositions, and we interpret texts out of an entire framework of preunderstanding.[110] Additionally, postmodernism has helpfully rebuked modernism for its elevation of individualism. Instead, postmodernism shows us the importance and value of community, a value that should resonate with Christians since

---

107. Ibid., 73.
108. Ibid., 72.
109. Ibid., 86.
110. D. A. Carson, *Collected Writings on Scripture* (Wheaton, IL: Crossway, 2010), 189.

the Bible highlights the significance of the interpretive community in the context of the local church. Postmodernism, whether it intended to or not, has helped Christians to see that modernism is no "sanctuary for the gospel."[111]

Yet postmodernism itself is plagued by massive problems. If true, postmodernism would spell the "death of God" as Nietzsche, the non-realist, predicted. The God of the Bible not only speaks, but claims to speak *the truth*, even sending his Son who is the way, the truth, and the light (John 14:6), the Logos who speaks the truth with authority (John 1:1), a truth that liberates the enslaved (John 8:32). Historic Christianity has argued that Scripture hands to us not just any narrative, but *the* metanarrative that interprets reality and judges all other competing narratives. This claim lies at the heart of *sola Scriptura* and the Bible's claim to authority. The Bible gives to us the supreme, final, truthful, objective, clear, and sufficient metanarrative, and this claim makes *sola Scriptura* offensive to the postmodernist mind. For many evangelicals, postmodernism and historic Christianity could not be more antithetical.

Nevertheless, some evangelicals believe postmodernism has something to offer. Accepting the label "postconservative," these evangelicals believe postmodernism is right in rejecting a realist-objectivist (i.e., foundationalist) view of knowledge, truth, and the world. Its advocates are diverse, but postconservatism is represented in the work of Stanley J. Grenz and John R. Franke.[112]

Grenz and Franke side with postmodernism's rejection of a realist-objectivist (i.e., foundationalist) understanding of knowledge and the world, and instead embrace a constructionist view (i.e., postfoundationalist view). They argue that no one possesses a God's-eye point of view, one that is objective. Language, including theological language, does not provide us with an objective lens through which we gain true, certain knowledge of the world. Language does not objectively picture

---

111. Ibid.

112. We will focus strictly on Stanley J. Grenz and John R. Franke, *Beyond Foundationalism: Shaping Theology in a Postmodern Context* (Louisville: Westminster John Knox, 2001). However, one should also consult Stanley J. Grenz, *Renewing the Center: Evangelical Theology in a Post-Theological Era* (Grand Rapids: Baker, 2000); John R. Franke, *Manifold Witness: The Plurality of Truth* (Nashville: Abingdon, 2009); idem, "Scripture, Tradition and Authority: Reconstructing the Evangelical Conception of *Sola Scriptura*," in Bacote et al., *Evangelicals and Scripture*, 192–210; idem, "Recasting Inerrancy: The Bible as Witness to Missional Plurality," in Merrick and Garrett, *Five Views*, 259–87.

reality or correspond to reality as it is, and our assertions do not provide us with objective truth claims about reality.[113]

Christians through the centuries have affirmed that Scripture, as God-breathed, is first-order language, and our theological formulation is second-order language. If the interpreter's theological formulation is based on Scripture, then it is true and trustworthy. *Sola Scriptura* is assumed in this entire hermeneutical process. Grenz and Franke seem to deny that one can move objectively from Scripture to theological formulation, and they are uncomfortable with the evangelical who draws theological conclusions based upon his exegesis of Scripture, only to believe that these conclusions are biblically accurate and definitive. The postfoundationalism of Grenz and Franke discards the belief that the Christian has in Scripture an "objective revelational foundation" from which he can draw sure theological conclusions.[114]

While at first appearing to affirm *sola Scriptura*, Grenz and Franke eventually scrap the traditional understanding of the formal principle. Scripture is inspired and authoritative only in the sense that the Spirit speaks to the community through the Bible, not because the Bible is inherently God-breathed.[115] It "is not the Bible as a book that is authoritative," they argue, "but the Bible as the instrumentality of the Spirit; the biblical message spoken by the Spirit through the text is theology's norming norm."[116] Again, sounding very Barthian: "The authority of scripture does not ultimately rest with any quality that inheres in the text itself but with the work of the Spirit who speaks in and through the text. Scripture is authoritative because it is the vehicle through which the Spirit speaks."[117] Therefore, the entire Reformation debate over authority is misguided, for "neither Scripture nor tradition is inherently authoritative in the foundationalist sense of providing self-evident, noninferential, incorrigible grounds for constructing theological assertions," but both derive their authority from the Spirit and are very much dependent upon each other.[118]

Not only are there three sources for theological formulation (Scripture, tradition, and culture), but the latter two appear to be just

---

113. Grenz and Franke, *Beyond Foundationalism*, 23–54.
114. Ibid., 49–51. This wording comes from Wellum, "Postconservatism," 172–74.
115. Grenz and Franke, *Beyond Foundationalism*, 65.
116. Ibid., 69.
117. Ibid., 114–15.
118. Ibid., 117.

as essential and authoritative as the first.[119] The community is needed and necessary, along with the assistance of the Holy Spirit, to make Scripture whole.[120] Since Grenz and Franke elevate these other norms to the level of Scripture, their affirmation of *sola Scriptura* fumbles out, somewhat tongue in cheek:

> Yet, while acknowledging the significance of sola scriptura as establishing the principle that canonical scripture is the *norma normans normata* (the norm with no norm over it), it is also true that in another sense scriptura is never *sola*. Scripture does not stand alone as the sole source in the task of theological construction or as the sole basis on which the Christian faith has developed historically. Rather scripture functions in an ongoing and dynamic relationship with the Christian tradition, as well as with the cultural milieu from which particular readings of the text emerge.[121]

In what sense, then, is Scripture the determining norm? For Grenz and Franke, the *text* of Scripture is not the determining norm, but only its *message*. This follows from their belief that the text of Scripture is *not* to be equated with the Word of God.[122] Scripture is the determining norm only in the sense that the Spirit uses the message of Scripture to impact the community.[123]

But even here the situation is far more complicated, for the meaning of the text is not restricted to the biblical author's intent. Following French philosopher Paul Ricoeur, Grenz and Franke believe that once the biblical author has finished his text, the text "takes on a life of its own."[124] The Spirit, they explain, is not bound to authorial intent when appropriating the text to the community's contemporary situation.[125] How the Spirit works through the text, therefore, is not restricted to the biblical text. The community's job is to listen to how the Spirit might be speaking today through the biblical message.[126] We must remember, say Grenz and Franke, that the Spirit is speaking to us today

---

119. On these three, see ibid., 64–68, 102–15.
120. Ibid.
121. Ibid., 112.
122. Ibid., 70–72.
123. Ibid., 74: "If the final authority in the church is the Holy Spirit speaking through scripture, then theology's norming norm is the message the Spirit declares through the text."
124. Ibid.
125. Ibid., 74–75.
126. Ibid., 74–90.

not only through Scripture but also through tradition and culture. Scripture, tradition, and culture, they assert, all speak together to the community, each being equally significant.[127]

The Evangelical Response to Postconservatism

How have evangelicals responded to postconservatism? At the start of the twenty-first century, one of the most instructive critiques can be seen in *Reclaiming the Center: Confronting Evangelical Accommodation in Postmodern Times*, edited by Erickson, Helseth, and Taylor, a book incorporating chapters by fourteen evangelicals from diverse evangelical denominations. Stephen Wellum's chapter on biblical authority is particularly representative of evangelicals dissatisfied with a postconservative view of Scripture.

Wellum agrees with Grenz and Franke that postmodernism "has been helpful in pointing out the inherent problems of modernism, namely, its hubris in thinking that finite human beings are self-sufficient, autonomous subjects who can discover, on their own apart from God and his revelation, truth in the metanarrative sense of universality and objectivity."[128] The best of the Christian tradition—thinkers like Herman Bavinck, Cornelius Van Til, Francis Schaeffer, Carl F. H. Henry—have rejected such an approach. But Grenz and Franke's reliance on postmodernism as an alternative is equally disastrous, for it has the same starting point: human autonomy. In other words, postmodernism falls into the same trap as modernism precisely because it does not begin with God and his revelation to mankind.[129]

Furthermore, Grenz and Franke fail to distinguish between *modernist* foundationalism and *biblical* foundationalism. "A scriptural foundationalism is *not* grounded in the finite human subject, as both modernism and postmodernism attempt to do, but instead it is rooted and grounded in the Bible's own presentation of the triune God—to use the famous words of Francis Schaeffer, 'the God who is there.'"[130] It is simply a mistake to assume that knowledge in the biblical foundationalism framework is the same view of knowledge adhered to by modernism. Unlike the latter, the former is rooted in the sovereign

---

127. Ibid., 161–63.
128. Wellum, "Postconservatism," 186.
129. Ibid.
130. Ibid., 186–87.

Lord, who is omniscient and has created his image bearers for the purpose of revealing himself to them. In short, Grenz and Franke have thrown the baby (biblical foundationalism) out with the dirty bathwater (modernist foundationalism).

Moreover, since language is a God-given gift, we can possess true knowledge of God, man, and the world around us even if this knowledge is not exhaustive.[131] Wellum strikes against the anti-realism and anti-objectivism of Grenz and Franke: "Why should we think that because our knowledge of God comes through revelation and then through our senses, reason, and linguistic means, it cannot be knowledge of God as he really is or of reality as it really is, but only a matter of linguistic construction? That is simply an unscriptural concept."[132] According to Scripture, God and his universe can be and are known. From the beginning, God did not endow man with reason and senses that obstruct, distort, or blockade knowledge of him and the world; instead, they serve as the very means God uses to bring us to a knowledge of the truth. As John Frame states, "God is Lord; He will not be shut out of His world."[133] In that light, man can possess an objective, true understanding of God, his Word, and the world even if this knowledge is not exhaustive, but limited. Because God has revealed himself, a God's-eye view of reality is possible.[134]

The postconservative view of Scripture is inconsistent with what Scripture says about itself. As we will see in the chapters that follow, Scripture not only presents itself as communicating an objective word from God, but Scripture itself is equated with God's Word and is considered God-breathed. Since Scripture is inspired by God and inerrant, it is first-order language. All second-order language is derivative and must be evaluated by Scripture.[135] The Bible holds first place, Wellum explains, "not merely because it is the community's book, nor merely due to its being utilized by the Spirit in some dynamic sense, but precisely because it is what it claims to be, God's Word written, that is,

---

131. Ibid., 187. See also Vern Poythress, *Inerrancy and Worldview* (Wheaton, IL: Crossway, 2012), 246; D. A. Carson, *Collected Writings on Scripture* (Wheaton, IL: Crossway, 2010), 191.

132. Wellum, "Postconservatism," 187.

133. John M. Frame, *The Doctrine of the Knowledge of God: A Theology of Lordship* (Phillipsburg, NJ: P&R, 1987), 33.

134. Therefore, Wellum, building off of Vanhoozer, advocates a type of "critical realism."

135. Wellum, "Postconservatism," 189.

divinely authorized discourse that gives us God's own interpretations of his own mighty actions."[136]

In this light, the postconservative view of Scripture does not do justice to *sola Scriptura*. Grenz and Franke do not actually treat the Bible as first-order language that is fully authoritative. Instead, for Grenz and Franke, "it is the 'Christian interpretive framework,' which is a combination of Scripture, experience, and interpretation, that is basic and foundational for them, but it is in the category of second-order."[137] Grenz and Franke sound much like Karl Barth on this point, for they do not believe that Scripture is inherently authoritative and self-authenticating. Instead, authority is present when the Spirit speaks through the text or appropriates the text in our communities, but Scripture is not authoritative because the Spirit has inerrantly breathed out the text in the first place.[138]

Both postconservatism and postfoundationalism leave the Christian on the all-too-shaky ground of hermeneutical subjectivism. Grenz and Franke "assert that 'the Spirit speaking through the Scripture' refers to the *Spirit's* illocutions, but these are *not* identical with those of the biblical authors."[139] Such a position "views the Spirit as speaking and creating a world independently of Scripture's speaking, instead of maintaining a correct view that the Spirit's speaking is *always* the speaking of Scripture."[140] This raises a host of problematic questions:

- How does one know what the illocutionary acts of the Spirit are, especially when it is possible for the Spirit to speak independently of the human authors' illocutionary acts?
- How is Scripture really serving as our final authority for theological construction?
- How, then, does one determine what the Spirit is actually speaking, except in the light of the *subjectivity* of the local community's hearing the Spirit's voice? And, furthermore, which community do we listen to?
- Given their rejection of *sola Scriptura* and their acceptance of a nonfoundationalist epistemology, how can we actually "check

136. Ibid.
137. Ibid.
138. Ibid., 190.
139. Ibid., 191.
140. Ibid.

and see" to know whether the world the Spirit is creating in and through our theological language belongs to the eschatological world?

• How can we falsify a world of our own idolatrous making that contradicts the Bible's world?[141]

In short, it is hard to see how the Christian is not left stuck in the black hole of relativism.[142]

The Bible under Fire Today

The battle over biblical authority is far from over. There continues to be an ever-growing number of books published on the subject every year, many questioning Scripture's authority, inspiration, inerrancy, clarity, necessity, and sufficiency. Consider the following sampling from representatives we will call "evangelical Bible critics"—a label that fits since they are critical of Scripture (in varying degrees) and identify themselves in some sense as evangelical (or at least did so at one time).[143]

• *Peter Enns*: The Bible is not reliable and factual in its historical narrative. What the Bible says happened didn't happen. Much of the Old Testament reads like fairy tales (e.g., Adam and Eve, God parting the Red Sea). Furthermore, many of its theological descriptions (even about God) and ethical instructions are disturbing, wrong, contradictory, and at times even immoral and barbaric (e.g., the Old Testament portrayal of God and genocide). Consequently, the Bible is not inerrant, clear, or sufficient, nor should we consider parts of it inspired at all.[144]

---

141. Ibid., 191–92.

142. Many other contemporary movements could be explored. For examples, see Grant Osborne, "Hermeneutics and Theological Interpretation," in *Understanding the Times: New Testament Studies in the 21st Century*, ed. Andreas J. Köstenberger and Robert W. Yarbrough (Wheaton, IL: Crossway, 2011), 62–86; Kevin J. Vanhoozer, *The Drama of Doctrine: A Canonical Linguistic Approach to Christian Theology* (Louisville: Westminster John Knox, 2005), 10–12.

143. The following are my summaries of these authors, though I have striven to closely parallel the words of the authors to represent their claims.

144. Peter Enns, "Inerrancy, However Defined, Does Not Describe What the Bible Does," in Merrick and Garrett, *Five Views*, 83–141; Peter Enns, *The Bible Tells Me So: Why Defending Scripture Has Made Us Unable to Read It* (New York: HarperCollins, 2014); Peter Enns, *Inspiration and Incarnation: Evangelicals and the Problem of the Old Testament* (Grand Rapids: Baker Academic, 2005). For a response, see John Frame, *The Doctrine of the Word of God* (Phillipsburg, NJ: P&R, 2010), 499–516; G. K. Beale, *The Erosion of Inerrancy in*

- *Kenton L. Sparks*: The Bible is primarily a human book, and since it was written by humans it naturally errs. Historical errors and contradictions are present throughout (e.g., Moses didn't write the Pentateuch, Paul didn't write many epistles bearing his name, the flood and exodus never happened, Nineveh never repented, Gospel writers contradict each other, the prophecy of Christ's return is mistaken). But these errors are not only historical in nature, but theological and ethical, as the Bible espouses values that are sinister and evil. Even Jesus's teachings were not immune from the fallen condition. Therefore, the Bible, being fallen and broken, has a dark side. Nevertheless, Scripture is still God's Word and authoritative in its main message, since God accommodates himself to error, redeeming and sanctifying man's broken word.[145]

Numerous other "evangelical Bible critics" could be mentioned, but we can make two observations based on the positions held by Enns and Sparks.[146] First, while the "evangelical Bible critics" mentioned above look at apparent Bible "problems" and conclude that the Bible is not inerrant but nonetheless remains the "word of God," skeptics (e.g., Bart Ehrman) look at the *same* Bible "problems" and conclude that the Bible most definitely is *not* the "word of God."[147] On this point, ironically, evangelical inerrantists and skeptics have much in common over against "evangelical Bible critics"—they agree that if the Bible errs, it cannot be the authoritative "word of God."

Evangelicalism: Responding to New Challenges to Biblical Authority (Wheaton, IL: Crossway, 2008); Michael Kruger, Review of *The Bible Tells Me So*, The Gospel Coalition, http://www.thegospelcoalition.org/article/the-bible-tells-me-so.

145. Kenton L. Sparks, *Sacred Word, Broken Word: Biblical Authority and the Dark Side of Scripture* (Grand Rapids: Eerdmans, 2012); Kenton L. Sparks, *God's Word in Human Words: An Evangelical Appropriation of Critical Biblical Scholarship* (Grand Rapids: Baker Academic, 2008). For a response, see Robert W. Yarbrough, "The Embattled Bible: Four More Books," *Themelios* 34, no. 1 (2009): 6–25. One author who takes this "dark side" accusation mentioned above to an extreme is Thom Stark, who says the biblical text is "evil" and has a "devilish nature." Thom Stark, *The Human Faces of God: What Scripture Reveals When It Gets God Wrong* (Eugene, OR: Wipf & Stock, 2011), 218–19.

146. For a sweeping overview of other critics, as well as a helpful critique, see D. A. Carson, "The Many Facets of the Current Discussion," in Carson, *Enduring Authority of the Christian Scriptures*, 3–42.

147. For example, Bart D. Ehrman, *God's Problem: How the Bible Fails to Answer Our Most Important Question—Why We Suffer* (New York: HarperOne, 2008); Bart D. Ehrman, *Misquoting Jesus: The Story behind Who Changed the Bible and Why* (New York: HarperOne, 2005); Bart D. Ehrman, *Forged: Writing in the Name of God—Why the Bible's Authors Are Not Who We Think They Are* (New York: HarperOne, 2011).

Second, for "evangelical Bible critics," not only is the historicity of the biblical accounts called into question (e.g., the historical Adam, the flood, the exodus, Mosaic authorship of Pentateuch, the miracles of Jesus), but the very theology and ethics of the Bible are questioned. We should not think that "evangelical Bible critics" have a problem with *minor* issues. Rather, their criticism of Scripture is with the Bible's own theology and ethical instruction; indeed, the Bible's own worldview.

How Shall We Then Proceed? The Self-Authenticating Nature of Scripture and the Internal Testimony of the Spirit

Having taken this brief history of modern and postmodern approaches to the Bible, what can we learn about the development of *sola Scriptura* and its application to our context today? To begin with, we must recognize that rationalistic modernism and subjectivist postmodernism are inadequate and inherently unbiblical. Each view makes the individual the starting point. Many Enlightenment thinkers began with the autonomous self apart from divine revelation. Liberalism did the same with man's experience. Postmodernism is no better and is the natural and logical outworking of modernism's rationalism. Postmodernism continues to elevate human reason as our "final authority" and "final arbiter of truth, even if that truth is only personal and self-created." Therefore, the "fundamental plank of the Enlightenment" has not been abandoned by the postmodernist.[148] It is not a surprise, then, when postmodernism turns Scripture into a wax nose and empties it of its divine authority in its exaltation of man's subjective experience.[149]

In contrast to rationalistic modernism and subjectivist postmodernism, we should begin by listening to what Scripture has to say about itself, for it "claims for itself an authority not derived from human beings but from God," and as "divine revelation it presents us with a meta-story that claims to communicate absolute truth that cannot be discovered by any other means."[150] Rather than imposing a modern or postmodern agenda upon the text, we will have an open ear to the biblical categories that Scripture itself provides in order to guide us in its interpretation.[151]

---

148. On postmodernism's elevation of man's subjective experience, see Robert Saucy, *Scripture: Its Power, Authority, and Relevance* (Nashville: Nelson, 2001), 28.

149. Ibid.

150. T. Desmond Alexander, *From Eden to the New Jerusalem: An Introduction to Biblical Theology* (Grand Rapids: Kregel, 2008), 9.

151. Notice how our approach differs from Sparks and Enns, who say we should approach

This means we cannot buy into the Enlightenment illusion that we can come to Scripture *neutral*, unbiased, and perfectly objective. No one comes to Scripture neutral. We all approach the text with certain traditions and preunderstandings in place. But neutrality is not our goal. While some preunderstandings may be misguided, others are right on target, guiding us to a correct understanding and interpretation of Scripture. Therefore, our aim will be to come to Scripture and allow its own voice to affirm *and* correct our preunderstanding of what Scripture is and how it should be read.[152]

Such an approach seeks to acknowledge the *self-authenticating* nature of Scripture.[153] Or as John Calvin and John Owen said, Scripture is *autopiston* (from *autopistos*, meaning trustworthy in and of itself).[154] While there is an important place for historical investigation, sometimes evangelicals approach Scripture making external data from historical investigation the ultimate judge over Scripture. In these approaches, the external data are necessary to validate whether the Bible is God's Word.[155] Ironically, such a starting point does not differ significantly from Liberalism, though the conclusions reached are vastly divergent. Both groups look to historical data as judge over Scripture.[156] Looking to Scripture itself becomes subservient to external proofs.

Scripture by interrogating it or as if we are engaging in a wrestling match. Sparks, *Sacred Word, Broken Word*, 30, 39; Enns, *The Bible Tells Me So*, 22–23.

152. J. Todd Billings, *The Word of God for the People of God: An Entryway to the Theological Interpretation of Scripture* (Grand Rapids: Eerdmans, 2010), 47–54.

153. It is sometimes referred to as the "self-attestation" of Scripture. Some, like James Barr, have rejected this doctrine (*Fundamentalism* [London: SCM, 1977], 78). However, many evangelicals in the Reformed camp have affirmed it: Sinclair Ferguson, "How Does the Bible Look at Itself?" in *Inerrancy and Hermeneutic*, ed. Harvie M. Conn (Grand Rapids: Baker, 1988), 47–66; Wayne Grudem, "Scripture's Self-Attestation and the Problem of Formulating a Doctrine of Scripture," in *Scripture and Truth*, ed. D. A. Carson and John Woodbridge (Grand Rapids: Baker, 1983), 19–59; John Frame, "Scripture Speaks for Itself," in *God's Inerrant Word: An International Symposium on the Trustworthiness of Scripture*, ed. John Warwick Montgomery (Minneapolis: Bethany Fellowship, 1973), 178–81.

154. John Calvin, *Institutes of the Christian Religion*, ed. John T. McNeill, trans. Ford Lewis Battles (Philadelphia: Westminster, 1960), 1.7.5. See also John Owen, *Divine Original*, in *The Works of John Owen*, ed. William H. Goold (Edinburgh: Banner of Truth, 1967), 16:309; Muller, *PRRD*, 2:257–58. Elsewhere Muller explains *autopistos*: "If Scripture is trustworthy in and of itself (*in se* and *per se*), no external authority, whether church or tradition need be invoked in order to ratify Scripture as the norm of faith and practice" (*DLGTT*, s.v. *autopistos*, 54).

155. Paul Helm, "Faith, Evidence, and the Scriptures," in Carson and Woodbridge, *Scripture and Truth*, 303–20.

156. Michael Kruger identifies these two approaches as the "canon-within-the canon" model (Liberalism) and the "criteria-of-canonicity" model (some evangelicals). Michael J.

Though addressing the larger subject of the canon of Scripture, Michael Kruger notes several problems with such an approach.[157] To begin with, it assumes that historical investigation is neutral. Scripture must be authenticated and proved only through biblical criticism's assured results. Christian and non-Christian alike must submit themselves to the neutral methods of historical research. But can one's method truly be worldview neutral? Such an approach is naive. Historical evidence does not interpret itself, but must be interpreted by somebody, and a "somebody" always has a worldview.[158] This means that there is no worldview-neutrality. The unbeliever comes at the biblical text with an entire non-Christian worldview in place, filled with unbiblical (and anti-biblical) presuppositions. His preunderstanding most definitely impacts his historical investigation. The methods of historical investigation are never neutral. They are "founded upon, and presuppose, some philosophical-religious system."[159] What appears convincing to the Christian appears foolish to the unbeliever.[160] So while historical arguments are important, they are supportive, not determinative. As Kruger writes, "Their effectiveness is always dependent upon the worldview of the one evaluating the evidence."[161]

That said, we are still left with the massive problem—one that appears to violate the spirit of *sola Scriptura*—that the Bible is subject to an external standard, in this case the assured (and neutral!) results of historical investigation.[162] To be clear, historical investigation is not a bad thing. "Historical-critical study," says Herman Bavinck, "may yield a clear insight into the origination, history, and structure of Scripture," but it can never lead "to a doctrine, a dogma of Holy Scripture."[163] Neither is it supposed to be the standard by which we judge Scripture. In doing so, we once again buy into an Enlightenment mentality that "allows autonomous human assessment of historical evidence to

---

Kruger, *Canon Revisited: Establishing the Origins and Authority of the New Testament Books* (Wheaton, IL: Crossway, 2012), 68–76.

157. Ibid., 77–87.

158. Ibid., 81.

159. Ibid., 78.

160. Ibid., 79.

161. Ibid.

162. Richard Gaffin, "The New Testament as Canon," in Conn, *Inerrancy and Hermeneutic*, 170; Herman N. Ridderbos, *Redemptive History and the New Testament Scripture* (Phillipsburg, NJ: P&R, 1988), 7.

163. Herman Bavinck, *Reformed Dogmatics*, vol. 1, *Prolegomena*, ed. John Bolt, trans. John Vriend (Grand Rapids: Baker, 2003), 424 (cf. 425).

become an external authority over God's Word."[164] So we are back to the key question, stated here by Kruger: "How can the Scriptures be the ultimate standard of truth if their reception is dependent upon some *other* (presumably more certain) standard?"[165]

We must begin by looking to Scripture itself for the answer, for Scripture is self-authenticating. In other words, we seek to ground authority in the greatest authority that we can find, namely, Scripture itself, for in doing so we are actually grounding Scripture's authority in God, for *he* is its divine author and it is *his* Word.[166] As Calvin said, "God alone is a fit witness of himself in his Word . . . Scripture is indeed self-authenticated."[167] Such an approach looks to the *content* of Scripture to discover what Scripture is and does, rather than looking ultimately or solely to the community (Roman Catholicism and postmodernism) or the autonomous individual's reason and experience (modernism and Liberalism). Scripture, as Bavinck notes, acts as our "first principle," meaning it must be "believed on its own account, not on account of something else." "Scripture's authority with respect to itself depends on Scripture."[168] Our approach is not to deny the value of historical investigation or evidence from outside of Scripture as "useful aids," as Calvin called them, but rather to say that such useful aids must come to us under the authority of Scripture itself.[169]

---

164. Kruger, *Canon Revisited*, 80.

165. Ibid.

166. Ibid., 89.

167. John Calvin, *Institutes of the Christian Religion*, ed. John T. McNeill, trans. Ford Lewis Battles (Philadelphia: Westminster, 1960), 1.7.4–5. See also Francis Turretin, *Institutes of Elenctic Theology*, trans. George Musgrave Giger, ed. James T. Dennison Jr., 3 vols. (Phillipsburg, NJ: P&R, 1992–97), 1:89.

168. Bavinck, *Reformed Dogmatics*, 1:458.

169. Kruger, *Canon Revisited*, 91. Some will object that such an approach is circular ("The Bible is God's Word because the Bible says so"). However, such an objection falls short: (1) Any appeal to an ultimate authority is necessarily circular. After all, there is no higher authority to appeal to. If there were a higher authority outside of Scripture to appeal to, then Scripture would no longer be the highest authority (and *sola Scriptura* would be compromised). See Packer, *"Fundamentalism" and the Word of God*, 76; John M. Frame, *Apologetics to the Glory of God* (Phillipsburg, NJ: P&R, 1994), 10; D. A. Carson, *Collected Writings on Scripture* (Wheaton, IL: Crossway, 2010), 35–36. (2) The objection does not recognize the heart of the argument. Ultimately, we are not saying the Bible is God's Word because the Bible says so (though that is true), but more precisely because *God* says so. In other words, the objection assumes that the Bible cannot be inspired because it divorces God from Scripture from the start. But our argument is different. The reason we can appeal to the Bible to understand the Bible is because we are ultimately appealing to the highest authority one can appeal to—God himself. (3) We believe the Bible on the authority of Christ and the apostles, which is the same basis on which we believe every doctrine. In short, we believe the

Second, and hand in hand with the self-authenticating nature of Scripture, we must possess the Spirit's internal testimony and witness. While Scripture is self-authenticating, due to our sinful minds we will fail to perceive its true nature apart from the work of the Spirit. "Scripture will ultimately suffice for a saving knowledge of God," Calvin said, "only when its certainty is founded upon the inward persuasion of the Holy Spirit."[170] The same Spirit who "has spoken through the mouths of the prophets must penetrate into our hearts to persuade us that they faithfully proclaimed what has been divinely commanded."[171]

For example, in 1 Corinthians 2 Paul says that the "natural person," the unregenerate person, "does not accept the things of the Spirit of God, for they are folly to him, and he is not able to understand them because they are spiritually discerned" (2:14 ESV). The Spirit is the one who gives spiritual sight, so that though the unbeliever previously saw the cross as folly, he now sees the cross as his salvation.[172] As Paul explains in 2 Corinthians 4:6: "For God, who said, 'Let light shine out of darkness,' has shone in our hearts to give the light of the knowledge of the glory of God in the face of Jesus Christ" (ESV; cf. Acts 26:18; Eph 1:13).[173]

Therefore, though the church or external evidences may be key, they bear only an ancillary testimony. The internal testimony of the Spirit is the "primary key to the authority and divinity of Scripture."[174]

Bible because Jesus did. See chapters 7 and 8. (4) Is it really fair for critics to tell evangelicals that they cannot look to Scripture to explain what Scripture is and what it does? D. A. Carson argues, "Surely part of the effort to find out what Scripture *is* requires that we read Scripture and see what it says of itself." D. A. Carson, *The Gagging of God: Christianity Confronts Pluralism* (Grand Rapids: Zondervan, 1996), 162, emphasis added.

170. Calvin, *Institutes*, 1.8.13.

171. Ibid., 1.7.4 (cf. 3.2.34).

172. F. W. Groshede, *The First Epistle to the Corinthians*, NICNT (Grand Rapids: Eerdmans, 1979), 73; Leon Morris, *The First Epistle of Paul to the Corinthians*, TBC (Grand Rapids: Eerdmans, 1958), 60.

173. Mark A. Seifrid, *The Second Letter to the Corinthians*, PNTC (Grand Rapids: Eerdmans, 2014), 200–204; George H. Guthrie, *2 Corinthians*, BECNT (Grand Rapids: Baker Academic, 2015), 243–46.

174. Richard A. Muller, *PRRD*, 2:266. Also see Calvin, *Institutes*, 1.7.5. "The Westminster Confession of Faith," in *Reformed Confessions of the 16th and 17th Centuries in English Translation, Volume 4, 1600–1693*, ed. James T. Dennison Jr. (Grand Rapids: Reformation Heritage, 2014), 235 (I.V), makes this point beautifully: "We may be moved and induced by the testimony of the Church to an high and reverent esteem of the Holy Scripture. And the heavenliness of the matter, the efficacy of the doctrine, the majesty of the style, the consent of all the parts, the scope of the whole (which is, to give all glory to God), the full discovery it makes of the only way of man's salvation, the many other incomparable excellencies, and the entire perfection thereof, are arguments whereby it does abundantly evidence itself to be the Word of God: yet notwithstanding, our full persuasion

Like Calvin before him, Puritan John Owen clarifies that this internal testimony of the Spirit is not new revelation but instead the illumination of the Word. The Spirit, Owen wrote, "gives no new light to Scripture." Rather, he "cleareth our understanding, to see the light of Scripture, by the very Scripture itself and by the light of the Scripture."[175] How essential is this internal testimony of the Spirit? If "the Holy Ghost, speaking in the Scripture, [does] not first of all inspire our minds, and open the eyes of our understanding . . . all other means shall profit us nothing at all."[176]

Where Shall We Begin? In the Beginning

One final consideration addresses the need to see Scripture in a holistic sense. Since Scripture comes to us in the form of a story—a redemptive-historical story—we will begin there. We will give special focus to Scripture's promise-fulfillment pattern as seen in the biblical covenants, only to then shift gears and look at its different attributes.[177] We will move from biblical theology to systematic theology, and in doing so we aim to read Scripture on its own terms and categories.[178] When the Bible's story is approached properly, it will act as our meta-narrative, transforming our understanding of Christianity and even providing us with a comprehensive worldview.[179]

We will take our cue from the text itself so that we are not making God think our thoughts after us, but rather we are thinking God's thoughts after him.[180] Throughout this entire process we will wear the spectacles of Scripture, as Calvin advised, and simultaneously aim to apply *sola Scriptura* afresh in light of today's hermeneutical challenges.

---

and assurance of the infallible truth and divine authority thereof, is from the inward work of the Holy Spirit bearing witness by and with the Word in our hearts." For a recent work on the self-authenticating nature of Scripture, see John Piper, *A Peculiar Glory: How the Christian Scriptures Reveal Their Complete Truthfulness* (Wheaton, IL: Crossway, 2016).

175. Owen, *Divine Original*, in Goold, *Works*, 16:325–326. See Calvin, *Institutes*, 1.9.1.

176. Robert Rollock, *Treatise of Effectual Calling*, trans. Henry Holland (London, 1603), 69–70; quoted in Muller, *PRRD*, 2:266. See also "The Westminster Confession of Faith," in Dennison, *Reformed Confessions*, 4:235 (I.V).

177. D. A. Carson, "Unity and Diversity in the New Testament: The Possibility of Systematic Theology," in Carson and Woodbridge, *Scripture and Truth*, 69.

178. Geerhardus Vos, *Biblical Theology* (Grand Rapids: Eerdmans, 1948; repr., Carlisle, PA: Banner of Truth, 2004); Peter J. Gentry and Stephen J. Wellum, *Kingdom through Covenant: A Biblical-Theological Understanding of the Covenants* (Wheaton, IL: Crossway, 2012), 32–34.

179. Carson, *Gagging of God*, 191, 194; Wellum, "Postconservatism," 196.

180. Another way to say this is that we will be "intratextual" rather than "extratextual" in our interpretation of the text.

PART 2

God's Word
in Redemptive
History

CHAPTER 4

God's Word in the Economy of the Gospel: Covenant, Trinity, and the Necessity of a Saving Word

> This God—his way is perfect; the word of the LORD proves true; he is a shield for all those who take refuge in him. *2 Samuel 22:31 ESV*

> The grass withers, the flower fades, but the word of our God will stand forever. *—Isaiah 40:8 ESV*

If God had never revealed himself, what would your life look like? Can you even begin to imagine what your world would be like if you possessed no word from God? You would have no way to know who he is or what he has done. You would have no way to know who you are and who he wants you to be. As a sinner, you would be spiritually lost, deaf, and blind. Apart from a word from God, you would have no salvation, no hope, and no relationship with your Creator and Redeemer.

The good news is that God is not silent. He has spoken! We are not left to ourselves in total confusion, despair, and death. We can understand, hope, and live, and all because he has made himself known to us in a saving way. What an important reminder this is to avoid the all-too-common temptation to think that divine revelation is God's response to us.[1] As we will see in this chapter, this is a reversal of the biblical order. We do not find God. God finds us and makes himself known to us. God is the speaker, we are the listeners. It's not enough

---

1. This chapter is a prolegomena to the two chapters that follow, which trace the word of God through Scripture's story line.

to say the biblical authors wrote about God or even wrote for God. We must say much, much more: God himself speaks! And he speaks for himself.[2] His best word has come to us in his own Son, the Word. In Jesus, God has a message for the world, a word that is meant for all people in all places. As the recipients, we are summoned to listen and embrace the good news of the Word with faith and repentance.

General Revelation's Insufficiency in Redemptive History

When talking about God's revelation of himself, we begin with general revelation. What does general revelation tell us about God, and how and to whom is it revealed?

First, general revelation is God's revelation of his divine attributes. As Paul says, through the created order God's "invisible attributes, namely, his eternal power and divine nature, have been clearly perceived" (Rom 1:20 ESV). When we put all of Scripture together, we see just how expansive this knowledge of God can be. God not only exists (Ps 19:1; Rom 1:19), but is

- uncreated (Acts 17:24).
- Creator (Acts 14:15).
- Sustainer (Acts 14:16; 17:25).
- universal Lord (Acts 17:24).
- self-sufficient (Acts 17:25).
- transcendent (Acts 17:24).
- immanent (Acts 17:26–27).
- eternal (Ps 93:2).
- great (Ps 8:3–4).
- majestic (Ps 29:4).
- powerful (Ps 29:4; Rom 1:20).
- wise (Ps 104:24).
- good (Acts 14:17).
- righteous (Rom 1:32; 2:15).
- sovereign (Acts 17:26).
- judge (Rom 2:15–16).[3]

---

2.   J. I. Packer, *God Has Spoken: Revelation and the Bible*, 3rd ed. (Grand Rapids: Baker, 1993), 47; Geerhardus Vos, *Biblical Theology* (Grand Rapids: Eerdmans, 1948; repr., Carlisle, PA: Banner of Truth, 2004), 4.

3.   For a similar list, see Bruce A. Demarest, *General Revelation: Historical Views and Contemporary Issues* (Grand Rapids: Zondervan, 1982), 243.

In light of all these, God alone deserves worship (Acts 14:15; 17:3).

Second, God's general revelation of himself, which is given to all mankind, is revealed both in nature and in man's conscience.[4] As for the created order, David sings:

> The heavens declare the glory of God,
>   and the sky above proclaims his handiwork.
> Day to day pours out speech,
>   and night to night reveals knowledge. (Ps 19:1–2 ESV)

Many other psalms give similar descriptions (Pss 8, 93, 104). Certainly nature's witness to God is affirmed by Paul too when he says in Romans 1:20 that God's invisible attributes "have been clearly perceived, ever since the creation of the world, in the things that have been made."[5] Therefore, Paul concludes, man is without excuse.

But general revelation is also manifested in man himself. As Calvin says, God has not only revealed "his perfection in the whole structure of the universe" but also placed "in our minds the seeds of religion."[6] Knowledge of a Creator is ingrained and embedded into man's moral nature, so that man possesses a sense of the divine (*sensus divinitatis*; Acts 17:22–28).[7] Biblically speaking, this also means that God's moral law is written on man's heart. Since man is made in the image of God, man not only knows intuitively that God exists but also knows right from wrong (Rom 1:32), for God has implanted such a moral compass within.

Man's sense of the divine becomes all the more apparent when he turns against God and sins. As Paul says in Romans 1:32, "Though they know God's righteous decree that those who practice such things deserve to die, they not only do them but give approval to those who practice them" (ESV). Or consider Romans 2:14–16:

> For when Gentiles, who do not have the law, by nature do what the
> law requires, they are a law to themselves, even though they do not

---

4. I have limited my discussion to these two—nature/creation and the human conscience—but one could also explore general revelation through divine providence over the created order (Acts 14:8–18) as well as "human history" (Acts 17:26–28; Dan 4:32, 34–37).

5. Also consider Acts 17:22–29.

6. The seed of religion: *semen religionis.* John Calvin, *Institutes of the Christian Religion*, ed. John T. McNeill, trans. Ford Lewis Battles (Philadelphia: Westminster, 1960), 1.5.1–2.

7. Calvin, *Institutes*, 1.3.2.

have the law. They show that the work of the law is written on their hearts, while their conscience also bears witness, and their conflicting thoughts accuse or even excuse them on that day when, according to my gospel, God judges the secrets of men by Christ Jesus.

Sadly, though man has a knowledge of God, he suppresses that knowledge and instead lives for himself (Rom 1:21–32), thereby leaving him guilty and condemned before God. Man is in desperate need of a saving revelation from God.

The Necessity of Special Revelation in Redemptive History

As mentioned earlier, we do not find God; God must find us and reveal himself to us. There are two reasons why this is the case. First, there is a *Creator-creature distinction* at play that requires God to take the initiative. God is infinite, self-existent, self-sufficient, transcendent, eternal, and incomprehensible (Gen 1–2; Acts 17:24–25).[8] In reference to the created order, God is the Creator of the universe, the only one who is uncreated. We are the creature, totally dependent upon our Creator. Unlike God, we are finite, limited, and needy creatures (Acts 17:28). Therefore, the only way we can know the one who made us is if he makes himself known to us. Our knowledge of God is completely dependent upon God to give it to us. Revelation is a gift from God since our Creator is choosing to manifest to us who he is for our benefit and his glory. However, a *general* revelation of God is insufficient for us to know God personally. It was not enough for God merely to give Adam and Eve the created order. If they were to know God intimately and relationally, they needed God to speak and communicate to them *directly*, which he did as they communed with him in the garden of Eden.[9] By speaking words to his image bearers, God made his will known so that they knew how to live in relation to him and to one another (Gen 1:26–28; 2:15). As important as general revelation is, it does not give us the specifics we need to have a personal relationship with God, but leaves us with only a general knowledge of God.

---

8.   Paul R. House, *Old Testament Theology* (Downers Grove, IL: IVP Academic, 1998), 59 (cf. 62).

9.   Robert Saucy, *Scripture: Its Power, Authority, and Relevance* (Nashville: Nelson, 2001), 45; Benjamin B. Warfield, *Revelation and Inspiration*, in *The Works of Benjamin Breckinridge Warfield*, 10 vols. (repr., Grand Rapids: Baker, 2003), 1:8.

Second, *mankind's sinfulness* makes it necessary for God to reveal himself to us in a saving way. The black cloud of our depravity hangs over all of history and is the massive barrier between us and God that we cannot overcome. God has made his awesome glory, power, deity, and eternity known to all people at all times through both the created order and the human conscience (Ps 19:1; Matt 6:26–30; Acts 14:16–17; 17:24–27; Rom 1:18–25; 2:1–15). Tragically, as children of Adam (Rom 5:12–21), we have suppressed general revelation and are blind to the beauty of God in front of us (Rom 1–2). We not only sin and disobey his moral law written on our conscience, but we shove the truth about God made manifest in the created order out of the way, disregarding it and pretending as if it is not there.

While general revelation is sufficient to condemn us (mankind is left "without excuse" before God, Rom 1:20–21; 2:14–16), it is insufficient to save us. "Nature cannot unlock the door of redemption."[10] General revelation gives us God, but it is as Creator and, due to our sin, as Judge.[11] God as "Savior" comes only through special revelation, through which God speaks a saving word for his people through his Son, Christ Jesus. It is in special revelation that God speaks directly, differently, and far more specifically about who he is and what he has done in redemptive history.[12] Special revelation is an act and communication of sovereign grace. We cannot make the first move to save ourselves, but depend entirely on a gracious word from God.[13] The royal king redeems rebel sinners, lost and damned on the dark paths of sin, and he does so by his Word, turning bad news into good news, condemnation into reconciliation, pardon, and peace.[14]

Special revelation, and Scripture in particular, is redemptive in nature, ultimately leading us to Jesus Christ, who is not only Creator but Redeemer as well. The Chicago Statement on Biblical Inerrancy states: "God, who is Himself Truth and speaks truth only, has inspired Holy Scripture in order thereby to reveal Himself to lost mankind through Jesus Christ as Creator and Lord, Redeemer and Judge. Holy

---

10. Vos, *Biblical Theology*, 21.
11. Packer, *God Has Spoken*, 55.
12. Notice, we not only need *more* revelation but a *different* revelation, one that will save us rather than condemn us. We are reminded, then, of the important distinction between law and gospel, and we dare not confuse the two. See Michael Horton, *Pilgrim Theology: Core Doctrines for Christian Disciples* (Grand Rapids: Zondervan, 2011), 39–40.
13. Vos, *Biblical Theology*, 4.
14. Packer, *God Has Spoken*, 61.

Scripture is God's witness to Himself."[15] Scripture is *Christocentric* and *Christotelic*.[16] It is through God's Word that the sinner comes to a saving knowledge of God, and knowing God *in Christ* is the chief aim of God's Word. Apart from God's Word, no sinner can know Christ (John 14:6; Acts 4:12).

The Form and Progression of Special Revelation in Redemptive History

What does God's special revelation of himself look like in redemptive history? How does God speak to those whom he has created and enter into a covenant relationship with them? And what is it that he conveys to his covenant recipients? These questions, and many others, will be the focus of future chapters as we embark on a survey of the story line of Scripture. It should be noted from the start that there are many different forms, or modes, of special revelation portrayed throughout Scripture. Throughout history God communicates through

- theophanies (Gen 12:7; 18:1–2, 22; 19:1; 32:24, 30).[17]
- dreams and visions (Gen 28:12–16; 37:5–9; 41:1–7).[18]
- angels (Dan 9:20–21; 10:10–21).[19]
- direct speech (Exod 33:11).[20]
- miracles and mighty acts/events (Mark 2:10–12).[21]
- Christ (Heb 1:1–2).
- Scripture (2 Tim 3:16–17).[22]

---

15. "The Chicago Statement on Biblical Inerrancy," in *Inerrancy*, ed. Norman L. Geisler (Grand Rapids: Zondervan, 1980), 494 (article 1 of "A Short Statement").

16. Robert W. Yarbrough, "Inerrancy's Complexities: Grounds for Grace in the Debate," in *Solid Ground: The Inerrant Word of God in an Errant World*, ed. Gabriel N. E. Flugher (Phillipsburg, NJ: P&R, 2012), 72.

17. See also Gen 16:9–13; 22:11–12; 31:11–13; Exod 3:2–4; Judg 6:11–24; 13:3–23; et al.

18. Num 12:6; 1 Sam 28:6; Dan 2:3, 31–35; 1 Kgs 3:5; Ezek 8:3; Joel 2:28; Amos 1:1; Matt 1:20; 2:13, 19.

19. Luke 2:10–13; Acts 7:53; Gal 3:19; 1 Pet 1:12.

20. Num 12:6–8; 1 Sam 3:4–14; Acts 9:4. Sometimes this direct speech was quiet and internal rather than loud and public. See Acts 8:29; 10:19; 13:2; Gal 1:11–17.

21. Acts 2:22; 2 Cor 12:12; Eph 2:19–20.

22. These different modes of special revelation teach us that revelation is *not* synonymous or identical with Scripture. The former is a much broader category under which the latter falls. Therefore, revelation and inspiration should be distinguished from each other, though never separated or divorced from each other. Also, it is just as important to understand that while revelation is progressive, developing and cumulating from old to new covenant, the same cannot be said of inspiration. Inspiration is not subject to varying degrees, nor does it develop,

As important as these are, God's special revelation through his own Son is truly the climax that all prior revelation pointed toward in great anticipation (Heb 1:1–2). The assumption, therefore, is that special revelation is *progressive* in nature, for with the incarnate Son came knowledge of God like never before (John 14:9; Col 2:9). As God incarnate, Christ did not merely arrive with a revelation from God, but he himself *is* the revelation from God.[23] In that light, it is appropriate that John gives Jesus the title the "Word" (John 1:1, 18; 3:2). But it would be a mistake to see Jesus merely as the climax of God's revelation; indeed, he is also the theme.[24] Indeed, he is the climax because he is the theme! All of Scripture pointed to Christ and found its fulfillment in Christ (Luke 24:25–27; John 5:39; Acts 2:14–40; 3:11–26; 1 Pet 1:10–12).

As significant as Christ is, God's *permanent* revelation of himself comes to us in written form. Jesus lived, died, resurrected, and then ascended into heaven. Nevertheless, it was good for him to leave (John 16:7–8), for in doing so he then sent the Holy Spirit to work in and through his disciples and their associates in order to leave to mankind God's final revelation. The New Testament Scriptures were not unprecedented. Over a long period of time and by means of his providential hand, God gave to his people, Israel, a written revelation of himself in the books of the Old Testament. The New Testament comes with the full force of the Messiah having fulfilled OT promises and as God's *final* and *definitive* revelation of himself, to which nothing can or should be added. Apart from God's written revelation, we have no access to Christ. Scripture is indispensable to how we know Christ, which is why the character and authority of Scripture is the main focus of this book as we explore its attributes in the chapters to come.

Word and Covenant in Redemptive History

So far we have said nothing specific about God's special revelation of himself in history. But as we look at God's actions and words throughout biblical history, what we discover is that they have an

---

as if the text is more inspired now than it was before. Herman Bavinck, *Reformed Dogmatics*, vol. 1, *Prolegomena*, ed. John Bolt, trans. John Vriend (Grand Rapids: Baker, 2003), 426–27.

23. Saucy, *Scripture*, 52.

24. Ibid.

inherently redemptive nature to them.[25] Another way to put this is that God's communication of himself (Word) comes to us in the context of covenants.[26] There is a pattern, a tapestry, to God's speech from Old Testament to New. Such a pattern revolves around the concept of God *covenanting* with his chosen people in order to bring about his kingdom rule and reign. We see this inseparable connection between Word and covenant in three ways.[27]

First, God declares what he will do through covenant promises. The word *covenant* is key. God makes himself known in a saving way by cutting a covenant with his people. As we see repeatedly throughout the story line of the Bible, it's in and through covenants that God communicates with us and we, in return, have communion with God. Even the climax of the story, the cross and resurrection of Christ, is the inauguration of the new covenant, whereby God communicates eternal life to his covenant recipients. The gospel itself is a covenantal work.[28]

While there may be a diverse list of characteristics to a divine covenant, at the core is the concept of promise and fulfillment. When God speaks covenantally, he makes promises he intends to keep. We will see this frequently as we trace God's speech through the Old Testament (see chapter 5). He is constantly appearing to different individuals to declare to them what he will do as their God and Lord.

Second, God accomplishes what he said he would do. Not only are his covenant promises properly called divine revelation but so are his mighty acts that bring about the fulfillment of his covenant promises.[29] God's trustworthiness is on the line, so he guarantees the veracity of his word by cutting a covenant (e.g., Heb 6:17–18). Salvation itself is entirely dependent upon God fulfilling his covenant words and promises. Should we doubt God's promises, his covenantal word, we essentially doubt his plan of redemption for his people.[30] This is a

---

25. To be extra clear, I am not referring to all of history (in general), as if what happens in other religions is redemptive. I am specifically referring to *redemptive* history as the Bible portrays it, especially in and through Jesus Christ.

26. Peter J. Gentry and Stephen J. Wellum, *Kingdom through Covenant: A Biblical-Theological Understanding of the Covenants* (Wheaton, IL: Crossway, 2012), 594.

27. John Frame, *Systematic Theology* (Phillipsburg, NJ: P&R, 2013), 519–20.

28. Scott R. Swain, *Trinity, Revelation, and Reading: A Theological Introduction to the Bible and Its Interpretation* (New York: T&T Clark, 2011), 7.

29. Peter Jensen, *The Revelation of God* (Downers Grove, IL: InterVarsity Press, 2002), 75.

30. Ibid., 77. A similar point is made by Carl F. H. Henry. See Kenneth Kantzer and Carl F. H. Henry, eds., *Evangelical Affirmations* (Grand Rapids: Zondervan, 1990), 77–78.

reminder that the gospel of Jesus Christ is inherently related to the truthfulness of Scripture. When we receive the gospel, we receive God's word of promise, and we believe that his word is true and that it is what it says it is: nothing less than the word of God.[31] This is a point we shall return to shortly.

Third, God does not leave it up to mankind to figure out what his mighty acts mean, but God follows up on his mighty acts with words that tell mankind what his acts mean and how we are to live in light of them. Word and act go together, the former interpreting the latter.[32] God is his own interpreter, and if we are to understand his revelation properly, we will be thinking God's thoughts after him. The fact that God not only makes and keeps his covenant promises but then interprets his covenantal actions is a reminder that Scripture is the *book of the covenant.* God has written down his revelation, giving us not only a living, active, and permanent witness to his covenantal actions but *the* authoritative interpretation of his covenantal actions (in contrast to postmodernism). No wonder the Torah is referred to as the "old covenant" and "the Book of the Covenant" (Exod 24:7; 2 Chr 34:14–31; 2 Cor 3:14), and the gospel is referred to as the "new covenant" (2 Cor 3:6).[33] By means of his covenant, God has restored his reign by means of his word. As Peter Jensen remarks, "The covenant is a characteristic form of the word of God, culminating in the gospel, the word of promise and demand that centres on Jesus Christ. The function of the Scripture is to record, expound, and apply this authority of God. That is why it is called the Word of God, the oracles of God, and the Holy Scriptures."[34]

What then does this mean for our relationship with God and his Word? It means that we are reconciled with God, entering into a saving relationship with him on the basis of his gracious covenant. It follows that our relationship is founded upon the God whose covenantal word has proved true in the gospel. Jensen writes that the Bible "functions as

---

31. Jensen, *Revelation of God,* 195. See also Robert Letham, *The Work of Christ* (Downers Grove, IL: InterVarsity Press, 1993), 102.

32. Geerhardus Vos, "The Idea of Biblical Theology," in *Redemptive History and Biblical Interpretation: The Shorter Writings of Geerhardus Vos,* ed. Richard B. Gaffin Jr. (Phillipsburg, NJ: P&R, 2001), 10. See also Vos, *Biblical Theology,* 6–7; John Frame, *Systematic Theology* (Phillipsburg, NJ: P&R, 2013), 542–43; Saucy, *Scripture,* 53–54; Gentry and Wellum, *Kingdom through Covenant,* 87–89.

33. Jensen, *Revelation of God,* 82.

34. Ibid.

both gospel and covenant in that it is intended to create and sustain our relationship with the living God on the right basis, namely on our being his covenant partners, bound to him in loyalty and obedience and relating to him through the mediator, Jesus Christ."[35] Scripture transports us to the living God as the Spirit immerses us in a saving relationship with Christ. The kingdom of God comes through covenant, specifically the book of the covenant. And with God's Word comes God's saving presence. Apart from God's Word, we are like Adam and Eve after the fall—east of Eden, cast out of the very presence of God, lost and without hope in the world.

The covenantal words of Scripture are absolutely essential. They are not museum pieces, but the authoritative Word of the living God, telling us who we are and what God has done to bring about our redemption. The Scriptures operate within the divine economy of salvation as the Bible communicates God's covenant promises to us, promises that create, by the power of the Spirit, new life within us.[36] The Bible tells us who we are (sinners) through a story of a people redeemed (Israel and the church) by a crucified and risen Savior (Jesus).[37] Indeed, we are rebels against our Creator. Only the Bible, the constitution of the covenant God has cut with us, can tell us how we can be right with God once more. Such was God's intention from the start.

Word and Trinity in Redemptive History

Not only is God's special revelation of himself coated in the context of redemptive covenants but this revelation is by nature Trinitarian.[38] In the Old Testament, God made himself known through his covenantal word, and in doing so foretold of his Son, the Messiah, who was to come (see chapter 5). Then, at the proper time, the Father sent his Son to take on human nature and come as the long-awaited Messiah, fulfilling the covenant promises God had made from Adam to the prophets (see chapter 6). After Christ established the new covenant in his blood, he rose victorious on the third day only to later ascend into

---

35. Ibid.

36. Mark D. Thompson, *A Clear and Present Word: The Clarity of Scripture* (Downers Grove, IL: InterVarsity Press, 2006), 136.

37. Ibid.

38. Chapter 6 of this book will draw out more thoroughly the implications the doctrine of the Trinity has for our understanding of God's revelation of himself, giving particular focus to Jesus's words in the Gospel of John.

heaven. The Father and Son then sent the Holy Spirit at Pentecost to communicate through the apostles as they explained who Christ is and what his life, death, and resurrection mean for all nations. As we will see, the Spirit, as with the prophets in the Old Testament, accomplished this work through the medium of the written Word (see chapter 6). Each member of the Trinity is active, therefore, in the communication of God's special revelation.

So while the entire Trinity is involved at each stage in redemptive history (the external works of the Trinity are undivided), each member of the Trinity takes on a focal role at one point or another.[39] Throughout redemptive history, we see each person of the Trinity participating in the delivery of divine revelation. In regard to Scripture, it is the Holy Spirit in particular who takes on the central role, carrying along the biblical authors in the act of inspiration so that they spoke from God (2 Pet 1:21). Appropriately, it is in and through the Scriptures that the triune God makes himself known to us in a saving way so that we, in turn, can have fellowship with God.[40] God's communication to us is the very means by which we have communion with him (1 John 1:3; 4:13). This means that the Bible is not just any type of revelation; it is the superlative written articulation of the triune God himself in redemptive history.[41]

The "Word of God" in Redemptive History

In the following chapters we will explore this covenantal Trinitarian pattern of God's speech that progressively unfolds from Old to New Testament, reaching its climax in the person and work of Christ.[42] It should be recognized that the phrase "word of God" is not limited to written revelation, but also refers to much more, including God's *power* (Gen 1:3; Pss 33:6–9; 46:6; 147:17–18; 148:8; Isa 30:30; Matt 8:8; Rom 4:17; Heb 1:3; 11:3), his *oral, authoritative speech* (Ps 147:19; Mark 1:11; John 10:35), the *content* of his revelation (Exod 9:20–21; Judg 3:20; Pss 33:4; 119:9–17; Isa 40:8; Rom 3:2), his *Trinitarian*

---

39. Gregory of Nyssa, *To Ablabius, on "Not Three Gods,"* in *NPNF*[2], 5:334.

40. Thompson, *A Clear and Present Word,* 7. See also Kevin J. Vanhoozer, *The Drama of Doctrine: A Canonical Linguistic Approach to Christian Theology* (Louisville: Westminster John Knox, 2005), 63–68.

41. Swain, *Trinity, Revelation, and Reading,* 8, 16.

42. Also consult Warfield's three stages of revelation: theophany, prophecy, and inspiration. Warfield, *Revelation and Inspiration,* in *Works of Benjamin B. Warfield,* 1:14–15.

personal presence (Deut 4:7–8; 30:11–14; Rom 10:9–10), his *Son, Christ Jesus* (John 1:1, 14–18; Rev 19:13), and his *gospel message* (Luke 5:1; John 3:34; 5:24; 6:63; 17:8–17; Acts 8:25; 13:7; 1 Thess 2:13; 1 Pet 1:25), also referred to as the *apostolic preaching of the gospel* (Acts 4:31).[43]

As we follow the many uses of God's *word*, it will become obvious that the actions performed by his word not only shed light on the character of God but also on the character of Scripture—the verbal, personal, and written *Word* of God.[44] Our approach, therefore, will situate our doctrine of Scripture in the economy of the gospel of Jesus Christ and the character of God himself.[45]

---

43. See Acts 13:5, 7; 15:36; 18:11; Col 1:5; 1 Thess 2:13; 1 Tim 6:3; 1 Pet 1:23, 25. On each of these, see Saucy, *Scripture*, 91.

44. For this reason, I will typically use "Word" to refer to Scripture, but "word" to refer to other uses. Exceptions are made when referring to Christ as the Word of God.

45. Vanhoozer, *Drama of Doctrine*, 45.

CHAPTER 5

God Speaks Covenantal Words: Creation, Fall, and the Longing for a Better Word

> And he gave to Moses . . . the two tablets of the testimony, tablets of stone, written with the finger of God.
>
> —*Exodus 31:18 ESV*

> I will raise up for them a prophet like you from among their brothers. And I will put my words in his mouth, and he shall speak to them all that I command him.
>
> —*Deuteronomy 18:18 ESV*

One blessing of living in the twenty-first century is the plethora of books available. Several of these helpfully trace key themes in the Bible from Genesis to Revelation, and utilizing the discipline of biblical theology, they track the story line of biblical history through the lens of themes—creation, judgment, temple, idolatry, mission, race, atonement, and innumerable others. But rarely will you find a biblical theology of the "word of God." While space limitations do not allow room here for an exhaustive study, nevertheless, we will attempt to lay a biblical foundation for what follows—a doctrinal articulation of the character of Holy Scripture (part 3).

In what follows, we will embark on a journey from Adam to the second Adam, and while we will touch on some of these other themes, our main focus will be how the story line of Scripture portrays the "word of God," particularly through the context of God's covenants. We will discover that the triune God speaks covenantal words, words that anticipate a better word, the Word (John 1:1). We will see that God cuts his covenants with his people by his words, and that the speech of God makes things happen. In our journey, it will also become clear

165

that God's covenantal word, both spoken and written, is authoritative, true, clear, necessary, and sufficient.

In the Beginning, God Speaks

"In the beginning God created the heavens and the earth" (Gen 1:1). At the genesis of time, what do we find? We discover that God's authoritative revelation of himself starts at the beginning of human existence. In fact, it is God's word that brings mankind into existence![1]

Genesis 1 tells us that God is the Creator of the universe, but the relevant question for our survey is, "*How* did God create?" The answer comes to us in two words: "God said" (1:3). God speaks and the universe comes into existence out of nothing. He wants light, and he gives the command: "'Let there be light,' and there was light" (1:3). He wants a canopy or expanse and gives the command: "Let there be an expanse in the midst of the waters, and let it separate the waters from the waters" (1:6 ESV). He wants plants and trees and gives the command: "Let the earth sprout vegetation, plants yielding seed, and fruit trees bearing fruit" (1:11 ESV). And to put lights in the heavens (1:14–19) and to have living creatures (1:20–25), he simply gives the command. As Psalm 33:6–9 beautifully explains:

> By the word of the LORD the heavens were made,
>   and by the breath of his mouth all their host.
> He gathers the waters of the sea as a heap;
>   he puts the deeps in storehouses.
> Let all the earth fear the LORD;
>   let all the inhabitants of the world stand in awe of him!
> For he spoke, and it came to be;
>   he commanded, and it stood firm. (ESV, emphasis added)[2]

Or, as the author of Hebrews says, "By faith we understand that the universe was created *by the word of God*" (Heb 11:3 ESV; emphasis added).[3] God's speech is powerful, creative, effective, personal, and majestic.

---

1.   N. H. Sarna, *Genesis*, The JPS Torah Commentary (Philadelphia: Jewish Publication Society of America, 1989), 7; Kenneth A. Mathews, *Genesis 1–11:26*, NAC 1A (Nashville: B&H, 1996), 145; Allen P. Ross, *Creation and Blessing: A Guide to the Study and Exposition of Genesis* (Grand Rapids: Baker Academic, 1996), 102.

2.   See also Pss 104:1–9; 119:89; 148:5; 2 Pet 3:5–7.

3.   See also Heb 1:2.

But as magnificent as light, water, and living creatures are, nothing compares to the one thing that has the privilege of being made in God's very image. The three persons of the Godhead speak and say, "Let us make man in our image, after our likeness. . . . So God created man in his own image, in the image of God he created him; male and female he created them" (Gen 1:26a, 27 ESV). Genesis 2 provides more detail: "The LORD God formed the man of dust from the ground and breathed into his nostrils the breath of life, and the man became a living creature" (2:7 ESV). The imagery used here is meant to communicate not only the power but the personal nature of God's words. His words bring life into existence and, as a result, he is completely satisfied, declaring his work of art "very good" (1:31).

Did God Actually Say?

Contrary to the deist position, God does not create the cosmos, including the first human pair, only to walk away into eternal solitude. Instead, the God of the Bible by his providential hand guides, directs, and controls the world by his word.[4] God then personally and intimately reveals himself to those made in his own image. This Creator talks!

After creating man, God spoke again, giving Adam instructions. Adam is given dominion over the created order (Gen 1:26), placed in the garden (2:8), and commanded "to work it and keep it" (2:15 ESV). Seeing that it is not good for him to be alone, God forms a woman from one of Adam's ribs (2:21–22). Notice that Adam is brought into a specific and special covenant with God from the start (Hos 6:7).[5] Though man is allowed to eat from every tree in the garden, God forbids him from eating from the tree of the knowledge of good and evil (2:17). So while God's speech creates everything good that man needs, his speech—which is clear—also warns, threatens, and promises death should they violate his command and forsake his word.[6] Will they choose life or death? This covenant of creation demonstrates that from the very beginning, God's word is to be taken seriously if man is to

---

4.   Gen 1:9–11, 22; 8:22; Pss 18:15; 29:3–9; 147:15–18; 148:6–8; Matt 8:26–27.

5.   "A *berit* is a relationship involving an oath-bound commitment" (Peter J. Gentry and Stephen J. Wellum, *Kingdom through Covenant: A Biblical-Theological Understanding of the Covenants* [Wheaton, IL: Crossway, 2012], 132).

6.   Paul House, *Old Testament Theology* (Downers Grove, IL: InterVarsity Press, 2008), 64.

remain in covenant relationship with God.[7] Obedience to the word of God results in ongoing fellowship with one's Creator, but disobedience results in separation, devastation, and disaster.

What happens next is tragic. While God's speech is true, pure, and perfect, along comes the serpent, whom Jesus called the "father of lies" (John 8:44).[8] Jesus attributed this title to Satan not only because he was a "murderer from the beginning" (8:44), but because his murder weapon was a word of deception (cf. Rom 16:20; Rev 12:9). He does not "stand in the truth," said Jesus, "because there is no truth in him. When he lies, he speaks out of his own character" (John 8:44 ESV). In contrast to the devil, God tells the truth. While the deceitfulness of the serpent's word reflects the wickedness of his character, the truthfulness of God's word reflects the purity of his character.[9]

The serpent's deception is evident in how he questions, distorts, and embellishes God's word: "Did God actually say, 'You shall not eat of any tree in the garden'?" (Gen 3:1). Already one can see his deception at work, painting God as if he had said they could not eat of any tree, when in fact God had given them great liberty to eat of every tree but one. The serpent "grossly exaggerates God's prohibition" and turns God from "beneficent provider to cruel oppressor."[10] The serpent "smuggles in the assumption that God's word is subject to our judgment."[11] Even when Eve clarifies which tree they are prohibited from touching, along with the deadly consequences that will follow should they disobey, the serpent denies the truthfulness and integrity of God's word, saying instead, "You will not surely die" (3:4 ESV). The serpent then counters God's promise with one of his own: "For God knows that when you eat of it your eyes will be opened, and you will be like God, knowing good and evil" (3:5 ESV).

The promise is enticing; Eve can liberate herself from God's oppression, gain the good God has kept from her, decide for herself what is

---

7. For a thorough defense of a covenant of works/creation, see Gentry and Wellum, *Kingdom through Covenant*, 612–18.

8. See also Isa 14:12–17; Ezek 28:2–5.

9. Scott R. Swain, *Trinity, Revelation, and Reading: A Theological Introduction to the Bible and Its Interpretation* (New York: T&T Clark, 2011), 21.

10. Victor P. Hamilton, *Book of Genesis, Chapters 1–17*, NICOT (Grand Rapids: Eerdmans, 1990), 188–89. See also Swain, *Trinity, Revelation, and Reading*, 21; Ross, *Creation and Blessing*, 135; Mathews, *Genesis 1–11:26*, 237.

11. Derek Kidner, *Genesis*, TOTC (Downers Grove, IL: IVP Academic, 1967; repr. 2008), 72.

good and evil, climb heavenward, and be more than God made her to be.[12] Seeing how "wise" the tree would make her, Eve ate, Adam followed, and together they demonstrated their neglect and mistrust of God's revelation of truth.[13] Ashamed and guilty, the couple suddenly knew whose word proved true, and it wasn't the serpent's.[14] What at first appeared to be a quest for wisdom turned out to be direct rebellion against the word of God.[15]

Too often we think of God's word in the most mechanical ways. However, God's revelation of himself is personal and relational. When Adam and Eve sinned and hid themselves from God's presence, knowing that they had distrusted God's word, the text tells us that they heard "the sound of the LORD God walking in the garden in the cool of the day" (3:8 ESV). The assumption is that the couple previously enjoyed God's presence in the garden. He was *with* them, walking alongside them. We can assume that his presence was accompanied by his words. Prior to the fall, they bathed in words of peace and friendship, but now the couple feared God's presence because they knew that with it would come words of death. And they were right. For when God calls on them, his words expose their nakedness and sinfulness. His words prove to be true, while the serpent's words prove to be false. God's words of judgment follow, cursing the woman, the serpent, and the man (3:14–19). No longer will they enjoy God's presence, but they are cast out of the garden with the promise that physical death will follow the spiritual death that has already taken root in their hearts.

But hidden in these words of condemnation are words of good news. Though he would have been perfectly just to speak only judgment, out of his grace and mercy God speaks a saving word, a gospel word that will change everything. Classically called the *protoevangelion* ("the first gospel"), God says, "I will put enmity between you and the woman, and between your offspring and her offspring; he shall bruise your head, and you shall bruise his heel" (3:15 ESV). While the serpent

---

12. Hamilton, *Book of Genesis, Chapters 1–17*, 190; Gerhard von Rad, *Genesis*, trans. J. H. Marks, OTL, rev. ed. (Philadelphia: Westminster, 1972), 89; John H. Sailhamer, "Genesis," in *Genesis–Leviticus*, ed. Tremper Longman III and David E. Garland, EBC 1 (Grand Rapids: Zondervan, 2008), 86.

13. House, *Old Testament Theology*, 64–65.

14. Mathews, *Genesis 1–11:26*, 237.

15. See Sailhamer, "Genesis," 86.

will produce offspring, so will the woman, and there will be continual enmity between the two as they wrestle for dominion.[16]

From the rest of Scripture we see the lineage of this promised seed narrowed, first to Abraham (Gen 12–15), then to the tribe of Judah (49:10–12), until we learn at the start of the New Testament that the seed or offspring of the woman who bruises the head of the serpent is ultimately found in the person of Christ (Ps 110:3, 5–6; Rom 16:20–27; 1 Cor 15:22–25; Gal 3:16; 4:4; Heb 2:14; Rev 12:1–13:1).[17] It's in these gospel words that the promise of the Word comes (John 1:1), the one who will save God's people from their sins (Matt 1:18–21) and deliver a fatal blow that crushes the head of the serpent (Col 2:15; Rev 12:7–12; 20:10). While Adam failed as an obedient covenant partner, Christ would not fail, proving God true to his promises.[18]

The story that unfolds will be one wrapped around the ongoing war between these two seeds/offspring.[19]

Revelation through Covenant

The story from Adam to Christ can be characterized by two words: *sin* and *grace*. Adam's sin ruined everything, and since Adam represented mankind, all of posterity inherited his guilt and corruption. Sadly, Adam's first sin plunged the human race into condemnation and sin (Rom 5:18–19). Not only did mankind inherit original sin, but the corruption of man's nature resulted in acts of sin as well.

Man's sinfulness is evident when we look at the history of Adam's children. Though God speaks directly to Cain, warning him not to be mastered by sin, Cain rebels, rejecting God's word, and kills his brother Abel, whose offering God had accepted (Gen 4). God confronts Cain and curses his labor, much as he did his father Adam (4:10–13). And like his father, Cain is sent away, separated from "the presence of the LORD" (4:16 ESV), though God graciously guarantees that Cain's life will be spared (4:15). As John observes, Cain and Abel picture the

---

16. Mathews, *Genesis 1–11:26*, 246.
17. T. Desmond Alexander, *From Eden to the New Jerusalem: An Introduction to Biblical Theology* (Grand Rapids: Kregel, 2008), 106; Stephen G. Dempster, *Dominion and Dynasty: A Biblical Theology of the Hebrew Bible* (Downers Grove, IL: InterVarsity Press, 2003), 68–69.
18. Gentry and Wellum, *Kingdom through Covenant*, 628.
19. Sailhamer, "Genesis," 91.

ongoing battle between the two seeds/offspring: the "children of the devil" and the "children of God" (1 John 3:10–12).[20]

Cain's rebellion is repeated in Noah's day. The Lord saw that the "wickedness of man was great in the earth, and that every intention of the thoughts of his heart was only evil continually" (Gen 6:5 ESV). So the Lord justly decided to wipe out man from the face of the earth by sending a massive flood (6:7, 17). Though sin abounds, grace abounds as well, for the Lord speaks a saving word to Noah (7:1). God had commanded Noah to build an ark to save a remnant and preserve the seed of the woman (6:13–21).[21] Unlike Cain, Noah "did everything just as God commanded him" (6:22), trusting in the word God had spoken to him.[22]

After the flood subsided, God spoke directly to Noah, but unlike before, when he had pronounced words of judgment, this time God spoke words of mercy through a covenant of his own making. Noah built an altar to the Lord and sacrificed burnt offerings whose aroma pleased the Lord. God promised never again to curse the ground or strike down every living creature (8:20–22). With arresting parallels to the creation story, God renews creation, commissioning Noah as a second Adam and charging him and his sons to multiply, fill the earth, and subdue it (9:1–7).[23] God established his covenant, promising never again to destroy the earth by flood (9:11). As a sign, God placed a bow in the sky, a visual, public, and colorful symbol of God's covenantal words of promise (9:12–17), a covenant that is "everlasting" (9:16). God put up his bow of war, promising to hold back the floodgates of destruction.[24] God demonstrated that his self-revelation is both gracious and personal.[25]

Man's rebellion against God did not cease after the flood. Lusting for fame and fearing dispersion (11:4), those at Babel began to build a great tower to heaven, an act that displayed outrageous hubris, self-exaltation, pretentious humanism, united autonomy, and rebel defiance against the Creator who had commanded man to multiply and fill the

---

20. Mathews, *Genesis 1–11:26*, 246, 248.
21. House, *Old Testament Theology*, 69.
22. Graeme Goldsworthy, *According to Plan: The Unfolding Revelation of God in the Bible* (Downers Grove, IL: IVP Academic, 1991), 114.
23. See Ross, *Creation and Blessing*, 202; Hamilton, *Book of Genesis, Chapters 1–17*, 313; Gentry and Wellum, *Kingdom through Covenant*, 629.
24. Von Rad, *Genesis*, 134; Hamilton, *Book of Genesis, Chapters 1–17*, 318.
25. House, *Old Testament Theology*, 70.

earth.[26] Authority is the issue at Babel (11:6). They desired to be God, for they rebelled against his word in their sinful efforts to seize God's authority for themselves.[27] Like Adam and Eve in Eden, those at Babel abandoned God's word and will.[28] God, bending low to "go down" to their tiny tower, confused their words and scattered them throughout the earth (11:7–9).

God Will Not Break His Covenantal Word of Promise

Though Babel resulted in mankind's dispersion throughout the earth, it is with Abraham that all of the earth would be blessed rather than cursed. The Lord came to Abraham and spoke to him directly, commanding him to leave his country and kindred and go to a land that God would show him (Gen 12:1).[29] The Lord promised to make him into a great nation, blessing him and cursing anyone who came against him (12:2–3). Through Abraham "all the families of the earth shall be blessed" (12:3 ESV).

In obedience, Abraham left Haran at the age of seventy-five, taking his wife Sarai and his brother's son Lot, setting their gaze on the land of Canaan. When he arrived, the Lord appeared again, speaking to him directly, elaborating upon his promise: "To your offspring I will give this land" (12:7), a land that would be a new Eden over which God's people would exercise dominion.[30] In Genesis 15 the "word of the LORD" came again, but this time in a vision: "Fear not, Abram, I am your shield; your reward shall be very great" (15:1). Abraham asked the Lord what he would receive since he had no heir through Sarai (15:2–3). Again, the "word of the LORD" came to him, promising that his son would be his heir.[31] Bringing him outside, the Lord showed him the stars, explaining that his offspring would be as many as

---

26. Ross, *Creation and Blessing*, 244–48; Hamilton, *Book of Genesis, Chapters 1–17*, 353–56; Geerhardus Vos, *Biblical Theology* (Grand Rapids: Eerdmans, 1948; repr., Carlisle, PA: Banner of Truth, 2004), 59; William J. Dumbrell, *Covenant and Creation: A Theology of the Old Testament Covenants* (Carlisle, UK: Paternoster, 1984), 63.

27. House, *Old Testament Theology*, 86, emphasis added.

28. Hamilton, *Book of Genesis, Chapters 1–17*, 356n.18. See also Mathews, *Genesis 1–11:26*, 467.

29. House observes how this encounter is "an act of direct, personal revelation" (*Old Testament Theology*, 72).

30. Thomas R. Schreiner, *The King in His Beauty: A Biblical Theology of the Old and New Testaments* (Grand Rapids: Baker Academic, 2013), 17.

31. Note the prophetic language used. In Genesis 20:7 Abraham is even called a prophet. See Sailhamer, "Genesis," 168.

the stars of heaven. Land, seed, universal blessing—this is the makeup of God's covenantal promises, occupying the attention of the rest of Scripture in its fulfillment with a great kingdom to come.[32]

Abraham believed the Lord. His faith was "not grounded in the old flesh of Sarah nor the tired bones of Abraham, but in the disclosing word of God."[33] Therefore, the Lord "counted it to him as righteousness" (Gen 15:6). God declared Abraham righteous not by works, but by faith (Rom 4:1–5). God's word pronounced Abraham justified in his sight. And, as Paul tells us in Romans 4:9–12, this word of justification, this "blessing," is not only for the Jew (the circumcised) but also for the Gentile (the uncircumcised). Righteousness is "counted" to both. God's "promise to Abraham and his offspring that he would be heir of the world did not come through the law but through the righteousness of faith" (Rom 4:13). Paul explains to the Galatians, "And the Scripture, foreseeing that God would justify the Gentiles by faith, preached the gospel beforehand to Abraham, saying, 'In you shall all the nations be blessed.' So then, those who are of faith are blessed along with Abraham, the man of faith" (Gal 3:8–9 ESV).

What happens next is critical to the nature of God's covenantal word. In order to reassure Abraham that God will do what he has promised, the Lord cuts a covenant with him. Typically, a covenant would be cut between a lesser ruler and a king.[34] Animals would be cut in two and it was the lesser ruler who would walk between the pieces, indicating to eyewitnesses that he would uphold his part of the pact lest he too be cut in half.[35] But what is remarkable about God's covenant with Abraham is that it is not the lesser party who walks between the bloody animals cut in two, but God himself, represented by a smoking firepot and a flaming torch, who passes between the carcasses! It is the greater party, God, who initiates the covenant and binds himself to it (Gen 15:7–21). Again, the word of God in covenantal form initiates and promises redemption. Abraham does not lift himself up to heaven, but God stoops down to Abraham and binds himself to his covenantal oath.[36]

---

32. Schreiner, *King in His Beauty*, 18.

33. Walter A. Brueggemann, *Genesis*, Interpretation (Atlanta: John Knox, 1982), 145.

34. Hamilton, *Book of Genesis, Chapters 1–17*, 430–33; Sailhamer, "Genesis," 173.

35. Gentry and Wellum, *Kingdom through Covenant*, 251.

36. Though this event emphasizes the strong unilaterial aspect of the covenant, we should not miss the conditional aspect in which God requires obedience from Abraham (Gen

We should not miss the fact that God's words in covenantal form are true words, words he promises will bring about his will. The truth of God's words to Abraham flows out of God's character. He is a God who is true and faithful, and when he makes a promise, he will fulfill his promise in every detail. His word will not return to him void. He is a God who swears by his own name, cutting his own covenant and binding himself to his own promises. The Abrahamic covenant tells us that God's word is truth, for the God of truth will see his promises fulfilled.

We should also note that the Abrahamic covenant is the first covenant where God's revelation is explicitly one of special saving grace, of God calling a specific people to himself, to be his own chosen people (Gen 17:1–14). While the word "everlasting" is used in God's covenant with both Noah and Abraham, with Abraham a special saving relationship is inaugurated between God and Abraham, his elect one. God will be God to Abraham and his offspring, a phrase that goes beyond Creator to Redeemer and Covenant Lord (17:7). God now has a specific people he will call his own—"And I will be their God" (17:8).

In the Abrahamic covenant, we see God's covenantal grace, which ultimately finds its fulfillment in Christ. As Paul explains, "Christ redeemed us from the curse of the law by becoming a curse for us—for it is written, 'Cursed is everyone who is hanged on a tree'—so that in Christ Jesus *the blessing of Abraham might come to the Gentiles*" (Gal 3:13–14 ESV). Paul tells us in Galatians 3:16 that the "offspring" or "seed" referred to is ultimately fulfilled in the coming of Christ. He is the offspring God promised to Adam in Genesis 3:15 (cf. Ps 110:1, 5–6), and he is also the promised seed who will fulfill the covenant promises made to Abraham (Acts 3:25; Gal 3:26–29; Heb 2:16).[37] Therefore, Paul can conclude that "if you are Christ's, then you are Abraham's offspring, heirs according to promise" (Gal 3:29 ESV; cf. Eph 2:11–22).

17:1; 18:19; 22:16–18). In my view, the covenants throughout Scripture have unconditional and conditional aspects to them. See Gentry and Wellum, *Kingdom through Covenant*, 634–35; House, *Old Testament Theology*, 72; Paul R. Williamson, *Sealed with an Oath: Covenant in God's Unfolding Purpose* (Downers Grove, IL: InterVarsity Press, 2007), 84–91; Schreiner, *King in His Beauty*, 44.

37. Gentry and Wellum, *Kingdom through Covenant*, 630–35.

"Thus Says the Lord"

From Abraham's line came Isaac (Gen 26:2–5), Jacob (Gen 27–35), and Joseph (Gen 37–50). Through revelation and promise, God continued to fulfill his covenant to Abraham through each of these men, sometimes in the most surprising and unthinkable ways.[38] Through these patriarchs, God repeatedly demonstrated that he was bringing to completion his promises to Abraham.[39] His word would not fail, as verified in Joseph's dying words: "I am about to die, but God will visit you and bring you up out of this land to the land that he swore to Abraham, to Isaac, and to Jacob" (50:24 ESV).

We cannot end our discussion of the Abrahamic covenant without understanding that God gave a prophetic word, specific in details that were immediately relevant to Abraham's descendants. The Lord declared to Abraham, "Know for certain that your offspring will be sojourners in a land that is not theirs and will be servants there, and they will be afflicted for four hundred years. But I will bring judgment on the nation that they serve, and afterward they shall come out with great possessions" (Gen 15:13–14 ESV). With the passing of Joseph and the multiplication of Abraham's offspring in Egypt, a nation blossoms, though in a context of severe and horrendous bondage to the pharaoh (Exod 1:8–22). Yet God's covenantal words to Abraham were not snuffed out. The Lord raised up Moses to deliver God's chosen people from the hand of this wicked, obstinate ruler. While Pharaoh no doubt thought he was in control, in light of Genesis 15:13–14, we learn that he was but a pawn in God's hand. At the proper time, God would liberate his "son" (Exod 4:22–23) in order to fulfill his promises made to Abraham, Isaac, and Jacob (3:6).

We must pause here to dwell on God's revelation of himself to Moses, one of the most amazing instances of God's direct personal speech in redemptive history. Having fled to Midian after killing an Egyptian, Moses became a shepherd. One day the "angel of the LORD appeared to him in a flame of fire out of the midst of a bush" (Exod 3:2 ESV), a bush that was not consumed. God called out to Moses from the bush and said, "'Do not come near; take your sandals off your feet, for the place on which you are standing is holy ground.' And he said,

---

38. House, *Old Testament Theology*, 78.

39. One should not overlook Genesis 35:1–15, where God blesses Jacob and reiterates his covenant promises at Bethel.

'I am the God of your father, the God of Abraham, the God of Isaac, and the God of Jacob'" (3:5–6 ESV). The God who had appeared to Abraham, Isaac, and Jacob now came face-to-face with Moses too. He is the covenant-keeping God, and Moses is the man God has chosen to bring his words of promise to fulfillment (3:7–12; 4:14–17).[40]

Unfortunately, Moses cowers at the thought of the job God has assigned to him (Exod 3:13; 4:1, 10, 13). God reassures Moses of his covenant faithfulness by revealing to Moses his divine name ("I AM WHO I AM" [3:14]) and by exhibiting his divine power through miracles (3:19–20; 4:1–9).[41] Moses is to be the mouthpiece of God, his ambassador and prophet. God will give to Moses the words he is to speak to Pharaoh (4:10–12).[42] When Moses continues to retreat in fear, the Lord reminds Moses who it was who made man's mouth, and who makes a man mute, deaf, seeing, or blind (4:11). God is in control, and what he has said he will do, he will accomplish.

Moses would learn this truth soon enough, becoming God's preeminent prophet until God would fulfill his promise to raise up a greater prophet to come. In Deuteronomy 18:18–19 we read, "I will raise up for them a prophet like you from among their brothers. And I will put my words in his mouth, and he shall speak to them all that I command him. And whoever will not listen to my words that he shall speak in my name, I myself will require it of him" (ESV). God himself puts clear, authorized words in his prophet's mouth, so that to disobey the prophet's word is to disobey God himself.[43] While a line of prophets in the heritage of Moses was appointed by God, ultimately this promise is fulfilled in the coming of the Messiah, who is not only a priest (Heb 5:5, 7–10) and king (Rom 1:3–4) but a prophet (Acts 3:22–26) who speaks the words of the Father (John 1:1).[44]

---

40. Goldsworthy, *According to Plan*, 136.

41. House, *Old Testament Theology*, 94; Schreiner, *King in His Beauty*, 29–32. On how the divine name is appealed to elsewhere, see Deut 32:39; Isa 41:4; 43:11–13; 45:18; 46:4; 48:12–13; 51:12; 52:6; Mark 14:61; John 8:24, 28, 58. See also Douglas K. Stuart, *Exodus*, NAC (Nashville: B&H, 2006), 122.

42. As the story goes on, technically it is Aaron who speaks the words God gave to Moses. Moses is like God to Aaron. See Exod 4:14–16.

43. Peter C. Craigie, *The Book of Deuteronomy*, NICOT (Grand Rapids: Eerdmans, 1976), 262; Daniel I. Block, *Deuteronomy*, NIVAC (Grand Rapids: Zondervan, 2012), 438–41; J. G. McConville, *Deuteronomy*, ApOTC 5 (Downers Grove, IL: InterVarsity Press, 2002), 303; Eugene H. Merrill, *Deuteronomy*, NAC (Nashville: B&H, 1994), 273.

44. See also John 1:21, 45; 6:14; 7:40; Acts 7:37. J. A. Thompson, *Deuteronomy*, TOTC (Downers Grove, IL: InterVarsity Press, 1974), 213.

As Moses headed back to Egypt, the Lord spoke to him again, telling Moses that he would harden Pharaoh's heart so that Pharaoh would keep refusing to let God's people go (Exod 4:21). Moses is to approach Pharaoh and perform the miracles God has put in his power. And when Pharaoh refuses, Moses is to threaten that which is most precious to him, his firstborn son. But notice how Moses is to speak to Pharaoh: "Then you shall say to Pharaoh, 'Thus says the LORD, Israel is my firstborn son, and I say to you, "Let my son go that he may serve me." If you refuse to let him go, behold, I will kill your firstborn son'" (4:22–23 ESV). "Thus says the LORD" is the phrase Moses is to use when speaking to Pharaoh. Moses is to use this phrase because it is not Moses who is commanding Pharaoh, but God himself. What Moses says, God says. To disobey Moses is to disobey God.[45]

Pharaoh does disobey, again and again, and God's word, through Moses and Aaron, brings judgment. One plague after another brought down the arrogance of Pharaoh and simultaneously displayed the power of God's hand against the Egyptian gods (Exod 7–12). The God who spoke and brought all creation into existence now spoke to unleash divine wrath. By the end of the plagues, Pharaoh and his people not only know God's voice but are begging him to speak a word of relief that they might live and not die (12:29–32).

This is a reminder that God's revelation of himself takes place not only when he speaks to an Abraham or a Moses but also in events like the plagues God brought down on the Egyptians. In his mighty acts, God is telling us about himself. He is communicating who he is through his deeds. As we will see, God reveals himself in events, but he also interprets those events for his people. He does not leave us to interpret his actions; he tells us exactly what his actions mean and how we should live in light of them.

Even before the plagues, Moses was showing a lack of faith in God's promises. When the people's work burden was increased by Pharaoh after Moses made his first request, the Israelites cried out in anger against Moses. Moses turned to the Lord and complained, "O Lord, why have you done evil to this people? Why did you ever send me?" (5:22 ESV). Even after God reiterated that he would fulfill his covenant promises to Abraham by bringing the Israelites into the land he

---

45. This same phrase will be used by God's prophets (Amos 1:3). See R. Alan Cole, *Exodus*, TOTC (Downers Grove, IL: InterVarsity Press, 1973), 80; Stuart, *Exodus*, 160.

had promised them as his people (6:2–9), Moses doubted. He said to God, "Behold, the people of Israel have not listened to me. How then shall Pharaoh listen to me, for I am of uncircumcised lips?" (6:12; cf. 6:30). What Moses failed to understand was that deliverance from Pharaoh was not dependent on his "uncircumcised lips" but on the lips of Almighty God. At God's word Pharaoh would bend and obey, for with the word of the Lord comes the presence and power of the Lord, and no one can thwart his will.

When God delivered his people from Egypt, he did not do so because the Israelites were better than the Egyptians (cf. Deut 7:6–11; 9:1–12). Even when God unleashed the tenth and final plague, the death of the firstborns, the Israelites would come under the wrath of the angel of death unless atonement was made. Once again, God spoke a word of mercy and grace. He commanded every household in Israel to slaughter a lamb without blemish and spread its blood over the doorposts, so that when the Lord passed through in judgment he would pass over the houses painted by this blood sacrifice (Exod 12:1–13). Here was a picture of what was to come, namely, the spotless, sinless lamb of God, Christ Jesus, who would one day take away the sins of the world (John 1:29; 1 Cor 5:7).[46]

God Writes with His Own Finger

Israel's exodus from Egypt is a story that puts on full display the mighty power of God's word. He delivers his people by bringing plagues on the Egyptians, guides them by pillars of cloud and fire, and when it looks as if there is no escape, he divides the Red Sea so that his people can pass into safety (Exod 14). The Lord hardens the "hearts of the Egyptians" so that he receives "glory through Pharaoh and all his army, through his chariots and his horsemen" by their destruction in the Red Sea (14:17; cf. 15:1). God's covenantal promises to Abraham are being fulfilled as Israel will be God's treasured possession, a kingdom of priests and a holy nation (19:6; cf. Gen 12:1–9).

When the Lord brought Israel out of Egypt and into the wilderness, he led them to Mount Sinai. There Moses met with God one-on-one. The Lord promised the Israelites, "You will indeed obey my voice and keep my covenant, you shall be my treasured possession among all peoples" (Exod 19:5 ESV). Moses then set before Israel everything

---

46. Alexander, *From Eden to the New Jerusalem*, 121–37; Schreiner, *King in His Beauty*, 34.

the Lord commanded, and the people answered, "All that the LORD has spoken we will do" (19:8 ESV). When Moses reported back to the Lord the people's answer, the Lord said, "Behold, I am coming to you in a thick cloud, that the people may hear when I speak with you, and may also believe you forever" (19:9).[47] On the third day, the people stood at the foot of the mountain, and God descended on it in fire and smoke (19:18). It was clear that when Moses came down to speak to the people, he was speaking the very words of God. By listening to Moses, they were listening to God.[48]

At the top of the mountain, God gave Moses the Ten Commandments (20:1–21). These commandments were written on two tablets of stone, and for the first time the people of God had the Word of God in *written* form (cf. 24:3–4).[49] What is astonishing about this account is that not only were God's words written down, but God himself did the writing. "And he gave to Moses, when he had finished speaking with him on Mount Sanai, the two tablets of the testimony, tablets of stone, written with the finger of God" (31:18 ESV; cf. 24:12; 32:16, 19; 34:1, 27–29). These tablets of the testimony do not come to Israel centuries later as man-made attempts to write out laws for governing the people. Instead, in one direct and instantaneous act, God writes his laws on stone with his own finger and then gives them to his servant Moses. It's hard to think of a more direct form of verbal and written inspiration than this!

Tragically, even while Moses was in the very presence of God, receiving the very words of God from the very finger of God, the people were violating the very laws they were about to receive. They were erecting a golden calf, a god made by their own hands (Exod 32). In their worship of this lifeless god of gold, they spoke words of blasphemy: "These are your gods, O Israel, who brought you up out of the land of Egypt!" (32:4 ESV). Israel had exchanged the Word of God, given to Moses on Sinai, for words of idolatry, betraying the one, true, and living God who had brought them up out of Egypt (20:2). Already they had violated God's commandments: "You shall have no other gods before me," and "You shall not make for yourself a carved

---

47. Cole, *Exodus*, 146. See also Stuart, *Exodus*, 424.

48. Moses's authority seems to be alluded to and assumed in John 5:45–47 and Luke 16:29–31. John Frame, *The Doctrine of the Word of God* (Phillipsburg, NJ: P&R, 2010), 548.

49. House, *Old Testament Theology*, 115–16.

image" (20:3–4 ESV). Israel had bucked divine authority in her human autonomy and idolatry.

Clearly Israel could not keep the law, which only served to expose her sinfulness. Though holy and righteous (Rom 7:12), the law could not save due to man's sin (Deut 27:26; Gal 3:10–12).[50] Israel was "held captive under the law," imprisoned by it (Gal 3:23 ESV; cf. Rom 3:19–20; Gal 3:10; Col 2:14). Therefore, the law proved to be a "guardian" until the coming of Christ "in order that we might be justified by faith" (Gal 3:24 ESV; cf. Rom 3:21–31). Israel's rebellion against God's law demonstrated that what they desperately needed was one who could obey the law and do so in their place. Such a law-keeper, however, would come only in Christ (Gal 3:21–22), God's faithful and obedient Son.

Holy Word, Holy Ark, Holy Place

Before we move on, it is crucial to observe that God intended his written Word to be reverenced as *holy*. Because its author is holy, the text is holy too. When Moses approached the burning bush, he had to take off his sandals. Why? Since the holy God is present (and speaking!), the ground beneath the bush is holy ground. How much more so, then, with the written Word, which is God's own words.

This covenant Word written on tablets of stone was not only permanent but holy and had to be placed in the holiest location, namely, the ark of the covenant (Deut 10:5; 1 Kgs 8:9). The "Book of the Law" was placed next to the ark (Deut 31:26 ESV), which sat in the Most Holy Place (Heb 9:3–4), the "focal point of the Lord's residence among his people."[51] The ark was "the most intense manifestation of God's presence."[52] On top of this "ark of the testimony" was the mercy seat, and it was there, between the two cherubim, that the Lord met with Moses and spoke to him (Exod 25:20–22).[53]

The sacred location of God's written tablets demonstrates not only that these words were covenant words but that they were written by God himself and must be placed in and beside the holy ark, in a holy

---

50. Gentry and Wellum, *Kingdom through Covenant*, 639.

51. Merrill, *Deuteronomy*, 404. See also Alexander, *From Eden to the New Jerusalem*, 32–33 (cf. 87).

52. John Frame, *Systematic Theology* (Phillipsburg, NJ: P&R, 2013), 566. See also McConville, *Deuteronomy*, 443.

53. Cf. Exod 30:6; 38:21; 39:35; 40:20; Num 4:5; 7:89; Deut 10:5; 31:26; Heb 9:4.

sanctuary, and touched only by a holy priest (Deut 31:9).[54] There they lay as God's written testimony and witness—indeed, God's holy constitution—for his people and against his people, should they disobey (Deut 31:26–28).[55] It makes sense that Paul, in 2 Timothy 3:15, would call the Old Testament the "sacred writings."

God's Word Is Near You

The rest of the history of Israel is one sad story after another, painfully demonstrating that Israel stubbornly refused to obey God's law or keep her end of the covenant. While God continues to keep his word, Israel fails to keep her word. God's law is a gift to his people, intended to lead them in righteousness and holiness, in purity and uprightness (Lev 11:44–45).[56] The tabernacle—wherein God dwells among his people—is built to provide, among other things, a system of offerings and sacrifices for the sins of the people, mediated by priests from the tribe of Levi (e.g., Exod 38–40; Lev 1–11; 16–17; 21–22).[57] God instructed his people to be holy as he is holy by keeping his rules and doing them, separating themselves from the other nations and their gods, as a people set apart and holy unto the Lord (Lev 19:1–37; 20:22–26). If they obey, there would be blessing (Lev 26:1–13), but if they disobey, punishment (Lev 26:14–39). The story of Israel unfolds the reality that characterizes this stiff-necked people. Though they have God's Word in the law, written on tablets of stone, what they need is God's Word written on their hearts instead (Jer 31:31–34; Ezek 11:19; 36:27).

The stubborn heart of that generation of Israelites culminated in their refusal to enter the Promised Land (Deut 1:1–33). Fearing man instead of God, the people rebel and fail to trust in God's word of promise. As a punishment, that generation never saw the land of promise (Deut 1:34–40). It would be the next generation who would enter the land (Deut 31:1–8; Josh 1).

---

54. Note how the psalmist praises God's word (Ps 56:4, 10), lifts up his hands toward God's commandments (Ps 119:48), stands in awe of God's word (Ps 119:161), and rejoices in God's word (Ps 119:161). Frame, *Systematic Theology*, 573.

55. McConville, *Deuteronomy*, 442; Block, *Deuteronomy*, 732; Frame, *Doctrine of the Word of God*, 108–9; House, *Old Testament Theology*, 194, 196. Kline observes how the two tablets were duplicate copies of the covenant in order to act as a legal, documentary witness to and against Israel. Meredith G. Kline, *The Structure of Biblical Authority*, 2nd ed. (Eugene, OR: Wipf & Stock, 1997), 121–25.

56. See also Lev 19:34–36; 22:31–33; 23:43; 25:38, 42, 55; 26:12–14, 45. Goldsworthy, *According to Plan*, 145.

57. Ibid., 144.

But with the transition from Moses to Joshua, the Lord says something through Moses to Israel that gives us a more vivid picture of how God's Word will work. In Deuteronomy 30, God promises that he "will circumcise your heart and the heart of your offspring, so that you will love the LORD your God with all your heart and with all your soul, that you may live" (30:6 ESV). With such a circumcised heart in mind, the Lord then says that his commandment "is not too hard," nor is it "far off" (30:11 ESV). "It is not in heaven, that you should say, 'Who will ascend to heaven for us and bring it to us, that we may hear it and do it?' Neither is it beyond the sea, that you should say, 'Who will go over the sea for us and bring it to us, that we may hear it and do it?' But the word is very near you. It is in your mouth and in your heart, so that you can do it" (30:12–14 ESV).

These questions presuppose that God's Word is inaccessible, remote, abstract, esoteric, unknowable, unreasonable, incomprehensible, impossible, and burdensome.[58] God rejects such excuses. Man does not have to climb up to heaven or travel across an ocean. God initiates, coming directly to man, delivering his divine words in all their clarity, sufficiency, and perfection. God has bowed low, as a Father does to his child, in order to tell Israel exactly what is required of them and the consequences that will occur depending on whether they obey or disobey (30:15–20).

The apostle Paul gives us further insight. Quoting Deuteronomy 30:11–14 in Romans 10:5–9, Paul connects everything to Christ. We do not have to ascend into heaven to bring Christ down or descend into the abyss to bring Christ up from the dead. God has done this for us. He has sent Christ (Immanuel; Matt 1:23) down to us to take on our human nature and has raised his Son from the dead, giving us victory in Christ and newness of life.[59] Therefore, says Paul, when God says in Deuteronomy 30:14 that the "word is very near you; it is in your mouth and in your heart," such a promise finds its fulfillment in the word of faith that Paul is proclaiming. The gospel of Jesus Christ is preached and those who confess and believe are saved (Rom 10:9).[60] The gospel

---

58. Merrill, *Deuteronomy*, 391; Block, *Deuteronomy*, 706–7; Frame, *Doctrine of the Word of God*, 208.

59. See Block, *Deuteronomy*, 714.

60. "Is Paul distorting the meaning of Deuteronomy 30:11–14? Superficially, it would seem that Moses' words speak of legal obedience, but Paul uses them to speak of grace. But recall that (1) the law itself proclaims the righteousness and grace of Christ (John 5:39–40). And (2) Deuteronomy 30 itself counsels Israel to rely, not on their own strenuous efforts, but on God's grace in bringing the Word near them, most significantly into their hearts" (Frame,

reminds us that God has come down to us and made his word clear, speaking as a Father would to his child (i.e., baby talk, as Calvin liked to say), so that blind eyes are opened to the glory of his Son.

Not One Word of God Has Failed

Israel did not enter into the lavish land of Canaan under Moses, but rather under Joshua, the new Moses. God told Joshua not only to be strong and courageous, but he warned Joshua to be careful to do all that was in the law of Moses, not letting the "Book of the Law" depart from his mouth. Joshua was to meditate on it day and night (Josh 1:7–8).[61]

As with Moses, God continued to reveal himself to Joshua, speaking to him, performing numerous mighty acts, and delivering Israel from her enemies (Josh 6, 8). God also renewed his covenant with Moses through Joshua, who engraved on stones a copy of the law (Josh 8:30–35). The people were reminded once again of the blessings or curses that would follow depending upon their obedience to the Torah. God's Word was in written form and was read to the people, reminding them that to disobey God's Word was to disobey God himself. Naturally, then, *every word and every detail* must be taken with utmost seriousness. No wonder Joshua read "all the words of the law," and there "was not a word of all that Moses commanded that Joshua did not read before all the assembly of Israel" (Josh 8:34–35 ESV).

Before Joshua went the way of his fathers, he reminded Israel that "not one word [of God] has failed of all the good things that the LORD your God promised concerning you" (Josh 23:14 ESV). In other words, God's Word has not miscarried. He is a God of truth, and he has been true to his word. This is reassuring and also frightening. It is reassuring because just as God has been true to his word in the past, so will he be true to his word in the future if Israel walks in uprightness. Yet God will be just as true to his promise to bring curses upon Israel if she transgresses the covenant (Josh 8:15–16).

The Word of the Lord Was Rare in Those Days

Though God continued to reveal himself not only through his words but also through his mighty acts of deliverance, Israel was on

---

Doctrine of the Word of God, 208–9). See also Block, *Deuteronomy*, 714–15.

61. On the "Book of the Law," see Deut 28:58; 29:21; 30:10; 31:26. See Robert L. Hubbard Jr., *Joshua*, NIVAC (Grand Rapids: Zondervan, 2009), 81–82.

a path to disobedience, with all the curses God promised to follow. Of course, even when Joshua renewed the covenant before his death, laying before Israel life and death, he made it clear that Israel could not obey. "You are not able to serve the LORD, for he is a holy God. He is a jealous God; he will not forgive your transgressions or your sins" (Josh 24:19 ESV). Israel's rebellion becomes painfully obvious during the time of the judges. We read in Judges 2:11–12 ESV, "And the people of Israel did what was evil in the sight of the LORD and served the Baals. And they abandoned the LORD, the God of their fathers, who had brought them out of the land of Egypt. They went after other gods, from among the gods of the peoples who were around them, and bowed down to them." They provoked God's anger against them, and just as he had "sworn to them," he gave them over to their enemies so that they were in "terrible distress" (2:15 ESV). Again, God remained faithful to his word. The last verse of Judges summarizes the situation: "In those days there was no king in Israel. Everyone did what was right in his own eyes" (21:25 ESV).

What is so remarkable is that even in spite of Israel's covenant-breaking idolatry, the Lord does not remain silent. The Lord takes a barren, childless woman named Hannah and blesses her with a child who will grow up for the purpose of serving the Lord (1 Sam 1:1–20). The Lord hears her cries and provides a son, Samuel. Faithful to her promise, Hannah devotes Samuel to the service of the Lord, taking him to Eli at Shiloh so that he would "appear in the presence of the LORD and dwell there forever" (1:22 ESV). Hannah's husband, Elkanah, recognizes that the Lord is establishing "his word" (1:23 ESV). They give Samuel to Eli the priest to serve the Lord, and Hannah recognizes that the Lord is one who keeps his promises, and Hannah kept her promise to give her child back to the Lord (1:11, 26–28).

As the story of Samuel unfolds, it is indisputable that he is the Lord's chosen priest and prophet in Israel. Even when Samuel was a young man ministering before the Lord under Eli, the Lord sent for him, revealing himself to Samuel in a special way. We read in 1 Samuel 3:1 that the "word of the LORD was rare in those days; there was no frequent vision" (ESV). Unquestionably, this was due to the sin of the people, which is especially seen in Eli's sons, who were leading the people into immorality, "blaspheming God" (3:13 ESV). When the Lord chose to be silent no longer, it was to Samuel that he "revealed himself . . .

by the word of the LORD" (3:21). True to the role of prophet, Samuel became the messenger and mouthpiece of God, declaring God's words to God's people.[62]

For instance, when the people cry out for a king, desiring to be like the other nations (1 Sam 8:19; 12:12), rejecting God as their king (8:7; 10:18–19), it is Samuel the Lord sends to anoint Saul as king. With Samuel, the Lord spoke directly (e.g., 8:6–9), giving him instructions for how to proceed with the Israelites, who had forsaken the Lord to serve other gods (8:8). So identical are the prophet's words with the Lord's words that to disobey Samuel and rebel against his word is to disobey the Lord. Samuel is the prophetic mediator, relaying the people's words to God and God's words to the people (8:21–22).

As a result, Saul is anointed king, but it turns out that Saul, as an offspring of the serpent, is a king who does not listen and obey the words of the Lord as the prophet Samuel does (e.g., 1 Sam 13:8–23; 14:24–46; 15:10–35). When Saul fails to listen and obey the Lord, Samuel declares that the Lord has rejected Saul as king because he has "rejected the word of the LORD" (15:23 ESV). Saul failed to obey the "voice of the LORD" through the prophet Samuel (15:19 ESV).[63] Again, Samuel's voice and the Lord's voice are equated with one another. To reject the words of God's prophet is to reject the very words of God.

By now, you are likely feeling the dreary repetition of Israel's rejection of God's Word (and it will be felt again as we move forward). No doubt, the story feels depressing, and we are not yet finished. Nevertheless, it is crucial for us to understand the entire biblical story in order to feel the full effect of this malaise. Only then will we understand how desperately we need a better, saving Word from God.

The Word of the Lord Proves True and Pure

Due to Saul's disobedience, the Lord raises up a new king, a king after his own heart, one who will exercise righteous dominion over the land. Unlike Saul, David is an offspring of the woman (Gen 3:15), for he believes God's Word and takes it seriously.[64] When Goliath defies

---

62. David T. Tsumura, *The First Book of Samuel*, NICOT (Grand Rapids: Eerdmans, 2007), 174.

63. Robert D. Bergen, *1, 2 Samuel*, NAC (Nashville: B&H, 1996), 173; House, *Old Testament Theology*, 234, 236.

64. Schreiner, *King in His Beauty*, 148.

the armies of the living God (1 Sam 17:26), David takes him on with much confidence because he knows that Goliath is no match for the God of Israel, who will not abandon his covenant people (17:45–47).

Though David had many shortcomings that resulted in great tragedy (e.g., 2 Sam 11–12; 24), unlike Saul, David's reign as a whole is characterized by his attention to the word of God. Here is a king who submits himself to God's three commands in Deuteronomy 17: (1) the king is to copy the Torah (17:18), (2) the king is to keep the Torah with him (17:19), and (3) the king is to read the Torah so that he "may learn to fear the LORD his God by keeping all the words of this law and these statutes, and doing them" (17:19).[65]

For example, consider the following psalms that highlight the character and nature of God's word as well as David's reverence for God's word:

> This God—his way is perfect;
>> the word of the LORD proves true;
>> he is a shield for all those who take refuge in him.
>> (2 Sam 22:31; Ps 18:30 ESV)

> Blessed is the man
> who walks not in the counsel of the wicked . . .
> but his delight is in the law of the LORD,
>> and on his law he meditates day and night.
>> (Ps 1:1–2 ESV)

> The words of the LORD are pure words,
>> like silver refined in a furnace on the ground,
>> purified seven times.
> You, O LORD, will keep them;
>> you will guard us from this generation forever.
>> (Ps 12:6–7 ESV)

> For I have kept the ways of the LORD,
>> and have not wickedly departed from my God.
> For all his rules were before me,
>> and his statutes I did not put away from me.
>> (Ps 18:21–22 ESV)

---

65. Peter J. Gentry and Stephen J. Wellum, *God's Kingdom through God's Covenant: A Concise Biblical Theology* (Wheaton, IL: Crossway, 2015), 195.

> The law of the LORD is perfect,
>> reviving the soul;
> the testimony of the LORD is sure,
>> making wise the simple;
> the precepts of the LORD are right,
>> rejoicing the heart;
> the commandment of the LORD is pure,
>> enlightening the eyes; . . .
> the rules of the LORD are true,
>> and righteous altogether.
> More to be desired are they than gold,
>> even much fine gold;
> sweeter also than honey
>> and drippings from the honeycomb.
> Moreover, by them is your servant warned;
>> in keeping them there is great reward.
>> (Ps 19:7–11 ESV)

> The voice of the LORD is powerful;
>> the voice of the LORD is full of majesty.
>> (Ps 29:4 ESV)

Perfect, true, righteous, sweet, powerful, majestic—all of these words are used by David to describe God's word. And notice the connection between God and his word.[66] Since God is a perfect God, his word is true and one that proves true rather than false.

Consider a few more psalms (and proverbs) that emphasize the righteousness, truthfulness, trustworthiness, purity, perfection, eternality, and power of God's word:

> For the word of the LORD is upright,
>> and all his work is done in faithfulness.
> He loves righteousness and justice;
>> the earth is full of the steadfast love of the LORD.
> By the word of the LORD the heavens were made,
>> and by the breath of his mouth all their host.
>> (Ps 33:4–6 ESV)

---

66. It is worth noting how many times David calls out to the Lord, even cries out to the Lord, and the Lord answers David: Pss 3:4; 4:3; 6:8–9; 16:7, 11; 17:6; 18:3, 6; 20:6; 28:6; 31:22; 32:5; 34:4, 6, 17; 55:16; 57:2; 61:1–3, 5; 86:1–7; 145:18.

He remembers his covenant forever,
>   the word that he commanded, for a thousand generations,
the covenant that he made with Abraham,
>   his sworn promise to Isaac,
which he confirmed to Jacob as a statute,
>   to Israel as an everlasting covenant. (Ps 105:8–10 ESV)

The works of his hands are faithful and just;
>   all his precepts are trustworthy;
they are established forever and ever,
>   to be performed with faithfulness and uprightness.
>   (Ps 111:7–8 ESV)

All your commandments are sure. (Ps 119:86 ESV)

Forever, O LORD, your word
>   is firmly fixed in the heavens. (Ps 119:89 ESV)

I will never forget your precepts,
>   for by them you have given me life. (Ps 119:93 ESV)

Your word is a lamp to my feet
>   and a light to my path. (Ps 119:105 ESV)

Your testimonies are wonderful;
>   therefore my soul keeps them. (Ps 119:129 ESV)

The sum of your word is truth,
>   and every one of your righteous rules endures forever.
>   (Ps 119:160 ESV)

Every word of God proves true;
>   he is a shield to those who take refuge in him.
>   (Prov 30:5 ESV)

According to the books of Psalms and Proverbs, God's Word, not only in its oral form but in its *written form* as well, is flawless, is trustworthy, gives life, and guides (cf. Pss 18:30; 78:5–7; 111:7).[67] It is wonderful and righteous, and it is truth, truth that endures forever. And because it proves true, God's people can find assurance in the Word God has spoken and written down.[68]

---

67. Frame, *Doctrine of the Word of God*, 116.
68. Allan Harman, *Psalms: Volume 1: Psalms 1–72* (Fearn, Ross-shire, Scotland:

Kingdom through Covenantal Words

We see many of these attributes at work when God makes a covenant with David in 2 Samuel 7 (cf. Ps 89:3–4), which expands on God's covenant with Abraham.[69] David will later reflect on this covenant, saying, "For he has made with me an everlasting covenant, ordered in all things and secure" (2 Sam 23:5). What does this covenant with David look like? It is a covenant in which God, through his prophet Nathan, speaks words of promise to David. David thinks he will build a house for the Lord, but to his surprise the Lord says he will build a house for David (7:11). "When your days are fulfilled and you lie down with your fathers, I will raise up your offspring after you, who shall come from your body, and I will establish his kingdom. He shall build a house for my name, and I will establish the throne of his kingdom forever. I will be to him a father, and he shall be to me a son" (7:12–14). This promise begins to sprout and blossom with the rise of Solomon (1 Kgs 3:6; Acts 7:47), who prays that Yahweh would remember his covenant faithfulness to his father David (2 Chron 1:8; 6:42), builds the temple, reigns over the kingdom with wisdom (1 Kgs 8:17–21, 24–26), and gives Israel rest in the Edenic land where God dwells.[70]

However, this kingdom promise, which expresses Yahweh's "covenant loyalty" (Ps 89:33; cf. Ps 132:8–12), finds its ultimate fulfillment in Christ, the royal son of David (Matt 1:1; Mark 10:47; Luke 1:32–33; Acts 2:29–30; 4:23–30; 13:23; Heb 1:5). Solomon's kingdom is but a type of the kingdom that is made "sure forever" and the King whose reign the Father "established forever" (2 Sam 7:16 ESV).[71] Jesus is the son, king, and seed/offspring who mediates, administers, and inaugurates the new covenant, thereby fulfilling God's covenant promises not only to David (Pss 2; 8; 45; 72; Isa 52:13–53:12; 55:3) but to Abraham (Gen 15:4) and Adam as well (Gen 3:15).[72] As Jesus himself indicates, he will build the temple (Matt 26:61; 27:40; Mark 14:58; 15:29; John 2:19–22; Heb 3:3), sit on the eternal throne (Matt

---

Christian Focus, 2011), 283; Willem A. VanGemeren, *Psalms*, rev. ed., EBC 5 (Grand Rapids: Zondervan, 2008), 319.

69. Schreiner, *King in His Beauty*, 157.

70. Ibid., 169.

71. Also consult Exod 4:22–23; 1 Chr 17:11–14; 2 Chr 13:5; 21:7; Pss 2:7–9; 89:3, 20–38; 132:11; Isa 55:3; Jer 33:17–22.

72. See Gentry and Wellum, *Kingdom through Covenant*, 640–44.

19:28–29), and rule over God's eternal kingdom and royal dynasty (Luke 22:29–30; John 18:36; Heb 1:8; Rev 19:11–16), thereby fulfilling God's covenantal word.[73]

How did David respond to this covenantal word of promise? David was humbled, and he recognized that God would accomplish what he had promised (2 Sam 7:18–29). So he praised the Lord, saying, "And now, O Lord GOD, you are God, and *your words are true*, and you have promised this good thing to your servant" (7:28 ESV). Solomon said the same: "Blessed be the LORD who has given rest to his people Israel, according to all that he promised. *Not one word has failed of all his good promise*, which he spoke by Moses his servant" (1 Kgs 8:56 ESV, emphasis added). God's words are true words. Not one of them will prove false. His words of promise will not fail.

They Did Not Obey the Voice of the Lord

Sadly, unlike King Jesus to come, King Solomon fell short just like his father David, and turned from the Lord (1 Kgs 11:1–8). His idolatry brought upon Israel the curses God had promised should he disobey (9:6–9; 11:9–43; cf. 2 Sam 7:14–15). In time, the kingdom was divided (1 Kgs 12:16–24). Whether the kings of Israel or Judah, few kings would follow the Lord, and even those who tried did not follow the Lord entirely.[74] But even in the midst of the wickedness of these kings, God was not silent, but spoke through his prophets Elijah (1 Kgs 17–19; 2 Kgs 1–2) and Elisha (1 Kgs 19:19–21; 2 Kgs 2–7). With Elijah and Elisha, God spoke directly (e.g., 1 Kgs 19:9–19), and in turn they communicated God's message to his people, a message that was sometimes accompanied by miracles and at other times filled with doom and gloom.

One king who stands out in a long line of ungodly kings is Josiah. Though only eight years old when he became king of Judah, his years as king were characterized by obedience, for he "did what was right in the eyes of the LORD and walked in all the way of David his father, and he did not turn aside to the right or to the left" (2 Kgs 22:2). When Josiah repaired the Lord's temple, Hilkiah rediscovered the

---

73. Bergen, *1, 2 Samuel*, 340; David G. Firth, *1 and 2 Samuel*, ApOTC (Downers Grove, IL: InterVarsity Press, 2009), 387–88; House, *Old Testament Theology*, 242–43.

74. For example, see kings such as Asa (1 Kgs 15:9–24), Jehoshaphat (1 Kgs 22:41–50), Hezekiah (2 Kgs 18–20), and Josiah (2 Kgs 22:11–23:30).

"Book of the Law" (22:8). So far had God's people strayed from the Lord that even the law was lost, which meant that it was not read, and if not read how could it be obeyed?[75] Considering the idolatry of the kings who preceded Josiah, especially Manasseh and Amon (2 Kgs 21), this neglect of God's law is not surprising. When Hilkiah found the book and sent Shaphan to read its words to the king, Josiah "tore his clothes" (22:11 ESV). He commanded Hilkiah the priest and the others, "Go, inquire of the LORD for me, and for the people, and for all Judah, concerning the words of this book that has been found. For great is the wrath of the LORD that is kindled against us, because our fathers have not obeyed the words of this book, to do according to all that is written concerning us" (22:13 ESV). The Lord then spoke through the prophetess Huldah, stating that disaster was coming because the people "have forsaken me and have made offerings to other gods" (22:17 ESV). However, the Lord told Josiah that because his "heart was penitent, and you humbled yourself before the LORD . . . you shall be gathered to your grave in peace, and your eyes shall not see all the disaster that I will bring upon this place" (22:19–20).

Josiah, hearing this word from the Lord, ignited a reformation, a return to the Word of God. Josiah went "up to the house of the LORD, and with him all the men of Judah and all the inhabitants of Jerusalem and the priests and the prophets, all the people, both small and great," and he "read in their hearing all the words of the Book of the Covenant that had been found in the house of the LORD" (23:2). Josiah then "made a covenant before the LORD, to walk after the LORD and to keep his commandments and his testimonies and his statutes with all his heart and all his soul, to perform the words of this covenant that were written in this book" (23:3 ESV). Josiah did what so many before him would not do; he took out of the temple all the vessels made for Baal and Asherah, and he burned them outside Jerusalem (23:4). He "broke down the houses of the male cult prostitutes who were in the house of the LORD, where the women wove hangings for the Asherah" and "defiled the high places where the priests had made offerings" (23:7, 8 ESV). Josiah also restored the Passover, for just as the Book of the Law had been lost, so also the Passover had not

75. Commentators are divided as to whether it was literally lost or just neglected. Either way, the Word did not have the present and active role it was supposed to have.

been practiced "since the days of the judges who judged Israel" (23:22 ESV). Indeed, when the Word of God was ignored and rejected, so also were its commandments. Josiah did not merely destroy all of the false idols. In their place he established "the words of the law that were written in the book" (23:24 ESV). No king like Josiah came before him, and no king like Josiah came after him until the arrival of King Jesus.

Though there were small shimmers of light over the centuries that followed, the story of Israel during the reign of the kings was primarily one tragedy after another. Justifiably, the wrath of God burned hot against his people, who had rejected his Word (and therefore rejected him), turning to false idols instead. The sin and idolatry of God's people resulted in Israel, like Adam, being expelled from the land, cast into exile just as God promised (2 Kgs 17:7–19).[76] First, Samaria fell to Assyria (2 Kgs 17:6), and then Judah fell to Babylon (2 Kgs 25). Why did they fall to their enemies? Why did God give them into the hands of their oppressors? They fell because they turned from the Lord and served idols. They failed to listen and obey the Word of the Lord and "believe in the LORD their God" (17:14 ESV). When 2 Kings 18:11–12 describes why the Israelites were carried away to Assyria, it says that it was because "they did not obey the voice of the LORD their God, but transgressed his covenant, even all that Moses the servant of the LORD commanded. They neither listened nor obeyed" (18:12 ESV). The same can be said regarding the captivity of Judah, whose idolatry resulted in Nebuchadnezzar, king of Babylon, burning down the temple and carrying the people away in chains to Babylon (2 Chr 36). Just before Nebuchadnezzar's siege of the temple, we read that even then the Lord had compassion and sent his messengers to his people. However, they "kept mocking the messengers of God, despising his words and scoffing at his prophets, until the wrath of the LORD rose against his people, until there was no remedy" (2 Chr 36:15–16). So connected was God to his Word that when his words were despised, God himself was offended.

Was all of this a surprise to the Lord? By no means. The Lord himself had brought Israel's enemies against her. Moreover, the Lord had sent his prophets, warning her of the destruction to come.

---

76. Schreiner, *King in His Beauty*, 100, 119.

I Am Watching Over My Word to Perform It: The Prophetic Word

At this point, we must take a more careful look at the prophets, major and minor, who spoke on behalf of God, especially in regard to their God-appointed role and function. The prophets were chosen by God to be the mouth and voice of God to the people of God.[77] What the prophet said, God said. The prophet announced, "Thus says the LORD," and obedience or disobedience to his words was obedience or disobedience to God.[78] For example, the opening chapter of Jeremiah reads:

> Now the word of the LORD came to me, saying,
>
>> "Before I formed you in the womb I knew you,
>> and before you were born I consecrated you;
>> I appointed you a prophet to the nations." (Jer 1:4–5 ESV)

Even when Jeremiah responds, as Moses did, out of fear, "I do not know how to speak, for I am only a youth" (1:6 ESV), the Lord reminds Jeremiah that it is not his word that he will deliver to the people but God's word, and therefore he should not be afraid:

> But the LORD said to me,
>
>> "Do not say, 'I am only a youth';
>> for to all to whom I send you, you shall go,
>> and whatever I command you, you shall speak.
>> Do not be afraid of them,
>> for I am with you to deliver you,
>>> declares the LORD." (Jer 1:7–8 ESV)

The text then says that the Lord "put out his hand and touched" Jeremiah's mouth, saying, "Behold, I have put my words in your mouth. . . . I am watching over my word to perform it" (1:9b, 12 ESV). Certainly any shortcoming in the humanity of Jeremiah was overcome because it was God who made sure his word was completely, satisfactorily, and truthfully communicated.[79]

---

77. Vos, *Biblical Theology*, 193; Bruce K. Waltke, *An Old Testament Theology: An Exegetical, Canonical, and Thematic Approach* (Grand Rapids: Zondervan, 2007), 805; House, *Old Testament Theology*, 185, 251.

78. Note the similarity between apostles and prophets in this regard. Swain, *Trinity, Revelation, and Reading*, 38; John Webster, *Holy Scripture: A Dogmatics Sketch* (Cambridge: Cambridge University Press, 2003), 9. For an extended treatment of the role of the prophets, see Edward E. Young, *My Servants the Prophets* (Grand Rapids: Eerdmans, 1985).

79. For an extensive study, see Andrew G. Shead, *A Mouth Full of Fire: The Word of God*

Consider Ezekiel, to whom the Lord gave a scroll of a book, with words of lamentation, mourning, and woe, only to then command him to eat the scroll, leaving Ezekiel with a sweet taste in his mouth (Ezek 2:7–10; 3:1–3). Ezekiel is then told to go to the house of Israel and "speak with my words to them" (3:4; cf. 3:10–11). Ezekiel demonstrates that when the prophets spoke, they spoke the word of God in all of its authority. God put his words in their mouths, so that their words were God's words.

Jeremiah and Ezekiel are just two examples.[80] Many other prophetic books confirm this God-appointed role as well. For example, consider how the following prophetic books begin:

The word of the LORD that came to Hosea (Hos 1:1).
The word of the LORD that came to Joel (Joel 1:1).
The word of the LORD came to Jonah (Jonah 1:1).
The word of the LORD that came to Micah (Mic 1:1).
The word of the LORD that came to Zephaniah (Zeph 1:1).
The word of the LORD came through the prophet Haggai (Hag 1:1).
The word of the LORD came to the prophet Zechariah (Zech 1:1).
A prophecy: The word of the LORD to Israel through Malachi (Mal 1:1).

When the prophets addressed the people, they used phrases like "Hear the word of the LORD" (Isa 1:10; Jer 2:4), "says the LORD" (Amos 1:5; Mal 1:2), or "Thus says the Lord GOD" (Isa 49:22 ESV). These phrases, especially the last one, were followed not merely with the prophet's words but with God's words (Amos 1:3, 6, 9, 11, 13; 2:1, 4, 6). More precisely, these phrases communicated that the prophet's words were God's words.

Consider how the prophets used such prefatory phrases, indicating that God had spoken in the first person. In Isaiah 49:22 we read, "Thus says the Lord GOD: 'Behold, I will lift up my hand to the nations, and raise my signal to the peoples'" (ESV). Isaiah was not merely reporting what God had said, but God himself was now speaking! God was addressing Israel, telling her what he would and would not do. So he spoke to them with tremendous force: "Listen to me . . ." (Isa 51:1) and

---

in the Words of Jeremiah, NSBT 29 (Downers Grove, IL: InterVarsity, 2012).
  80. Also consider Isa 8:11; Amos 3:11.

"Give attention to me, my people" (51:4 ESV). While the prophet was the messenger, the message was directly from the Lord.

The word from God through the prophets addressed Israel's present circumstances, warning and instructing them how to live in covenant relationship with Yahweh and with one another (e.g., Jer 2–6; Hosea 1–3; Amos 2:6–3:8). Given the idolatry and covenant disobedience of the people, however, the prophets also warned of God's judgment and wrath.[81] Their word from God was not limited to the present but also spoke of what was to come, predicting future events that would come to fruition, bringing God's promises to pass. And not just events but persons as well, as evident in the messianic promises sprinkled throughout the prophetic books.[82]

Those who were false prophets were known as such because they spoke "visions of their own minds, not from the mouth of the LORD" (Jer 23:16; cf. 23:26–32). Their prophetic word would prove to be untrue (Deut 18:22). When someone claimed to be a prophet and his message was false, he could not be from God. If the prophet taught the people something that contradicted God's commandments, then that prophet was false no matter how many miracles he claimed to pull off. God put his own words in the mouths of his prophets (Num 22:35; 23:5, 12, 16; Jer 1:9, 14; Isa 51:16; 59:21; Ezek 3:4), and since God's word is always true, Israel would know a false prophet from a true prophet by the accuracy (or lack thereof) of the prophet's message.[83] As Moses explained in Deuteronomy 13:1–11, if a prophet sought to persuade the people to worship other gods, he was a false prophet and should be put to death. He was one who spoke lies, the "deceit" of his own mind rather than the truth of God (Jer 14:14 ESV). He followed his own spirit and had not been sent by the Spirit of God (Ezek 13:3).[84] As the Lord asked in Ezekiel 13:7, "Have you not seen false visions and uttered lying divinations when you say, 'The LORD declares,' though I have not spoken?"

---

81. For example, Isa 1:21–31; 7:1–14; Jer 7:1–15; Hos 4:2; Ezek 8:1–18; Amos 4:6–11; cf. "day of the LORD" language: Isa 2:12–22; 13:6, 9; 24:1–23; Jer 46:10; Ezek 7; 13:5; 30:3; Joel 1:15; 2:1–11, 31; 3:14; Amos 5:18, 20; Obad 15; Zeph 1:7–18; Mal 4:5.

82. Isa 9:2–7; 11:1–16; 52:13–53:12; 61:1–3; Jer 33:14–16; Dan 7:9–14; Mic 5:1–5.

83. House, *Old Testament Theology*, 263–64; Benjamin B. Warfield, *Revelation and Inspiration*, in *The Works of Benjamin Breckinridge Warfield*, 10 vols. (repr., Grand Rapids: Baker, 2003), 1:20.

84. The prophets are spoken of as those who have the Spirit of Yahweh. See Neh 9:30; Isa 42:1; Hos 9:7; Joel 2:28–29; Mic 3:8; Zech 7:12.

The prophets also spoke about a covenant to come, a new covenant that God would cut with his people. But this covenant would be different from the Mosaic covenant. As the Lord says through Jeremiah, "It will not be like the covenant I made with their ancestors when I took them by the hand to lead them out of Egypt" (Jer 31:32). The Lord declares: "'I will put my law in their minds and write it on their hearts. I will be their God, and they will be my people. No longer will they teach their neighbor, or say to one another, "Know the LORD," because they will all know me, from the least of them to the greatest,' declares the LORD. 'For I will forgive their wickedness and will remember their sins no more'" (31:33–34; cf. Heb 8:8–12). The Word of God, his law, will not be written on tablets of stone, but on the heart, so that every one of God's children will know him in a saving way and have their sins forgiven. The power of the Word of God will accomplish this new covenant work of salvation (Ezek 36:22–37; 2 Cor 3). As the Lord declared through the prophet Ezekiel, "I the LORD have spoken, and I have done it, declares the LORD" (Ezek 37:14).[85]

Though the new covenant was prophesied in the Old Testament, it's in the New Testament that this new covenant is identified with the coming of Christ and is accomplished by Christ. The early church understood that Jesus, as the long-awaited Messiah, had fulfilled the Old Testament promises of God to bring about this great redemption. The entire history of Israel reaches its consummation in the person and work of Jesus Christ.[86] As the author of Hebrews explains, "For this reason Christ is the mediator of a new covenant, that those who are called may receive the promised eternal inheritance—now that he has died as a ransom to set them free from the sins committed under the first covenant" (Heb 9:15). Paul says he was "set apart for the gospel of God—the gospel he promised beforehand through his prophets in the Holy Scriptures regarding his Son, who as to his earthly life was a descendant of David, and who through the Spirit of holiness was appointed the Son of God in power by his resurrection from the dead: Jesus Christ our Lord" (Rom 1:1–4).[87] While the prophets of old longed to see the day of the Messiah, their office pointed ahead to a

---

85. See also Isa 10:20–23; Amos 9:11–14.
86. Peter Jensen, *The Revelation of God* (Downers Grove, IL: InterVarsity Press, 2002), 40.
87. Compare Rom 15:4, 8–12; 16:25–27; 1 Cor 10:11.

prophet to come in Jesus Christ (Deut 18:18–22; Acts 3:22–23). Jesus came with the words of the Father put in his mouth. The word of this prophet is far greater because his message is one of salvation through his own blood, which inaugurates the new covenant. He is not only a prophet but a priest as well.

Ears Attentive to the Book of the Law

Tragically, the period of the prophets was a time of great turmoil due to the people's disobedience. The people were exiled, and all hope seemed to be lost as they lived under the hand of their enemies. Yet even in the middle of exile, the Lord was not silent, but spoke once again through his prophets, promising deliverance and redemption.

Second Chronicles ends with a heavy weight, describing the horrific siege of Jerusalem by the Babylonians and the subsequent exile, reminding the reader that God's people "despised his words and scoffed at his prophets" (2 Chr 36:16). Though all seemed lost, one small paragraph concludes the book, stating that God's word would speak life into existence once again. Cyrus, king of Persia, would come into power "to fulfill the word of the LORD spoken by Jeremiah" (36:22). At the proper time, the Lord "moved the heart of Cyrus . . . to make a proclamation throughout his realm" that "the LORD, the God of heaven, has given me all the kingdoms of the earth, and he has appointed me to build a temple for him at Jerusalem in Judah. Any of his people among you may go up, and may the LORD their God be with them" (36:22–23; cf. Ezra 1:1–4).

Cyrus, king of Persia, did capture Babylon (Dan 5:30–31), and though he did not know it, he was an instrument in the hands of Almighty God. Long before Cyrus was born, God promised through Isaiah that he would raise up this "shepherd" in order to bring about the restoration of his people and temple (Isa 44:28; 45:1–7). Such predictive prophecy is once again a reminder that God's word proves true. Prophecy became reality when three waves of exiles returned to the land during the days of Haggai, Zechariah, and Malachi.

When the returned exiles began to rebuild the temple (Ezra 3:1–6:22), a long and difficult project ensued, one that would start under Cyrus, stop due to opposition (Ezra 4:1–5, 24), then resume under King Darius (Ezra 5:2; cf. Hag 1:14) and continue until its completion (Ezra 6:15). However, it would not be until the reign of Artaxerxes that

Ezra, along with a second group of exiles, would travel from Babylon to Jerusalem with the authority to reestablish the Mosaic law (Ezra 7:1–8:36). Ezra, we are told, was "a scribe skilled in the Law of Moses . . . for the hand of the LORD his God was on him" (7:6 ESV). When he arrived in Jerusalem, the text says he "set his heart to study the Law of the LORD, and to do it and to teach his statutes and rules in Israel" (7:10 ESV). Ezra reestablished the Mosaic law among the people (7:26).

We also see a reemphasis on the law of God during a third wave of returning exiles. Under the leadership of Nehemiah, not only were the walls of Jerusalem rebuilt, but the law was read to the people by Ezra (Neh 8:1–8). "And all the people listened attentively to the Book of the Law" (8:3). The people even "worshiped the LORD with their faces to the ground" (8:6).

Unfortunately, the waves of exiles now returning home did not obey the Word of God completely. For example, in Malachi's day, the priests made polluted offerings and profaned the name of the Lord (Mal 1:6–14). They did not fear the Lord, but angered him, and if they continued to disobey the Word of God, he promised to curse their blessings, rebuke their descendants, and "smear on your faces the dung from your festival sacrifices" (2:2–3). The priests violated God's covenant with Levi, a covenant "of life and peace . . . [that] called for reverence," a covenant that resulted in Levi revering the Lord, standing in "awe of my name" (2:5). The priests did not lead the people according to the Word of God. They failed to "preserve knowledge" as messengers of the Lord (2:7). Not only did they stumble, but worse, by their instruction they caused the people to stumble (2:8). The Lord listened to those who feared him and honored him (Mal 3:16–18). With the day of the Lord approaching (4:1–3), the Lord commanded them, "Remember the law of my servant Moses, the decrees and laws I gave him at Horeb for all Israel" (4:4).

Though Israel was unfaithful, the Lord remained faithful (Mal 3:6). He promised to send a future messenger, one who would prepare the way of the Lord (3:1), a second Elijah (4:5). Elijah would come in the person of John the Baptist (Matt 11:10–14; 17:10–13), who prepared the way for the Lamb of God (John 1:29). Unlike the priests in Malachi's day, however, this great high priest would not offer a polluted sacrifice, but a perfect, spotless sacrifice as the spotless Lamb who would be slain. He would be the "sun of righteousness" who would "rise with healing in its rays" (Mal 4:2; cf. John 1:4–6; 8:12).

What are we to conclude from this overview of the prophets? The prophets believed God was speaking through them. Each prophet was God's mouth, God's messenger. When the prophet spoke, God himself spoke, and the prophet's word was God's word. Their books, which we have today, are God's Word written for us to read. As 2 Peter 1:21 asserts, "For no prophecy was ever produced by the will of man, but men spoke from God as they were carried along by the Holy Spirit" (ESV).

God's Word in Written Form

Lying beneath the surface of this quick overview of the Old Testament is the obvious reality that God's word was written down. The temptation for us is to think of the Old Testament as a dusty, dry, dead book of stories. But Scripture is the *viva vox Dei*, the living voice of God. It was crucial not only that God communicate to his people through events, theophanies, proclamations, and persons, but also through the written Word.[88] Why? By putting it down in writing, God was ensuring the perpetual endurance of his word. As the psalmist poetically says, "The grass withers, the flower fades, but the word of our God will stand forever" (Isa 40:8 ESV). So God commanded Isaiah (Isa 8:1–2; 30:8–11), Jeremiah (Jer 25:13; 30:2; 36:32; 51:60–61), and Daniel (Dan 9:1–2) to write down his words.

Such a decision fits with how God makes himself known. The purpose of certain signs and symbols in the Old Testament (e.g., the rainbow for Noah, circumcision for Abraham) was to verify, confirm, and establish God's covenantal promises not only for those participating in that moment but for future Israelites as well. Something similar is true of God's verbal and written Word given to Moses at Mt. Sinai. The written Word stood as an everlasting witness that God's promises are true, effecting either the blessings or curses of the covenant (Deut 31:26).[89] God's written Word carries authority. In it God speaks, calling his people to attention and to decision.

It makes sense, then, that when Jesus came on the scene, he knew

---

88. In theology we might say that God revealed himself not only through event-revelation and person-revelation but through word-revelation as well. See Vos, *Biblical Theology*, 6–7.

89. Swain, *Trinity, Revelation, and Reading*, 56.

that the Old Testament was the written Word of God. He could quote David's psalms with confidence that they pointed ahead to the work he was about to accomplish (Matt 22:42–45).[90] The New Testament authors did the same (e.g., Heb 1:5–13). The generations that followed viewed Scripture not merely as an ancient record of divine revelation but as God's authoritative written Word through which he still spoke to his covenant people (e.g., Rom 15:4; Heb 3:7–19).[91] We should not conclude, Herman Bavinck says, that Scripture is an "arid story" or an "ancient chronicle." Rather, Scripture is an "ever-living, eternally youthful Word of God, which God now and always issues to his people."[92]

---

90. Note how one prophet will quote another prophet whose words are in writing (Jer 26:17–18 and Mic 3:12–13; Isa 2:2–4 and Mic 4:1–5; Isa 11:9 and Hab 2:14) and how OT authors will reference the written Law of Moses (Dan 9:9–15; Pss 19:7; 94:12; 119). Frame, *Doctrine of the Word of God*, 111.

91. Swain, *Trinity, Revelation, and Reading*, 56.

92. Herman Bavinck, *Reformed Dogmatics*, vol. 1, *Prolegomena*, ed. John Bolt, trans. John Vriend (Grand Rapids: Baker, 2003), 384.

CHAPTER 6

God's Covenantal Word Proves True: Christ, the Word Made Flesh

The Word was God.

—*John 1:1*

We ought to believe that Christ cannot be properly known in any other way than from the Scriptures; and if it be so, it follows that we ought to read the Scriptures with the express design of finding Christ in them.

—*John Calvin*

The Son . . . is the Word of the Father.

—*The Thirty-Nine Articles*

Revelation and Redemption

In our journey through the Old Testament, we saw that God's revelation of himself to mankind takes on many forms. To Adam, Abraham, Isaac, Jacob, and many others, God spoke directly, even coming down or appearing in one form or another so that his divine presence was manifested. Furthermore, his revelation of himself often came in and through covenants. For example, God bound himself to his covenant with Abraham, giving his own word that what he had promised he would accomplish.

Yet it is in his covenant with Moses that God not only spoke directly but put down his words in written form. With his own finger, God wrote down his commandments on tablets of stone for the people of Israel. The words of these tablets were always to be on the minds and lips of God's chosen people. Due to their sinfulness, however, God's

201

law exposed his people's wickedness. Their inability to keep the law served to expose their guilt before a holy God as well as their desperate need for a redeemer and mediator. God promised Moses that he would raise up one like Moses and put his words in his mouth. Such a prophet would be found in the Messiah.

God's revelation of himself did not end with Moses. God revealed himself to David, establishing his covenant and kingdom with him, carrying on the promises to Abraham, even guaranteeing to raise up a son from David whose kingdom would have no end. Again, such a promise would ultimately come to fruition in the advent of the Davidic son, the Messiah.

Sadly, after David and Solomon, Israel rejected the Lord, which eventually resulted in her exile. Yet the Lord was not silent but continued to make himself known through his appointed prophets, whom he sent to Israel, not only commanding his people to repent but also promising that he would bring about a new covenant, one in which God's words would be written not on stone but on the human heart, causing man to walk in love and obedience to God (Jer 31:29–34; Ezek 36; 2 Cor 3). This new covenant would come through the messianic suffering servant, who would be pierced for the transgressions of God's people and crushed for their iniquities (Isa 52:13–53:12). This new covenant would be the fulfillment of all previous covenants. "It is the new covenant which all the previous covenants anticipate and typify, and it is in this way that the new covenant supersedes all the previous covenants."[1]

When we open the pages of the New Testament, we see that God's covenant promises to Adam, Abraham, Moses, and David are finally realized in the person and work of Jesus (2 Cor 1:20). Christ is the one who cuts the new covenant as the last Adam, the seed of Abraham, the new Moses, the true Israel, and, especially, the kingly Son of David (Isa 9:6–7; 11:1–10; Jer 23:5–6; 33:14–26; Ezek 34:23–24; 37:24–28).[2] This new covenant is accomplished and made effectual through his atoning blood that was shed on the cross for the forgiveness of sins, since he is not only the sinless, mediating high priest but the spotless sacrifice itself (Matt 1:1; Luke 22:20; 1 Cor 11:25; Heb 2:17–18;

---

1. Peter J. Gentry and Stephen J. Wellum, *Kingdom through Covenant: A Biblical-Theological Understanding of the Covenants* (Wheaton, IL: Crossway, 2012), 644–45.

2. See ibid., 650–51; Thomas R. Schreiner, *The King in His Beauty: A Biblical Theology of the Old and New Testaments* (Grand Rapids: Baker Academic, 2013), 164–65.

8–10). It is no surprise then that Christ comes as one who not only announces the arrival of the kingdom by his words (Matt 3:2; Luke 4:43) but is himself *the Word*, the very voice of God (John 1:1).[3] The Word of God climaxes in tangible, human form. The speech of God is so valuable that when God describes his only Son, he emphasizes his importance by saying that he is himself the very Word of God. We are reminded that in the story of salvation history, *redemption comes through revelation, and revelation through redemption.*

The Word *Is* God

The synoptic Gospels in innumerable ways show us that Jesus is the long-awaited Messiah whom God promised through his oral and written Word in the Old Testament era. This especially stands out when we read the fourth Gospel, the Gospel of John. John's Gospel begins by referring to Jesus as the "Word." And though we will touch on each Gospel as we look at the New Testament teaching on God's revelation and written Scriptures, our main focus will be on John's Gospel as we seek to understand what it means for Jesus to be called the "Word" and what implications this has for the written Word.

"In the beginning was the Word, and the Word was with God, and the Word was God" (John 1:1). John's language echoes Genesis 1 where God brought the world into existence by his creative word.[4] As we saw in chapter 5, God's speech is powerful. He spoke creation into existence, and by his word his people were saved. In the Old Testament, God's word creates (Gen 1:3; Ps 33:6), reveals (Isa 9:8; Jer 1:4; Ezek 33:7; Amos 3:1, 8), and redeems (Ps 107:20; Isa 55:1).[5] Here too, in John 1:3, God's Word is said to be the means by which the cosmos comes into existence. But what is astonishing about John 1:1 is that the "Word" is *a person*, one who not only was with God but *was* God. The eternal Word is divine, and it is through this eternal, divine Word that the Father brought the cosmos into existence. Morris writes that the "Word is God's creative Word."[6] John proves this when he says,

---

3. John Frame, *Systematic Theology* (Phillipsburg, NJ: P&R, 2013), 558.

4. Allen P. Ross, *Creation and Blessing: A Guide to the Study and Exposition of Genesis* (Grand Rapids: Baker Academic, 1996), 108; C. John Collins, *Genesis 1–4: A Linguistic, Literary, and Theological Commentary* (Phillipsburg, NJ: P&R, 2006), 94.

5. D. A. Carson, *The Gospel according to John*, PNTC (Grand Rapids: Eerdmans, 1991), 115–16.

6. Leon Morris, *The Gospel according to John*, NICNT (Grand Rapids: Eerdmans, 1971), 118.

"Through him all things were made; without him nothing was made that has been made" (John 1:3; cf. Ps 102:25–27; Heb 1:10–12). Jesus himself refers to his eternal existence as the Word and even claims the divine name ("I AM") in numerous passages, motivating his opponents to execute him (Mark 14:61–64; John 8:24, 28, 58; 18:5–6).[7]

But why apply this title in particular to Jesus? The Word conveys that Jesus is the supreme revelation of God himself (i.e., the self-expression of God). Just as a man reveals his hidden thoughts by speaking, so God reveals himself by his Word.[8] Amazingly, the Word of the Father is the *person* of the Son. Just as the Father created the world through his Son, now the Father speaks to the world through his Son. This should eliminate any idea that revelation is static. The Word conveys information and knowledge of God, but it also conveys life itself, for to know the Word is to receive life eternal from the one who is life (John 1:4; 3:36; 1 John 5:11–12).[9]

Not only does John 1:1–3 tell us about the Word's preexistence as Creator God, but verse 14 teaches that "the Word became flesh and made his dwelling among us. We have seen his glory, the glory of the one and only Son, who came from the Father, full of grace and truth." The eternal Word became flesh (Phil 2:6–7) and tabernacled (i.e., pitched his tent; encamped) in our very presence, manifesting God's *shekinah* glory, which previously indwelled the tabernacle and temple (Exod 25:8–9; 33:7–11; 40:34–35; Lev 26:11–12; Matt 1:23).[10] The Word is none other than the Son, the second person of the Trinity, who was sent from the Father. While the law came through Moses, the Word brought grace and truth (John 1:17). And lest one doubt that the Word is fully divine, John tells us that he is the "one and only Son, who is himself God and is in closest relationship with the Father" (1:18). We then read that the Word has made the Father known (1:18b). It is precisely because the Word is God that he can make the Father known in a way that has never been done before.

---

7. On Jesus as the eternal and divine Word, see F. F. Bruce, *The Gospel of John* (Grand Rapids: Eerdmans, 1983), 205–6.

8. Morris, *Gospel according to John*, 75. See also Andreas J. Köstenberger, *John*, BECNT (Grand Rapids: Baker Academic, 2004), 25.

9. See also John 3:16; 5:40; 6:51, 53; 10:28; 11:25; 14:6. Morris, *Gospel according to John*, 75, 83.

10. Morris shows how the tabernacle was a type of the presence of Christ. Morris, *Gospel according to John*, 103–4. On what this "glory" looks like, see Carson, *John*, 127–28; Köstenberger, *John*, 41–42.

We can conclude that while God made himself known throughout the Old Testament writings and through his work with Israel, it is in the coming of his Son that we receive the most incredible revelation of all because the Son of God himself has opened the heavens, stepped down, and dwelt among us *as one of us* (Matt 1:23). Jesus not only came as a priest and king, but as a prophet, proclaiming the arrival of the kingdom of God (Matt 5:17; Mark 1:14–15; 6:4; Luke 4:16–24; Heb 1:1–2).[11] He is the great prophet God promised to Moses in Deuteronomy 18:15–18, as Peter explains in Acts 3:15–26. He is a prophet like no other prophet before him. Jesus comes as the prophet whose authority is inherent, for he is the Word who is identified with God (John 1:1–5). His teaching carries a unique, one-of-a-kind authority; indeed, a divine authority.[12] The entire prophetic witness in the OT pointed forward to Christ as the one who would be God's final and definitive Word (Luke 24:25–47; John 5:45–47; 1 Pet 1:10–12), bringing a message and work of redemption and reconciliation (John 3:16–18). It is impossible to improve upon the words that open the letter to the Hebrews:

> Long ago, at many times and in many ways, God spoke to our fathers by the prophets, but in these last days he has spoken to us by his Son, whom he appointed the heir of all things, through whom also he created the world. He is the radiance of the glory of God and the exact imprint of his nature, and he upholds the universe by the word of his power. After making purification for sins, he sat down at the right hand of the Majesty on high, having become as much superior to angels as the name he has inherited is more excellent than theirs. (Heb 1:1–4 ESV)

Jesus is the ultimate proof that God's covenantal word has come true (Rom 1:1–6; 16:25–27; 1 Pet 1:10–12).[13]

Our purpose in this chapter is to understand the significance of Jesus as the Word of God. As we transition from the Old to the New

---

11. Graeme Goldsworthy, *According to Plan: The Unfolding Revelation of God in the Bible* (Downers Grove, IL: IVP Academic, 1991), 205.

12. On this point, see Robert Letham, *The Work of Christ* (Downers Grove, IL: InterVarsity Press, 1993), 92–93.

13. Kevin J. Vanhoozer, "Augustinian Inerrancy: Literary Meaning, Literal Truth, and Literate Interpretation in the Economy of Biblical Discourse," in *Five Views on Biblical Inerrancy*, ed. J. Merrick and Stephen M. Garrett (Grand Rapids: Zondervan, 2013), 217–18.

Testament, three points (structured around the three persons of the Trinity) will guide us in better understanding the advent of Christ leading up to the written Word of the New Testament Scriptures:

1. Christ, the Word, fulfilled the promises of God in the Old Testament, which he affirmed as the very Word of God.
2. Christ, as the Son of God and the Word of God, is the ultimate, climactic, and full revelation of God, and his word is true because it came from the Father.
3. The Father and Son sent the Spirit of truth with a word of truth.

The Word Fulfills God's Word

First, Christ, the Word, fulfilled the promises of God in the Old Testament, which he affirmed as the very Word of God.[14] In countless ways, by means of who he is, what he taught, and what he accomplished, Jesus fulfilled God's promises.

At the beginning of his ministry, Jesus entered Nazareth and attended the synagogue on the Sabbath. When Jesus stood up to read from the scroll that was handed to him, he "found the place where it is written" in the book of the prophet Isaiah that the "Spirit of the Lord is on me, because he has anointed me to proclaim good news to the poor" (Luke 4:18; cf. Isa 61:1). When he was through reading, he sat down and all eyes were on him. Jesus made a shocking statement: "Today this scripture is fulfilled in your hearing" (Luke 4:21).

Consider what Jesus said concerning the "Law and the Prophets" in Matthew 5:17–18: "Do not think that I have come to abolish the Law or the Prophets; I have not come to abolish them but to fulfill them. For truly I tell you, until heaven and earth disappear, not the smallest letter, not the least stroke of a pen, will by any means disappear from the Law until everything is accomplished" (cf. Luke 16:16–17). The Pentateuch, the first five books of the OT, as well as the Prophets, generally the rest of the OT (cf. Ps 78:2; Matt 7:12; 11:13; 13:35; 22:40; Rom 3:21), are fulfilled by and in Christ.[15] All of the OT pointed to the coming of the Messiah, and his advent signaled the fulfillment not only of that which was predicted but that which was a type of the

---

14. This is not to deny, however, that there are OT prophecies awaiting future fulfillment. Rather, this chapter's focus is directed toward the fulfillment of salvation in Christ.

15. It is debated as to what exactly it means for Christ to fulfill the law. For the various views, see Grant Osborne, *Matthew*, ZECNT (Grand Rapids: Zondervan, 2010), 182.

Messiah to come (the sacrificial system, the tabernacle and temple, the priesthood, Israel, etc.).

Jesus in no way undermined the authority of the OT but rather brought the old covenant to its intended and appointed end (see Heb 8:13). The truth of the Torah is not doubted but is confirmed in Jesus's words.[16] R. T. France paraphrases Jesus's words in Matthew 5:17–18: "Far from wanting to set aside the law and the prophets, it is my role to bring into being that to which they have pointed forward, to carry them into a new era of fulfillment."[17] So while the authority of the Law and the Prophets is not discarded or contradicted by Jesus, they will function differently since what they foreshadowed has now come in the person and work of Christ and his new covenant (Heb 9:11–28).[18] It is in the Word made flesh that the Word of God prior to Christ finds its *telos*.

Jesus did not hesitate to affirm the abiding authority and permanence of God's Word. Not "the smallest letter" or "the least stroke of a pen" will pass from the Law until "everything is accomplished."[19] The point is that not the smallest detail will go unfulfilled. David Turner writes, "It would be hard to make a stronger statement about the ongoing authority of the Torah than that made in Matthew 5:18."[20] Jesus's words demonstrate that all Scripture, even the minutest detail, is authoritative, inspired, and truthful, and each element of Scripture finds its purpose accomplished in Christ. Jesus warns that anyone who ignores even the least of the commandments and teaches others to do so "will be called least in the kingdom of heaven" (5:19).

Elsewhere we learn that Jesus was conscious of how his own death and resurrection fulfilled the Old Testament. When Jesus cleansed the temple, his Father's house, his disciples remembered what was said in Psalm 69:9, "Zeal for your house will consume me" (John 2:17). And when the Jews responded by demanding a sign, Jesus predicted the death and resurrection of the temple of his body (2:19–21).[21] When he was raised from the dead, his disciples remembered what he had

---

16. Leon Morris, *The Gospel according to Matthew*, PNTC (Grand Rapids: Eerdmans, 1992), 108.

17. R. T. France, *The Gospel of Matthew*, NICNT (Grand Rapids: Eerdmans, 2007), 183.

18. Ibid.

19. In the Hebrew alphabet, the *yod* is the smallest letter, and the smallest stroke is the Hebrew letter *waw*. David L. Turner, *Matthew*, BECNT (Grand Rapids: Baker Academic, 2008), 163; Morris, *Matthew*, 109.

20. Turner, *Matthew*, 163.

21. See also Mark 11:15–19 where Jesus quotes from Isa 56:7 and Jer 7:11.

said and "believed the scripture and the words that Jesus had spoken" (2:22). Not only did the Old Testament Scriptures point to Jesus, but Jesus himself recognized that he was fulfilling the Word of God in his life, death, and resurrection.[22]

Or consider John 3. After teaching Nicodemus about the necessity of the new birth, Jesus said, "No one has ever gone into heaven except the one who came from heaven—the Son of Man. Just as Moses lifted up the snake in the wilderness, so the Son of Man must be lifted up, that everyone who believes may have eternal life in him" (3:13–14). Jesus was referring to the events of Numbers 21:4–9, and he saw his death as the antitype of the bronze serpent Moses erected for the people's healing.[23] This is a reminder that not only prophetic predictions but events and symbols in the Old Testament prefigured Christ and what he would accomplish.

Matthew's Gospel also demonstrates that Jesus considered his own death and resurrection to be orchestrated, planned, and determined by God in fulfillment of the Scriptures. In Matthew 16 Jesus "began to explain to his disciples that he must go to Jerusalem and suffer many things at the hands of the elders, the chief priests and the teachers of the law, and that he must be killed and on the third day be raised to life" (16:21; cf. 17:12).[24] Jesus predicted his own suffering as the Messiah, much to the dismay of his disciples (16:22–23). He is the suffering servant Isaiah foretold (Isa 53).

His identity also came to light when he was transfigured before Peter, James, and John, when he spoke with Moses and Elijah as well (Matt 17:2–4; cf. Mark 9:2–13). Moses represented the Law and Elijah the Prophets. Both the Law and the Prophets pointed forward to the coming of the Messiah (e.g., Mal 4:5–6), and now that he had arrived these two representatives talked with Jesus, perhaps about what he was about to do at Calvary to fulfill the Scriptures.

Next, Jesus discussed John the Baptist in order to demonstrate that

---

22. John Wenham, *Christ and the Bible*, 3rd ed. (Grand Rapids: Baker, 1994), 111.

23. A "type" can be a person, object, event, etc. that symbolically points forward to something or someone greater to come (antitype), the latter of which fulfills and brings to completion the former. In other words, a type foreshadows and prefigures the antitype to come. For example, the sacrificial system in the Old Testament is a type of the final, sufficient sacrifice of Jesus on the cross. The book of Hebrews is an excellent example of how OT types reach their fulfillment in Christ and the new covenant.

24. See also John 12:27–36; Mark 8:31–33; 9:30–32; 10:32–34; Luke 18:31–34; 22:37–38.

the Old Testament was being fulfilled. When the disciples, puzzled, asked Jesus why the teachers of the law said that Elijah must come first, Jesus answered that "Elijah has already come, and they did not recognize him, but did to him whatever they pleased" (Matt 17:12 ESV). As Jesus says in Matthew 11:13–14, "All the Prophets and the Law prophesied until John," and John was Elijah, fulfilling the prophecy of Malachi 4:4–6. Jesus made it clear that God's Word through his prophets was now being fulfilled in his own day.

This pattern continued with Jesus coming down from the mountain after being transfigured and instructing his inner circle not to tell anyone about the vision until after "the Son of Man has been raised from the dead" (Matt 17:9). And in case the other disciples missed his prediction, Jesus once again foretold his death and resurrection while in Galilee. "The Son of Man is going to be delivered into the hands of men. They will kill him, and on the third day he will be raised to life" (17:22–23; cf. 20:17–19). Jesus was on a mission to fulfill God's Word, which could not and would not return void.[25]

We see evidence of this mission when we look at how Jesus prepared to go to the cross, eating his final meal with his disciples. His words spoken at the close of the meal are especially important. As we saw, the Old Testament prophets promised a day to come when God would cut a new covenant with his people. This new covenant was now at hand. Jesus took the bread, broke it and gave it to his disples, and said, "Take and eat; this is my body." Then he took the cup, gave thanks and gave it to them, and said, "Drink from it, all of you. This is my blood of the covenant, which is poured out for many for the forgiveness of sins" (Matt 26:26–28; cf. Luke 22:17–20). The blood of the covenant harkens back to John the Baptist's words at the start of Jesus's ministry: "Look, the Lamb of God, who takes away the sin of the world!" (John 1:29). In fulfillment of the Old Testament, Jesus acted as the spotless Passover lamb, slain for the forgiveness of sins. Jesus could say prior to his death that the new covenant had arrived through his blood, which would be spilled to accomplish redemption. He then drank the cup of God's wrath to secure the new covenant and its promises (Matt 26:39).

---

25. Other passages where Jesus sees his actions or his personal identity fulfilling the OT include Matt 21:4–5, 13–16, 42–44; 22:41–45; Mark 2:23–28; 12:1–12, 35–37; Luke 6:1–5; 20:9–18, 41–47; 22:37–38. Additionally, one should take note of the birth narrative in Luke's Gospel, which is presented as a fulfillment of many OT prophecies: Luke 1–2.

What the Old Testament prefigured in the sacrificial system, and what the prophets predicted (Isa 53) was now brought to pass on the cross of Calvary (Heb 8–10). The promise-fulfillment pattern of God's Word could not be more evident than in Jesus's last words: "It is finished" (John 19:30).[26] By raising Jesus from the dead three days later, God declared his satisfaction with and approval of the payment Christ made on our behalf, for our sins, on the cross. There is no greater indicator that God's covenant promises have been fulfilled than the empty tomb.

After his resurrection from the dead, Jesus once again verified that what had happened to him was to fulfill everything the Scriptures predicted. On the road to Emmaus, Jesus joined two men, one being Cleopas (Luke 24:18), who were talking about everything that had happened in Jerusalem. With his identity concealed, Jesus asked them about their conversation, and the men began telling him about "Jesus of Nazareth, a man who was a prophet mighty in deed and word before God and all the people, and how our chief priests and rulers delivered him up to be condemned to death, and crucified him" (24:19–20 ESV). These men had hoped Jesus was the one "to redeem Israel" (24:21). Now they were not only disappointed but confused, for some women had found the tomb empty and were told by angels that Jesus had risen (24:23). What was Jesus's response? "'O foolish ones, and slow of heart to believe all that the prophets have spoken! Was it not necessary that the Christ should suffer these things and enter into his glory?' And beginning with Moses and all the Prophets, he interpreted to them in all the Scriptures the things concerning himself" (24:25–27 ESV). Later on, when he appeared to his disciples, Jesus would say something similar: "These are my words that I spoke to you while I was still with you, that everything written about me in the Law of Moses and the Prophets and the Psalms must be fulfilled" (24:44 ESV). Jesus then "opened their minds to understand the Scriptures" and said to them, "Thus, it is written, that the Christ should suffer and on the third day rise from the dead, and that repentance and forgiveness of sins should be proclaimed in his name to all nations, beginning from Jerusalem" (24:45–47 ESV). Unquestionably, Jesus knew that the entire Old Testament spoke of him and what he had accomplished, further demonstrating that the covenant promises of God were true and trustworthy.

---

26. One should also observe Jesus's cry of dereliction in Matt 27:46, where he is quoting from Ps 22:1.

The New Testament writers believed the same. When Paul attests to the historicity of the resurrection and its necessity for the credibility of the Christian gospel, he says Christ was raised on the third day "in accordance with the Scriptures" (1 Cor 15:4 ESV). Indeed, the apostolic testimony to the gospel and the resurrection of Christ (Acts 17:31) is entirely dependent upon the inspiration of the Old Testament. "To become a Christian through this gospel," says Peter Jensen, "is not to abandon historical reality, but to accept the testimony of those whom we regard as trustworthy; it is to put our trust in their words, or, rather, to trust the one to whom their words testify, through their words."[27]

Jesus not only asserted that his words and actions were in fulfillment of the Old Testament but that the *Old Testament Scriptures themselves were divinely given and therefore true and authoritative*. While we will explore this point in more depth in chapter 8, here it should be recognized that from the beginning to the end of his ministry, Jesus was clear that the Old Testament he was claiming to fulfill was breathed out by God and authoritative as the Word of God. For example, when he was tempted in the wilderness by Satan at the start of his ministry, it was to the Old Testament that Jesus appealed, as that which is from God and therefore authoritative (Matt 4:1–17). Jesus said that the Old Testament had been divinely given. When Satan tempted Jesus to turn stones into bread, Jesus quoted Deuteronomy 8:3, saying, "Man does not live by bread alone but on every word that comes from the mouth of the Lord." While Israel failed in the wilderness, Jesus, the last Adam (Rom 5:12–21) and the true Israel, succeeded in his wilderness temptation, obeying the Father rather than listening to the ancient serpent. Jesus paid heed to what was written in the Scriptures, believing that these words were from the Father's very mouth and were man's sustenance and life source. While Satan tried to use God's Word to deceive Jesus, Jesus used God's Word as a weapon of truth. While Satan twisted the Scriptures, Jesus remained faithful to their true meaning. The Word of God is not only one's bread but one's sword, fending off the devil's lies (Eph 6:17).

Jesus asserted the divine inspiration of the Old Testament in countless ways. He referred to its writings as "Scripture" (Mark 12:10; Luke 4:21; John 7:38), used the phrase "it is written" (Matt 4:4–10; 11:10; 21:13; 26:24, 31), cited the Old Testament writings as the "Law" and

---

27. Peter Jensen, *The Revelation of God* (Downers Grove, IL: InterVarsity Press, 2002), 41.

"Prophets" (Matt 5:17–18; 7:12; 11:13; 12:5; 22:40; 23:23; John 10:34), and appealed to the Scriptures for support against his opponents (Matt 5:17–19; John 5:45–47; 10:34–36).[28] Jesus considered not only the Old Testament *message* as a whole to be God-breathed but the *actual writings* as well. While each of these books has a human author, God is the divine author who chose to work through the human author, revealing himself covenantally, even foretelling the coming of his Son, the Messiah.

The point in all of this is clear: *God's Word is true.* What God promised in the old covenant, he brought to completion in the new covenant through the person and work of his Son. And when we look at what Christ himself said, it is unmistakable that he believed the Old Testament to be the very Word of God, fulfilled in his own ministry and teaching.

The Word of Truth from the Father

Second, as the Son of God and the Word of God, Christ is the ultimate, climactic, and full revelation of God, and his word is true because it came from the Father.[29] We mentioned this point when we discussed John 1:1 where Jesus is called the "Word." However, we need to press this idea further because there are numerous places where Jesus lucidly told his listeners not only that he had a unique relationship to the Father as the Son but that he had come *to make the Father known.* In John 5:19 Jesus said that "the Son can do nothing of his own accord, but only what he sees the Father doing" (ESV). The Father "loves the Son and shows him all that he himself is doing" (5:20 ESV). And in John 14:24 Jesus confirms that "the word that you hear is not mine but the Father's who sent me" (cf.14:10). There is an intra-Trinitarian revelation at play between the Father and the Son, with the Father showing his Son all that he is doing and the Son doing only that which he saw the Father doing.

Jesus also demonstrates that he makes the Father known, both in word and in deed. "Just as the Father raises the dead and gives them life, even so the Son gives life to whom he is pleased to give it" (John 5:21). Furthermore, says Jesus, "Whoever hears my word and believes him

---

28. On this subject, see Frame, *Systematic Theology,* 574ff.

29. Space constrains me, but for a more in-depth treatment of this second point than I can make here, see Herman N. Ridderbos, *Redemptive History and the New Testament Scriptures,* trans. H. De Jongste (Phillipsburg, NJ: P&R, 1963).

who sent me has eternal life" (5:24). Because of his relationship to the Father, the Son speaks words of life for the salvation of sinners. So powerful is the word of the Son that a day is coming when the dead "will hear the voice of the Son of God and those who hear will live" (5:25; cf. 11:25–26). Again, the power of the word of the Son is rooted in the Son's relation to his Father. "For as the Father has life in himself, so he has granted the Son also to have life in himself" (5:26). The Father has also granted the Son authority to execute judgment (5:27; cf. 5:22). At the command of his voice, the dead will rise from the tombs to either resurrection life or resurrection judgment (5:29). There is an efficacy and power to the word of the Son, one that is tied to the Son's revelation of the Father and the Father's revelation of his Son. As Jesus explains in John 5:32, the Father bears witness about his Son. Is this witness fallible? Not at all, for Jesus says that the Father's witness about his Son is "true."[30] It is a word that is trustworthy through and through.[31]

According to Jesus, the Old Testament had everything to do with this Trinitarian revelation between the Father and the Son. When Jesus said that John "testified to the truth" (John 5:33), he qualified this by adding that his own testimony was greater than John's (5:36). How so? "For the works that the Father has given me to finish—the very works that I am doing—testify that the Father has sent me" (John 5:36). Not only did Jesus's works reveal that the Father had sent him, but the Father "has himself testified concerning me" (5:37; 1 John 5:9). Jesus explained that unlike Moses, his listeners have not heard the Father's voice (5:37; cf. Exod 33:11; Deut 4:12); unlike Jacob, they have not seen his form (5:37; cf. Gen 32:30–31); and unlike Joshua or the psalmist, they do not have "his word" abiding within them (Josh 1:8–9; Ps 119:11), for they "do not believe the one whom he has sent" (John 5:38 ESV).[32] They "search the Scriptures" because they think that in them they "have eternal life." However, they have failed to see

---

30. Morris, *Gospel according to John*, 325–26.

31. The Son has "accomplished the work" the Father gave him to do (John 17:4 ESV). In doing so, says Jesus, "I have manifested your name to the people whom you gave me out of the world. . . . For I have given them the words that you gave me, and they have received them and have come to know in truth that I came from you; and they have believed that you sent me" (17:6, 8). The Father has manifested his word through the Son, resulting in the salvation of his elect.

32. See Morris, *Gospel according to John*, 329; J. Ramsey Michaels, *Gospel of John*, NICNT (Grand Rapids: Eerdmans, 2010), 330; Carson, *John*, 262.

that the Scriptures bear witness about Christ, the one who is the truth and the life (John 5:39). Therefore, since they refuse to come to Jesus that they may have life (5:40), their accuser is Moses, "on whom you have set your hope" (5:45 ESV). "If you believed Moses, you would believe me, for he wrote about me" (5:46; cf. 1:45). So the Father has revealed his Son not only by giving him works to accomplish (5:36) but by sending his Son just as he said he would when he spoke through prophets like Moses (5:37, 39, 45–47).[33]

As one who possessed the full authority of the Father, Jesus spoke "words" that were "full of the Spirit and life" (John 6:63; cf. 6:68). His revelation was a life-giving revelation (John 8:31–32; cf. Luke 8:21). Yet Jesus and his words of life were rejected and hated. Why? Jesus gave the reason: "You seek to kill me because my word finds no place in you" (8:37 ESV). And again, "Why do you not understand what I say? It is because you cannot bear to hear my word" (8:43 ESV). Their father, said Jesus unapologetically, was the devil, the father of lies (8:44). In contrast, Jesus was one who was telling the truth (8:45). His word is truth, and there is no falsehood mixed in it. Therefore, those who keep "my word will never see death" (8:51). They are those whom Jesus called his "sheep." "My sheep hear my voice, and I know them, and they follow me. I give them eternal life, and they will never perish, and no one will snatch them out of my hand" (10:27–28 ESV). The sheep are the ones whom the Father would sanctify in the truth. And as Jesus said in John 17:17, the Father was able to sanctify them in the truth because his "word is truth."[34] If it were a *false* word, a word that proved untrustworthy, unreliable, and tainted by falsehood, then the sheep could not have confidence in the Father to sanctify them in the truth.[35]

The authority of Jesus's words and their origin from the Father are also evident in the fact that his words will judge unbelievers on the last day.

---

33. Compare Luke 24:27, 44; Acts 13:27; 1 John 5:9. For passages where Jesus makes the same point, see John 7:14–24; 8:39–47; 10:25; 12:44–50; 14:10–11.

34. "By 'your word' he does not mean the written Scriptures (as in [John] 10:35 ['the word']) but the 'word' or message from the Father which he has given the disciples. . . . The identification of 'your word' and 'the truth' is thoroughly in keeping with Jesus's identification of himself as 'the Truth' (14:6), the coming Advocate, as 'the Spirit of truth' (14:17; 15:26; 16:13), and the Father as 'the only true God' (v. 3)" (Michaels, *Gospel of John*, 872).

35. On the connection between sanctification and the trustworthiness of divine revelation, see Morris, *Gospel according to John*, 731.

If anyone hears my words and does not keep them, I do not judge him; for I did not come to judge the world but to save the world. The one who rejects me and does not receive my words has a judge; the word that I have spoken will judge him on the last day. For I have not spoken on my own authority, but the Father who sent me has himself given me a commandment—what to say and what to speak. And I know that his commandment is eternal life. What I say, therefore, I say as the Father has told me. (John 12:47–50 ESV)

Jesus speaks, but his authority is from the Father who sent him. It is the Father who has told him "what to say and what to speak," and the words he speaks are either life or death. They are eternal life for those who believe his words and eternal death and judgment for those who reject them. So synonymous are Jesus and his words that to reject the words of Jesus is to reject the Son, and not only the Son but the Father who sent him.

Some neo-orthodox theologians would say that Jesus *is* the Word, but Scripture itself is not. However, were we to be critical of Jesus's words, then we would be inconsistent to then appeal beyond his words to his person, as if one can be had apart from the other. It is also illegitimate, notes John Frame, to "appeal to the substance or content of Jesus's words, beyond the forms in which they are presented."[36] To do so is to fail to take Jesus's words seriously. The importance of the words of Jesus is reiterated by Paul when he warns against anyone who "teaches a different doctrine and does not agree with the *sound words of our Lord Jesus Christ* and the teaching that accords with godliness" (1 Tim 6:3 ESV, emphasis added). If we truly love Christ, we will obey his words (John 14:15–23).[37]

The Spirit of Truth Comes with a Word of Truth

Third, the Father and Son sent the Spirit of truth with a word of truth. That there is a trinitarian nature to divine revelation is undeniable. We have learned that what the Father planned long ago, the Son brought to completion. However, we must not forget the Spirit. In John 14 Jesus says that though he will not be physically with his disciples any longer, he will send the Holy Spirit to be with them. "I will ask the

---

36. Frame, *Systematic Theology*, 559. Similarly, see Carson, *John*, 302, 453.
37. Compare 15:7–14; 17:6, 17; 1 John 2:3–5; 3:22; 5:2–3; 2 John 6; Rev 12:17; 14:12. Frame, *Systematic Theology*, 559.

Father, and he will give you another advocate to help you and be with you forever—the Spirit of truth. The world cannot accept him, because it neither sees him nor knows him. But you know him, for he lives with you and will be in you" (John 14:16–17).

Jesus calls the advocate the "Spirit of truth" (cf. 15:26). Like the Father and the Son, the Spirit speaks, and when he speaks he does not lie, make mistakes, or speak falsely in his witness to Christ.[38] His word is truth, just as the Father's word is truth (17:17), because the Spirit is the Spirit of the Father. And not only is he the Spirit of the Father but the Spirit of the Son who is the way, the truth, and the life (14:6). If the Spirit were to speak falsely or incorrectly about Christ, it would compromise the character of all three—the Father, Son, and the Holy Spirit.

The Spirit of truth, Jesus promised, would not only help the disciples remember what Jesus had taught them but assist them in comprehending its significance and meaning.[39] As Jesus explains, "But the Advocate, the Holy Spirit, whom the Father will send in my name, will teach you all things and will remind you of everything I have said to you" (14:26). Jesus's words were truer than the disciples at that time realized, for the Spirit would come at Pentecost to permanently indwell them.

Jesus said something similar in John 16 when he told his disciples that unless he went away, the Holy Spirit would not come (16:7). Jesus then said:

> I still have many things to say to you, but you cannot bear them now. When the Spirit of truth comes, he will guide you into all the truth, for he will not speak on his own authority, but whatever he hears he will speak, and he will declare to you the things that are to come. He will glorify me, for he will take what is mine and declare it to you. All that the Father has is mine; therefore I said that he will take what is mine and declare it to you. (16:12–15 ESV)

Jesus calls the Spirit the "Spirit of truth." With the Spirit comes a truthful testimony and witness to the things of Christ (i.e., the Spirit's work is Christocentric).[40] He came as the one who guided the disciples

---

38. For more on the Paraclete as the Spirit of truth, see Carson, *John*, 500.

39. "The Spirit's ministry in this respect was not to bring qualitatively new revelation, but to complete, to fill out, the revelation brought by Jesus himself" (Carson, *John*, 505). See also Köstenberger, *John*, 442.

40. Morris, *Gospel according to John*, 701.

into all truth. And just as Jesus did not speak on his own authority but declared the word that the Father gave to him (14:24), so also the Spirit did not speak on his own authority but was sent by the Father and the Son (15:26) and spoke the word of truth given to him by the Father and the Son (16:13).[41] In other words, there was a Trinitarian handoff of truth (16:15). It began with the Father who gave his words to his Son, only for the Son to give these words to the Spirit, who testified concerning the Son. Not only did the Father testify concerning his Son (5:32, 37; 6:27; 8:18) and the Son testify concerning his Father (17:6), but the Spirit also testified about the Son (15:26).

As we will see in the chapters to follow, there are major implications here for one's doctrine of Scripture. We have seen that the Spirit of truth came upon the biblical authors with a word from the Father and the Son. The Spirit of truth guided the biblical authors to write down the truth.[42] The word of the gospel, therefore, was not only proclaimed but written down.

Just as Jesus promised, the Holy Spirit did come at Pentecost (Acts 2), and in those early years of the new covenant church, the Spirit ensured that the gospel of Jesus Christ advanced not only among the Jews but also among the gentiles. Indeed, the apostles strove tirelessly to make disciples of all nations, teaching them all that Christ commanded (Matt 28:19–20). And they did so by relying extensively on the Old Testament Scriptures, demonstrating time and again that what took place at Calvary was prophesied about long ago through kings like David and prophets like Joel, and that now the fulfillment had arrived (e.g., Acts 2:15–36).

Consider Peter's proclamation in Solomon's portico: "What God foretold by the mouth of all the prophets, that his Christ would suffer, he thus fulfilled" (Acts 3:18 ESV). Peter then appealed to God's word to Moses, Samuel, and Abraham:

> Moses said, "The Lord God will raise up for you a prophet like me from your brothers. You shall listen to him in whatever he tells

---

41. Regarding the phrase "he will declare to you the things that are to come," commentators are divided as to its meaning. Some believe it is eschatological, while others believe it refers to what is yet to happen after this point in Jesus's ministry. Köstenberger, *John*, 473–74, may pave a middle way when he says the emphasis is not on predictive prophecy, "but on helping the believing community understand their present situation in light of Jesus's by-then-past revelation of God."

42. Letham, *Work of Christ*, 101–2.

you. And it shall be that every soul who does not listen to that prophet shall be destroyed from the people." And all the prophets who have spoken, from Samuel and those who came after him, also proclaimed these days. You are the sons of the prophets and of the covenant that God made with your fathers, saying to Abraham, "And in your offspring shall all the families of the earth be blessed." (Acts 3:22–25)[43]

Sounding much like the Old Testament prophets, Peter exhorted the people to listen to the Word of God spoken through the prophets of old, now fulfilled in the coming of Jesus.[44]

Paul said the same when he went into the synagogue in Antioch:

"Of this man's [David's] offspring God has brought to Israel a Savior, Jesus, as he promised. . . . Brothers, sons of the family of Abraham, . . . to us has been sent the message of this salvation. For those who live in Jerusalem and their rulers, because they did not recognize him nor understand the utterances of the prophets, which are read every Sabbath, fulfilled them by condemning him. . . . And when they had carried out all that was written of him, they took him down from the tree and laid him in a tomb. But God raised him from the dead. . . . And we bring you the good news that what God promised to the fathers, this he has fulfilled to us their children by raising Jesus, as also it is written in the second Psalm, 'You are my Son, today I have begotten you.'" (Acts 13:23, 26–27, 29, 30, 32–33 ESV; cf. Ps 2:7)

Paul quoted from Old Testament passages (Isa 55:3; Pss 2:7; 16:10; Hab 1:5) to demonstrate that the Word of God has proven to be true and men everywhere are to receive this good news of salvation (Acts 13:38). As Peter said after realizing the gospel was to go forth to the gentiles too, "To him [Christ] all the prophets bear witness that everyone who believes in him receives forgiveness of sins through his name" (Acts 10:43 ESV). With each new opportunity, these Christ-followers, by the power of the Holy Spirit, would boldly "speak the word of God"

---

43. Compare Gen 22:18; Deut 18:15–19; 1 Sam 3:20. See Wenham, *Christ and the Bible*, 111–12.

44. One should especially see the martyrdom speech of Stephen in Acts 7 and his many OT quotations from the prophets. See also Philip's interaction with Isa 53:7–8 in Acts 8:32–35.

(Acts 13:46; 14:3), the gospel. After all, God had put in their mouths the "words of this Life" (Acts 5:20 ESV). Not even persecution and death could thwart God's will and stop his gospel-word from advancing (Acts 5:27–42).

Throughout the book of Acts, we hear phrases used repeatedly to emphasize that God's gospel has been communicated to his apostles and is now advancing. The apostles and early leaders of the church were those who preached the "word of God" (Acts 6:2, 7; 8:4; 10:36, 44; 13:5, 46; 17:13; 18:11) or the "word of the Lord" (Acts 8:25; 13:44, 48–49; 15:25, 36; 16:32; 19:10, 20), who devoted themselves to the "ministry of the word" (Acts 6:4), who spoke boldly for the Lord and bore witness to the "word of his grace" (Acts 14:3 ESV; 20:32), and who then watched as the Spirit worked in the hearts of sinners so that they "received the word of God" (Acts 11:1; cf. 12:24) and heard "the word of the gospel and believe[d]" (Acts 15:7). These phrases demonstrate that the apostles believed that their own gospel message, and not just that of the Old Testament Scriptures, was from God and could rightly be called the word of God.[45] The apostles assumed and asserted that what they were passing on was given to them by Christ himself and was fully authoritative (see John 13:20).[46] Sinclair Ferguson writes, "Ultimately, therefore, the authority of the NT rests on the authority of Jesus himself."[47]

A tradition was being handed down by the triune God. The Father handed over this tradition to the Son (Matt 11:27). Then the Son revealed this tradition to those whom the Father had given to him (John 14:26; 17:20). After he ascended, the Spirit brought to remembrance all that Jesus taught, teaching his disciples all things (John 14:26).[48] Having received this tradition from Christ (1 Cor 15:3) and the Spirit (John 16:12–15), the apostles then delivered it to the first-century churches, instructing them to "guard what has been entrusted to your care" (1 Tim 6:20). Paul says in 2 Thessalonians 2:15, "So then, brothers, stand firm and hold to the traditions that you were taught by us,

---

45. Other related texts include Acts 11:16, 19; 13:7, 15; 14:25; 16:6; 17:11; 18:5. Many of these texts simply refer to "the word."

46. For more on the authority given to the apostles by Christ, see Bavinck, *Reformed Dogmatics*, 1:394–402.

47. Sinclair B. Ferguson, *From the Mouth of God: Trusting, Reading, and Applying the Bible* (Edinburgh: Banner of Truth, 2014), 33.

48. The Spirit not only brought to remembrance the words of Jesus but also what those words meant. Michaels, *Gospel of John*, 792.

either by our spoken word or by our letter" (ESV; cf. 2 Tim 1:12–14; 2:2; 2 Pet 1:21).[49] And again: "Now we command you, brothers, in the name of our Lord Jesus Christ, that you keep away from any brother who is walking in idleness and not in accord with the tradition that you received from us" (2 Thess 3:6 ESV). Or consider Jude 3: "Beloved, although I was very eager to write to you about our common salvation, I found it necessary to write appealing to you to contend for the faith that was once for all delivered to the saints" (ESV). At first the faith was delivered orally, but then it was put in writing. As Paul indicates in 2 Thessalonians 2:15, the traditions he passed on were not only through "our spoken word" but "by our letter" (ESV). This written tradition was meant by God to be permanent, and the churches were to receive it as authoritative (e.g., Col 4:16). The job of the church, then, was to defend this God-given tradition, this gospel-word that was handed down in Scripture.[50]

We see, then, that the triune God communicates through the permanence of the Scriptures. The Bible is the authoritative Word of Jesus to us, for Jesus sent his Spirit to inspire human authors so he might speak to you and me today. While all else fades away, God's Word stands forever (Isa 40:8). As John Frame explains, "In Scripture itself, God ensures the sovereignty of his revelation, not by making it momentary and evanescent, but by establishing it as a permanent part of the human landscape, like the pillars and altars of the patriarchs."[51] God's Word stands over us, speaking to us, holding us accountable, piercing our hearts, and giving us the words of eternal life. We cannot take away from it or change it. When we read the Scriptures, the only proper response to its divine author is worship. Only then do we take God and his Word seriously, as he intended.

---

49. Frame, *Systematic Theology*, 564.
50. Ibid.
51. Ibid.

PART 3

The Character of God's Word and Contemporary Challenges

PART

The Character
of God's
Word and
Contemporary
Challenges

CHAPTER 7

God Speaks with Authority: The Inspiration of Scripture

> For no prophecy was ever produced by the will of man, but men spoke from God as they were carried along by the Holy Spirit.
>
> —*2 Peter 1:21 ESV*

> The authority of the Holy Scripture . . . dependeth not upon the testimony of any man or church, but wholly upon God (who is truth itself), the Author thereof; and therefore it is to be received, because it is the Word of God.
>
> —*The Westminster Confession of Faith*

In the previous two chapters, we journeyed from Old Testament to the New and saw that the triune God communicated his covenantal Word in order to redeem his people. We learned that God's Word proved true, as he fulfilled his covenantal promises made in the old covenant through the Word, his Son, in the new covenant. This Trinitarian drama of redemption played itself out not only with the advent of the Word, Christ Jesus, but also with the commissioning of the Holy Spirit, who came upon the authors of the New Testament so that Scripture was breathed out by God.

In this chapter we shift gears from biblical to systematic theology, as we further explore the Spirit's work in the inspiration of Scripture, seeking to understand in what sense the Bible is inspired by God and what importance this has for the authority of Scripture. As we do so, we should keep in mind Calvin's insight, namely, that the authority of Scripture is grounded in its inspiration. Following Paul's logic in 2 Timothy 3:16, we will aim to uphold the authority of Scripture by demonstrating that it is God-breathed and therefore deserves our utmost reverence.[1]

How Should We Approach Inspiration?

How should we approach the doctrine of inspiration? One's answer to this question makes all the difference, largely determining one's outlook toward God and the Bible. According to the Enlightenment man, we are to approach Scripture like any other book, with a pair of critical glasses, determining for ourselves whether Scripture meets our modern-day criteria or suffers from a primitive lack of intelligence and ignorance. Scripture does not stand in judgment over us, but we stand over and above Scripture, deciding for ourselves whether Scripture is reasonable. Our thoughts are not to be captive to Scripture, but Scripture is to undergo the scrutiny and judgment of our enlightened reason.

In contrast, we must come to the text with open ears, asking ourselves what Scripture claims about itself. The Bible itself should be consulted as it tells us the type of book it is.[2] After all, Scripture claims to be the final authority, an authority from God himself. The burden of proof rests on those critical of Scripture, for they must answer the question, "Why shouldn't Scripture's voice in the matter be the first one we listen to?"

This will be our approach going forward: We will allow Scripture to speak for itself, rather than placing an extrabiblical (and possibly unbiblical) grid on top of Scripture. Instead of judging Scripture by preconceived modern or postmodern categories and presuppositions, we will sit at the feet of Scripture, listening to its own claims about its identity and allowing these claims to correct and shape our preunderstandings.[3] In this, we will join Augustine and Anselm and many others in church history by adopting the mind-set of faith seeking understanding.[4]

What Is Inspiration?

The Bible claims to be breathed out by God (2 Tim 3:16). But that raises a difficult question: In what sense is Scripture God-breathed? To answer this, we must understand the term *inspiration*. Throughout

---

1. Richard A. Muller, *PRRD*, 2:257.
2. E. J. Young, *Thy Word Is Truth: Some Thoughts on the Biblical Doctrine of Inspiration* (Edinburgh: Banner of Truth, 1957; repr. 1997), 17.
3. J. Todd Billings, *The Word of God for the People of God: An Entryway to the Theological Interpretation of Scripture* (Grand Rapids: Eerdmans, 2010), 45–46.
4. *Credo ut intelligam* and *fides quaerens intellectum*. For my response to those who object that such an argument is circular, see page 148.

history there have been many theories of inspiration, and we will examine six in particular.[5]

The *intuition theory* teaches that the biblical authors possessed a religious instinct, or intuition, one that is also present in other ancient pagan philosophers. This view rejects the universal, absolute truth claims made by the biblical authors. The *illumination theory* goes a step further, suggesting that the Holy Spirit was active, having influenced the biblical authors, increasing their insight. However, while the Spirit's impression may have been different in degree, it was not any different in kind, for he leaves his impression on others too. The *encounter theory* argues that though the Bible is not that different from other religious books, nevertheless it is unique when the Spirit utilizes it as a means of revelation within the community of God. Though the Bible is not inherently the Word of God in this theory, it becomes the Word of God when applied by the Spirit, which entails that inspiration is an ongoing process.[6] The *dynamic theory* takes us a step further, arguing that God left a unique, one-of-a-kind impression on the biblical authors. Yet the Spirit's influence in this view was at the conceptual level; the exact words were left up to the human authors.[7] The fifth theory, the *verbal plenary inspiration theory*, argues that there is a dual authorship to Scripture. In this view the human authors wrote exactly what they intended in their own distinct style, yet at the same time what they wrote was superintended by the Holy Spirit so that what the human author said, God said, down to the exact words and phrases. Since the author's words are God-breathed, they are without error. Finally, the *dictation theory* believes that God literally dictated his words to each human author. Since the mode is strictly mechanical, the human authors were mere secretaries. Unfortunately, some confuse the dictation view with the verbal plenary inspiration view.[8]

Several of these theories have been alluded to already in previous chapters, and while there are many views, only one is faithful to what

---

5.   For more on these, see Millard Erickson, *Christian Theology*, 3rd ed. (Grand Rapids: Baker Academic, 2013), 174–75; David S. Dockery, "Special Revelation," in *A Theology for the Church*, ed. Daniel L. Akin (Nashville: B&H, 2014), 129–31; Robert L. Plummer, *40 Questions about Interpreting the Bible* (Grand Rapids: Kregel, 2011), 31–32.

6.   For example, Karl Barth, and to varying degrees Emil Brunner, Reinhold Niebuhr, and Rudolf Bultmann.

7.   For example, A. H. Strong, E. Y. Mullins, G. C. Berkouwer, Paul Achtemeier, William Abraham, Clark Pinnock, and Donald Bloesch.

8.   I have limited our discussion to six historical views, but one might add a recent view: the *appropriated discourse theory* (e.g., Nicholas Wolterstorff, Stanley Grenz, John Franke).

Scripture says about itself. The aim of this chapter is to demonstrate that when we look at what Scripture says about inspiration, the corresponding view is verbal, plenary inspiration.[9]

The word *inspiration* can be traced back to 2 Timothy 3:16. The King James Version reads, "All scripture is given by inspiration of God," and the word "inspiration" is taken from the Greek: θεόπνευστος (*theopneustos*; *theos* meaning "God" and *pneō* meaning "to blow, breathe on"). Other Bible versions provide us with a more precise translation of θεόπνευστος. The NIV says, "All Scripture is God-breathed," and the ESV reads, "All Scripture is *breathed out* by God." These translations get to the heart of the phrase—the words of Scripture are God's own words.

While some have tried to limit inspiration to the human authors, Paul attributes inspiration to the *very words* themselves. It is the γραφή (*graphē*) itself that is breathed out by God, and this means that we should never pit *plenary* inspiration against *verbal* inspiration.[10] Paul does not say that "every Scripture" breathed out by God is inspired, or "Every inspired Scripture is also useful." Such a translation would mean that only a select portion of the text is breathed out by God (whatever portion that is), while the rest is not. While the grammar of the text is technically open to this translation, strong arguments from the text itself and its context have been made against this view and in support of the view that Paul's grammar intends to communicate that Scripture is all-extensive in its inspiration.[11] There is nothing in the immediate or larger context that indicates Paul was trying to distinguish between inspired and uninspired Scripture. Such a distinction would have been totally foreign to Paul, who elsewhere (as we shall soon see) affirmed that the entire Old Testament is breathed out by God.[12] Moreover, the

---

9.   This book is not meant to be a full doctrine of Scripture, so I will not be critiquing these views, but only presenting a positive case for verbal, plenary inspiration.

10.   See Carson's response to such a view in D. A. Carson, *Collected Writings on Scripture* (Wheaton, IL: Crossway, 2010), 64–66.

11.   Towner explains the debate over the grammar: "*Theopneustos*, however, might be understood as an attributive adjective modifying *graphē* ('every [all] *inspired* Scripture is useful . . .'), or as a predicate adjective coordinate with 'useful' ('every [all] Scripture is *inspired* and useful . . .')." Towner is in favor of the latter, arguing that the "scope is extensive, leaving no text of 'Scripture' unaccounted for" (Philip H. Towner, *The Letters to Timothy and Titus*, NICNT [Grand Rapids: Eerdmans, 2006], 585, 587). Space will not permit an exploration of these debates, but see Towner, 585–89; George W. Knight III, *The Pastoral Epistles*, NIGTC (Grand Rapids: Eerdmans, 2013), 445–48; Benjamin B. Warfield, *Revelation and Inspiration*, in *The Works of Benjamin Breckinridge Warfield*, 10 vols. (repr., Grand Rapids: Baker, 2003), 1:229–82.

12.   "Taking θεόπνευστος as attributive would imply that Paul did not regard all γραφὴ

rest of the sentence in 2 Timothy 3:16–17, which affirms the sufficiency of Scripture, would be undermined if Paul first indicated that only those texts that are inspired turn out to be profitable.[13]

The emphasis of this text falls on what God has done, stressing God's initiative in giving us the Scriptures. Paul's point is that the Bible's origin is to be traced back to God, not man.[14] The Holy Spirit is the Trinitarian person who breathed out God's words through the human authors. What a great comfort this must have been to Timothy! Edward Young writes that Paul is telling Timothy "to place his confidence not in writings which merely express the hopes and aspirations of the best of men, but rather in writings which are themselves actually breathed out by God, and consequently of absolute authority."[15] We should understand Paul to be saying "all Scripture" is breathed out by God, meaning all of the Old Testamet is inspired *in toto*, not in part.[16]

Today the word *inspiration* can mean a host of things that do not accurately capture the biblical concepts we've just covered. For example, many people assume that inspiration is synonymous with a strong feeling. One might say with great excitement, "I find the Beatles' music to be inspiring." Or "That home run was inspirational!" Or "I love her so much I was inspired to write her a poem." We tend to use the word to say that something moved us to *feel* a certain way, and applied to the Scriptures, one might be misled to think that the inspiration of Scripture merely refers to the human authors feeling inspired about what had happened and choosing to write about it. In this view, the biblical authors were inspired in the same sense that a pupil might be inspired by his teacher and therefore pass on what he has learned.[17] If that were the case, inspiration may not have much to do with God after all, since Scripture is merely a document that tells us about the religious experiences and feelings individuals had.

as God-breathed—a position that would be incredible, since by γραφὴ he always means scripture" (Knight, *Pastoral Epistles*, 447).

13. Knight, *Pastoral Epistles*, 445.

14. Young, *Thy Word Is Truth*, 20.

15. Ibid., 21.

16. See Paul Feinberg, "The Meaning of Inerrancy," in *Inerrancy*, ed. Normal L. Geisler (Grand Rapids: Zondervan, 1980), 277–79.

17. See William J. Abraham, *The Divine Inspiration of Holy Scripture* (Oxford: Oxford University Press, 1981). Abraham's view does not entail inerrancy, infallibility, or verbal inspiration, for he denies that the pupil passes on his teacher's material perfectly. For a critique, see D. A. Carson, "Recent Developments in the Doctrine of Scripture," in *Hermeneutics, Authority, and Canon*, ed. D. A. Carson and John D. Woodbridge (Eugene, OR: Wipf & Stock, 2005), 29–30.

Undoubtedly, the apostles were moved to their core after seeing Jesus again after his resurrection, and they chose to act on that experience. But this inspired feeling is not what we are referring to when we say Scripture is inspired. Instead, we are referring to God's act in superintending the human authors, causing them to write what he desired. This is why the phrase "God-breathed" more acutely conveys what we mean when we say Scripture is inspired. We are not merely reading a story about the religious experience an individual decided to write down; we are reading accounts that God himself has authored through these individuals who reported what took place.

To complicate matters further, modern usage of the word tends to communicate something being *breathed in* or inhaled. Yet the context of 2 Timothy 3:16 clearly conveys something being exhaled. God's words are not breathed in; they are breathed out! God's words come out from him to us, not vice versa.[18] This clarification has led some to use words like *spiration* or *expiration* instead of *inspiration*.[19]

This is important because some may be tempted to think that the human authors wrote their books, and God, like a Johnny-come-lately, saw what they wrote after the fact and decided he would adopt it.[20] This view is comparable to the early christological heresy known as Adoptionism, which argued that Jesus was an ordinary man whom God decided to adopt (most likely at Jesus's baptism) and implant his divine spark within.[21] Adoptionism was seen as heretical because it undermined and compromised the full divine identity of Christ as the second person of the eternal Trinity. By comparison, such a view cannot be applied to the Scriptures because 2 Timothy 3:16 does not convey that God breathed something divine into the human writings after the fact, but rather the reason the Scriptures exist is because God himself

---

18. Some have suggested the word *spiration* instead in order to correct such a misconception. For example, see David S. Dockery, *Christian Scripture* (Eugene, OR: Wipf & Stock, 1995), 41. I disagree, however, with the way McGowan uses the word to argue against inerrancy. See A. T. B. McGowan, *The Divine Authenticity of Scripture: Retrieving an Evangelical Heritage* (Downers Grove, IL: InterVarsity Press, 2008). For an excellent critique, see Frame, *Doctrine of the Word of God*, 525–53.

19. For example, see Warfield, *Revelation and Inspiration*, 1:77–114; John Stott, *The Message of 2 Timothy* (Downers Grove, IL: InterVarsity Press, 1984), 101–2.

20. Warfield, *Revelation and Inspiration*, 1:99 (cf. 100 on "breathing out" versus "breathing into").

21. Unashamedly, Sparks identifies his view of inspiration as comparable to adoptionism. See Kenton L. Sparks, *Sacred Word, Broken Word: Biblical Authority and the Dark Side of Scripture* (Grand Rapids: Eerdmans, 2012), 29, 53–55.

breathed them out.[22] While the books of the Bible are written by man, their origin, or genesis, is from God. They are God's creative acts. They are the products of divine inspiration.[23]

The actual ins and outs of how inspiration works remain mysteries to us. It is difficult to explain *how* God breathes out Scripture, yet at the very least we can say it means that the words penned by the human authors of Scripture are, without qualification, God's words.[24] As John Frame explains, inspiration "is a divine act creating an identity between a divine word and a human word."[25] Frame's definition recognizes the fundamental truth of inspiration, namely, that there is a relationship between the divine author's words and the human author's words, a relationship God himself initiates and creates. With that in mind, I offer the following definition of inspiration:

> The inspiration of Scripture refers to that act whereby the Holy Spirit came upon the authors of Scripture, causing them to write exactly what God intended, while simultaneously preserving each author's writing style and personality. This supernatural work of the Holy Spirit upon the human authors means that the author's words are God's words and therefore are reliable, trustworthy, and authoritative.[26]

Scripture: Divine *and* Human

This definition indicates that there are divine and human aspects to Scripture, though the former is primary. God is the divine author and Scripture comes from him. However, God did not drop the Bible down from heaven, nor did he give it to man mechanically. He used ordinary human beings—often in the ordinary affairs of everyday life—to communicate over a long period of time what he intended. There is a *dual authorship* to Scripture, which means that each biblical book has both a divine author and a human author. The divine author is in full control,

---

22. Young, *Thy Word Is Truth*, 22–23.

23. Warfield, *Revelation and Inspiration*, 1:269 (cf. 280).

24. I believe a compatibilist view of divine sovereignty and human freedom explains the mystery best. See Stephen J. Wellum, "The Importance of the Nature of Divine Sovereignty for Our View of Scripture," *Southern Baptist Journal of Theology* 4, no. 2 (2000): 76–90.

25. Frame, *Systematic Theology*, 595.

26. For similar definitions, see Archibald A. Hodge and Benjamin B. Warfield, *Inspiration* (Grand Rapids: Baker, 1979), 17; Robert Saucy, *Scripture: Its Power, Authority, and Relevance* (Nashville: Nelson, 2001), 134; Young, *Thy Word Is Truth*, 27.

guiding, directing, and providentially and supernaturally superintending everything so that his exact words are communicated.[27] Benjamin Warfield says it best: "The Bible is the Word of God in such a sense that its words, though written by men and bearing indelibly impressed upon them the marks of their human origin, were written, nevertheless, under such an influence of the Holy Ghost as to be also the words of God, the adequate expression of His mind and will."[28] Consider the prophets. Scripture speaks of them as under "the hand" or "the strong hand" of the Lord (2 Kgs 3:15; Ezek 1:3; 3:14, 22; 33:33; 37:1; 40:1). God's control is both "complete and compelling, so that, under it, the prophet becomes not the 'mover,' but the 'moved' in the formation of his message."[29]

It is crucial to reiterate this emphasis on divine control in inspiration. Those critical of the Bible have argued that the Christianity of the Bible begins and originates with man and his creative genius (or lack thereof). They say the Bible is man-made, revealing each author's religious thoughts and aspirations about the supernatural.[30] However, Scripture presents Christianity in the exact opposite way, namely, as a *revealed religion*, one that comes from God to man, not vice versa. Warfield explains:

> The religion of the Bible thus announces itself, not as the product of men's search after God, if haply they may feel after Him and find Him, but as the creation in men of the gracious God, forming a people for Himself, that they may show forth His praise. In other words, the religion of the Bible presents itself as distinctively a revealed religion. Or rather, to speak more exactly, it announces itself as the revealed religion, as the only revealed religion; and sets itself as such over against all other religions, which are represented as all products, in a sense in which it is not, of the art and device of man.[31]

And Warfield astutely concludes:

---

27. This is not to imply that the human authors were out of control. Not at all. Rather, I am merely asserting that God, being God, was totally sovereign over the entire process.

28. Warfield, *Revelation and Inspiration*, 1:173.

29. Ibid., 1:23 (cf. 1:26–27).

30. This approach was seen with Liberalism in chapter 3. Today it is once again seen with individuals like Sparks who view the Bible as primarily human and therefore fallible, broken, fallen, impure, and in need of redemption and sanctification. See Sparks, *Sacred Word, Broken Word*, 46–48, 63–66, 107, 115, 157.

31. Warfield, *Revelation and Inspiration*, 1:4.

We should bear in mind that the intellectual or spiritual quality of revelation is not derived from the recipient but from its Divine Giver. The fundamental fact in all revelation is that it is from God. This is what gives unity to the whole process of revelation, given though it may be in divers portions and in divers manners and distributed though it may be through the ages in accordance with the mere will of God, or as it may have suited His developing purpose—this and its unitary end, which is ever the building up of the kingdom of God. In whatever diversity of forms, by means of whatever variety of modes, in whatever distinguishable stages it is given, it is ever the revelation of the One God, and it is ever the one consistently developing redemptive revelation of God.[32]

The question that naturally follows is: "What role, then, does the human author play?" Some have argued that man hardly plays any role in this process, and those who have gone in this direction tend to affirm the dictation theory of inspiration in which the human author was totally passive as God directly and unilaterally dictated his words. The human author merely wrote down what God dictated, much like a secretary. Anything human that might contribute to the Scriptures is suspended in the process. This view has understandably been criticized. When applied to Scripture as a whole, it does not take into consideration the human role, but makes man mechanical and robotic in the entire process. As Warfield warns, we should not think of inspiration as an event where the human author is in "strict ecstasy, involving the complete abeyance of all mental life."[33]

The Bible does not present us with a dictation theory of inspiration. On the contrary, man's mind is attentive and active in the reception of God's revelation. The recipient's mind is not a barrier to the process (nor an embarrassment), but is the very means God uses to bring about his Word.[34] Here is where distinctions must be made. While man's intelligence was active in the process, we should not go so far as to think that it was the human mind that invented Scripture, only for God to come along and put his support behind it. As Warfield puts the matter, while the intelligence of the biblical authors may be the "instrument of revelation," their intelligence cannot be "active in the *production* of

---

32. Ibid., 1:16.
33. Ibid., 1:21.
34. Peter Jensen, *The Revelation of God* (Downers Grove, IL: InterVarsity Press, 2002), 39.

their message."[35] They can be "receptively active," Warfield explains, but not "creatively" active.[36] The former concept conveys that man is actively receiving revelation, while the latter insinuates that man, not God, is the author of the message.

For example, when we look at the major and minor prophets, we find the prophets insisting that their message is not their own but is from God. This is precisely what distinguishes them from false prophets. The false prophet, as we saw in chapter 5, comes in his own spirit with his own words and his own message, whereas the true prophet comes in the Spirit of God as the mouthpiece of God. But being a mouthpiece does not preclude the prophet's own activity. The prophets were active, not only in receiving divine revelation but in delivering it. Yet what they proclaim is not their own but belongs to God and is from God. As Peter asserts, "For prophecy never had its origin in the human will, but prophets, though human, spoke from God as they were carried along by the Holy Spirit" (2 Pet 1:21).

What Peter describes has been labeled *concursus* by theologians, a term borrowed from the doctrine of providence.[37] Concursive involvement, says Warfield, means that "the whole of Scripture is the product of divine activities which enter it, however, not by superseding the activities of the human authors, but confluently with them; so that the Scriptures are the joint product of divine and human activities, both of which penetrate them at every point."[38] Much like God's providential involvement in the contingent, fallen world, God's concursive operation in inspiration does not entail the abandonment of his divine freedom, sovereignty, holiness, or truthfulness.[39] As we've seen in chapters 2 and 7, the incarnation of our Lord proves that the intrusion of the divine does not compromise the human, nor does the adoption of that which is human necessarily profane the divine. As Peter Jensen notes,

---

35. Warfield, *Revelation and Inspiration*, 1:23, emphasis added.
36. Ibid.
37. The word *concursus* comes from Latin *concurro*. It refers to two people cooperating with each other in a single action or event. On "concurrence" to describe inspiration, see Hodge and Warfield, *Inspiration*, 14–17.
38. Benjamin B. Warfield, "The Divine and Human in the Bible," in *Selected Shorter Writings of Benjamin B. Warfield*, ed. John E. Meeter, 2 vols. (Nutley, NJ: P&R, 1970–73), 2:547. At other times Warfield uses the term *confluence*. See Hodge and Warfield, *Inspiration*, 16.
39. Mark D. Thompson, "The Divine Investment in Truth: Toward a Theological Account of Biblical Inerrancy," in *Do Historical Matters Matter to Faith? A Critical Appraisal of Modern and Postmodern Approaches to Scriptures*, ed. James K. Hoffmeier and Dennis R. Magary (Wheaton, IL: Crossway, 2012), 88.

"God's sovereign involvement in the created order need not be seen as jeopardizing genuine human agency, nor need it be taken as ensnaring God in the real limitations and moral failures of the human agents."[40]

We more clearly see man's activity in this divine-human concursus when we look at how God frequently used the ordinary means of human life, even the peculiar and unique personalities, traits, background, and individual gifts of each author to bring about his message. Luke was a physician and a historian. David was a king, a warrior, and a poet. The apostles were mostly fishermen. We see God's providence at work when we read that prior to God calling Moses to go to Pharaoh, he was raised in the courts of Egypt by Pharaoh's daughter. Prior to David officially reigning as king, he was a servant in the house of King Saul. And prior to Paul encountering unbelieving Jews, he received instruction under the rabbi and teacher Gamaliel. Inspiration does not require God to wipe out or obliterate human personalities or cultural upbringing. On the contrary, the unique personalities of the human authors color each book of the Bible as God utilized each author's cultural, social, educational, and linguistic characteristics in a unique way to bring about exactly what he wanted to say.[41]

With God's use of ordinary human means in mind, Abraham Kuyper and Herman Bavinck clarify that there is an *organic* (as opposed to *mechanical*) nature to the inspiration of Scripture.[42] God does not merely communicate information through the human author, but he communicates the perspective, tone, and voice of the author as well. God often utilized the diverse experiences and personalities of the human authors,[43] yet God's use of human language and real human persons does not lessen the quality of Scripture or make it impure. To the contrary, God's use of human language and human persons gives Scripture a rich diversity. Human authorship does not distort Scripture, like light passing through a dirty window, thereby causing it to cease being pure and holy. Rather, God prepares the path for Scripture by providentially forming the very personalities of those through whom

---

40. Ibid.

41. Herman Bavinck, *Reformed Dogmatics* (Grand Rapids: Baker, 2003), 1:432–33, 438; Warfield, *Revelation and Inspiration*, 1:101; Scott R. Swain, *Trinity, Revelation, and Reading: A Theological Introduction to the Bible and Its Interpretation* (New York: T&T Clark, 2011), 67.

42. Bavinck, *Reformed Dogmatics*, 1:428–48.

43. Frame, *Systematic Theology*, 596.

he has chosen to communicate his Word.[44] Surely if God can providentially control, sustain, and govern the cosmos, he can bring about his Word through human flesh. He did it with the incarnation; he did it again with Scripture.[45]

In light of the human role in the inspiration of Scripture, we must avoid thinking that we can cut up Scripture, parceling out its pieces as "divine" and "human," as if we could somehow assign a certain percentage to each. The biblical authors never thought of Scripture in this way. "In their view," says Warfield, "the whole of Scripture in all its parts and in all its elements, down to the least minutiae, in form of expression as well as in substance of teaching, is from God; but the whole of it has been given by God through the instrumentality of men." Warfield concludes, "There is, therefore, in their view, not, indeed, a human element or ingredient in Scripture, and much less human divisions or sections of Scripture, but a human side or aspect to Scripture; and they do not fail to give full recognition to this human side or aspect."[46] Warfield's point is supported by 2 Peter 1:21, where man participates, but it is only because he speaks from God, carried along by the Holy Spirit. Balance is necessary. We do not want to so emphasize the human contribution that we make Scripture a human product. At the same time, we do not want to so emphasize the divine that human instrumentality is irrelevant.

Nevertheless, there is still some truth in the dictation theory that we cannot immediately dispense with. While it is fair to say that the normal or typical pattern of inspiration is not dictation, there are occasions when God does directly dictate his words. For example, when God gathered Israel at Mount Sinai to make a covenant with his people, God spoke directly to Moses, giving him the Ten Commandments (Exod 19:1–20:21; 34:27–28). In the book of Revelation we discover that God sent his angel to his servant John who "bore witness to the word of God and to the testimony of Jesus Christ" (Rev 1:1–2 ESV). The words of this prophecy were given to John and were addressed to the seven churches in Asia (1:4; cf. 2–3). John recalls how he was on the island of Patmos, and when he was in the Spirit on the Lord's Day "a loud voice like a trumpet" said, "Write on a scroll what you see and

---

44. Warfield, *Revelation and Inspiration*, 1:102.
45. Swain, *Trinity, Revelation, and Reading*, 70.
46. Warfield, *Revelation and Inspiration*, 1:96.

send it to the seven churches" (1:11). John turned around and saw one like a son of man (1:13), who is "the First and the Last. . . . the Living One" who died and rose again, who has the keys of death and Hades (1:17–18). John then receives his instruction: "Write, therefore, what you have seen, what is now and what will take place later" (1:19). John's experience certainly qualifies for divine dictation.[47]

Some have protested that divine dictation is denigrating because it turns the human author into a mere instrument, like a pen in the hand of the author or an instrument in the hand of a musician. But how wonderful and glorious it would be if the Lord chose to use us in this way![48] Furthermore, we must ask critics what, exactly, is their problem with dictation (the concept, not the theory). Wouldn't dictation, after all, provide *more* certainty, as opposed to less, when it comes to the reception of an inspired Word from God? As Peter Jensen asks, "Is it the baldness of the claim, the brute fact of so fearful a thing as the actual word of God, that is the underlying problem?"[49] Jensen wonders if underlying the allergic reaction critics and many evangelicals have to dictation is a prejudice against the miraculous, an attempt to restrict God from acting directly and supernaturally. In our attempts to accommodate human involvement in the inspiration of the Scriptures, we must be careful not to swing the pendulum too far to the other side. Though it is not the normal mode of inspiration, God has used dictation in redemptive history, as rare as it might be, and while we should reject a dictation *theory* of inspiration, we should recognize the diverse ways God breathes out Scripture.

Inspiration Is Verbal *and* Plenary

We have affirmed that inspiration involves God creatively making the human author's words his words. It should be evident that inspiration is not some abstract, stoic, impersonal act of God. Rather, it is intensely *personal* in nature. We can say that Scripture is *God's* Word, but we can also say that Scripture is God's *Word*. In other words, the personal nature of inspiration is apparent in God's use of ordinary

---

47. Dictation also occurred when a biblical author used a secretary to write down his words. For example, the prophet Jeremiah called the son of Neriah, Baruch, to write down on a scroll all the words of the Lord that Jeremiah dictated to him (Jer 36:4). Also consider Isaiah 6:9; 38:4–6.

48. Frame, *Systematic Theology*, 595.

49. Jensen, *Revelation of God*, 159.

human language rather than heavenly language that is unintelligible to finite and fallible human beings.

Inspiration has an inherently *verbal* nature to it; it is not merely the concepts and ideas that are God-breathed, but the very words themselves. These words are what make up the ideas and concepts, and this is why bifurcating the two is unjustified. Without words, there would be no message. The words of Scripture are indispensable and essential.[50]

Inspiration is *plenary*, or all-extensive, as well. Not only does inspiration extend to the very words of Scripture but to *all* the words of Scripture (*tota Scriptura*). And by "all" we mean absolutely everything. We cannot decide for ourselves what parts of Scripture are inspired and what parts are not. Scripture never limits its inspiration to only some of its parts (say, the big ideas or concepts but not the historical details). Nor does Scripture give us hermeneutical autonomy and sovereignty to decide for ourselves which parts are God's Word and which parts are not.[51]

Inspiration and Divine Accommodation

Because there is a dual authorship to Scripture, we can genuinely say that while God breathes out his words, he does so through human authors, all the while preserving each one's human personality and agency. Redemptive history is a unified story of how the triune God has revealed himself through covenantal acts, persons, and words—words not merely spoken but intentionally written down. God has condescended to our level to manifest his divine character and saving will to his people. As Calvin says, it is as if God uses baby talk, lisping as a father does to his child.[52] Even the medium used to reveal himself displays the beauty of divine accommodation. The wonder of divine condescension is apparent in the diverse styles of language God utilized to communicate his message. The flow of the Hebrew in a book like Deuteronomy is smooth, making its narrative a pleasure to read, and Psalm 23 is written in a way that has a quiet tenderness to it.[53] When you turn the page to Psalm 90 or to the book of Daniel, it is startling just how rough and rugged the Hebrew can be.

---

50. Hodge and Warfield, *Inspiration*, 21–23; Frame, *Systematic Theology*, 596.
51. See chapter 8 where I critique such approaches in detail.
52. John Calvin, *Institutes of the Christian Religion*, ed. John T. McNeill, trans. Ford Lewis Battles (Philadelphia: Westminster, 1960), 1.13.1.
53. Young, *Thy Word Is Truth*, 116.

Or consider the *Koine* Greek of the NT. The opening verses of the Gospel of Luke are beautifully constructed, displaying a linguistic crescendo. Yet verse 5 abruptly changes pitch, and the reader is suddenly "thrust into another world."[54] No longer does the text resemble classical Greek but instead the "simplicity of the Semitic."[55] Diversity exists across the NT canon as well. The Greek of Luke, the physician, or of the writer of Hebrews is often eloquent and elevated. In contrast, Peter's language is simple, not necessarily the most eloquent.

There is beauty in this diversity. God did not wipe out the uniqueness of the human authors, but accommodated himself, using different literary styles and grammatical constructions to communicate to different types of people in the first century. The use of poor grammar doesn't reveal errancy but shows how far God will accommodate himself to the common language of the people.[56] The Bible is far from monotonous; it is a majestic mosaic.

Some have concluded that if God accommodated himself to humanity in the writing of Scripture, then there must be errors in Scripture.[57] But there is a theological jump in that logic. It automatically assumes that *to err is human*. Theologically speaking, error, and even sin, is not something essential to humanity.[58] One does not cease to be human if error or sin is absent. Adam and Eve were created by God without flaw, without sin. One day believers will spend eternity in a glorified state, with fully human, resurrected bodies, without sin. So while sin and error certainly characterize our present in-between state, neither is essential to our human essence and existence.

Furthermore, we must not forget that God is sovereign. Why

---

54. Ibid., 117.

55. Ibid.

56. Frame, *Systematic Theology*, 601; Young, *Thy Word Is Truth*, 117.

57. See Karl Barth, *Church Dogmatics* I, part 2, *The Doctrine of the Word of God* (Edinburgh: T&T Clark, 1956), 531; Clark Pinnock, *The Scripture Principle* (San Francisco: Harper & Row, 1984), 97, 100; Bruce Vawter, *Biblical Inspiration* (Philadelphia: Westminster, 1972; London: Hutchinson, 1972), 169. Other authors who take this view include Bernard Ramm, Daniel Fuller, Donald McKim, and Jack Rogers. For a critique, see Carson, "Recent Developments in the Doctrine of Scripture," 26–27; Wayne Grudem, "Scripture's Self-Attestation and the Problem of Formulating a Doctrine of Scripture," in *Scripture and Truth*, ed. D. A. Carson and John Woodbridge (Grand Rapids: Baker, 1983), 53–57.

58. For an extensive defense of the compatibility of the humanity of Scripture and inerrancy against those who argue for incompatibility—Karl Barth, Emil Brunner, Reinhold Niebuhr, Richard Niebuhr, Paul Tillich, Herry Boer, Charles Davis, Leslie Dewart, Hans Küng, G. C. Berkouwer, see Gordon R. Lewis, "The Human Authorship of Inspired Scripture," in Geisler, *Inerrancy*, 229–64.

couldn't a sovereign God accommodate himself to human authors yet guarantee that his Word remain flawless? Why must human fallibility or error be mixed in with his Word? He is the God of the universe. As the Creator of all things, he can accommodate himself to mankind without imbibing human error into his revelation. Inspiration through divine accommodation need not incorporate human fallibility. God has communicated his words through the commonplace speech of man, and at the same time has done it in such a way that man's fallen tendencies toward error were avoided and overcome. The greatest example of this is seen in the incarnation itself, where the Son took on human flesh, was tempted, and then was crucified as an atoning sacrifice, and yet "did not sin" (Heb 2:17; 4:15).[59]

Others have taken divine accommodation in a distinctly christological direction. Jesus, they argue, accommodated himself to the erroneous beliefs of his listeners to get his message across. They say he quoted from the Old Testament not because he thought the Scriptures were God-breathed, but only because he knew his audience held this belief. This view is mistaken for several reasons. Jesus was very clear that everything he said and did was in fulfillment of the Old Testament. Jesus referred to the Old Testament as that which is from God and is authored by God and is fully trustworthy and authoritative. Jesus never had a problem challenging the religious leaders (and others) when he disagreed with them, showing them that they were in error and in need of correction (Matt 3:7; 12:34; 23:33). Why would we think that he would be any less bold if he thought his opponents held a high view of Scripture that was uncalled for?[60]

The Inspiration of the Old Testament

The most important question for us to consider is this: Does Scripture portray itself as inspired in the way we have described? We have already taken a close look at 2 Timothy 3:16. The perspective

---

59. Compare 2 Cor 5:21; 1 Pet 3:18. See Thompson, "Divine Investment in Truth," 90.

60. Saucy, *Scripture*, 122–23; Thompson, "Divine Investment in Truth," 91–92. It should also be noted that such a view of accommodation runs contrary to the understanding of accommodation held from the patristic to post-Reformation period. See Muller, *DLGTT*, s.v. *accommodatio*, 19; Carson, "Recent Developments in the Doctrine of Scripture," 27; John D. Woodbridge, "Some Misconceptions of the Impact of the Enlightenment on the Doctrine of Scripture," in Carson and Woodbridge, *Hermeneutics, Authority, and Canon*, 237–70; Glenn S. Sunshine, "Accommodation Historically Considered," in *The Enduring Authority of the Christian Scriptures*, ed. D. A. Carson (Grand Rapids: Eerdmans, 2016), 238–65.

we find there is also evident when we look at the whole testimony of Scripture.

The Witness of the Old Testament

In chapter 5 we saw that the God of the Bible is a speaking God. Countless times God spoke in order to be heard and obeyed (e.g., Gen 1:28–30; 3:9–19; 12:1–3).[61] His speech to and through his prophets was clear, and when the prophets delivered God's message to God's people, it came with a divine stamp of authority, as evident in the opening phrase, "Thus says the LORD," a phrase used hundreds of times. The very words of God were put in the mouths of God's prophets (e.g., Exod 4:12; 24:3; Num 22:38; 23:5, 16).[62] What the prophet said, God said (1 Kgs 13:21, 26; 21:19; Hag 1:12; 1 Sam 15:3, 18), which is apparent in how many times the prophets spoke on God's behalf in the first person (see 2 Sam 7:4–16; 1 Kgs 20:13, 42).[63] Therefore, to disobey the prophet was to disobey God himself.[64]

Not only did God speak through his prophets to be heard but he also commanded that his words be written down. These written words were considered authoritative precisely because they were from God (i.e., they were *his* words).[65] In Exodus 31:18, God gave to Moses the "two tablets of the covenant law"; these were "tablets of stone inscribed by the finger of God." They were the work of God and the writing was the writing of God (Exod 34:1, 28; Deut 4:13; 10:4).[66] Moses was told numerous times to write down all the words of the Lord (Exod 17:14; 24:4; 34:27; Num 33:2; Deut 31:22, 24), and Joshua, the new Moses, was also told to write down God's words in the "Book of the Law of God" (Josh 24:26; cf. Neh 8:1–3). When the prophet Samuel finished telling Israel the rights and duties of the king, he "wrote them down on a scroll and deposited it before the LORD" (1 Sam 10:25). King David's acts are said to be "written in the records of Samuel the seer, the records of Nathan the prophet and the records of Gad the seer" (1 Chr 29:29), as are the acts of Solomon "in the records of Nathan"

---

61. Exod 3:1–4:23; 20:1–4; 1 Sam 3:10–14; 1 Kgs 19:9–18; Job 38–41; Isa 6:8–13; Jonah 1:1–2; 3:1–2; 4:1–11.

62. Deut 18:18–22; Jer 1:9; 37:2; Ezek 2:7; 3:27. See also 1 Kgs 16:34; 2 Kgs 9:36; 14:25; 17:23; 24:2; 2 Chr 29:25; Ezra 9:10–11; Neh 9:30; Zech 7:7, 12.

63. 2 Kgs 17:13; 19:25–28, 34; 21:12–15; 22:16–20; 2 Chr 12:5; Isa 45:5.

64. Deut 18:19; 1 Sam 8:7 [2 Chr 20:20]; 1 Sam 13:13–14; 15:19–23; 1 Kgs 20:25–26.

65. Bavinck, *Reformed Dogmatics*, 1:391.

66. Grudem, "Scripture's Self-Attestation," 25–26.

(2 Chr 9:29), and many others.[67] The prophets were no exception. God told Isaiah, Jeremiah, Ezekiel, Habakkuk, and Daniel to write everything he had spoken to them, so that it would be a witness forever (Isa 30:8; Jer 30:2; Ezek 43:11; Dan 7:1; Hab 2:2).[68]

God's purpose in his oral and written communication was to enter into and maintain his covenantal relationship with his chosen people. The prophets' written words served as an authoritative record of the covenant's provisions.[69] They also bore public testimony to the agreement made by both sides. In short, their written words stood tall as a living witness to God's covenant, and we see references to the book of the covenant (Exod 24:7; 2 Kgs 23:2–3, 21; 2 Chr 34:30). This is why Isaiah's writings can serve as a witness against Israel should they disobey (Isa 30:8; cf. Deut 31:19, 26), since the stipulations regarding one's behavior as a covenant member are conveyed in a written book (Exod 34:27; Josh 24:26; 1 Sam 10:25; Ezek 43:11), and the Bible's historical narratives can be identified as records of whether the covenant bond has been broken or kept.[70] Even the latter prophets are listed as covenant messengers reiterating the covenant provisos so that covenant obedience results.[71] The covenantal nature of God's communication in written form would have been an obvious indicator to Israel that the words they heard and read were from God, breathed out by God, and authoritative. Certainly Jesus believed this was true.

Jesus Believed the Old Testament Was Inspired by God

One of the most powerful arguments for the inspiration of the OT is that Jesus himself affirmed such a belief in a variety of ways.

1. *Jesus attributed the Old Testament writings to the Holy Spirit.* Consider Mark 12:35–37. Jesus was teaching in the temple when asked the question, "Why do the teachers of the law say that the Messiah is the son of David?" (12:35). Jesus then quoted from Psalm 110:1:

---

67. For example, Rehoboam (2 Chr 12:15), Abijah (2 Chr 13:22), Jehoshaphat (2 Chr 20:34), Ussiah (2 Chr 26:22), Hezekiah (2 Chr 32:32).
68. See also Jer 29:1; 36:1–32; 45:1; 51:60. For a more in-depth defense of the inspiration of the prophetic writings, see Bavinck, *Reformed Dogmatics*, 1:389–94.
69. Grudem, "Scripture's Self-Attestation," 27.
70. Ibid.
71. Ibid.

David himself, speaking by the Holy Spirit, declared:

> "The Lord said to my Lord:
> 'Sit at my right hand
>   until I put your enemies under your feet.'"

David himself calls him "Lord." How then can he be his son? (Mark 12:36–37)

This passage has far more to do with the deity of Jesus than with the Spirit, but we cannot miss what Jesus says about the Spirit. Jesus did not deny that David was the author of Psalm 110. However, Jesus says that David did not speak on his own, but he spoke "by the Holy Spirit" (Mark 12:36; cf. 2 Sam 23:2; Acts 1:16; 4:25), for he was a "prophet" of God (Acts 2:30–31). In other words, his psalm was not the product of his own invention, but he was moved along by the Spirit to put down these words.[72] We know that inspiration is in view when we consider exactly what David said "by the Holy Spirit," referring not to one but to two Lords. This passage was used by Jesus to assert his own divine identity as Lord and Messiah.

2. *Jesus referred to Old Testament books as "Scripture(s)" from God.* Not only are Old Testament books attributed to the Spirit, but Jesus also identified them as God-breathed "scripture." Consider Luke 4, where Jesus entered the synagogue on the Sabbath and read from the scroll of the prophet Isaiah (4:16–19). After reading this passage from Isaiah, Jesus sat down and, with all eyes on him, said, "Today this scripture (ἡ γραφὴ) is fulfilled in your hearing" (4:21). What is astonishing about this narrative is that Jesus claimed that such a prophecy was now fulfilled in him, the Spirit-anointed Messiah. But don't miss the fact that Jesus referred to this Old Testament passage as "scripture." Isaiah's words were God's words, and so they could be referred to as "scripture."

A similar passage is John 7:37–38. On the last day of the

---

72. See Robert H. Stein, *Mark*, BECNT (Grand Rapids: Baker Academic, 2008), 570; James R. Edwards, *The Gospel according to Mark*, PNTC (Grand Rapids: Eerdmans, 2002), 376; R. T. France, *The Gospel of Mark*, NIGTC (Grand Rapids: Eerdmans, 2002), 487; William L. Lane, *The Gospel of Mark*, NICNT (Grand Rapids: Eerdmans, 1974), 436–37; Thomas R. Schreiner, *The King in His Beauty: A Biblical Theology of the Old and New Testaments* (Grand Rapids: Baker Academic, 2013), 139.

feast Jesus cried out, "If anyone thirsts, let him come to me and drink. Whoever believes in me, as the Scripture [ἡ γραφή] has said, 'Out of his heart will flow rivers of living water'" (ESV). Once again, Jesus said that the Old Testament was being fulfilled through him. The passage, in this case possibly Zechariah 14:8, Proverbs 4:23, or Isaiah 44:3, 55:1, 58:11, is referred to as "the Scripture."[73] Here Jesus incorporates the words of "Scripture" as his own authoritative promise.[74]

In Matthew 21, after telling the parable of the wicked tenants, Jesus quoted from Psalm 118:22–23 to apply the parable to his own day.[75] Jesus then asked, "Have you never read in the Scriptures [ταῖς γραφαῖς] . . ." (v. 42). Not only the prophets but the psalms too were labeled as Scripture by Jesus.

Jesus did the same in Matthew 26 at his arrest. When one of his disciples cut off the ear of the soldier arresting him, Jesus told his zealous follower to put his sword away, for if he wanted to use violence he could easily call down twelve legions of angels. But if he did so, how "then would the Scriptures [αἱ γραφαὶ] be fulfilled that say it must happen in this way?" (26:54). The "Scriptures" Jesus had in mind were none other than the Old Testament writings (specifically Zech 13:7–9), and these "Scriptures" were being fulfilled in the suffering of Christ.[76] As Jesus said in John 5:39, "These are the very Scriptures that testify about me."

Numerous other passages do the same.[77] John Wenham's observation here is on target: "Scripture is Scripture to Christ because it has (in a way which other writing has not) God as its primary author."[78]

---

73. Köstenberger believes Jesus may be referring to not just one particular OT passage but to the "common prophetic teaching." If he is right, Jesus's reference to "Scripture" would be even broader. See the texts that Jesus may have in mind in Andreas J. Köstenberger, *John*, BECNT (Grand Rapids: Baker Academic, 2004), 240.

74. J. Ramsey Michaels, *The Gospel of John*, NICNT (Grand Rapids: Eerdmans, 2010), 467.

75. Compare Mark 12:10; Luke 20:17.

76. Others may include Pss 22; 69; Isa 52–53.

77. One might also consult passages where the word "Scripture" is not used, but it is assumed that the OT referred to is under divine inspiration. See Matt 12:3; 19:4; 21:16; 22:31; Mark 2:25; 12:10, 26; Luke 6:3. See also passages where the phrase "it is written" is used: Matt 11:10; 21:13; 26:24, 31; Mark 9:12, 13; 11:17; 14:21, 27; Luke 7:27; 19:46. See John Wenham, *Christ and the Bible*, 3rd ed. (Grand Rapids: Baker, 1994), 33.

78. Ibid., 34.

3. *Jesus used "Scripture" and "God" interchangeably.* Since Jesus repeatedly referred to the Old Testament as Scripture, we should also consider how Jesus used "Scripture" and "God" synony- mously. In doing this, Jesus was following the pattern of the Old Testament, where innumerable times the Torah and Yahweh are spoken of interchangeably, word/command/Torah being sub- stituted for the divine name, Yahweh (e.g., Ps 119:19–20, 31, 41–42, 46–48).[79]

While numerous passages could be listed, consider Matthew 19 where the Pharisees tested Jesus, asking him whether it was lawful to divorce one's wife.[80] Jesus responded by quoting Gen- esis 1:27 and 2:24. "Have you not read that he who created them from the beginning made them male and female, and said, 'Therefore a man shall leave his father and his mother and hold fast to his wife, and the two shall become one flesh'?" (Matt 19:4–5 ESV).[81] What is assumed in Jesus's quotation is that God is the primary author of Genesis. In other words, Jesus did not say, "Moses said," but rather "he [God] . . . said."[82] Jesus believed that Genesis was a book that had God as its author and architect.[83] So assumed is this truth that Jesus felt no need to explain it; he simply assumed its validity, as did the Pharisees and any other Jew at the time (cf. Matt 19:7–8). As R. T. France says, "Jesus attributes this comment by the author of Genesis to God himself. Such an attribution would have caused no surprise in first-century Judaism, for which Scripture as a whole was the Word of God, so that its contents, even if narratively spoken by someone else, are God's statements."[84]

We will soon see that such interchangeability is found not only in Jesus's teachings but throughout the New Testament. Still, it is clear that for Jesus, God and Scripture can be spoken

---

79. Daniel I. Block, *Deuteronomy*, NIVAC (Grand Rapids: Zondervan, 2012), 715.

80. Other passages to consider in the Gospels include Matt 1:22; 4:4; 22:29–32; Mark 7:9–13; Luke 1:70; 24:25; John 5:45–47.

81. Compare Mark 10:3; Deut 24:1–4.

82. John Nolland, *The Gospel of Matthew*, NIGTC (Grand Rapids: Eerdmans, 2005), 771.

83. Wenham, *Christ and the Bible*, 35.

84. R. T. France, *The Gospel of Matthew*, NICNT (Grand Rapids: Eerdmans, 2007), 717. Some have translated "and said" (καὶ εἶπεν) in verse 5 not as part of Jesus's argument whereby he refers to what God said in the Genesis narrative but rather as Matthew introduc- ing an additional statement by Jesus. For why such a translation is misguided, see France, *Gospel of Matthew*, 711n.4; 717.

of synonymously, demonstrating that Scripture *is* the very Word of God. We should not attempt to drive a wedge between the two.[85]

4. *Jesus believed the Old Testament was fulfilled because it had God as its author.* We will treat this point briefly here since it was covered in greater detail in chapter 6.

If Jesus believed the Old Testament was God-breathed, wouldn't we expect him to appeal to it, even to its tiniest stipulations, to show that his own ministry was in fulfillment of God's promises? And that is what we find. For instance, in Matthew 5:17–18 Jesus says he did not come to abolish the Law or the Prophets (i.e., the whole OT) but to fulfill them, and not even the smallest detail of the Law would pass away until all was accomplished. Likewise, at the start of his ministry, Jesus read from the scroll of Isaiah in the synagogue only to sit down and say that these words were fulfilled in himself (Luke 4:18–21; cf. Isa 61:1). And when John the Baptist wondered whether Jesus was the one prophesied about in the OT, Jesus told John to look at Jesus's miracles. Why? Because his miracles demonstrated that he was fulfilling Isaiah's prophecy concerning the coming of the Messiah (Matt 11:1–6; Isa 35:5–6).

Jesus also saw his own sacrificial, atoning death as fulfillment of the salvation God promised through the prophets (Mark 10:45; Isa 53:10–11).[86] Even in his dying moments Jesus, "knowing that all was now finished, said (to fulfill the Scripture), 'I thirst'" (John 19:28 ESV; cf. Ps 69:21). He then cried out, "It is finished" (John 19:30), demonstrating that he had fulfilled all that Scripture foretold would take place through the suffering servant.

Is it any surprise, then, that after Jesus was resurrected, he rebuked two disciples on the road to Emmaus for not perceiving his redeeming work in the Old Testament (Luke 24:25–27)?[87] Not only did Jesus refer to the entirety of the Old Testament as the "Scriptures," but these Scriptures were fulfilled because God

---

85. Wenham, *Christ and the Bible,* 34.

86. Before his death, Jesus explained that he could appeal to his Father and his Father would at once send twelve legions of angels to deliver him, "but how then would the Scriptures be fulfilled that say it must happen in this way?" (Matt 26:54).

87. Compare John 20:9; Acts 4:24–25; 13:26–41.

himself was the author, bringing to completion the promises he had made to Israel's fathers. Stated otherwise, Jesus believed the entire Old Testament pointed forward to his death and resurrection, a belief that not only depends upon the divine authorship and inspiration of the Old Testament but also the divine orchestration of the events of the Old Testament leading up to the cross. The author of Hebrews confirms this when he explains that God, at many times and in various ways, "spoke to our ancestors through the prophets . . . but in these last days he has spoken to us by his Son" (Heb 1:1–2; cf. 1:6–10; 3:7). Not only did Jesus assume the inspiration of the Old Testament, but he believed and taught that it was fulfilled precisely because it was God-breathed. [88]

5. *Jesus's enemies never questioned his belief that the Old Testament was inspired.* Jesus's enemies may have disagreed with his interpretation of Scripture, and they may have despised his application of Scripture, but nowhere do we find them rejecting his belief in the inspiration of Scripture. Scholars have observed at least three tests of orthodoxy for traditional Judaism: (1) loyalty to the Sabbath, (2) loyalty to the temple, and (3) loyalty to the Torah.[89] The Jewish religious leaders challenged Jesus on his understanding of the Sabbath and the temple, but we never find them infuriated by his loyalty to the Torah.[90] They never seek to stone Jesus because he was asserting that the Old Testament was inspired by God and therefore authoritative. The same can be said of Christ's disciples after his ascension. In the book of Acts we read of the apostles being persecuted, but never for their belief in the inspiration of Scripture. This is because there was a consensus not only among Jesus and his followers but among all first-century Jews that the Old Testament was divine revelation and authoritative in every way.

6. *Jesus submitted himself to the authority of the Old Testament.* When he was tempted in the wilderness, Jesus submitted to Scripture rather than to Satan (Matt 4:1–11). When the religious leaders accused Jesus of breaking the law (Mark 2:24–28;

---

88. Wenham, *Christ and the Bible*, 31; Warfield, *Revelation and Inspiration*, 1:212. For more passages than those listed here, see Saucy, *Scripture*, 116–18.

89. Wenham, *Christ and the Bible*, 96–97.

90. Geerhardus Vos, *Biblical Theology* (Grand Rapids: Eerdmans, 1948; repr., Carlisle, PA: Banner of Truth, 2004), 360.

3:4; Luke 13:14–17), he appealed to the correct meaning of the Old Testament in order to validate that he had not broken the law at all (John 7:21–24). While the religious leaders elevated their own traditions over the Word of God (Matt 15:6; Mark 3:1–4), Jesus argued that his teaching was consistent with what the Old Testament said, even believing the Old Testament bore witness concerning him (Matt 3:15; 26:54; Luke 18:31–33; 22:37; 24:44; John 5:39).[91] Not only did Jesus assume the inspiration of the Old Testament, but in his life and ministry he consistently and persistently submitted to the Old Testament because he believed it was under divine inspiration.

Furthermore, Jesus revealed his submission to the Old Testament as the authoritative Word of God countless times in how he questioned the religious leaders and their understanding of the Scriptures. For example, Jesus asked:

- Haven't you read what David did? (Matt 12:3)
- Or haven't you read in the Law? (Matt 12:5; cf. 19:4–6; 21:16)
- Have you never read in the Scriptures? (Matt 21:42)
- Have you not read what God said to you? (Matt 22:31)
- What did Moses command you? (Mark 10:3)
- What is written in the Law? (Luke 10:26)
- Then what is the meaning of that which is written? (Luke 20:17)
- In your own Law it is written (John 8:17)
- Is it not written in your Law? (John 10:34)[92]

Again, Jesus submitted himself to the authority of the Old Testament because he believed it was God-breathed.

How serious, then, is it to deny Jesus's high view of Scripture? We cannot claim to believe in the authority of Jesus and then reject the authority of Scripture. Our trust in Jesus is intrinsically and inseparably connected to our trust in Scripture. As Robert Saucy explains, "If we believe the Bible's record of Christ—that He is who He said He was, namely, the very revela-

---

91. Geerhardus Vos, *The Teaching of Jesus concerning the Kingdom of God and the Church* (New York: American Tract Society, 1903), 12; Saucy, *Scripture*, 113–14.

92. Saucy, *Scripture*, 115.

tion of God, the truth incarnate—then we must accept Him as our authoritative Teacher in all things, including the nature of the Bible."[93] To believe in one is to believe in the other. And to reject one is to reject the other. To put this simply, we believe Scripture is God-breathed because our Lord did.[94]

The New Testament Authors Believed the Old Testament Was Inspired by God

We see the full case for inspiration when we grasp that this perspective on the Old Testament is not limited to Christ but extends to his apostles and their associates as well. Like Jesus, the New Testament authors affirmed that the Old Testament was God-breathed. Benjamin Warfield captures their belief well:

> Whenever they carried the gospel it was as a gospel resting on Scripture that they proclaimed it (Acts 17:2; 18:24, 28); and they encouraged themselves to test its truth by the Scriptures (Acts 17:11). The holiness of life they inculcated, they based on Scriptural requirement (1 Pet. 1:16), and they commended the royal law of love which they taught by Scriptural sanction (Jas. 2:8). Every detail of duty was supported by them by an appeal to Scripture (Acts 23:5; Rom. 12:19). The circumstances of their lives and the events occasionally occurring about them are referred to Scripture for their significance (Rom. 2:26; 8:36; 9:33; 11:8; 15:9, 21; 2 Cor. 4:13). As Our Lord declared that whatever was written in Scripture must needs be fulfilled (Mt. 26:54; Lk. 22:37; 24:44), so His followers explained one of the most startling facts which had occurred in their experience by pointing out that 'it was needful that the scripture should be fulfilled, which the Holy Spirit spake before by the mouth of David' (Acts 1:16). Here the ground of this constant appeal to Scripture, so that it is enough that a thing "is contained in scripture" (1 Pet. 2:6) for it to be of indefectible authority, is plainly enough declared: Scripture must needs be fulfilled, for what is contained in it is the declaration of the Holy Ghost through the human author. What Scripture says, God says.[95]

---

93. Ibid., 123.
94. For more on this point, see Hodge and Warfield, *Inspiration*, 24.
95. Warfield, *Revelation and Inspiration*, 1:91.

So what are some of the ways in which the New Testament writers assert the inspiration of the Old Testament?

1. *The New Testament authors appealed to the Old Testament as Scripture, which is apparent in the type of phrases and labels they used to identify the Old Testament.* When the New Testament writers quote from the Old Testament, typically to persuade others of Christ's divine identity as the Messiah, they often would say, "it is written," "it is said," or "in accordance with the Scriptures" (e.g., Matt 2:5; 4:4; Mark 1:2; Luke 4:12; 24:46; John 10:34).[96] At other times they simply refer to the Old Testament writings as the "sacred oracles" or "oracles of God" (Acts 7:38; Rom 3:2; Heb 5:12; 1 Pet 4:11) or as the "perfect law" and "royal law" (Jas 1:25; 2:8).[97] Paul even called the Scriptures "sacred" (2 Tim 3:15) and the law "holy" (Rom 7:12). With Warfield we can conclude from these phrases that the Bible's "authority rests on its divinity and its divinity expresses itself in its trustworthiness; and the New Testament writers in all their use of it treat it as what they declare it to be—a God-breathed document, which, because God-breathed, as through and through trustworthy in all its assertions, authoritative in all its declarations, and down to its last particular, the very word of God, His 'oracles.'"[98]

2. *The New Testament authors used "Scripture" and "God" interchangeably.*[99] For example, when Paul unfolds the mystery of election in Romans 9:17, he appeals to Exodus 9:16 where not only did the Lord harden Pharaoh's heart but then said, through Moses and Aaron, that he raised Pharaoh up in order to show Pharaoh his divine power so that his name might be proclaimed throughout all the earth. However, when Paul quotes this passage, he introduces it by saying, "For Scripture says to Pharaoh" (Rom 9:17). Again, "God" and "Scripture" can be used interchangeably because when Scripture speaks, God speaks.[100]

---

96. Acts 13:35; Rom 1:17; 3:4; 4:18; 15:10; 1 Cor 6:16; 15:3–4; 2 Cor 6:2; Gal 3:16; Eph 4:8; 5:14; Heb 1:7–10; 3:7, 15. Warfield points us to a number of other texts, including Acts 8:35; 17:3; 26:22; Rom 1:17; 3:4, 10; 4:17; 11:26; 14:11; 1 Cor 1:19; 2:9; 3:19; 15:45; Gal 3:10, 13; 4:22, 27. See Warfield, *Revelation and Inspiration*, 1:91.

97. On the phrase "oracles of God," see ibid., 1:335–91.

98. Ibid., 1:96 (cf. 1:404–5).

99. It is not "simple personification" that is in view, but the "outgrowth of a deep-seated conviction that the word of Scripture is the word of God" (ibid., 1:92).

100. John Murray, *The Epistle to the Romans*, NICNT (Grand Rapids: Eerdmans, 1968), 27.

In countless other passages we see that (1) *the Scriptures are used as if they were God* (e.g., Gal 3:8 [Gen 12:1–3]),[101] and (2) *God is spoken of as if he is the Scriptures* (e.g., Acts 13:34–35 [Isa 55:3; Ps 16:10]).[102] Such passages show that the New Testament authors believed the Old Testament was inspired by God, just as Jesus did.[103]

3. *The New Testament authors attributed the Old Testament writings to the Holy Spirit.* We saw this point demonstrated with Jesus in Mark 12:35–36. However, the New Testament authors are no different. For example, just prior to Pentecost the apostles were seeking God's will to find a replacement for Judas. We read in Acts 1:16, "Brothers, the Scripture had to be fulfilled, which the Holy Spirit spoke beforehand by the mouth of David concerning Judas, who became a guide to those who arrested Jesus." Notice that David did not prophesy on his own (Pss 69:25; 109:8; cf. Acts 1:20), but the Spirit spoke through him so that his words were in fact God's words.[104]

The same pattern reoccurs in Acts 4:24–26. When Peter and John were released and reported how they testified about the Christ, the believers who heard praised God, saying, "Sovereign Lord, who made the heaven and the earth and the sea and everything in them, who through the mouth of our father David, your servant, said by the Holy Spirit, 'Why did the Gentiles rage, and the peoples plot in vain?'" (cf. Ps 2:1). Again, David did not just speak on his own accord. Rather, the Lord spoke through him so that his words were words from the Spirit.[105]

Similarly, when the apostle Paul was in Rome preaching the

---

101. Rom 9:15 (Exod 33:19); Rom 15:10 (Deut 32:43; Ps 107:1); Gal 3:8 (Gen 12:1–3); Gal 3:16 (Gen 13:15); Eph 4:8 (Ps 48:18); Eph 5:14 (Isa 60:1); 1 Cor 6:16 (Gen 2:24); 1 Cor 15:27 (Ps 8:7); 2 Cor 6:2 (Isa 49:8); Heb 8:5 (Exod 25:40); Jas 4:6 (Prov 3:34).

102. Acts 2:16–17 (Joel 2:28–32); Acts 3:18–21; 4:25 (Ps 2:1); Rom 1:2; 3:2; 1 Cor 9:8–10; Heb 1:5–13 (Ps 2:7; 2 Sam 7:14; Deut 32:43; Pss 45:6–7; 97:7; 102:25–27; 104:4; 110:1); Heb 3:7 (Ps 95:7); Rom 15:9 (Deut 32:43; Pss 18:49; 117:1; Isa 11:10). In other passages God's name is omitted, but it is more or less assumed: Job 20:23; 21:17; Ps 114:2; Lam 4:22. Also consider passages where "it says" and "he says" are used interchangeably: Rom 15:10; 1 Cor 6:16; 15:27; 2 Cor 6:2; Gal 3:16; Eph 4:8; 5:14; Heb 8:5; Jas 4:6.

103. Warfield, *Revelation and Inspiration*, 1:302 (cf. 283ff).

104. Eckhard J. Schnabel, *Acts*, ZECNT (Grand Rapids: Zondervan, 2012), 97; Darrell L. Bock, *Acts*, BECNT (Grand Rapids: Baker Academic, 2007), 82; Craig S. Keener, *Acts: An Exegetical Commentary, an Introduction and 1:1–2:47*, vol. 1 (Grand Rapids: Baker Academic, 2012), 758.

105. Schnabel, *Acts*, 255; Warfield, *Revelation and Inspiration*, 1:98.

kingdom of God, he was "trying to convince them about Jesus both from the Law of Moses and from the Prophets" (Acts 28:23 ESV). Paul believed the Old Testament was fulfilled in the person and work of Christ, demonstrating that God's covenantal word proved to be true. However, while some were convinced, others disbelieved. Paul's response is telling: "And disagreeing among themselves, they departed after Paul had made one statement: 'The Holy Spirit was right in saying to your fathers through Isaiah the prophet: "Go to this people, and say, 'You will indeed hear but never understand, and you will indeed see but never perceive'"'" (28:25–26 ESV). So while it was Isaiah who spoke (Isa 6:9–10), Paul believed that it was not ultimately Isaiah but the Spirit speaking through Isaiah, exposing the hardness of the people's hearts.[106]

Or consider Hebrews 3:7. The author makes his case that Jesus is far greater than Moses, for Christ was faithful over God's house as a son (3:6). He concludes that we are his house if we hold fast our confidence. But then the author quotes from Psalm 95:7–11 in order to warn his readers not to harden their hearts as their fathers did, failing to enter into God's rest. Notice how the author introduces Psalm 95: "Therefore, as the Holy Spirit says" (Heb 3:7; cf. 10:15–16). Again, we see that the New Testament authors referred to the human author and the divine author interchangeably. What the human author said, God said. His words were God's words. In this case, the Holy Spirit is specifically mentioned as the author and speaker of the text (cf. Heb 9:8; 10:15).[107]

We can also consider the words of Peter, who says in his first letter that the prophets "who prophesied about the grace that was to be yours searched and inquired carefully, inquiring what person or time the Spirit of Christ in them was indicating when he predicted the sufferings of Christ and the subsequent glories" (1 Pet 1:10–11 ESV). Peter says that the Old Testament prophets examined (1) the Scriptures they had in their possession, (2) their own prophecies, and (3) the circumstances of

---

106. Schnabel, *Acts*, 1072.

107. Peter T. O'Brien, *The Letter to the Hebrews*, PNTC (Grand Rapids: Eerdmans, 2010), 140.

their own day. And they did so to understand what was to come. They understood that there was a Messiah to come, though they did not know who he would be or when he would arrive. This is what Peter means when he says they inquired "what person or time." But notice, they even looked at their own prophecies in their investigation. Peter says that the "Spirit of Christ," which is another way of referring to the Holy Spirit (Acts 16:7; Gal 4:6; Phil 1:19), is the one who predicted the sufferings of Christ.[108] Through their prophecies the Spirit was predicting what was to come in the suffering of the Messiah. We don't know how aware the prophets were of this while they were giving these prophecies. Certainly they did not understand everything the Spirit was prophesying through them, and this is why they inquired into their own prophecies to see what the Spirit was saying about the Messiah and the time of his arrival. What is certain is that Peter believed that the prophets were inspired by God. These prophets were not delivering their own opinions or messages but were speaking the very words of God. Their prophetic writings were God-breathed.

No passage is as explicit in affirming this as 2 Peter 1:21: "For no prophecy was ever produced by the will of man, but men spoke from God as they were carried along by the Holy Spirit" (ESV). Peter's words here, along with Paul's in 2 Timothy 3:16, teach that Old Testament prophecy was not the product or invention of man. Rather, the Holy Spirit spoke through the prophets, causing them to say exactly what God wanted them to say so that the Word of God was proclaimed to the people of God. Nowhere does Peter qualify his statement, as if the Old Testament prophets and their writings should not be equated with God's revelation of himself. To the contrary, the Old Testament prophets were carried along by the Spirit so that their prophecy was the very Word of God. Warfield describes the Spirit's work precisely when he writes:

> The Spirit is not to be conceived as standing outside of the human powers employed for the effect in view, ready to supplement any inadequacies they [the human authors] may

---

108. Thomas R. Schreiner, *1, 2 Peter, Jude*, NAC, vol. 37 (Nashville: B&H, 2002), 73.

show and to supply any defects they may manifest, but as working confluently in, with and by them, elevating them, directing them, controlling them, energizing them, so that, as His instruments, they rise above themselves and under His inspiration do His work and reach His aim. The product, therefore, which is attained by their means is His product through them.[109]

4. *The New Testament's use of the Old assumed inspiration.* When we look at how the New Testament authors used the Old Testament, we find that they not only assumed the inspiration of the Old (cf. Acts 24:14; Rom 15:4) but also believed there was but one divine author who held all of Scripture together as a unit. The story of redemption is characterized by covenant promises followed by God's fulfillment of those covenant promises (see chapters 5 and 6). When the New Testament authors appealed to the Old Testament, they were appealing to God himself, who orchestrated all of history, progressively bringing to fruition his gospel plan.

We see this when we reflect on a passage like Galatians 3, where Paul teaches that justification is through faith alone, not based upon works of the law (Gal 3:10–11). Paul then appeals to God's covenant promises to Abraham, showing that it is in Christ that the Abrahamic blessings have come to the gentiles (3:12–14). Paul writes, "Now the promises were made to Abraham and to his offspring. It does not say, 'And to offsprings,' referring to many, but referring to one, 'And to your offspring,' who is Christ" (3:16 ESV).[110] For Paul, the one word "offspring" (σπέρματι), used in the singular, is significant. Paul was well aware that "offspring" is a collective singular (he uses the singular as a collective in 3:29, after all). Paul is not turning to allegory or twisting the text to fit his agenda. Instead, he pinpoints the singular in order to show that the promise in Genesis 3:15 and 17:8 should be interpreted typologically.[111] The "offspring" God promised is ultimately found in Christ. His coming

---

109. Warfield, *Revelation and Inspiration*, 1:27.

110. Note the similarities between Gen 15:3 and Gal 3:16–17 and the "offspring" promise made to David in 2 Sam 7:12, which is also fulfilled in Christ (Heb 1:5).

111. It should be observed that it is not unprecedented for the singular to be used. See Seth in Gen 4:25 as well as Isaac in Gen 21:12 and Rom 9:6–9.

is first promised in Genesis 3:15, and this promised seed or off-spring "narrows" from Abraham to Isaac to David to the son of David, Jesus the Messiah.[112] Thomas Schreiner writes, "The 'off-spring' texts should be interpreted, then, in terms of corporate representation. Jesus is the representative offspring of Abraham and David and the fulfillment of the original redemptive prom-ise in Gen 3:15."[113] Paul sees the Abrahamic covenant promises reaching their fulfillment in the one offspring of Christ.[114]

Galatians 3:15–17 demonstrates that inspiration is both verbal *and* plenary. Those who argue that *only* the message is inspired and inerrant but not the words need to consider Paul's argument here, which hinges not only on a word but on its singular or plural use.

Even more to the point, what is axiomatic in Paul's quota-tion of Genesis 15:13, 18 and 17:8 is this: if the Bible's inscrip-turation was limited to the construction of the human authors, then there would be no plan of redemption, nor would this divine plan reach its fulfillment.[115] It is precisely because the divine author was behind each human author that Paul could even appeal to the grammatical construction of a single word to show that God intended to use the singular in order to point for-ward to one single man (offspring), namely Christ, who fulfilled God's covenant promises made to Abraham so long ago.[116] And lest we think such a principle is limited to this text, we should recall that this was how God worked in all the Old Testament as it crescendoed in the New, as articulated by Wenham:

> The Holy Spirit knew beforehand the course of history with
> its consummation in Christ, and so in guiding the writers
> he intended a deeper meaning than they understood. Not
> only was the ritual typical, but also the history. The first
> Adam was typical of the last Adam, the Flood typified the
> Last Judgment, Isaac and Hagar typified the church made
> free by the Spirit and Israel seeking justification by the law,

---

112. Thomas R. Schreiner, *Galatians*, ZECNT (Grand Rapids: Zondervan, 2010), 229.
113. Ibid., 230.
114. Wenham, *Christ and the Bible*, 106.
115. See also Gen 12:7; 22:18; 24:7.
116. For the broader context and argument of Paul, see Douglas J. Moo, *Galatians*, BECNT (Grand Rapids: Baker Academic, 2013), 228–31.

the Exodus typified redemption, the Red Sea baptism, the
brazen serpent the cross. . . . The prophets "were serving
not themselves, but you" (1 Pet. 1.10–12). "These things
happened to them as a warning, but they were written
down for our instruction, upon whom the end of the ages
has come" (1 Cor. 10.11). . . . The biblical revelation is an
organism—the essential elements of the whole are to be
found in every part.[117]

The parts matter for they make up the whole. If we divorce
the parts from the whole, then we are left with a fragmented
document where one author contradicts another, and the whole
does not relate to its parts.[118] But as seen in Galatians 3:17,
Scripture is not divided. There is a historical unity throughout,
and this is due to its divine authorship. Indeed, one can barely
get through a chapter in the New Testament without hearing
phrases like, "This happened that the Scripture might be fulfilled" (John 19:24), or "This took place to fulfill what was
spoken through the prophet" (Matt 21:5). We conclude with
Warfield that the "whole New Testament is based on the divinity of the Old, and its inspiration is assumed on every page."[119]

The Inspiration of the New Testament

Now that we have seen that Jesus and the New Testament authors
firmly believed in the inspiration and authority of the Old Testament,
we should ask: Is it also true that they believed in the inspiration and
authority of the New Testament?

Jesus Believed His Own Teaching Was from God

Chapter 6 established that Jesus certainly believed that his own
teaching was from God. He was not merely reflecting on God or making observations about God, but as the Son of God, he came from the
Father and therefore was speaking the very words of God (e.g., John

---

117. Wenham, *Christ and the Bible*, 107–8.
118. This is not to deny the importance of comparing biblical authors and their theologies with one another. However, we should not assume that a diversity of authors entails
disunity in the Bible. To the contrary, Scripture is a unified book due to its one primary and
divine author.
119. Warfield, *Revelation and Inspiration*, 1:404.

12:48–50). His words are God's words (John 3:34; 14:10, 24; 17:8, 14). There is no higher authority.[120]

This is important because what the Gospel writers committed to writing was, in part, the teachings of Jesus. When you open your Bible and read the words of Jesus, you are reading words that Jesus himself believed were from God and were authoritative.[121]

The New Testament Authors Believed Their Own Writings Were Inspired and Authoritative

Some will deny that the New Testament authors believed that they were writing the inspired Word of God. They will argue that the biblical authors had no clue that what they were writing was inspired by God and would at a later date be recognized as part of the canon of Scripture. And there is some truth to this view, though it goes too far. Most likely, the New Testament authors did not have a comprehensive, exhaustive, or holistic understanding of the inscripturation of their writings as we have today.[122] Yet this does not mean that they were ignorant of the fact that their writings and the writings of their fellow apostles were inspired by God and therefore authoritative. When we look at what they said concerning their writings, we find that they were confident that what they had received was from God, much like the prophets in the Old Testament.

Let's begin with the apostle Paul. Repeatedly Paul makes mention of the fact that what he has passed along is not his own but is from God himself. To the Ephesians, Paul writes of the "stewardship of God's grace . . . given to me for you" and the "mystery ... made known to me by revelation" (Eph 3:2–3 ESV).[123] Paul makes himself

---

120. See John 5:19 and 14:24. Leon Morris, *The Gospel according to John*, NICNT (Grand Rapids: Eerdmans, 1971), 313, 655.

121. For example, Jesus believes his words bring life and are life (John 5:24; 6:63, 68; 8:51). To reject his words is to invite judgment and condemnation (John 12:47). Morris, *Gospel according to John*, 125.

122. In other words, they wrote in a particular place and time, in the first century, and therefore could not have envisioned everything God was doing and would do in his inspiration of the entire NT canon. We, on the other hand, can see how God providentially brought the entire canon together to form another authoritative testament. Nevertheless, this fact in no way precludes the biblical authors from understanding to some degree that their own particular writings were God-breathed and therefore authoritative for the church(es) they addressed.

123. Paul may very likely have in mind how Christ appeared to him on the Damascus road. Clinton E. Arnold, *Ephesians*, ZECNT (Grand Rapids: Zondervan, 2010), 187.

perfectly clear: "When you read this, you can perceive my insight into the mystery of Christ, which was not made known to the sons of men in other generations as it has now been revealed to his holy apostles and prophets by the Spirit" (Eph 3:4–5 ESV).[124] What is this mystery? The mystery is that "the Gentiles are fellow heirs, members of the same body, and partakers of the promise in Christ Jesus through the gospel" (Eph 3:6 ESV). What is especially relevant for our purposes is how Paul says he received this message. It is not something he concocted, but something God himself revealed to Paul through the Holy Spirit, and not just to Paul but to the other apostles as well (e.g., Peter in Acts 10:9–48).[125]

In Galatians 1:11–12 Paul says, "I want you to know, brothers and sisters, that the gospel I preached is not of human origin. I did not receive it from any man, nor was I taught it; rather, I received it by revelation from Jesus Christ."[126] Rather than receiving the gospel from others, Paul received it directly from Christ on the Damascus road.[127]

Or consider Paul's first letter to the Corinthians where he says he imparts "a secret and hidden wisdom of God, which God decreed before the ages for our glory" (2:7 ESV). These things, says Paul, "God has revealed to us through the Spirit" (2:10 ESV). "And we impart this in words not taught by human wisdom but taught by the Spirit" (2:13 ESV). Again, Paul believes what he is passing on is of divine origin.

Paul says something similar in his doxology at the end of Romans:

> Now to him who is able to strengthen you according to my gospel and the preaching of Jesus Christ, according to the revelation of the mystery that was kept secret for long ages but has now been disclosed and through the prophetic writings has been made known to all nations, according to the command of the eternal God, to bring about the obedience of faith. (Rom 16:25–26 ESV)

Paul is very bold to assert that God will strengthen the church "according to my gospel" (Rom 16:25 ESV). Paul attached his name to this gospel precisely because it was revealed to him by the Holy Spirit, and Paul has now communicated this gospel to the nations. Where did

---

124. For four ways the plan of God was unknown, see ibid., 190.
125. Ibid., 191.
126. See also Gal 1:1.
127. On the nature of this revelation, see Schreiner, *Galatians*, 96–97.

this message that Paul proclaimed and wrote down come from? Paul says it was revealed in the Old Testament through the prophetic writings. Not only does Paul assert the inspiration of the Old Testament in this passage, but he ties his own message to this Old Testament revelation, confirming that now this revelatory mystery is being manifested across the globe. Again, it is hard to avoid Paul's strong language, which seems to place his own message and revelation on par with the Old Testament.

Additionally, at the end of his first letter to the Corinthians, Paul asserts the *authority* of his message, saying, "If anyone thinks that he is a prophet, or spiritual, he should acknowledge that the things I am writing to you are a command of the Lord. If anyone does not recognize this, he is not recognized" (1 Cor 14:37–38 ESV). A true prophet will recognize that what Paul is teaching is divinely given. Paul even refers to his own writings as a "command of the Lord" and therefore equal in authority to the Old Testament (1 Cor 14:37 ESV).[128]

Similarly, in 1 Thessalonians 2:13 Paul writes, "And we also thank God constantly for this, that when you received the word of God, which you heard from us, you accepted it not as the word of men but as what it really is, the word of God, which is at work in you believers" (ESV; cf. 4:15). Paul does not think his words are ordinary human words. He has not delivered to the church "the word of men." Instead, Paul's gospel message is the very "word of God."[129] Therefore, in his second letter to the Thessalonians he can warn them, "If anyone does not obey what we say in this letter, take note of that person, and have nothing to do with him, that he may be ashamed" (3:14 ESV). Apparently Paul's written letter has authority![130]

Paul's opening greeting to Titus likewise captures the authority of the apostle Paul:

> Paul, a servant of God and an apostle of Jesus Christ, for the sake of the faith of God's elect and their knowledge of the truth, which accords with godliness, in hope of eternal life, which God, who never lies, promised before the ages began and at the proper

---

128. On the binding nature of Paul's commands, see 1 Cor 7:40; 1 Thess 4:2, 11; 2 Thess 3:6–14.

129. Gary S. Shogren, *1 and 2 Thessalonians*, ZECNT (Grand Rapids: Zondervan, 2012), 110.

130. See also 1 Thess 5:27 where Paul puts the Thessalonians under an oath before the Lord to have his letter read to all the brothers and sisters.

time manifested in his word through the preaching with which I have been entrusted by the command of God our Savior. (Titus 1:1–3 ESV)[131]

Paul was not the only one who believed that his preaching and writing were given to him from God and therefore authoritative. Peter also believed Paul's writings were on equal par with the rest of Scripture. In 2 Peter 3 he writes:

> And count the patience of our Lord as salvation, just as our beloved brother Paul also wrote to you according to the wisdom given him, as he does in all his letters when he speaks in them of these matters. There are some things in them that are hard to understand, which the ignorant and unstable twist to their own destruction, as they do the other Scriptures. (2 Pet 3:15–16 ESV)

Not only does Peter say that Paul wrote to the church with wisdom that God himself gave to him, but Peter also implies that Paul's writings are Scripture when he says that there are some who twist Paul's epistles "as they do the other Scriptures."[132]

Paul not only views his writings as God-given and authoritative, but the writings of others as well. For example, in 1 Timothy 5:17 Paul reminds Timothy that the elders who rule well are worthy of "double honor." To support his claim, Paul quotes two sources: "For Scripture [γραφή] says, 'Do not muzzle an ox while it is treading out the grain,' and 'The worker deserves his wages'" (1 Tim 5:18). Where are these two quotations from? The first is from Deuteronomy 25:4. But what is shocking is that the second quote is from Luke 10:7.[133] What is implied is that Paul considered Jesus's words as well as Luke's written statements of Jesus's words to be Scripture! According to Paul, Luke is not merely recording a Gospel account, but his writings are God-breathed.[134]

Luke himself had some understanding of this concept, for he begins his Gospel by saying that he has received his material from those who

---

131. Also note how Paul commands "Scripture" to be read in the church, but it is very likely that he includes his own letters in this command (1 Tim 4:13; 1 Thess 5:27; Col 4:16).

132. One might also consider the authority Paul speaks with: 1 Cor 4:21–5:5; 12:28; 14:36–37; 15:5–11; 2 Cor 12:1; 13:10; Gal 1:8; Eph 4:11; 1 Thess 4:2, 11; 2 Thess 2:15; 3:6–15. Also consider John: 2 John 10; Rev 1:3; 22:18.

133. See also Matt 10:10.

134. Wenham, *Christ and the Bible*, 125.

"from the first were eyewitnesses and servants of the word" (Luke 1:2). What matters is not whether it's an apostle writing, but whether this Gospel is characterized by the authoritative apostolic tradition, which is certainly true with Luke's Gospel.[135] The New Testament authors were self-consciously aware that they were passing on the authoritative tradition that they received from Jesus either directly or, in Luke's case, indirectly (cf. John 14:26; 16:12–15; 1 Cor 11:2, 23; 15:2–5; 2 Thess 2:15; 3:6). In Luke's circumstance, he intends his readership to identify his Gospel as bearing the marks of an authoritative apostolic message.[136]

Not only are Luke's writings considered Scripture, but Peter verifies that what he has passed on is directly from God as well. In light of false teachers questioning the second coming of Christ (2 Pet 3:3–7), Peter tells his readers:

> For we did not follow cleverly devised myths when we made known to you the power and coming of our Lord Jesus Christ, but we were eyewitnesses of his majesty. For when he received honor and glory from God the Father, and the voice was borne to him by the Majestic Glory, "This is my beloved Son, with whom I am well pleased," we ourselves heard this very voice borne from heaven, for we were with him on the holy mountain. (2 Pet 1:16–18 ESV)

In other words, what Peter declared concerning Christ's future return was factual, not fictional. It was not mythical, but "anchored in history."[137] His readers could be certain of this since Peter (as well as James and John) heard the voice of the Father with their own ears and saw Jesus transfigured with their own eyes (Matt 17:1–13), a transfiguration that anticipated the power and glory of Christ in his second coming.[138] It is on this reliable, apostolic tradition and testimony that the churches were established.[139]

Peter goes on to explain, "And we have the prophetic word more

---

135. Michael J. Kruger, "Recent Challenges to the New Testament Writings," in *Did God Really Say? Affirming the Truthfulness and Trustworthiness of Scripture*, ed. David B. Garner (Phillipsburg, NJ: P&R, 2013), 62.

136. Ibid.

137. Schreiner, *1, 2 Peter, Jude*, 314.

138. As one who was there with Peter, the apostle John confirms the same: "That which was from the beginning, which we have heard, which we have seen with our eyes, which we looked at and our hands have touched—this we proclaim concerning the Word of life" (1 John 1:1).

139. Schreiner, *1, 2 Peter, Jude*, 312.

fully confirmed, to which you will do well to pay attention as to a lamp shining in a dark place, until the day dawns and the morning star rises in your hearts, knowing this first of all, that no prophecy of Scripture comes from someone's own interpretation" (2 Pet 1:19–20 ESV). By the "prophetic word" (ESV) Peter is referring to the "prophetic message" (NIV), that is, the Old Testament Scriptures, specifically Old Testament prophecies concerning the future day of the Lord. The transfiguration would have verified the truthfulness of these Old Testament prophecies about the second coming of Christ as interpreted by the apostles. This is why Peter can say that we have the prophetic word "more fully confirmed" (ESV) or "made more sure" (NASB).[140] Schreiner writes, "Since believers have in the Old Testament Scriptures a prophetic word that is more reliable because of the interpretive confirmation of the transfiguration, they should pay close attention to the word and heed what it says."[141] Peter compares the prophetic word to a "light shining in a dark place" (2 Pet 1:19), echoing Psalm 119:105 and Proverbs 6:23 to show that the prophetic word has an illuminating power concerning what is to come.

This brings us to the final part of this section: "knowing this first of all, that no prophecy of Scripture comes from someone's own interpretation" (1:20 ESV). Interpreters have taken two sides on this verse: (1) Peter is talking about the *origins* of prophecy (i.e., the vision/dream the prophet received and his interpretation of that vision/dream as from God).[142] (2) Peter is talking about the *interpretation* of prophecy (i.e., in contrast to the false teachers, the apostles' interpretation of prophecy is not their own but from God).[143] Regardless of which position we adopt, biblical authority and inspiration are affirmed, the former view affirming the Old Testament and the latter view affirming the apostles.

Verse 21 brings everything to a climax, arguing that prophecy is not man's invention but comes from God himself. They are God's

---

140. Ibid., 320.

141. Ibid., 320–21.

142. For example, Jer 1:11–14; Dan 7:2; 8:1; Amos 7:1; Zech 1:8–11. This first position is taken by Richard J. Bauckham, "James, 1 Peter and 2 Peter, Jude," in *It Is Written: Scripture Citing Scripture: Essays in Honour of Barnabas Lindars*, ed. D. A. Carson and H. G. M Williamson (Cambridge: Cambridge University Press, 1988), 303–17. This view also seems to be taken by the NIV, NET, and NLT.

143. This second view is argued by Schreiner, *1, 2 Peter, Jude*, 322. It also seems to be the view of the ESV, HCSB, NKJV, and NRSV.

words, and he has given them to us through his appointed prophets. What should not be missed is Peter's assertion that the *writings* of the prophets ("prophecy *of Scripture*," v. 20) are breathed out by God.[144] These men "spoke from God as they were carried along"—like a boat in the wind, Acts 27:15, 17—"by the Holy Spirit." This is not a dictation theory, but a divine-human encounter and concursus, with verbal and plenary inspiration being the result. And while Peter's focus may be on the inspiration of the prophetic writings, by logical extension his point can be applied not only to the rest of the Old Testament but to the New Testament as well (e.g., Rev 1:10–11; 2:7–29; 3:6–22).[145]

Finally, consider 2 Peter 3:2 where Peter exhorts his readers to remember the "predictions of the holy prophets and the commandment of the Lord and Savior through your apostles" (ESV). Peter assumes once again the inspiration and authority of the Old Testament prophets, but he also alludes to the authority of the apostles.[146] Not only does Peter place the apostles (himself included) as equals to the prophets (as does Paul in Eph 2:20), but Peter is clear that it is Jesus himself, who is Lord and Savior, who speaks through his apostles.[147] Should we then think any differently about their apostolic writings?

In summary, the New Testament writers did not view the revelation they had received as somehow subordinate to the Old Testament. Quite the contrary, in various ways they understood that God had given to them a revelatory word, equal in authority with the Old Testament.[148] Furthermore, because the new covenant superseded the old—for the old covenant was full of types and shadows that pointed forward to the antitype—there is a sense in which the apostles could speak with even greater authority. As those who were with Christ himself, they experienced the arrival of the kingdom of God, witnessed the shedding of his blood of the new covenant, and were recipients of the Spirit at Pentecost.[149] Their writings, therefore, were

---

144. Ibid., 324.

145. Ibid.

146. Wayne A. Grudem, *1 Peter*, TNTC, vol. 17 (Downers Grove, IL: IVP Academic, 1988), 77.

147. Schreiner, *1, 2 Peter, Jude*, 371; Keith A. Mathison, *The Shape of Sola Scriptura* (Moscow, ID: Canon, 2001), 170.

148. Wenham, *Christ and the Bible*, 118.

149. See Rom 16:25–26; Eph 1:3–14; 3:3–12; 2 Tim 1:9–11; Titus 1:1–3; 1 Pet 1:18–23. Ibid.

received by the church, who recognized that what the apostles said was from God.[150]

How Serious Is a Rejection of Inspiration?

Throughout this chapter we have seen that the Bible itself teaches us that it is the inspired Word of God. Yet many today reject this idea. How serious are the consequences, then, of rejecting inspiration? If we reject inspiration, we are rejecting the Bible's own testimony concerning itself. While this may seem obvious, it deserves repeating because some have claimed that the Bible never claims its own verbal, plenary inspiration. They conclude that we are forcing an extrabiblical grid upon the Bible, making it say something it never said.[151] However, it is difficult to ignore the evidence that the Bible does affirm its own inspiration. Scripture is not silent on its identity and origin. While a skeptic may reject the Bible, he has no grounds for doing so on the assumption that the Bible does not make the claim to be God-breathed (2 Tim 3:16).

This means that to reject inspiration is to abandon the authority of Christ and the apostles as our doctrinal authorities, for they themselves taught this doctrine. If Scripture is not inspired, as some argue, then the claims and exhortations of Christ and the apostles no longer hold water. When inspiration is rejected, other doctrines fall as well (or at least they should, if one is to be consistent).[152] Warfield's words are sobering:

> No wonder we are told that the same advance in knowledge which requires a changed view of the Bible necessitates also a whole new theology. If the New Testament writers are not trustworthy as teachers of doctrine and we have to go elsewhere for the source and norm of truth as to God and duty and immortality, it will not be strange if a very different system of doctrine from that delivered by the Scriptures and docilely received from them by the Church, results.[153]

---

150. Ibid., 125.

151. For example, Craig D. Allert, *A High View of Scripture? The Authority of the Bible and the Formation of the New Testament Canon* (Grand Rapids: Baker Academic, 2007), 147–72.

152. For example, Protestant Liberalism (and those who would borrow from it today).

153. Warfield, *Revelation and Inspiration*, 1:180.

In addition, to reject inspiration is to reject biblical authority itself. Some try to have biblical authority without verbal, plenary inspiration,[154] but this is impossible because the authority of Scripture is based upon the inspiration of Scripture. Without the latter, the former ceases to exist.[155] If the Bible is not God's inspired Word, why should it be our authority? Why submit to a merely human book? In that case, Scripture is reduced to a man-made collection of man-made reflections, and Scripture can no longer be the determining norm.

We need to remember this, for many Christians today are tempted to think they can retain biblical authority without affirming verbal, plenary inspiration. They locate authority in Christ, in the church, or in their own reason and experience. But should we go down this path, we will be disappointed. We will be grounding God's authority in something other than what God intended—his written Word. As we saw from Jesus himself, our final authority resides in the God-breathed Word.[156]

---

154. Sparks, *Sacred Word, Broken Word*, 6 (cf. 42, 44, 47, 48, 58, 66, 107).
155. Bavinck, *Reformed Dogmatics*, 1:460, 462.
156. Ibid., 1:462.

CHAPTER 8

God Speaks Truthfully: The Inerrancy of Scripture

> Did God actually say . . . ?
>
> —*The serpent*

> Your word is truth.
>
> —*John 17:17*

> This is the Word of God, which can not lie nor err, of this I am certain.
>
> —*Martin Luther*

> The trustworthiness of the Scriptures lies at the foundation of trust in the Christian system of doctrine, and is therefore fundamental to the Christian hope and life.
>
> —*B. B. Warfield*

"The real reason why men oppose the doctrine of an infallible Scripture is that they are not willing to embrace the Biblical doctrine of inspiration. There is no such thing as inspiration which does not carry with it the correlate of infallibility. A Bible that is fallible—and we speak of course of the original—is a Bible that is not inspired. A Bible that is inspired is a Bible that is infallible. There is no middle ground."[1] These assertive words by the late E. Y. Young in his classic 1957 book *Thy Word Is Truth* give a taste of this chapter. We have waited to address inerrancy until now because the inerrancy of Scripture naturally flows out of the inspiration of Scripture, and the former is a biblical corollary

---

1. E. J. Young, *Thy Word Is Truth: Some Thoughts on the Biblical Doctrine of Inspiration* (Edinburgh: Banner of Truth, 1957; repr. 1997), 108. See also Carl F. H. Henry, *God, Revelation, and Authority*, vol. 4, *God Who Speaks and Shows, Fifteen Theses, Part Three* (repr., Wheaton, IL: Crossway, 1999), 181–94.

of the latter. To believe in inerrancy is to affirm that the true God has breathed out a true Word. While some will deny this logic, in this chapter I aim to show that it is biblical logic.

What Is Inerrancy?

What does it mean for Scripture to be inerrant? In the most basic sense, inerrancy means that Scripture, in its original manuscripts, does not err in all that the biblical authors assert. While this short definition gets at the heart of the matter, defenders of inerrancy have fleshed out additional details. Let's start by considering two definitions, the first from Paul Feinberg and the second from David Dockery:

> When all facts are known, the Scriptures in their original auto-graphs and properly interpreted will be shown to be wholly true in everything they affirm, whether that has to do with doctrine or morality or with the social, physical, or life sciences.[2]

> The Bible (in its original writings) properly interpreted in light of which culture and communication means had developed by the time of its composition will be completely true (and therefore not false) in all that it affirms, to the degree of precision intended by the author, in all matters relating to God and his creation.[3]

These definitions are noteworthy for several reasons. First, they show that inerrancy requires humility. Critics of the Bible love to point out that there are many problems and contradictions in the Bible.[4] What these critics misunderstand is that defenders of inerrancy do not deny these apparent problem passages in Scripture, but they do believe—since God is the divine author and Scripture therefore is a unitary whole—that while there may be Bible difficulties or apparent contradictions, "when all the facts are known" and when Scripture is "properly interpreted," it is "wholly true." We recognize that we are finite and sinful, and so we are often either ignorant of or blinded to the truth of the matter. Sometimes the best solution to an apparent Bible

---

2.   Paul Feinberg, "The Meaning of Inerrancy," in *Inerrancy*, ed. Norman L. Geisler (Grand Rapids: Zondervan, 1980), 293.

3.   David S. Dockery, *Christian Scripture: An Evangelical's Perspective on Inspiration, Authority, and Interpretation* (Nashville: B&H, 1995), 64.

4.   For example, Kenton L. Sparks, *Sacred Word, Broken Word: Biblical Authority and the Dark Side of Scripture* (Grand Rapids: Eerdmans, 2012); Peter Enns, *The Bible Tells Me So: Why Defending Scripture Has Made Us Unable to Read It* (New York: HarperOne, 2014).

problem is time and prayer. Many of the "contradictions" that scholars found problematic a century ago have now been resolved with time and study. Nor can we neglect the role of the Spirit. What at first appears to be an insurmountable hurdle later becomes a small speed bump when the Spirit illumines the Word so that we can better understand its meaning. Therefore, the Bible, "properly interpreted," is inerrant. As Kevin Vanhoozer states, inerrancy means one has faith "not only that the biblical authors speak truthfully but that they will eventually be seen to have spoken truly (when right readers read rightly)."[5]

Second, inerrancy means that Scripture is true in everything it affirms. Scripture does not address everything, but in everything it does address, it speaks the truth. So whether it is doctrine, morality, history, or even life sciences, its assertions are truthful and trustworthy. As Vanhoozer puts it, "To say that Scripture is inerrant is to confess faith that the authors speak the truth in all things they affirm (when they make affirmations)."[6] Of course, it takes a keen eye to discern what exactly Scripture is affirming and asserting and what it is not (hence the importance of hermeneutics). We must work hard to consider the various biblical genres to ensure that we do not make Scripture say something it is not saying, and we must also distinguish between the inerrant text and our fallible interpretations of the text. Should our interpretation pose a contradiction between two biblical texts, we should first assume that our interpretation needs correction, not the text. And in seeking a more accurate interpretation, we should allow Scripture to interpret Scripture, using the clear texts to interpret those that appear ambiguous.[7]

Third, we must remember that inerrancy applies to the original autographs. When Paul says all *Scripture* is breathed out by God, he has the actual *document* in mind (2 Tim 3:16), not merely the biblical authors. This means that it is not the copies that are inerrant, but the original manuscripts of the biblical authors.[8] However, this should not be used to create an attitude of doubt, suspicion, or distrust toward our

---

5.   Kevin J. Vanhoozer, "Augustinian Inerrancy: Literary Meaning, Literal Truth, and Literate Interpretation in the Economy of Biblical Discourse," in *Five Views on Biblical Inerrancy*, ed. J. Merrick and Stephen B. Garrett (Grand Rapids: Zondervan, 2013), 207.

6.   Ibid.

7.   On inerrancy and hermeneutics, see J. I. Packer, "Infallible Scripture and the Role of Hermeneutics," in *Scripture and Truth*, ed. D. A. Carson and John Woodbridge (Grand Rapids: Baker, 1992), 325–58.

8.   Greg L. Bahnsen, "The Inerrancy of the Autographa," in Geisler, *Inerrancy*, 182 (cf. 173).

contemporary translations. The translations we have today are incredibly accurate, and where there are uncertainties as to what the original autograph said, it is always in matters insignificant, never having to do with Christian doctrine or the credibility of the biblical text. Moreover, faith in the inerrancy of the original autographs also entails faith in our current translations as far as they are consistent. Where our contemporary translations are faithful to the original manuscripts—and we can accurately say this is the case with the vast majority of biblical texts—we can rest assured that we are reading an inerrant text.[9] Finally, we should have no hesitation trusting the copies since Solomon (Deut 17:18; 1 Kgs 2:3), the men of King Hezekiah (Prov 25:1), Ezra (Ezra 7:14; Neh 8:8), Jesus (Luke 4:16–21), Paul (Col 4:16; 2 Tim 3:16; 4:13), and the apostles (Luke 4:16–21; John 5:39; Acts 17:2, 11; 18:28; 2 Tim 3:15–16) all used, trusted, and relied upon copies of Scripture, treating them as canonical and authoritative for faith and practice.[10]

Before moving on from this point, we must acknowledge what a terrible state we would be in should the original *autographa* not be inerrant.[11] If the *autographa* is inerrant, then through the discipline of textual criticism we can properly discern where errors in transmission occurred precisely because we are confident that there was an inerrant text and it will show itself through the copies we possess. However, if inerrancy of the *autographa* were denied, then such a task would be impossible for there would be no objective textual basis on which to distinguish fact from fancy.[12] Many fail to distinguish between "an original that is inerrant but to which errors have been added through transmission and an original that has substantive errors and has been further corrupted in transmission." Feinberg concludes, "With respect to the former, an inerrant text can be approached through textual criticism, while in the latter case, any attempt to discover an inerrant text would be hopeless."[13]

---

9. Craig L. Blomberg, *Can We Still Believe the Bible? An Evangelical Engagement with Contemporary Questions* (Grand Rapids: Brazos, 2014), 124. Contra John J. Brogan, "Can I Have Your Autograph? Uses and Abuses of Textual Criticism in Formulating an Evangelical Doctrine of Scripture," in *Evangelicals and Scripture: Tradition, Authority, and Hermeneutics*, ed. Vincent Bacote, Laura C. Miguélez, and Dennis L. Okholm (Downers Grove, IL: InterVarsity Press, 2004), 108–9.

10. See Bahnsen, "Inerrancy of the Autographa," 160–65.

11. To clarify, we must not confuse the autographic *text* (the words) with the autographic *codex*. While the codex may be lost, that does not mean the words have been lost.

12. Carl F. H. Henry, *God, Revelation, and Authority* (Wheaton, IL: Crossway, 1979), 4:231, 234.

13. Feinberg, "Meaning of Inerrancy," 297.

With these three points in place, it is necessary, due to misunder-standings and caricatures, to also say what inerrancy does *not* mean. Feinberg is helpful here, providing eight qualifications on inerrancy and what it does not mean:

1. Inerrancy does not demand strict adherence to the rules of grammar.
2. Inerrancy does not exclude the use either of figures of speech or of a given literary genre.
3. Inerrancy does not demand historical or semantic precision.
4. Inerrancy does not demand the technical language of modern science.
5. Inerrancy does not require verbal exactness in the citation of the Old Testament by the New.
6. Inerrancy does not demand that the *logia Jesu* (the sayings of Jesus) contain the *ipsissima verba* (the exact words) of Jesus, only the *ipsissima vox* (the exact voice).[14]
7. Inerrancy does not guarantee the exhaustive comprehensive-ness of any single account or of combined accounts where those are involved.
8. Inerrancy does not demand the infallibility or inerrancy of the noninspired sources used by biblical writers.[15]

In order to understand some of these qualifications better, we will start with the issue of "precision."

Inerrancy and Precision

As we read and interpret the Bible, we must always be careful that we do not read our modern views of truth and precision into our understanding of the Bible's inerrancy. Unfortunately, too often critics of inerrancy do this very thing by imposing a modern standard onto Scripture, only to conclude that Scripture is errant because it fails to match up with modern standards of precision.[16] The critic sees places

---

14. To clarify: "When a New Testament writer cites the sayings of Jesus, it need not be that Jesus said those exact words. Undoubtedly the exact words of Jesus are to be found in the New Testament, but they need not be so in every instance" (Feinberg, "Meaning of Inerrancy," 301).

15. Feinberg, "Meaning of Inerrancy," 299–302.

16. Take Sparks, for example, who says the Bible is errant because its descriptions do not picture the universe in a way that is consistent with the assured results of modern science. He

in Scripture that are not as precise as he thinks they should be, and he concludes that the biblical author has misspoken and committed an error.

But truth and precision are *not* the same thing.[17] Scripture can be completely truthful in what it asserts and affirms, without being totally precise. To be clear, truth and precision can and often do relate to one another. In mathematics or fields of science, for example, there are many times when a statement must be precise if it is to be true. But other fields and other aspects of life do not work this way. Imagine trying to force mathematical precision into everyday speech and conversation.

For example, consider what people commonly say when they are asked the time. We need not say it is 2:04 and one tenth of a second. Instead we can respond by saying that it is two o'clock. Have we been precise? No. Have we been untruthful? Not at all. Or consider the distance a jogger runs in his morning workout. Suppose a fellow jogger were to ask, "How far did you run this morning?" If he replies that he ran two miles when in reality it was 1.913 miles, has he been imprecise? Yes. Untruthful? No. Or take a biblical example. Was Jesus untruthful when he said the mustard seed "is the smallest of all seeds on earth" (Mark 4:31)? The answer is no. Why? Because Jesus was not trying to be scientifically precise; he was communicating truth by using hyperbole that would have been understandable to his audience and perfectly truthful.[18] While we want to affirm "literal truth," we must be careful to avoid "literalism," which "runs roughshod over the intent of the author and the literary form of the text."[19] We must "specify the author's communicative intent in order rightly to say what he is doing with his words."[20]

In countless areas of life, one is not untruthful, nor in error, when he or she is imprecise. Applying this distinction between truth and precision to the Bible helps with many interpretive questions

---

goes so far as to say Genesis is an example of "primitive science and anthropology." Sparks, *Sacred Word, Broken Word*, 92.

17. John Frame, *Systematic Theology* (Phillipsburg, NJ: P&R, 2013), 599–600; John Wenham, *Christ and the Bible*, 3rd ed. (Grand Rapids: Baker, 1994), 98.

18. Vanhoozer, "Augustinian Inerrancy," 219; "The Chicago Statement on Biblical Inerrancy," in Geisler, *Inerrancy*, 496, 497 (articles 13 and 18).

19. Vanhoozer, "Augustinian Inerrancy," 219.

20. Ibid. Vanhoozer defines literalism as "the view that equates *what is said* (that is, meaning) with *semantic content* (that is, the proposition semantically expressed by the sentence regardless of context)."

that commonly arise. A biblical author may paraphrase a quotation from the Old Testament, give a general number of attendees at one of Jesus's miracles, or structure his book thematically rather than chronologically. To conclude that the biblical author is in error for not being precise in the mathematical or scientific sense is to force a straitjacket onto Scripture that would never be forced on any other piece of literature.

God has chosen not to speak in the scientific or mathematical language of a modern textbook, but rather in the ordinary, common language of everyday people, a language engulfed in a historical, cultural, social, and religious milieu. The Old Testament was written in Hebrew since God's people were Israelites, not Egyptians. The New Testament was written in *Koine* Greek, which was the vernacular tongue of the people at the time.[21] In other words, God utilized the everyday language of the people to make his gospel universally known. God does not always choose to communicate in modern technical language, nor is he obligated to do so, as it would be highly restrictive and suffocating. When we open Scripture, we read history, but we also find biographical, epistolary, homiletic, and apocalyptic literature. One author may speak in prose, and another in poetry or parables. While biblical authors may sometimes speak in a technical sense, at other times they choose to use hyperbole or generalization. Imprecision, in other words, does not necessarily compromise truth. The Chicago Statement on Biblical Inerrancy gets it right: "Scripture is inerrant, not in the sense of being absolutely precise by modern standards, but in the sense of making good its claims and achieving that measure of focused truth at which its authors aimed."[22]

The God of Truth Speaks Words of Truth

"Scripture is trustworthy because the God behind Scripture is trustworthy."[23] This statement by Carl Trueman gets at the core idea behind biblical inerrancy. Scripture is flawless because its divine author is perfect. The holiness of Scripture is derived from the holiness of God. Albert Mohler states the matter well:

---

21. "The Chicago Statement on Biblical Inerrancy," 500–501.
22. Ibid.
23. Carl R. Trueman, "The God of Unconditional Promise," in *The Trustworthiness of God: Perspectives on the Nature of Scripture*, ed. Paul Helm and Carl R. Trueman (Grand Rapids: Eerdmans, 2002), 178.

The focus on God's trustworthiness underlines the personal nature of God's gift of his own self-revelation. God intended not merely to give the church a collection of infallible and inerrant facts but also to reveal himself—and to do so in a manner that is completely trustworthy. Our trust in the Scriptures is entirely dependent upon our trust in God. In the same way, a lack of confidence in the truthfulness and trustworthiness of the Bible reveals a lack of confidence in either God's ability or his intention—or both—to give his people a trustworthy revelation.[24]

Chapters 5 and 6 labored to show this very point. God and his Word are inseparably tied together. They rise and fall together, the Word flowing out from God. This is why Scripture is properly called the Word *of God*. Were Scripture to err, it not only would communicate that Scripture is deeply flawed but that God himself is untrustworthy. On the other hand, if Scripture is pure, such purity speaks volumes about God.[25] Critics tend to miss this point, thinking that an errant Word is of no consequence for the character of God.[26] But this divorces God from his Word, making one irrelevant to the other. In contrast, *the doctrine of Scripture is inherently located within the doctrine of God.*[27]

Hans Küng once wrote, and many since have wrongly agreed, that "there is not a passage in Scripture that speaks of its inerrancy."[28] This idea stems from a failure to do good systematic theology. If we took such an approach with other doctrines of the faith, we would have to abandon the Trinity, the hypostatic union, and the imputation of Christ's righteousness as well.[29] Though the exact term, *inerrancy*, is

---

24. R. Albert Mohler Jr., "When the Bible Speaks, God Speaks: The Classic Doctrine of Biblical Inerrancy," in Merrick and Garrett, *Five Views*, 44.

25. Frame, *Systematic Theology*, 602.

26. For example, Sparks, *Sacred Word, Broken Word*, 6, 32, 60, 98, 103, 128.

27. Mark D. Thompson, "The Divine Investment in Truth: Toward a Theological Account of Biblical Inerrancy," in *Do Historical Matters Matter to Faith? A Critical Appraisal of Modern and Postmodern Approaches to Scripture*, ed. James K. Hoffmeier and Dennis R. Magary (Wheaton, IL: Crossway, 2012), 73.

28. Hans Küng, *Infallible? An Enquiry*, trans. Eric Mosbacher (London: Collins, 1971), 181. See also James D. G. Dunn, "The Authority of Scripture according to Scripture," *Churchman* 96 (1982): 107; John Goldingay, *Models for Scripture* (Grand Rapids: Eerdmans, 1994), 273; Dennis E. Nineham, "Wherein Lies the Authority of the Bible?," in *On the Authority of the Bible*, ed. Leonard Hodgson (London: SPCK, 1960), 88; James Barr, *Fundamentalism* (London: SCM, 1977), 277.

29. Francis Turretin, *Institutes of Elenctic Theology*, ed. James T. Dennison Jr., trans. George Musgrave Giger, 3 vols. (Phillipsburg, NJ: P&R, 1992–97), 1:37; Thompson, "Divine Investment in Truth," 74–75.

not found in the Bible, it logically follows from what Scripture says about itself. Good systematic theology synthesizes the biblical material into a coherent whole, and we can do this because though there are various human authors, there is *one* divine author behind them all.[30] Again, our doctrine of Scripture is rooted in our doctrine of God. When we construct our doctrinal house, we do not look for a golden proof-text but seek to put together what all of Scripture has to say about God and how he has revealed himself.

In a variety of ways, we see throughout Scripture this unbreakable chain between God's trustworthiness and the trustworthiness of his Word, between the purity and perfection of God and the holiness of his Word.

First, the God of the Bible is a God of truth, not falsehood. Truthfulness is one of God's communicable attributes (i.e., God *is* truth), and it plays a significant role in identifying the true God from false gods. For example, consider how God portrays himself to Israel in the OT, particularly in light of Israel's temptation to worship false gods. The God of Israel is not like the gods of the nations because he is a speaking God (1 Kgs 18:24–46; Pss 115:5–8; 135:15–18; Hab 2:18–20; 1 Cor 12:2). No other religion can claim that their God speaks to his people; only Christianity can do that. As a result, the God of Scripture can claim to be near his people and to be with his people since he is a God who speaks to his people. On the other hand, the silent, mute gods of other religions are not present because they cannot talk. But the God of the Bible is one who stoops down and tabernacles among us by means of the Word (Matt 1:23; John 1:14).[31] Not only does our God speak, but it is because he is a God of truth that he speaks words of truth. Indeed, his Son, the Word, is even said to be the truth (John 14:6).

If the Lord were ever to speak falsely, his words would be no better than the gods he competes with, gods who are mute and whose prophets speak false prophecies (Pss 115:5–7; 135:16). It is Yahweh's ability to speak *truth* (and words that come true; see ch. 6) that distinguishes him from every other religion and their god(s). Genuine believers are those who have turned away "from idols to serve the living and true

---

30. Thompson, "Divine Investment in Truth," 74–75.
31. Frame, *Systematic Theology*, 522, 523; Scott R. Swain, *Trinity, Revelation, and Reading: A Theological Introduction to the Bible and Its Interpretation* (New York: T&T Clark, 2011), 15.

God" (1 Thess 1:9). And how do we know he is both "living" and "true"? By whether his Word *is* truth.[32]

Countless times we read that the Lord is the "true God" (Jer 10:9–10; John 17:3). The same is said of Christ, the Son of God, who is full of grace and truth (John 1:14, 17), bears witness to the truth (1:18; 8:40; 17:17; 18:37), speaks the truth (8:44), and is himself the truth (14:6). The Holy Spirit is referred to as the "Spirit of truth" and identified as the one "who is the truth" (14:17; 15:26; 16:14; 1 John 5:6, 20). The "Spirit of truth" is even distinguished from the "spirit of error" (1 John 4:6). There is a Trinitarian nature to truth, for Father, Son, and Holy Spirit are the one true God who speaks words of truth.[33]

Not only is God identified as the God of truth, he is also spoken of as the one who is trustworthy in all he says. He is not a God who lies (Num 23:19; 1 Sam 15:29; Rom 3:4; Titus 1:2; Heb 6:17–18), nor is he one who can err (Heb 4:12–13) or deny his own holy character (2 Tim 2:13). Rather, he is faithful in all he says and does, fulfilling his promises (e.g., Deut 32:4; 1 Cor 1:9; 10:13).[34] His ways are holy, just, and true (Rev 6:10; 15:3; 16:7; 19:2, 11). Unlike man, God is reliable, unswerving, and dependable (1 Sam 2:2; Pss 18:2; 62:2; Isa 26:4).[35] As we read in Proverbs 30:5, "Every word of God proves true; he is a shield to those who take refuge in him" (ESV). Truth so characterizes God's words that Psalm 12:6 can say God's words are "pure," like "silver refined in a furnace" and "purified seven times" (ESV). The image of a furnace means to convey that no flaw can be found. God's words are clean, even perfect, as the number seven indicates. No falsehood can be found in them (Ps 119:140). And as Psalm 18:30 affirms, not only is God's way "perfect," but his word "proves true" as well, a great comfort to those who take refuge in him (119:96). Indeed, the "sum" of God's "word is truth" (Ps 119:160; cf. Prov 8:8). The proper response is to be humble and tremble at God's word (Isa 66:2).

In light of this biblical affirmation of God's truthfulness, why would we be surprised to discover that the God of truth communicates

---

32. I cannot stress this enough: apart from the veracity of his divine revelation, we have nothing to stand upon, for the foundation of our faith has been removed. No longer can we know whether or not our God has spoken to us truthfully.

33. See chapter 4.

34. Also see 1 Thess 5:24; 2 Thess 3:3; Heb 10:23; 11:11; 1 John 1:9.

35. Frame, *Systematic Theology*, 522–23.

words of truth as opposed to error? Why would we expect anything less from a truthful God?[36]

Second, the words of the true God reflect his character and are even identified with God himself. So closely related are the character of God and the character of his word that Scripture can even speak of God's word as the object of our praise and worship (Pss 56:4, 10; 119:120, 161–62; Isa 66:5). Throughout the Old Testament, the text commands its readers to praise the name of the Lord, which is significant because the name of the Lord is typically identified with the word of the Lord (e.g., Pss 9:2; 34:3; 68:4; 138:2).[37] Therefore, as Paul does in Romans 1:2, it is appropriate to label Scripture *holy*, for the God who breathes it out is a holy God. The purity of his Word naturally mirrors the purity of his character, so much so that his Word and his name can be used interchangeably, as we saw in chapter 7.[38]

Third, the connection between the trustworthiness of God and the trustworthiness of his speech is rooted in the doctrine of inspiration. What Scripture says, God says. The words of Scripture are God's words, given to the human authors through inspiration. The character of God is the source and fountain of the character of his words. The perfection of Scripture, then, is grounded in the perfection of its divine author. That such a relationship is common sense becomes all the more obvious when we consider how we think about God's speech in and of itself. As J. I. Packer explains, "No Christian will question that God speaks truth and truth only (that is, that what He says is infallible and inerrant). But if all Scripture comes from God in such a sense that what it says, He says, then Scripture as such must be infallible and inerrant, because it is God's utterance."[39]

Scripture's Testimony to Its Own Truthfulness

Does Scripture itself affirm that it is free from error? Does Scripture assert its own purity? Many critics today say no.[40] Let's look at the biblical witness.

---

36. Roger Nicole, "The Biblical Concept of Truth," in Carson and Woodbridge, *Scripture and Truth*, 287–302.

37. Frame, *Systematic Theology*, 522.

38. Young, *Thy Word Is Truth*, 45 (cf. 50, 87, 88, 92, 93, 123).

39. J. I. Packer, *God Has Spoken: Revelation and the Bible*, 3rd ed. (Grand Rapids: Baker, 1993), 104.

40. For example, Craig D. Allert, *A High View of Scripture? The Authority of the Bible and the Formation of the New Testament Canon* (Grand Rapids: Baker Academic, 2007), 147–72.

Jesus Believed the Old Testament Was Inerrant

As with our discussion of inspiration, the place to begin with inerrancy is with Jesus himself. Consider the many ways in which he saw the OT to be inerrant.

1. *Jesus approached the Old Testament as true and factual.* Today critics typically turn to the narratives of the Old Testament to expose what they believe is Scripture's inaccuracy, implausibility, or lack of coherence.[41] They balk at the Old Testament's historical record and witness to figures like Adam and Eve, Jonah and the big fish, or Noah and the flood. Ironically, Jesus does the exact opposite. He appeals to the historical narratives of the Old Testament as reliable, trustworthy, and essential components in the drama of redemption.[42] For example, consider the host of persons, places, events, and acts that Jesus considers historically accurate:

   • Adam and Eve as the first historical persons (Matt 19:4–6)
   • Cain and Abel (Matt 23:35; Luke 11:51)
   • Noah and the flood (Matt 24:37–38)
   • Tyre, Sidon, and Sodom (Matt 11:21–24; Luke 17:29)
   • Death of Lot's wife (Luke 17:31–32)
   • Abraham (John 8:56)
   • Isaac and Jacob (Matt 8:11)
   • Moses as the author of the Law (Luke 24:44; John 7:19)
   • God's appearance to Moses in the burning bush (Mark 12:26–27)
   • God's miracle of providing manna to Israel in the wilderness (John 6:32, 49, 58)
   • Moses and the bronze serpent (John 3:14)
   • David and Solomon (Matt 12:3, 42)
   • Queen of Sheba (Matt 12:42)
   • Elijah and Elisha (Luke 4:25–27)
   • Isaiah as the author of the book of Isaiah (John 12:38–41)
   • Zechariah's martyrdom (Matt 23:35)
   • Jonah being swallowed by the great fish (Matt 12:40–41)

---

41. For example, Enns, *The Bible Tells Me So.*
42. Wenham, *Christ and the Bible*, 18.

- Historical events, figures, and narrative from Abel to Zechariah son of Berekiah (Matt 23:25; Luke 11:50–51)[43]

Jesus had no hesitation appealing to the Old Testament as historical and accurate. Jesus is not referencing these individuals and events in a way that assumes they are merely spiritual illustrations, but rather to show that his messianic identity depends upon these individuals and events as historical types of what was to come—in his life, his death, and his resurrection.[44]

2. *Jesus treated the Old Testament as a unitary, comprehensive whole that does not contradict itself.* According to Jesus, Scripture does not contradict Scripture. Rather, one part of Scripture is always in perfect consistency with the rest of Scripture. For Jesus, there is a *coherence* to Scripture that cannot be broken, and so Scripture must be treated as a unitary whole.[45] Such coherence and unity were explained extensively in chapter 6. Here it will suffice to observe just how often Jesus makes mention of the fact that Scripture must be fulfilled.

For example, consider the hours leading up to Jesus's crucifixion. As Jesus prepared to go to the cross, he shared a final meal with his disciples. In holding up the bread and wine, Jesus was clear that these represent his body and blood, the latter being referred to as the "blood of the covenant, which is poured out for many" (Mark 14:24). After singing a hymn, they went to the Mount of Olives, where Jesus said to them, "You will all fall away, *for it is written*: 'I will strike the shepherd, and the sheep will be scattered'" (Mark 14:27, emphasis added). Jesus was quoting from Zechariah 13:7, telling his disciples that what was occurring was happening to him precisely as Scripture had predicted.

---

43. A similar list can be found in Robert Saucy, *Scripture: Its Power, Authority, and Relevance* (Nashville: Nelson, 2001), 110–11; Wenham, *Christ and the Bible*, 12–16; Craig L. Blomberg, "Reflections on Jesus' View of the Old Testament," in *The Enduring Authority of the Christian Scriptures*, ed. D. A. Carson (Grand Rapids: Eerdmans, 2016), 680.

44. See the numerous texts, for example, where Jesus and the Gospel writers see the OT fulfilled in the life of Jesus: Matthew 2:15, 18; 4:15–16; 8:17; 12:18–21; 13:35; 27:9–10; John 12:38; 19:14, 28, 36–37. See Blomberg, "Reflections on Jesus' View of the Old Testament," 689; Saucy, *Scripture*, 111.

45. Wenham, *Christ and the Bible*, 25.

The closer we get to the cross, the more Jesus makes this apparent. After Jesus prayed in Gethsemane, Judas and his gang came at Jesus with swords and clubs. He was betrayed by Judas, who kissed him as a signal, and the men "arrested him" (Mark 14:46). What is telling is how Jesus responded: "Have you come out as against a robber, with swords and clubs to capture me? Day after day I was with you in the temple teaching, and you did not seize me. *But let the Scriptures be fulfilled*" (Mark 14:49 ESV, emphasis added; cf. Matt 26:54–56). Again, Jesus saw his death as the fulfillment of what was prophesied long ago in the OT. In other words, what God said through his prophets in the Old Testament was now coming true in the suffering of Jesus. The fulfillment of the Old in the New is a pillar that undergirds the doctrine of inerrancy.

As the story continues with Jesus's trial and crucifixion, the Gospel writers make it clear that what happened took place to fulfill the Scriptures. Even the smallest details are important, a reminder that inerrancy applies to the small matters just as much as it does to the big ones. For example, in John's account we read that the soldiers, after crucifying Jesus, "took his garments and divided them into four parts, one part for each soldier; also his tunic. But the tunic was seamless, woven in one piece from top to bottom, so they said to one another, 'Let us not tear it, but cast lots for it to see whose it shall be'" (John 19:23–24 ESV). While these may seem like insignificant details, John, quoting Psalm 22:18, tells us otherwise: "This was to *fulfill the Scripture* which says, 'They divided my garments among them, and for my clothing they cast lots'" (John 19:24 ESV, emphasis added).

The fulfillment of the Old Testament in the New reiterates that Jesus's words in John 5:39 are true. The Scriptures, Jesus said, "testify about me." Even Moses, Jesus says in John 5:46–47, "wrote about me."[46] Certainly Jesus thought that even the smallest details in the Old Testament were true and demanded fulfillment in his coming lest the promises of God be compromised (Matt 5:17, 36).

---

46. One should also observe how Jesus quotes the OT to support his mission and identity (e.g., Matt 4:1–10).

3. *Jesus taught that the Old Testament could not be broken.* In John 10 the Jews were infuriated with Jesus, ready to stone him for his claims to deity. When Jesus asked them for which of his works he was about to be stoned, they responded, "We are not stoning you for any good work, but for blasphemy, because you, a mere man, claim to be God" (John 10:33). Jesus replied, in John 10:34–35, by quoting from Psalm 82:6: "Is it not written in your Law, 'I said, you are gods'? If he called [Israel] gods to whom the word of God came—and Scripture cannot be broken—do you say of him whom the Father consecrated and sent into the world, 'You are blaspheming,' because I said, 'I am the Son of God'?" (ESV).[47]

Notice how Jesus equated "your Law" with "Scripture." And since Jesus is quoting the Psalter (Ps 82:6), "Law" in this instance is not limited but refers to the whole Old Testament.[48] The assumption is that the Old Testament *is* the Word of God. Additionally, Jesus says that Scripture cannot be broken. Here Jesus is using a syllogism: "Scripture cannot be broken; Psalm 82:6 is Scripture; therefore Psalm 82:6 cannot be broken."[49] What does this demonstrate? It shows that "it was sufficient proof of the infallibility of any sentence or phrase of a clause, to show that it constituted a portion of what the Jews called 'the Scripture.'" Furthermore, the word "broken" means that Scripture cannot be "annulled, set aside, or deprived of its force."[50] Scripture cannot be breached, ruptured, or falsified, nor can it fail in its fulfillment (cf. Matt 5:17–18).[51] Here, says Andreas Köstenberger, is "evidence for his [Jesus's] belief in the inviolability of God's written word."[52]

---

47. "If Israel can in some sense be called 'god' in the Scriptures, how much more is the designation appropriate for him who truly is the Son of God" (Andreas J. Köstenberger, *John*, BECNT [Grand Rapids: Baker Academic, 2004], 315). See also D. A. Carson, *The Gospel according to John*, PNTC (Grand Rapids: Eerdmans, 1991), 397–98.

48. See John 12:34; 15:25; 1 Cor 14:21. Carson, *John*, 397.

49. This syllogism comes from Donald Macleod, "Jesus and Scripture," in Helm and Trueman, *Trustworthiness of God*, 76.

50. Ibid., 77. Jesus uses the same word in Matthew 5:19: "Therefore whoever *relaxes* one of the least of these commandments and teaches others to do the same will be called least in the kingdom of heaven" (ESV).

51. Macleod, "Jesus and Scripture," 77. Jesus no doubt offends the Pharisees, for in Mark 7:13 he accuses them of "making void the word of God by your tradition" (ESV).

52. Köstenberger, *John*, 315.

4. *Jesus appealed to the Old Testament as that which is authoritative.* Since Jesus not only believed the Old Testament was God-breathed but also true and cohesive, a unity not to be broken but to be fulfilled in the new covenant, it follows that he also believed it was authoritative. This is exactly what one would expect if Jesus believed the Old Testament was inerrant. Precisely because the Old Testament was not only inspired but inerrant, Jesus saw it as authoritative, demanding Israel's allegiance, obedience, and reverence.[53]

What are we to conclude after this brief look at Jesus? We must conclude that since our Lord affirmed Scripture's inerrancy, then so should we. We can believe in doctrines like inspiration and inerrancy fundamentally because they are doctrines our Lord himself believed and taught. Those who reject inerrancy in reality are rejecting the very view held by our Lord.[54] You cannot have the Jesus of the Bible and reject the Bible of Jesus. It's all or nothing.

The New Testament Authors Believed the Old Testament Was Inerrant

A common maneuver today is to pit Christ against his apostles and the apostles against Christ, as if the two held different views of Scripture. But the apostles were endorsed and commissioned by Jesus (John 16:12–15) and were teaching the very things Jesus himself had taught them. Their authority as apostles was derived from Christ. The result: to reject the apostles' teaching on Scripture is to reject Jesus's teaching on Scripture.[55] One cannot say, I want the apostles' teaching on Scripture, but not Christ's. Or I want Christ's teaching on Scripture, but not the apostles'. No, the two go hand in hand, for Christ gives us his apostles and the apostles give us Christ in their writings.[56]

Note that the apostles, like Jesus, never (not once!) take a critical

---

53. According to Jesus, the God who spoke in the Old Testament was the living God, and Jesus considered the words and promises of the Old Testament the authoritative and binding words and promises of the one, true, and living God. See Wenham, *Christ and the Bible*, 17, 23; John Warwick Montgomery, "Biblical Inerrancy: What Is at Stake?," in *God's Inerrant Word: An International Symposium on the Trustworthiness of Scripture*, ed. John Warwick Montgomery (Minneapolis: Bethany Fellowship, 1973), 28–29.

54. Warfield makes this very point repeatedly. See Fred Zaspel, *The Theology of B. B. Warfield: A Systematic Summary* (Wheaton, IL: Crossway, 2010), 161–65, 173.

55. Ibid., 161.

56. Ibid.

stance toward the Old Testament. Whenever it is referenced, alluded to, or relied upon, it is always seen as authoritative, inspired, true, and trustworthy (Rom 15:4; 2 Tim 3:16; 1 Pet 1:10–12; 2 Pet 1:19–21). When the New Testament books are studied, we see that the authors' trust in the reliability of the Old Testament is overwhelming:

- The NT authors referenced persons, places, and events in the OT as real and historical (Matt 12:42; Mark 2:25–26; Luke 11:31–32; John 3:14; Heb 7:2; 1 Pet 3:20; 2 Pet 2:16), and sometimes this included even the minutest facts (Matt 22:41–46; Mark 12:35–37; Gal 3:16).[57]
- The NT authors believed the promises and types in the OT were fulfilled in the new covenant (Acts 2:17; 3:22; 7:37; 8:32; 1 Cor 5:7; 10:4; 2 Cor 6:16; Gal 3:13; 4:21; Heb 2:6–8; 7:1–10).
- The NT authors repeatedly appealed to the OT to prove and support their beliefs and conduct (Acts 15:16; 23:5; Rom 1:17; 3:10; 4:3–7; 9:7–17; 10:5; Gal 3:10; 4:30; 1 Cor 9:9; 10:26; 15; 2 Cor 6:17).
- The NT authors, as well as Jesus (Matt 5:18; 22:45; Luke 16:17; John 10:35), believed even the smallest detail (even a single word) of the OT was authoritative and trustworthy (Gal 3:16).
- The NT authors believed the OT was an organic whole with God as its divine author, as seen in the way the NT authors attributed OT authorship to God or the Holy Spirit (Matt 19:5; Heb 1:5; 3:7; 4:3–5; 5:6–7; 7:21; 8:5–8; 10:16, 30; 12:26; 13:5).[58]

Previously, we looked at Matthew 22:42–45 and saw how Jesus buttresses his divine identity as Messiah, son of David, by appealing to Psalm 110:1 ("The Lord said to my Lord"). Jesus insinuates, as do Peter (Acts 2:33–35) and the author of Hebrews (1:13; 5:6, 10; 6:20; 7), that the second "Lord" referred to is the Messiah, and this Messiah is none other than Jesus himself. What I wish to point out is that both Jesus and Peter attribute this psalm to David, who is named as its author in the superscription of the psalm. Jesus even says David

---

57. For a long list of historical details the NT authors thought reliable, see Grudem, "Scripture's Self-Attestation and the Problem of Formulating a Doctrine of Scripture," in *Scripture and Truth*, ed. D. A. Carson and John Woodbridge (Grand Rapids: Baker, 1983), 42–44.

58. On this last point, see Herman Bavinck, *Reformed Dogmatics*, ed. John Bolt, trans. John Vriend (Grand Rapids: Baker Academic, 2003), 1:394.

spoke this psalm "in the Spirit," thereby asserting biblical inspiration and authority.[59] In other words, Jesus assumes that not only is the text accurate in its messianic reference, but even the superscription is trustworthy.[60] If David is not the author, Jesus's argument that David spoke of the Messiah is void.[61]

This text, in light of the inerrancy debate, serves as a case in point. John Goldingay, professor of Old Testament at Fuller Seminary, can be commended for striving to interpret the Old Testament text within its own context. Yet Goldingay goes astray in his failure to take into account the broader, canonical context. In his treatment of Psalm 110, he denies that this text is from David despite the fact that the New Testament authors say so.[62] Goldingay rebukes those who would read the psalm messianically in light of the New Testament. What, then, should we do with the New Testament authors, including Jesus himself, who believed David was the author and who applied the psalm to Jesus? Goldingay says that the Spirit must have inspired "people [in the NT] to see significance in the OT that was never there before."[63] Goldingay goes even further, saying, "The text's theological implications then do not lie in its application to Jesus; that is to ignore its meaning."[64] We must not, he argues, "neutralize the psalm's insights by claiming that we interpret it in light of the rest of the canon." He is saying that Jesus's and the New Testament authors' trust in and interpretation of the Old Testament should not color our reading (i.e., we should not read an OT text in its canonical context).[65]

In this, Goldingay has undermined the unity of the canon of Scripture and the authority of Jesus and the New Testament authors.

---

59. Leon Morris, *The Gospel according to Matthew*, PNTC (Grand Rapids: Eerdmans, 1992), 565; R. T. France, *The Gospel of Matthew*, NICNT (Grand Rapids: Eerdmans, 2007), 850.

60. Kidner observes, "In the Heb. Text there is no break between these words [A Psalm of David] and those which we normally print as the first line. Our custom of placing the title above the psalm, rather than as part of verse 1, is a matter of convenience, which does not alter its status as part of the text" (Derek Kidner, *Psalms 73–150*, TOTC [Downers Grove, IL: IVP Academic, 1975; repr. 2008], 426n.10).

61. D. A. Carson, *Collected Writings on Scripture* (Wheaton, IL: Crossway, 2010), 25–26. The same point is made by France, *Matthew*, 851–52.

62. John Goldingay, *Psalms, Volume 3: Psalms 90–150*, BCOTWP, ed. Tremper Longman III (Grand Rapids: Baker Academic, 2008), 291.

63. Ibid., 3:299.

64. Ibid., 3:300.

65. Goldingay makes a similar claim in *Do We Need the New Testament? Letting the Old Testament Speak for Itself* (Downers Grove, IL: IVP Academic, 2015), 97: "The hermeneutical guidance the New Testament offers us is that we should not be looking to it for hermeneutical guidance."

If Goldingay is right, we might wonder if Jesus got it wrong, not only in his attribution of the psalm to David but in seeing Psalm 110 as speaking prophetically of his own divine messianic identity. And if Jesus got Psalm 110 wrong, certainly the New Testament authors did as well (Rom 8:34; 1 Cor 15:25; Eph 1:20; Col 3:1; Heb 1:3, 13; 5:6–10; 7:10–28; 8:1; 10:12–13; 12:2).

In contrast to Goldingay, whose approach ruptures the unity and authority of the canon that Jesus and the New Testament authors assumed, Derek Kidner's conclusion on Psalm 110:1 is far more in step with the biblical text itself. "To amputate this opening phrase [A Psalm of David], or to allow it no reference to the authorship of the psalm, is to be at odds with the New Testament, which finds King David's acknowledgement of his 'Lord' highly significant." Kidner continues, "Our Lord gave full weight to David's authorship and David's words, stressing the former twice by the expression 'David himself', and the latter by the comment that he was speaking 'in the Holy Spirit' (Mark 12:36f.) and by insisting that his terms presented a challenge to accepted ideas of the Messiah, which must be taken seriously."[66]

In summary, when the diversity of Old Testament passages cited by New Testament authors is taken into consideration, it is undeniable that the New Testament authors, following Jesus himself, believed the Old Testament was without error and therefore authoritative and trustworthy. In short, the New Testament authors held the Old Testament in such reverence that they would have been shocked by many today who claim that the Old Testament is fallible, corrupt, and even misleading. Their apostolic testimony depended upon the Bible's trustworthiness.

Jesus Believed His Own Teaching Was Inerrant

Jesus not only believed the Old Testament was true and trustworthy, but he believed the same concerning his own teaching as well. Jesus said that until heaven and earth pass away, not one letter or pen stroke will pass from the Law until all is accomplished (Matt 5:18), and he elevates his own words when he says that while heaven and earth will pass away, *his* words will not (Matt 24:35; Mark 13:31; Luke 21:33). Jesus repeatedly speaks with divine authority, introducing his teaching with phrases such as "truly I say to you" (used 31 times in Matthew, 13 times in Mark, and 6 times in Luke) and "truly, truly, I say to you"

---

66. Kidner, *Psalms*, 73–150, 426–27.

(used 25 times in John).[67] Jesus treats not only the Old Testament as God's Word but his own words as well. They carry the same authority. In fact, it is shocking how many times Jesus's words even supersede them, as seen in how many times Jesus says "I say to you . . ." in contrast to the Old Testament's "The Lord spoke to . . ." or "Thus says the Lord . . ." Jews hearing such phrases from the mouth of Jesus would have been startled, understanding him to be either truly speaking *as* God or blaspheming the name of God.[68]

Jesus viewed his own words and obedience to them as a matter of spiritual life and death (e.g., Matt 7:24–26; 13:3–23). Those who do not believe his words, he says, are foolish and do not have the truth. His words carry divine authority (Matt 11:25–27; 28:18) and are to be obeyed and followed (Matt 28:19–20). Jesus can make such a claim only if (1) he truly is who he says he is (i.e., the eternal Son of God), and (2) his words are true. It is no accident, then, that inerrancy is wrapped tightly around Christology and vice versa. The truth of Jesus's words, and the authority of his words, is entirely dependent upon his divine identity (e.g., John 5:24–25; 6:63).[69] As the Son of God, the divine Word, Jesus is not only full of grace but "truth" (John 1:14; cf. 5:32).[70] His identity as "the truth" (John 14:6) is consistent with the identity of the Father, the "only true God" (John 17:3) whose "word is truth" (John 17:17), as well as the "Spirit of truth" (John 14:17; 15:26; 16:13).[71]

This raises a dilemma for those who oppose the inerrancy of Christ's words. If they find error in what Christ has spoken, what are they to make of Christ's person? Can they really quarantine off the person of Christ from the words of Christ? Can they say that the truthfulness (or untruthfulness) of Christ's words is of no consequence for the truthfulness of his person? I think not. The Gospels present Christ and his words together. For example, Matthew, in his Gospel, puts Jesus forward as one who speaks with a new authority, an authority that can be placed on the same level as the Old Testament itself. What is even more remarkable is how Jesus affirms the authority and inspiration of the

---

67. Wenham, *Christ and the Bible*, 58.

68. Ibid., 55 (cf. 63).

69. John 7:15–17; 8:26–28, 37–38, 40, 43–47; 12:48–50; 14:10; 15:3, 7, 15; 18:37.

70. Leon Morris, *The Gospel according to John*, NICNT (Grand Rapids: Eerdmans, 1971), 107. Michaels connects John 1:14 (Jesus is full of truth) to Exod 34:6, where Moses confesses God as great in truth. J. Ramsey Michaels, *The Gospel of John*, NICNT (Grand Rapids: Eerdmans, 2010), 83.

71. Michaels, *Gospel of John*, 872.

of the Law and the Prophets, at times showing submission to these Scriptures while also indicating that his word transcends the Old Testament, bringing the OT prophecies to completion and fulfillment. When Jesus taught, he spoke with his own authority, not simply with an authority derived from the Old Testament.[72] His authority resides in his own person as the incarnate God-man. This is the only explanation for why Christ can speak the way he does.[73] It is an injustice to the biblical text to divorce the person of Christ from the words of Christ, to deny the truthfulness and reliability of his words. This does harm to his person, for the two are codependent. "Consequently," says N. B. Stonehouse, "not his words only but his person and life also come as a new revelation. . . . To fail to comprehend him as constituting a divine disclosure is to fail utterly to understand him at all."[74]

The New Testament Authors Believed Their Writings Were Inerrant

The apostles believed the words of Christ were true and trustworthy. They certainly demonstrated this by the sacrifices they made to take the words of Christ to the nations, even laying down their lives to spread the gospel.

Those commissioned by Christ and then by the Spirit at Pentecost (John 14:26; 15:26–27; 16:7–14; 20:22; Acts 2) saw their own writings as true as well. No one is as forthright as the apostle John. At the end of his Gospel, John identifies himself and lucidly states the purpose of his narrative: "This is the disciple who is bearing witness about these things, and who has written these things, and *we know that his testimony is true*" (John 21:24 ESV, emphasis added; cf. 19:35; 3 John 12). John ends with this affirmation. Luke begins with it:

> Inasmuch as many have undertaken to compile a narrative of the things that have been accomplished among us, just as those who from the beginning were eyewitnesses and ministers of the word have delivered them to us, it seemed good to me also, having followed all things closely for some time past, to write an orderly account for you, most excellent Theophilus, that you may have certainty concerning the things you have been taught. (Luke 1:1–4)

---

72. Wenham, *Christ and the Bible*, 58–59.
73. Ibid.
74. As quoted in ibid., 59.

Why is it that Luke is writing to Theophilus? So that he will have *certainty*. Notice that this certainty concerns doctrinal *and* historical matters. Luke, under the inspiration of the Holy Spirit, set out to "compile a narrative" of what took place based on the eyewitness accounts of those who were with Jesus.[75] Historical truth is important to Luke (the historian) if Theophilus is to gain certainty in the things he has been taught.[76]

That the New Testament authors thought their own teaching and letters were true and trustworthy is manifested in the authority they believed they carried. Paul argued for the truth of his teaching on subjects like justification against the Judaizers of his day (Gal 1–2; 1 Cor 1:10–4:21; 2 Cor 10:13).[77] As one whom Jesus himself appeared to (1 Cor 9:1; 15:8), giving Paul his gospel (Gal 1:12; Eph 3:2–8; 1 Tim 1:12), Paul was called by God to apostleship (Gal 1:1, 15) and even given revelations and visions (2 Cor 12; Acts 26:16). Paul emphasized repeatedly that he spoke not by himself but by the Spirit (1 Cor 7:40) and Christ (1 Cor 2:10, 16; 2 Cor 2:17; 5:20; 13:3), and therefore his word was true (1 Cor 7:25). The truthfulness of his word was not limited to his oral speech, but extended to his writings (Col 4:16; 1 Thess 5:27; 2 Thess 2:15; 3:14). Paul believed his word and letters were authoritative, binding, and to be obeyed (1 Cor 7:40; 1 Thess 4:2, 11; 2 Thess 3:6–14). Indeed, when he wrote them, it was as if the Lord himself had written to the churches.

It is hard to imagine the New Testament churches submitting themselves to the authority of the apostolic writings and the apostles' associates (Acts 15:22; Col 4:16) if these same letters were not trustworthy, true, and reliable, as some now claim. Authority has everything to do with inerrancy, and this leads us to an important question.

What Does Inerrancy Have to Do with *Sola Scriptura*?

We've spent several chapters looking at the Reformation cry of *sola Scriptura*. And we've traced the history of this doctrine through the Enlightenment to the present day. We've also looked at the biblical

---

75. "The verb ἔδοξε(ν) [it seemed good] is used in Acts 15:22, 25, 28 for a decision that is prompted by the Holy Spirit." David E. Garland, *Luke*, ZECNT (Grand Rapids: Zondervan, 2012), 54.

76. On the meticulous historical process Luke went through to write an orderly account, see ibid., 53–56.

77. Bavinck, *Reformed Dogmatics*, 1:399–400.

evidence for inspiration and inerrancy. All of this leads to a question that is seldom asked but enormously important: What does inerrancy have to do with *sola Scriptura*? The answer: everything.

As we saw in part 1, *sola Scriptura* since the Reformation came under fire. The sixteenth-century Reformers opposed Rome because she questioned the sufficiency and authority of Scripture by elevating Tradition, believing it to be divine revelation and just as authoritative as Scripture itself. As a result, the distinctiveness and uniqueness of biblical inerrancy was challenged. Rome claimed there was a *second* source of divine revelation, namely, Tradition. To be clear, Rome did not oppose the inerrancy of Scripture. She affirmed it. The point is that Rome's elevation of Tradition as a second inerrant source of revelation was perceived by the Reformers as a major threat to the exclusivity and uniqueness of Scripture as the *sole* inerrant source of written revelation and final authority for the church. The consequences were devastating: No longer could Scripture be sufficient and authoritative in and of itself. Scripture was no longer the final authority. For Rome, Tradition was equally authoritative because it was considered not only revelatory but also inerrant. Rome's elevation of Tradition to the level of inerrancy had significant consequences for her denial of scriptural sufficiency and final authority.

The situation worsened with the advent of the Enlightenment, Liberalism, and eventually postmodernism. The very trustworthiness and truthfulness of the Bible *itself* was brought into question, something Rome in the sixteenth century had not been willing to do.[78] As we saw in chapters 2 and 3, history demonstrates that when Scripture's trustworthiness is rejected, it is not long before Scripture's sufficiency and authority are abandoned as well. Again, notice the inseparable and natural connection between inerrancy, authority, and sufficiency. Critics of the Bible saw no reason why they should believe the Bible was authoritative when they believed that the Bible was not inspired by God but was errant in numerous ways. To them, there could be no

---

78. It should be qualified that movements like the Enlightenment, Liberalism, and Postmodernism have influenced Roman Catholicism today so much so that some post-Vatican II Catholics will question inerrancy. However, other Roman Catholics reject such a move. On Vatican II and Rome's shift to stress human authorship, as well as its sympathies for Protestant Liberalism, see Anthony N. S. Lane, "Roman Catholic Views of Biblical Authority from the Late Nineteenth Century to the Present," in Carson, *Enduring Authority of the Christian Scriptures*, 292–320.

"Thus says the Lord" when the Lord didn't really speak and the text that says he did speak was errant to begin with. It made little sense to them to believe the biblical text was authoritative in what it addressed and asserted when that same biblical text, they believed, was errant and uninspired. Whenever this thinking took root, the Reformation understanding of *sola Scriptura* was seriously undermined.[79]

Many of these approaches to Scripture continue today. What makes our day unique—particularly in the world of evangelicalism—is that some have tried to pave a middle way (*via media*) by holding on to biblical authority and sufficiency while denying biblical inerrancy. While some have abandoned the concept of inerrancy completely, others are dissatisfied with it but are unwilling to dispense with the term or idea. This "limited inerrancy" position (as we can call it) may take on a variety of forms and includes a diverse group of advocates. It essentially argues that there are errors in Scripture, but when it comes to the Bible's central spiritual message, there are no errors. Limited inerrancy advocates maintain that while Scripture may not be perfect in all of its details (especially those of historical or cosmological nature) or in every subject it addresses, it is trustworthy in its main message and thus the Bible remains authoritative and sufficient. Notice that advocates of limited inerrancy do not necessarily believe their view precludes the doctrine of *sola Scriptura*. In their view, the two remain mutually compatible. As we saw in chapter 3, this was the view taken by the progressive Neo-Evangelicals at Fuller Seminary in the 1960s, who denied Scripture's full inerrancy yet insisted that Scripture remains the Christian's final authority.[80] Such an approach continues to pervade the academic world today and has infiltrated many church pews.

How should we evaluate the "limited inerrancy" position? It is a

---

79. This was not the case with every individual, obviously. However, I would argue that it proved to be a consistent pattern. See chapters 2 and 3.

80. See chapter 3 with regard to Fuller Seminary. For example, Jack Rogers, *Biblical Authority* (Waco, TX: Word, 1977); Jack Rogers and Donald McKim, *The Authority and Interpretation of the Bible: An Historical Approach* (San Francisco: Harper & Row, 1979). It is also an approach that has been utilized by progressive Roman Catholics since Vatican II. Some would argue that there was deliberate ambiguity in its statement so that Scripture was no longer said to be inerrant in all its assertions. Some saw this ambiguity as a victory for the progressives. See Clark H. Pinnock, "Limited Inerrancy: A Critical Appraisal and Constructive Alternative," in Montgomery, *God's Inerrant Word*, 146–48. For the inerrancy debate between Catholics at Vatican II, see Cardinal Alois Grillmeier, "The Divine Inspiration and the Interpretation of Sacred Scripture," in *Commentary on the Documents of Vatican II*, vol. 3, ed. Herbert Vorgrimler (New York: Crossroad, 1989), 199–246.

view riddled with inconsistency. As we have seen, to question Scripture's reliability is also to question Scripture's sufficiency and authority. These attributes are intertwined, inseparable, and essential to the existence of one another. One cannot consistently affirm and practice *sola Scriptura* while abandoning inerrancy. Indeed, it is because *all* of Scripture is verbally inspired by God, and therefore without error, that it carries final and ultimate authority and is fully sufficient.

If we think back to chapter 1 and the narrative of Luther's progress to the Diet of Worms, we recall that the issue of *sola Scriptura* rested on who does and does not err.[81] As we saw in each of Luther's debates, Luther strongly believed that what set Scripture apart in terms of authority was not only its divine inspiration but specifically its absolute perfection and flawlessness, much in contrast to the imperfection of ecclesiastical tradition. Luther believed Scripture alone is our *flawless* authority. "For Luther," observes R. C. Sproul, "the *sola* of *sola Scriptura* was inseparably related to the Scriptures' unique inerrancy. It was because popes could and did err and because councils could and did err that Luther came to realize the supremacy of Scripture. Luther did not despise church authority nor did he repudiate church councils as having no value. . . . Luther and the Reformers did not mean by *sola Scriptura* that the Bible is the only authority in the church. Rather, they meant that the Bible is the only *infallible* authority in the church."[82]

It is precisely because God's Word is God-breathed and therefore inerrant (i.e., God does not breathe out error) that it possesses unconditional and final authority.[83] *Sola Scriptura* means that the Bible alone

---

81. See Gordon Rupp, *Luther's Progress to the Diet of Worms* (New York: Harper, 1964), 69.

82. R. C. Sproul, *Sola Scriptura: The Evangelical Doctrine* (Phillipsburg, NJ: P&R, 2005), 17. See also Rupp, *Luther's Progress to the Diet of Worms*, 69; Paul Althaus, *The Theology of Martin Luther*, trans. Robert C. Schultz (Philadelphia: Fortress, 1966), 6–7.

83. An important point must be made to avoid misunderstanding. I am not assuming that inerrancy is the sufficient ground or basis for authority. While inerrancy is necessary for authority, it is not in and of itself sufficient. To say so would be to deny the role of inspiration as the foundation upon which biblical authority is built. At the same time, this should not lead us to conclude that a denial of inerrancy does not affect authority. It does! Remember, inerrancy is the necessary and natural corollary of inspiration (see chapter 5). As B. B. Warfield demonstrated throughout his writings, if the Bible truly is God's Word, then, *ipso facto*, it is without error. After all, it is the Word *of God*, and God is a God of truth, perfect in all that he says. Therefore, inerrancy is necessarily bound up with biblical authority because it is inseparably connected to biblical inspiration. It is inconceivable, then, to say that Scripture could be authoritative but errant. To the contrary, when we say Scripture speaks with authority, what we are really saying is that it speaks with *flawless* authority. All in all, when it comes to Scripture, there is no authority without inspiration, and there is no inspiration without inerrancy. They all go together and necessarily entail

is our *flawless* authority, something that cannot (and should not) be said of anything else.[84] The Bible alone is the inerrant source of written divine revelation from God. As Luther believed so emphatically, since church councils, fathers, and, yes, even popes err, they cannot possess an equal authority to Scripture. Their authority is contingent upon their faithfulness to the biblical text, which alone is inspired and inerrant. At best, they possess a *derivative* authority. Where they are consistent with Scripture, they speak authoritatively. As Luther said, "But everyone, indeed, knows that at times they [the fathers] have erred as men will; therefore, I am ready to trust them only when they prove their opinions from Scripture, which has never erred."[85] The Reformers considered inerrancy to be a corollary to *sola Scriptura*.[86] In his description of Luther's theology, Paul Althaus explains, "We may trust unconditionally only in the Word of God and not in the teaching of the fathers; for the teachers of the Church can err and

one another. I must give credit to Fred Zaspel, who helped me work through this point in personal correspondence. See also Zaspel's chapter "Bibliology" in *The Theology of B. B. Warfield*, 111–78.

84. What about general revelation? It too is a flawless authority, for it is from God. Moreover, there are other forms of revelation outside of the written canon, such as OT and NT miracles, teachings from Jesus not recorded in the Bible, lost epistles by some apostles, etc. However, none of these are canonical and none of these, including general revelation, are sufficient. Therefore, we can conclude that none of these are *sufficiently authoritative* for Christians today. This role belongs to Scripture alone. This point is made beautifully by "The Westminster Confession of Faith (1646)," in *Reformed Confessions of the 16th and 17th Centuries in English Translation, Volume 4, 1600–1693*, ed. James T. Dennison Jr. (Grand Rapids: Reformation Heritage, 2014), 233 (I.I).

85. *LW* 32:11. For other places where Luther affirms the inerrancy of Scripture, see *LW* 1:121; 4:14; 22:254, 259; 31:11, 282; 32:98; 35:128, 150; 36:136–37; 39:165. For Luther's affirmation of Scripture's perfection in relation to *sola Scriptura*, see Mark D. Thompson, *A Sure Ground on Which to Stand: The Relation of Authority and Interpretive Method in Luther's Approach to Scripture* (Eugene, OR: Wipf & Stock, 2004), 249–82.

86. As mentioned in previous chapters, the Reformers did not use the term *inerrant*, but this does not mean that the *concept* was not affirmed. For defenses of the Reformers' affirmation of inerrancy, see Robert D. Preus, "Luther and Biblical Infallibility," in *Inerrancy and the Church*, ed. John D. Hannah (Chicago: Moody Press, 1984), 99–142; J. Theodore Mueller, "Luther and the Bible," in *Inspiration and Interpretation*, ed. John F. Walvoord (Grand Rapids: Eerdmans, 1947), 87–114; Thompson, *Sure Ground on Which to Stand*; James I. Packer, "John Calvin and the Inerrancy of Holy Scripture," in Hannah, *Inerrancy and the Church*, 143–88; Kenneth Kantzer, "Calvin and the Holy Scriptures," in Walvoord, *Inspiration and Interpretation*, 115–55; W. Robert Godfrey, "Biblical Authority in the Sixteenth and Seventeenth Centuries: A Question of Transition," in Carson and Woodbridge, *Scripture and Truth*, 225–43, 391–97; Roger R. Nicole, "John Calvin and Inerrancy," *JETS* 25 (1982): 425–42; Eugene F. Klung, "Word and Spirit in Luther Studies since World War II," *TJ* 5 (1984): 3–46; John D. Woodbridge, *Biblical Authority: A Critique of the Rogers/McKim Proposal* (Grand Rapids: Zondervan, 1982), 49–100; Muller, *PRRD*, 2:289–90.

have erred. Scripture never errs. Therefore it alone has unconditional authority."[87] Sproul is right to conclude, "The Reformation principle of *sola Scriptura* involved inerrancy."[88] While some, like Jack Rogers and Donald McKim, have popularized the myth that inerrancy was an invention of Reformed scholasticism and Old Princeton, John Woodbridge exploded this myth, demonstrating not only that inerrancy was taught by the Reformers but has a heritage all the way back to the fathers (see chapters 1 and 3).

All of this explains why it is necessary to highlight inerrancy in our explanation and defense of *sola Scriptura*. And it explains why inerrancy is prominently featured in our definition of *sola Scriptura*, that only Scripture, because it is God's inspired Word, is our *inerrant*, sufficient, and final authority for the church. It's not just the Reformers who saw (and assumed) this connection between inerrancy and biblical authority. The Reformed tradition at large has followed suit. The Belgic Confession (1561) calls Scripture the "infallible rule" for the church, a statement that combines both Scripture's perfection and authority in one phrase.[89] Or consider the Church of England, whose Thirty-Nine Articles (1563) assert that councils "may err, and sometimes have erred, even in things pertaining unto God."[90] Only Scripture, as God's inspired Word, does not err, and so it stands supreme in its authority over councils.[91] Similarly, the Westminster Confession of Faith (1646) states that the *"infallible rule* of interpretation of Scripture is the *Scripture itself*," and by "infallible" these Westminster divines did not mean something less than inerrancy as limited inerrantists do today. Therefore, as the "infallible rule," Scripture alone is the "supreme judge."[92] The London Baptist Confession (1677), which is largely based on the Westminster Confession of Faith, is just as explicit: "The Holy Scripture is the *only*

87. Althaus, *Theology of Martin Luther*, 6–7.

88. R. C. Sproul, *Scripture Alone: The Evangelical Doctrine* (Phillipsburg, NJ: P&R, 2005), 18.

89. "The Belgic Confession (1561)," in *Reformed Confessions of the 16th and 17th Centuries in English Translation, Volume 2, 1552–1566,* ed. James T. Dennison Jr. (Grand Rapids: Reformation Heritage, 2010), 428 (article VII).

90. "The Thirty-Nine Articles (1562/63)," in ibid., 761 (article XXI).

91. This is, in part, why the next sentence reads, "Wherefore things ordained by them [councils] as necessary to salvation have neither strength nor authority, unless it may be declared that they be taken out of Holy Scriptures" (ibid.).

92. "The Westminster Confession of Faith (1646)," in Dennison, *Reformed Confessions, Volume 4,* 236 (I.IX).

sufficient, certain, and *infallible rule* of all saving knowledge, faith, and obedience."[93]

Reformed theologians and councils today also see inerrancy as essential to our definition and articulation of *sola Scriptura*. One of the best examples can be found in the Chicago Statement on Inerrancy (1978), which declares:

> Recognition of the *total truth and trustworthiness* of Holy Scripture is essential to a full grasp and adequate confession of its *authority*.[94]

> Holy Scripture, being God's own Word, written by men prepared and superintended by His Spirit, is of *infallible divine authority* in all matters upon which it touches.[95]

> The *authority* of Scripture is inescapably impaired if this total divine *inerrancy* is in any way limited or disregarded.[96]

> Great and grave confusion results from ceasing to maintain the *total truth* of the Bible whose *authority* one professes to acknowledge. The result of taking this step is that the Bible which God gave *loses its authority*, and what has authority instead is a Bible reduced in content according to the demands of one's critical reasonings and in principle reducible still further once one has started.[97]

More recently, this explicit inclusion of inerrancy in an articulation of *sola Scriptura* was also affirmed by the Cambridge Declaration (1996), signed by a host of leading Reformed thinkers. Toward the start of this declaration we read: "Scripture alone is the *inerrant* rule of the church's life," and we "reaffirm the *inerrant* Scripture to be the *sole* source of written divine revelation, which alone can bind the conscience."[98]

---

93. "The London Baptist Confession (1677)," in ibid., 532 (I.1).

94. Preface, "Chicago Statement," in ibid., 493.

95. "Chicago Statement," in Geisler, *Inerrancy*, 494, emphasis added. One might say the Chicago statement is not necessarily Reformed. True. At the same time, most of its representatives were Reformed or at least came out of the Reformation tradition (Lutheran, Reformed, Baptists, etc.).

96. Ibid.

97. This statement is from the statement's "Exposition," in ibid., 502, emphasis added.

98. "The Cambridge Declaration," http://www.alliancenet.org/cambridge-declaration; emphasis added. The declaration was signed by council members such as John Armstrong, Alistair Begg, James M. Boice, W. Robert Godfrey, John D. Hannah, Michael S. Horton, R. Albert Mohler Jr., R. C. Sproul, David Wells, among others. Similarly, consider Reformed theologian Keith Mathison who states that Scripture "is the only inspired and

As can be seen from this brief summary of the historical evidence, it would have been unthinkable in ages past to say that Scripture is authoritative but *not* inerrant. For those who have come out of the Reformation heritage, one includes the other.[99] After all, how could we trust and submit to the authority of the Bible if we do not believe it is true? Our knowledge is derivative of the Scriptures. Limiting or abandoning Scripture's total trustworthiness would inevitably bring down the entire structure of theology.[100]

In the midst of the ongoing controversy over inerrancy, Sproul raises an interesting hypothetical (though not one he himself adopts). He notes how someone could argue that Scripture's elevation as the sole and final authority does not "carry with it the necessary inference that it is inerrant."[101] One might believe, for example, that popes, councils, and Scripture all err, but that Scripture is the first among equals. Sproul writes, "Or Scripture could be regarded as carrying unique authority solely on the basis of its being the primary historical source of the gospel."[102] Either way, *sola Scriptura* is affirmed in this view, but not because Scripture is perfect but rather because it is primary either in quality or in origin.

Two points need clarification concerning this limited inerrancy position. First, this was not the historic position of the Reformers. Scripture was the sole and final authority not because it was the best of all errant authorities or because it came first, but because its supremacy was derivative of its perfection as divine revelation. Second, it is doubtful

---

inherently *infallible* norm, and therefore Scripture is the only final *authoritative* norm. . . . It is because the Scripture alone is God's inspired and *infallible* Word that Scripture carries unique authority—binding *final authority* of God Himself." He goes on to add: "Scripture's unique, infallible and final authority means that it stands as the Church's supreme norm. This was a primary element of early classical Protestant formulations of the doctrine of *sola Scriptura*. To Scripture alone can we ascribe the term *norma absoluta*—"absolute norm"— because it is Scripture alone that is God-breathed. The supreme normativity of Scripture is the logical corollary of its inspiration, infallibility, and unique authority. If Scripture truly is the divinely inspired Word of the living God; if it is therefore completely, absolutely, and unconditionally infallible; if it does carry the very authority of God Himself, then it is self-evident that Scripture is our supreme norm or standard" (Keith Mathison, *The Shape of Sola Scriptura* [Moscow, ID: Canon, 2001], 260, 264, 266; emphasis added). See also Muller, *DLGTT*, s.v. *sola Scriptura*, 284.

99. "To say that the Holy Scripture is the sole source of normative apostolic revelation today is to say that the Holy Scripture has the qualities of perfection and sufficiency" (Mathison, *Shape of Sola Scriptura*, 256).

100. Pinnock, "Limited Inerrancy," 150.

101. Sproul, *Sola Scriptura*, 18.

102. Ibid.

that those who believe in limited inerrancy are actually affirming *sola Scriptura* (and here I place the emphasis on the word *sola*). Perhaps their belief is that Scripture, popes, and councils all err; nevertheless, Scripture is the supreme authority because it is the only one of the three that is from God as divine revelation. Scripture, for them, is the first among errant sources.[103] But does this solve the problem for the limited inerrantists? Have they found a way to affirm *sola Scriptura* even though they reject the inerrancy of Scripture?

The answer must be no. For Reformers like Luther and Calvin, to say that Scripture is the sole or final source of authority is an incomplete definition of *sola Scriptura*. *Sola Scriptura* must mean that Scripture is the sole and final *inerrant* source of authority. If we take out the word *inerrant*, we no longer have the doctrine of *sola Scriptura* in its totality. Perhaps the point is best seen in the following table, which seeks to pinpoint the dividing line:

Two Views of Authority and Inerrancy

Full Inerrancy View	Limited Inerrancy View
All Scripture is our inerrant authority.	Only when Scripture addresses matters of faith is it our inerrant authority.

Which one is affirming *sola Scriptura*?[104] It is the full inerrancy position. Why? Because the limited inerrancy view can consistently utilize *sola Scriptura* only when it believes Scripture's main spiritual message of the Bible is in view. In other areas, where that view believes Scripture errs, Scripture is neither inerrant, nor authoritative, nor sufficient.[105]

---

103. Ibid.

104. Sproul gives a similar comparison. Ibid., 21.

105. Limited inerrantists typically use the phrase "faith and practice" in a way that is contrary to how the Reformers used it. They use it to say that the Bible is inerrant *only when it addresses* matters of faith and practice (notice how this assumes not *all* of the Bible is in view). By contrast, the Reformation tradition has used it to say that the Bible is the only inerrant rule of faith and practice. Notice, however, that the limited inerrantists divide the Bible into two categories: one that addresses issues of faith and practice and one that is occupied with everything else. This is convenient because it then allows the limited inerrantists to affirm inerrancy while simultaneously denying that inerrancy applies to *all* of the Bible. In contrast, the Reformers and the Reformed tradition have never divided Scripture up like this, and nor should we (see chapters 1 and 3). As I will explain shortly, Scripture itself never imposes this distinction. Instead, we should say that the Bible is inerrant in all that it addresses (see chapter 8). Saying that the Bible is the inerrant rule of faith and practice was never meant to limit inerrancy, but rather to expand it so that the Bible applies to all of life. (To clarify, I am not saying that the Bible explicitly or directly addresses every detail of life and the world.

Those parts of Scripture believed to be errant don't fall under the banner of *sola Scriptura*. Indeed, they cannot. Where they believe the Bible is misguided and wrong, it would be impossible for it to speak authoritatively and sufficiently on matters it addresses erroneously. Why would anyone listen, let alone obey, those parts of the Bible they believe are in error and will somehow mislead them? While the limited inerrantist might appeal to other parts of the Bible—the true parts, that is—he is inconsistent to appeal to the errant parts as "Thus says the Lord" passages. Why? Whether he will acknowledge this or not, it is because authority and sufficiency are naturally bound up with inerrancy. Should one be compromised, the others will follow.

Therefore, because the limited inerrantist limits inerrancy, he must also limit *sola Scriptura*. The two are inseparable. For the limited inerrantist, it is not just inerrancy that is limited but authority and sufficiency as well.

Canon Reduction: Who Can Rightfully Claim *Sola Scriptura*?

A final question remains: Can the limited inerrantist truly claim to follow in the legacy of *sola Scriptura*? I have sought to demonstrate that the answer must be no because in limiting inerrancy, one must necessarily limit authority as well (if one is going to be consistent).[106] But what is the limit that some are placing on the Bible? Typically we find the limit defined as the main salvation message of the Bible. Scripture is no longer the sole and final *flawless* authority in *all* it addresses. The only way for a limited inerrantist to still affirm *sola Scriptura* is to modify its meaning to something like: Scripture is the sole and final authority *as far as it is inerrant*.[107]

It does not [e.g., physics]. However, in what the Bible does address it does so inerrantly. Furthermore, we should pay heed to the Westminster Confession [I.VI] when it says that the Bible is authoritative not only in a direct sense [what is expressly set down in Scripture] but also in what may be deduced from Scripture by good and necessary consequence.) For more on this point, see chapter 10 on sufficiency.

106. It should be qualified that an affirmation of inerrancy does not guarantee that one affirms *sola Scriptura*. Roman Catholicism is a case in point. See John D. Woodbridge, "Evangelical Self-Identity and the Doctrine of Biblical Inerrancy," in *Understanding the Times: New Testament Studies in the 21st Century*, ed. Andreas J. Köstenberger and Robert W. Yarbrough (Wheaton, IL: Crossway, 2011), 113–22.

107. Limited inerrantists will prefer to use the word *infallible* instead because they mean by it something far less than inerrancy (i.e., Scripture is infallible in its spiritual message, but not in its totality). However, their appeal to use the word *infallible* for such a purpose only

For the full inerrantist, inerrancy and authority extend to all of Scripture, but for the limited inerrantist, inerrancy and authority extend only to certain parts of Scripture. For the full inerrantist, there is no limit to the canon's sufficiency because there is no limit to its perfection, but for the limited inerrantist the sufficiency of the canon is limited to those places where they believe it is perfect.

The position held by the limited inerrantist presents several additional challenges. First, since the limited inerrantist has limited Scripture's perfection and therefore its authority, Scripture must be supplemented. Scripture alone is not enough.[108] Because the perfection and authority of Scripture have been restricted, there has been a canon reduction.[109] Wherever they determine that Scripture is lacking in perfection and authority, there must be a supplemental authority to take its place (e.g., reason, experience, tradition, science). At this point the limited inerrantist has deviated from the Reformation, from the evangelical path.

Moreover, those who travel down such a path have now elevated themselves and their own reason above Scripture. Once they declare that Scripture is in error, they stand above the Bible as a superior authority, acting as judge and declaring the verdict. Unfortunately, this is exactly the position the limited inerrantist has taken, declaring which parts are acceptable and which parts are not. Yet if Scripture truly is our supreme authority, then, *ipso facto*, no one (and I mean no one!) can stand over and above Scripture as judge.[110] The minute we do so, we have removed the *sola* from *Scriptura* and have placed our own human reason there instead. We simply cannot say that Scripture is our supreme authority and simultaneously judge (as the limited inerrantist does) certain parts of Scripture untrustworthy, unreliable, and errant. If we do, we have now become the supreme, final authority, not Scripture.

Second, canon reduction is not a sustainable option for evangelicals.

---

proves my point above, namely, that for the limited inerrantist, authority cannot apply to the Bible in its totality but must be restricted to those portions we know are true.

108. Limited inerrantists may object that they believe Scripture *is* enough for *faith and practice*. But this only brings us back to the original problem of canon reduction. If Scripture can err in apparently insignificant historical details, for example, why would we assume it will "get it right" when it comes to the significant matters of life, like faith and practice? It is hard not to conclude that the limited inerrantist is determining his own canon within a canon.

109. Sproul, *Sola Scriptura*, 33.

110. Credit must be given to Fred Zaspel who thought through this point with me in personal correspondence. Not surprisingly, this is a very Warfieldian point!

If we limit inerrancy to some parts of Scripture but not others, then two questions arise: (1) What parts of Scripture are inerrant and therefore authoritative, and what parts are not? (2) Who gets to determine what parts of Scripture are inerrant and therefore authoritative and what parts are not? To answer the first question, limited inerrantists respond by saying that those parts of Scripture that address our faith are inerrant and authoritative. But this presents more problems than solutions. To begin with, how much must we know to be saved? This opens the door for a wide variety of opinions, including those who would answer: very little! And if very little is needed for salvation, then very little of the Bible is actually inerrant.[111]

Additionally, it is hard to avoid the conclusion that we are now seeking to create a canon within a canon. Given the long history of Protestant Liberalism, how do we avoid repeating the practice of throwing away the husk of Scripture in order to find the kernel? For limited inerrantists, the husk is typically the historical or scientific data, while the kernel concerns matters related to the main message of Scripture (i.e., matters of "faith and practice").

However, Scripture never divorces faith from history, the spiritual from the historical. When we look at the big picture of the Bible, what we see is that all of redemption is rooted in history, from Adam to the last Adam, from Eden to the New Jerusalem. It is called redemptive *history* for a reason.[112] We cannot bifurcate matters of faith from matters of history because the two go hand in hand. Moreover, if we were to do so, Scripture no longer would be the determining norm, but our human reason would have taken on that role. In the end, the individual decides what parts are from God and what parts are not.

Finally, the limited inerrancy viewpoint, with its emphasis on the macropurpose of the Bible, can be misleading. We do not deny the distinction between primary and secondary, fundamental and nonfundamental material in Scripture. Indeed, one could go so far as to say that not every passage is directly or explicitly soteriological in nature. Distinctions like these have historically aided Christians and councils in determining what does and does not count as heresy. These distinctions should not lead us to conclude, however, that the Bible is inerrant only in its fundamental, soteriological aspects. This is a misuse of theological

---

111. Pinnock, "Limited Inerrancy," 150.
112. Sproul, *Sola Scriptura*, 34.

categories. As we saw previously, Jesus and his apostles, having an attitude of total trust and confidence, approached *all* of the Old Testament as the very Word of God. Jesus and his apostles not only trusted the soteriological macromessage of the Old Testament but assumed in every way the reliability of its secondary details (even those historical in nature). In other words, they understood *all* of it to be trustworthy and true.[113]

To conclude, to affirm *sola Scriptura* is to affirm inerrancy. These two are mutually dependent upon each other, and it is inconsistent to abandon inerrancy and argue that you maintain *sola Scriptura*, at least in the original sense of its meaning. Were we to abandon *sola Scriptura*, we would no longer stand in the heritage of the Reformation and the evangelical movement. As Greg Bahnsen wisely suggests, "It is impossible to maintain the theological principle of *sola Scriptura* on the basis of limited inerrancy, for an errant authority—being in need of correction by some outside source—cannot serve as the only source and judge of Christian theology."[114]

No Inerrancy, No Assurance

Often those who reject inerrancy yet insist on retaining an evangelical identity will say that their rejection of inerrancy is inconsequential, and our Christian faith remains untarnished by its absence.[115] What do we make of this claim?

It is true that a denial of inerrancy does not preclude one from being a true Christian or a Christian who may biblically understand a host of other doctrines. Hodge, Warfield, and Machen refused to make inerrancy *the* badge that determined whether one was a Christian or not. Likewise, Carl F. H. Henry noted that a rejection of "inerrancy does not automatically drive one to repudiate other evangelical doctrines," though it may mean that "consistent evangelical faith is maintained thereafter only by an act of will rather than by persuasive epistemological credentials."[116]

---

113. Pinnock, "Limited Inerrancy," 149.

114. Bahnsen, "Inerrancy of the Autographa," 183–84. Also consider Saucy, who says that inerrancy "logically upholds the final authority of all of Scripture. Only truth has authority, and because the Scriptures are completely true they command ultimate authority" (Saucy, *Scripture*, 161). Likewise Sproul: "*Sola Scriptura* as the supreme norm of ecclesiastical authority rests ultimately on the premise of the infallibility of the Word of God" (Sproul, *Sola Scriptura*, 21).

115. For example, Peter Enns, "Inerrancy, However Defined, Does Not Describe What the Bible Does," in Merrick and Garrett, *Five Views*, 91, 114; Sparks, *Sacred Word, Broken Word*, 6, 60.

116. Carl F. H. Henry, *Evangelicals in Search of Identity* (Waco, TX: Word, 1976), 55.

With this in mind, we would go too far if we said that a rejection of inerrancy was inconsequential. If we take the gospel as our starting point, which is basic to being an "evangelical," then the reliability of God's Word proves crucial. To accept and receive this gospel is to instinctively accept and receive it as a word of promise, genuinely believing that this word of promise is what it says it is, namely, the word of the true and living God.[117] This same principle is at work in our everyday relationships. Faith is absolutely essential if we are to have a relationship with another person. Such a relationship, if it is to work properly, must rest confidently on the basis of a promise made (e.g., marriage vows). But if we were to discover that our faith has been rooted in a lie, our faith is undermined. In such a case, the object of our faith proves counterfeit.[118]

In similar fashion, this principle of faith translates into our relationship with God and his Word. We may be zealous and devoted, and our conversion may be remarkable. However, if the object of our faith (Christ) and the instrument through which that object comes to us (the Word of God) prove untrustworthy, then our relationship with God is compromised in a significant way, for it is no longer based upon the truthfulness of his Word. Our relationship with God must rest upon the truth. Just as our relationship with someone is degraded if we cannot trust their word, our relationship with God falters should he prove to be deceptive or unreliable. In short, we cannot divorce who we are from what we say, nor can God, lest he violate his holy character.[119]

The opposite is true as well. If a relationship is built upon trust, and with it the trustworthiness of one's word, then that relationship flourishes. Trust proves to be liberating. We are now free and able to enjoy the many blessings that come from trusting in one another.[120] Trust strengthens the relationship and is the foundation upon which any relationship is built. Reliability, proving trustworthy over time, further solidifies the relationship. This is equally true of our relationship with God and his Word. Because inerrancy is inherently *relational* in nature, it is the glue that holds the gospel and the Christian's faith together. "If we are to have real faith," Peter Jensen says, "we must have infallible

---

117. Peter Jensen, *The Revelation of God* (Downers Grove, IL: InterVarsity Press, 2002), 195.
118. Ibid.
119. Ibid., 195–96.
120. Ibid., 196.

words; that is, words whose truth we can rely upon absolutely and from which we do not dissent; words we can study, learn from, assimilate, use, obey and trust. These are the infallible words of God."[121]

If we were to abandon inerrancy, not only would the building blocks of our gospel-centered relationship with God be called into question but so would our basic fundamental trust in all of Scripture's assertions and affirmations. We would face not only a vertical problem (can we trust the divine author?) but a horizontal one as well (how do we know what parts of Scripture are true?). This is the Achilles' heel of the limited inerrancy position, which seeks to maintain inerrancy of some parts of Scripture but not others. If God erred in one place, which they believe, how can they know he has not erred in other places?[122] Assurance seems to be lost and one's trust in Scripture (or at least in *all* of it) is stripped away.[123]

Limited inerrantists reassure us that Scripture is not errant on major issues, only on minor ones.[124] But how can we *know* this? After all, we have already been told that we are handling an *errant* text. Moreover, even if we did know this, what is to reassure us that Scripture does not err on the major matters too? If Scripture cannot get the small things right, as limited inerrantists claim, can anyone really trust it to get the big things right?[125] And if limited inerrantists cannot trust the Bible with regard to what it says about itself, then how can they have any assurance when the Bible speaks to matters of this world? The problem is not only internal but external.[126]

Inerrancy Meets Real Life

As one might imagine, when trust in the reliability of *all* of Scripture crumbles, practical ministry becomes extremely difficult to navigate. Consider preaching. No longer can one preach the *whole* counsel of God. Instead, we must first discern which texts are worthy

---

121. Ibid., 197.

122. Young, *Thy Word Is Truth*, 263.

123. It is true that an error in one part of Scripture does not *necessarily* entail errors in other parts. However, the existence of error naturally raises the possibility of other errors in Scripture. So we can conclude with Saucy that "to say the Bible has errors undermines our confidence in the whole of Scripture" (Saucy, *Scripture*, 159).

124. Sparks claims that Scripture's errors do not impact theology. Sparks, *Sacred Word, Broken Word*, 6, 60.

125. Turretin, *Institutes of Elenctic Theology*, 1:71; Young, *Thy Word Is Truth*, 75–76, 89.

126. Young, *Thy Word Is Truth*, 29.

and which ones lack authority and credibility. True preaching, argues Packer, occurs when the preacher becomes a "mouthpiece for his text, opening it up and applying it as a word from God to his hearers, talking only in order that the text may speak for itself and be heard."[127] When doubt seeps in, the preacher begins to wonder (and understandably so) whether the text he is preaching is in fact trustworthy. Are these *really* God's words? Lamentably, once such doubt is entertained, preaching with authority becomes impossible. The preacher is simply sharing his own opinions or summarizing what the church has said in ages past.[128] [129] But in that case one cannot, with any confidence, say, "Hear the Word of God." Could this be why the heritage of evangelical preaching has faded away in many churches today? Could this be why so many Christians have such little confidence in preaching as a means of grace?[130]

Counseling suffers from the same disease. One must now decide what parts of Scripture are acceptable and applicable to the Christian life and which ones should be ignored, even repudiated, as unethical.[131]

It is only a matter of time until the relativism of postmodernism takes hold. In an attempt to rip off the husk to get down to the kernel, subjectivity reigns. One man's textual treasure may be another man's textual trash. While some may see texts describing the historicity of Jesus's resurrection as golden, others, utilizing the *same* methodology, see those resurrection texts as deeply flawed and find no credibility in the claim to a historical resurrection.

A rejection of inerrancy turns things upside down. Man, not God, has become the arbiter of truth. The reader, not the author, now determines what is good and necessary for the Christian faith. "To say that some parts are more 'inspired' than others," observes Jensen, "is to treat inspiration as a response by the reader rather than as a characteristic of the text."[132] Believing that God has not revealed himself in a completely truthful and trustworthy manner, each individual must decide for himself what parts of God's self-communication stay and

---

127. J. I. Packer, *God Has Spoken: Revelation and the Bible*, 3rd ed. (Grand Rapids: Baker, 1993), 32. See also Young, *Thy Word Is Truth*, 264.

128. Packer, *God Has Spoken*, 32.

129. Packer, *God Has Spoken*, 32.

130. Ibid.

131. For example, Enns, *The Bible Tells Me So*.

132. Jensen, *Revelation of God*, 161.

what parts are to be dispensed with. Without inerrancy, what we are left with is a doctrine of Scripture that looks and feels more like a theology of glory than a theology of the cross.[133] Rather than God stooping down to us (theology of the cross), we are climbing our own ladder up to God (theology of glory).

Eventually, deviating from *sola Scriptura* leads to a fork in the road. As we elevate man, we see ourselves as the arbiter of truth (modernism) or as the inventor and creator of truth (postmodernism). History teaches us that either road is a dead end. We are no longer thinking God's thoughts after him, but have reinterpreted God's thoughts into our own image.[134] Turretin warns, "Unless unimpaired integrity characterize the Scriptures, they could not be regarded as the sole rule of faith and practice."[135] The truthfulness of Scripture is critical and fundamental to our faith.[136] While belief in inerrancy does not determine whether one is a Christian or not, it is crucial to the Christian faith. It represents the historic position of the Western church and aligns with what the prophets, apostles, and Christ himself all believed about God's Word. What do we gain by discarding it?[137] Or perhaps the more troubling question is: What do we lose by forsaking it?

---

133. Kevin Vanhoozer, "Augustinian Inerrancy: A Well-Versed Account," paper presented at the Evangelical Theological Society, November 2013.

134. For other aspects of the faith undermined by a rejection of inerrancy, see Packer, *God Has Spoken*, 32–33.

135. Turretin, *Institutes of Elenctic Theology*, 1:71.

136. Swain, *Trinity, Revelation, and Reading*, 79.

137. Robert W. Yarbrough, "Inerrancy's Complexities: Grounds for Grace in the Debate," in *Solid Ground: The Inerrant Word of God in an Errant World*, ed. Gabriel N. E. Flugher (Phillipsburg, NJ: P&R, 2012), 75.

CHAPTER 9

God Speaks to Be Heard: The Clarity of Scripture

Your word is a lamp for my feet, a light on my path.

—*Psalm 119:105*

The Holy Spirit . . . has generously and advantageously planned Holy Scripture in such a way that in the easier passages He relieves our hunger; in the more obscure He drives away our pride. Practically nothing is dug out from those obscure texts which is not discovered to be said very plainly in another place.   —*Augustine*

You shall believe God who speaks plainly in his Word.

—*John Knox*

The Bible is a plain book. It is intelligible by the people.

—*Charles Hodge*

Postmodernism's Murky Waters

"There is one thing a professor can be absolutely certain of: almost every student entering the university believes, or says he believes, that truth is relative."[1] This statement by Alan Bloom in his well-known book *The Closing of the American Mind* is startling when we read it. And yet, speaking as a professor, I have to admit that there is truth to it. Our age is drenched in a postmodern worldview, and in interpreting a text, meaning is seen as something the reader, influenced by his community, creates and constructs, rather than something that originates inherently in the author.[2] This leads to multiple interpretations of a

---

1. Alan Bloom, *The Closing of the American Mind* (New York: Simon & Schuster, 1987), 25.

2. For example, Stanley Fish, *Is There a Text in This Class? The Authority of Interpretive Communities* (Cambridge: Harvard University Press, 1980).

text. This plurality of interpretations exists because there is a plurality of readers and communities, each constructing their own meaning, each equally valid and "true." No objective, fixed, inherent meaning exists in the text. When this mind-set is applied to the text of Scripture, the Bible becomes a tool for our own agendas. Or to switch metaphors, God's Word is submerged under the murky waters of postmodernism. No objective clarity exists, only a plurality of equally valid, even contradictory, interpretations.[3]

When we open Scripture, we see a fundamentally different conception of language and meaning. God speaks and there is meaning in everything he has said. He expects not only to be heard and understood but to be obeyed. His covenantal words are not ambiguous but clear and straightforward—so straightforward that one's response to them is a matter of life and death (Josh 24:15; John 3:36). Today's Christian, armed with a Bible, faces an enormous challenge. How can we remain firmly planted on the solid ground of what God says while all around us postmodernist readings of the Bible try to undermine the ground we stand upon? Our prayer is this: Even though I walk through the valley of the shadow of postmodernism, I will fear no subjectivism, for you have communicated clearly, and your Word and Spirit help me.[4]

The Clarity of God and His Covenantal Word

As we saw in the last chapter, the truthfulness of Scripture stems from the truthfulness of God. The same is true of the clarity of Scripture. It stems from the clarity of God, from the fact that God is an effective communicator.[5] God does not leave us to guess what he wants or thinks. He has revealed and communicated his will for his people in his own words. Once again, we must not think that what God does and says can somehow be divorced from who God is.[6] There is no chasm, gulf, or valley dividing God from his Word. What is characteristic of

3. Additionally, the clarity of Scripture is being abandoned today by those who have worn or still do wear the label "evangelical." For example, Christian Smith, *The Bible Made Impossible: Why Biblicism Is Not a Truly Evangelical Reading of Scripture* (Grand Rapids: Brazos, 2011); Kenton L. Sparks, *God's Word in Human Words: An Evangelical Appropriation of Critical Biblical Scholarship* (Grand Rapids: Baker Academic, 2008), 72, 101–2, 142.

4. I am playing off of a comment in Kevin J. Vanhoozer, "Triune Discourse: Theological Reflections on the Claim That God Speaks (Part 2)," in *Trinitarian Theology for the Church*, ed. Daniel J. Treier and David Lauber (Downers Grove, IL: IVP Academic, 2009), 52.

5. Mark D. Thompson, *A Clear and Present Word: The Clarity of Scripture* (Downers Grove, IL: InterVarsity Press, 2006), 49.

6. Ibid., 64 (cf. 111).

one is characteristic of the other. His Word is clear in what it communicates because God himself is clear.

This is radically different from the gods of the nations. Moses, reflecting on Israel's obedience and disobedience, says in Deuteronomy 4:11 that when Israel came to the foot of the mountain, which burned with fire to "the heart of heaven," the Lord spoke to Israel. "Then the LORD spoke to you out of the midst of the fire. You heard the sound of words, but saw no form; there was only a voice" (4:12 ESV). Israel did not see God, but they heard his voice. In contrast, the nations saw their gods, but their gods could not speak. This is the point Moses makes in verses 15–31. Should Israel disobey, she shall be scattered among the nations. "And there you will serve gods of wood and stone, the work of human hands, that neither see, nor hear, nor eat, nor smell" (Deut 4:28).[7] It is not a blessing but a curse to serve gods who cannot see or hear, or gods you can see but cannot hear. These things are indicators that these gods have been fabricated; they are speechless and powerless.[8] The true God not only hears and sees, but he speaks and can be heard. This God honors the one who listens when he speaks and trusts in the redemptive promises he has made.[9] Of course, all this assumes that the God who reveals himself through words does so clearly.

This clarity in communication is not limited to the *audible* words that Moses heard from Yahweh or the apostles heard from Jesus (Matt 3:16–17; 17:5; Mark 1:14; John 12:27–30), but applies to the *written* Word as well. As we saw in chapter 7, Scripture is God-breathed. What Scripture says, God says, and when we read Scripture, we are reading the very Word of God. His Word does not come to us wrapped in code, nor is it coated in some type of heavenly dialect. It comes to us in plain language, for God used ordinary individuals, under the superintendence of the Holy Spirit, to bring about exactly what he intended to say to his people. God had a purpose behind the delivery of Scripture, that his people might be instructed in his ways. The message has to be clear. The clarity of Scripture is connected to the clarity of God's speech.

If Scripture is not clear in the way we need it to be clear for our salvation, then essentially God's intentions, as genuine as they are, will

---

7.   See Isa 41:6–7; 44:12–20; 46:6–7; Jer 2:27; 3:9; Hos 4:12.

8.   Eugene H. Merrill, *Deuteronomy*, NAC, vol. 4 (Nashville: B&H, 1994), 128; J. G. McConville, *Deuteronomy*, ApOTC 5 (Downers Grove, IL: InterVarsity Press; Leicester, England: Apollos, 2002), 110.

9.   Thompson, *A Clear and Present Word*, 61.

fail. Should his message in Scripture be unreadable and unintelligible, it remains ineffective. God's Word comes back void. The consequences for God's character follow. Is he really a God who can speak clearly and effectively? If not, what does this say about him? Should this be true, Christians are left with a gospel message that is confusing at best and empty at worst.

But God *has* spoken clearly and his Word *is* effective in the way he intends it to be. His Word is not only understood cognitively, it also ignites saving change in the heart of the sinner when accompanied by the Holy Spirit.[10] God's written Word is not merely a revelation (though it's certainly not less), but a *communication*. His words don't just convey information; they do something. To borrow from speech-act theory, with any given utterance, there is not only a *locution* (words spoken) but an *illocution* (the action performed by words) as well as a *perlocution* (the consequence or effect of the performed words).[11] For example, if I were to enter an airport, point to a man sitting near a terminal, and yell "bomb" or "terrorist," my words would not merely provide information but would inspire and incite action.

God's spoken and written Word does the same. As an example, consider God's salvific speech. The Father effectually *calls* his elect to his Son. Such a calling is not resistible, but irresistible. In other words, God's wooing of his elect does not fail but is always successful (e.g., John 6:44, 65; Rom 8:28–30).[12] Having been effectually called and regenerated by the power of the Holy Spirit (John 3:5–8) through the word of the gospel (1 Pet 1:23; James 1:18), the elect is then granted by the Spirit not only repentance (2 Tim 2:24–26; Acts 5:31; 11:18) but faith (Acts 13:48–50; Eph 2:8–10; Phil 1:29–30; 2 Pet 1:1), working these two gifts within. Upon faith in Christ, that elect sinner is then justified (Gal 3:10–14). Justification itself is a legal, forensic

---

10. Some might object that God's Word sometimes goes out and does not create change. I would argue that in these instances God *intends* his Word to harden hearts or declare judgment. Scripture indicates that there are times when the purpose of God's Word is not to save but actually to blind and condemn (e.g., Matt 13:10–17). But even here God's speech is effective, for it accomplishes his purpose, which in these cases is judicial.

11. On speech-act theory, see J. L. Austin, *How to Do Things with Words* (Cambridge: Harvard University Press, 1962); John Searle, *Speech Acts: An Essay in the Philosophy of Language* (Cambridge: Cambridge University Press, 1969), 110; Jeannine K. Brown, *Scripture as Communication: Introducing Biblical Hermeneutics* (Grand Rapids: Baker, 2007), 32–35.

12. For a biblical defense of effectual calling, see Matthew Barrett, *Salvation by Grace: The Case for Effectual Calling and Regeneration* (Phillipsburg, NJ: P&R, 2013).

declaration; God pronounces the sinner not guilty, but righteous on the basis of the redeeming work of Jesus Christ. The righteousness of Christ is imputed or reckoned to the believer's account (Rom 4:3–6; 5:17; Phil 3:9).[13] God's words are effective covenantal words, words that perform a saving action. They do not merely convey information but bring into existence a new state of affairs: new life as well as a new identity in Christ.

However, all this is possible only if God's covenantal words are clear. If they are inherently unclear, his covenantal words fail to accomplish what he sent them out to accomplish. His words fall short, and he has no chosen and transformed recipient. To the contrary, Scripture everywhere attests to the efficacy of God's speech. As the Lord said through the prophet Isaiah:

> As the rain and the snow come down from heaven,
>   and do not return to it without watering the earth
> and making it bud and flourish,
>   so that it yields seed for the sower and bread for the eater,
> so is my word that goes out from my mouth:
>   It will not return to me empty,
> but will accomplish what I desire
>   and achieve the purpose for which I sent it. (Isa 55:10–11)

The same efficacy, reliability, and dependability apply to God's written Word.[14] Scripture is not merely transmitting information, but the Spirit uses God's inscripturated speech to pierce the heart (Heb 4:12).[15]

Therefore, God's Word is *effective*, successfully accomplishing the purpose for which it was sent. We can speak of irresistible/effectual grace, but we can also speak of irresistible/effectual speech, and Scripture falls within this category. God's Word does not fail because it is the instrument of his omnipotent will, and his Word does not fail because God's Word is clear. Because it is clear, the Spirit can use it to penetrate the mind and heart, much as light pierces darkness.

---

13. See Thomas Schreiner, *Faith Alone: The Doctrine of Justification*, The Five Solas Series, ed. Matthew Barrett (Grand Rapids: Zondervan, 2015).

14. Rain in the ancient Near East was a sign that crops would come, and crops meant life. The effectiveness of the rain is then compared to God's word, which achieves its purpose of bringing blessing and life. John N. Oswalt, *The Book of Isaiah: Chapters 40–66*, NICOT (Grand Rapids: Eerdmans, 1998), 446.

15. Thompson, *A Clear and Present Word*, 133.

Contrary to the beliefs of Karl Barth, God's speech in written form does not weaken divine omnipotence but shows just how powerful God is.[16] Only an omnipotent God can communicate his will both clearly and irresistibly in a pure and undefiled written text. Mark Thompson writes, "God has something to say and he is very good at saying it."[17]

To reject or attack the clarity of Scripture is to assault God himself. To say that God's Word is unclear is to convey that God himself has not been clear. Those who say his Word is unintelligible are left to conclude that either God is a poor communicator or he has no desire or intention for people to know him.[18] If the latter is true, then we face a terrible reality: God is a liar, for he has said in Scripture that he does desire for us to know him. Both of these options do harm to the character of God. Notice that it is not merely our doctrine of Scripture that is on the line, but our doctrine of God as well. And not just our doctrine of God, but our doctrine of salvation too. If we cannot understand God's saving Word, then how can we be saved?[19]

Scripture's Witness to Its Own Clarity

The Roman Catholic Church has argued through the centuries that Scripture is unclear, and because it is unclear believers everywhere must depend upon the infallible interpretation of the Church. Individual believers cannot interpret Scripture themselves but must depend entirely upon Rome, who is never mistaken in its official teaching and doctrine.

It is hard to find this argument in Scripture. Instead, what we see in Scripture is that the Word of God is presented to the people of God as clear in its salvific message. The recipients of God's Word are expected not only to understand it but to apply it to their daily lives and in their local churches. We have every indication that the biblical authors, including Jesus himself, believed Scripture was clear, for it alone is the infallible and inerrant authority for the Christian life.

First, consider how God intended his Word to be presented to his people in the Old Testament. When God delivered his people from the Egyptians,

---

16. Ibid., 101.

17. Ibid., 170. See also John Webster's use of Isaiah 29 in *The Domain of the Word: Scripture and Theological Reason* (London: T&T Clark, 2012), 21.

18. Philip Graham Ryken, "The Accessible Word," in *Solid Ground: The Inerrant Word of God in an Errant World*, ed. Gabriel N. E. Flugher (Phillipsburg, NJ: P&R, 2012), 121, 123.

19. Ibid.

he gave them his Law, the Ten Words (or Ten Commandments). These commandments were not for an elite few. They were to be obeyed by the whole assembly, young and old, rich and poor, male and female, by parents and their children alike. While the Ten Commandments may have needed reiteration, elaboration, or interpretation, there was never any indication that they were obscure or incomprehensible. It was assumed that they were understandable and applicable, so much so that obedience was expected to follow.[20] In fact, the clarity of these commands showed itself when God could at a later date hold his people accountable, even discipline them for their disobedience to his commands. Culpability was built on the assumption that there was clarity.

The clarity of God's Law in the Old Testament is supported by passages like Deuteronomy 6:6–7, where the Lord, having given his people his Law, said, "These commandments that I give you today are to be on your hearts. Impress them on your children. Talk about them when you sit at home and when you walk along the road, when you lie down and when you get up." What is so astonishing about this passage is that God's covenantal commands were so clear that parents could teach them to their children. God's Word was not restricted to the educated adult but could be understood and absorbed by little boys and girls.[21] For this reason, the Lord could instruct Moses in Deuteronomy 31 to assemble the people—men, women, and little ones, as well as foreigners—to listen as his law was read before all of Israel so "they can listen and learn to fear the LORD your God, and follow carefully all the words of this law" (31:12). No one in Israel was excluded from listening and embracing God's Word. Like a river, God's Word is deep enough for an elephant to swim in but shallow enough for a lamb to find its footing.[22]

God's commands were not designed for the classroom. They were to be the topic of everyday, public conversation. In the rudimentary business of family life, God's Word was to be the conversation piece. Whether one was eating, relaxing, or working, God's Word was to be

---

20. The call to listen and obey is repeated in Scripture, demonstrating its clarity (Deut 4:1–2; 6:4–9; 31:9–13; Ps 19:7–11; Rom 4:22–25; 15:4; 1 Cor 10:1–11; Col 3:16; 1 Tim 4:13; 2 Tim 3:14–17; 1 Pet 1:22–2:3). See D. A. Carson, *Collected Writings on Scripture* (Wheaton, IL: Crossway, 2010), 180.

21. Daniel I. Block, *Deuteronomy*, NIVAC (Grand Rapids: Zondervan, 2012), 184–85.

22. Gregory the Great, *Moralia in Iob*, ed. E. B. Pusey et al., A Library of Fathers of the Holy Catholic Church Anterior to the Division of the East and West, 3 vols. (Oxford: Parker Society, 1844–50), 9.

on the tip of the tongue.[23] "Tie them as symbols on your hands and bind them on your foreheads. Write them on the doorframes of your houses and on your gates" (Deut 6:8–9). There is no evidence here that God's Word is murky or unintelligible.

Consider Deuteronomy 30:9–14. God's covenant had just been renewed at Moab and the people were then promised that the Lord would bring them into the land their fathers had possessed, and he would be the one to circumcise their hearts so that they would love the Lord (30:5–7). Yahweh commanded his people to repent that they might return to the Lord and obey his voice (30:9–10). Where has God's voice been heard? It has been heard in his commandments and in "his commands and decrees that are written in this Book of the Law" (30:10). One can anticipate the objection to come: "Yes, Lord, but your Word is not clear enough, nor is it accessible!" Listen to the correction:

> For this commandment that I command you today is not too hard for you, neither is it far off. It is not in heaven, that you should say, "Who will ascend to heaven for us and bring it to us, that we may hear it and do it?" Neither is it beyond the sea, that you should say, "Who will go over the sea for us and bring it to us, that we may hear it and do it?" But the word is very near you. It is in your mouth and in your heart, so that you can do it. (Deut 30:11–14 ESV)

While the speech of the pagan gods was enigmatic, inaccessible, unreasonable, incomprehensible, and impenetrable, Yahweh's Word was not.[24] Instead, his Word was covenantal and not only authoritative but close at hand and palatable.[25] Rather than concealing it from us, God has made his will known to us, and he has done so in a way that we can understand and comprehend.[26] Therefore, choosing life did not mean Israel was jumping into the dark unknown, but it meant leaning upon the sure and ever-present Word of God. Ultimately, Israel was to direct her gaze ahead to the advent of Christ, who would come down, take on human flesh, and make the Father known in order to save sinners (Rom 10:5–9).

Or consider the book of Joshua. When Moses was succeeded by

---

23. Merrill, *Deuteronomy*, 167.
24. See Block, *Deuteronomy*, 707–8; Merrill, *Deuteronomy*, 391.
25. See Merrill, *Deuteronomy*, 391–92; McConville, *Deuteronomy*, 429.
26. Thompson, *A Clear and Present Word*, 95.

Joshua, the Lord made sure Joshua also understood just how clear and effective his Word would be for his people. The Lord said to this new leader:

> Only be strong and very courageous, being careful to do according to all the law that Moses my servant commanded you. Do not turn from it to the right hand or to the left, that you may have good success wherever you go. This Book of the Law shall not depart from your mouth, but you shall meditate on it day and night, so that you may be careful to do according to all that is written in it. For then you will make your way prosperous, and then you will have good success. Have I not commanded you? Be strong and courageous. Do not be frightened, and do not be dismayed, for the LORD your God is with you wherever you go. (Josh 1:7–9 ESV)

One cannot miss the connection between God's Word and God's presence. The presence of the "Book of the Law" was the presence of the Lord their God. His law was always to be in Israel's mouth. Israel was to meditate on it every day, careful to do what it said. The Lord could not give such a command if his law was vague, elusive, and encased in impenetrable mysteries. Only a clear Word, such as this, could have such an effect on the life of a believer.

The psalmists also assumed the clarity of Scripture in their many songs of worship and lamentation. The clarity of God's Word reflects God himself. He is a God who shines his light in an otherwise dark place. David, for example, says in Psalm 36:7–9:

> How precious is your steadfast love, O God!
>   The children of mankind take refuge in the shadow of your
>   wings.
> They feast on the abundance of your house,
>   and you give them drink from the river of your delights.
> For with you is the fountain of life;
>   in your light do we see light. (ESV)

It is because God provides light—blessing, redemption, divine presence, etc.—that we see and live rather than remain in spiritual blindness and die.[27]

---

27. Willem A. VanGemeren, *Psalms*, rev. ed., EBC 5 (Grand Rapids: Zondervan, 2008), 339. Also note David's use of "light" in Ps 27:1: "The LORD is my light and my

The same imagery of "light" is applied to God's Word. Consider Psalm 119:105: "Your word is a lamp for my feet, a light on my path." Apart from God's Word, we walk in utter darkness, but with it we walk down the path of light (cf. Prov 6:23).[28] This imagery applies not only to God's spoken word (i.e., oral/verbal commands, promises) but to his written Word as well. Scripture is like a light that shines bright, showing us the way ahead to salvation. Without it, we stumble around in darkness, straying off the path that leads to life. The image of "light" conveys how *clear* God's word is for the believer. As Psalm 119:130 says, "The unfolding of your words gives light; it gives understanding to the simple." The same is true of God's inscripturated Word, for it makes wise the simple (Ps 19:7).

With great excitement Josiah had all the words of the "Book of the Covenant" read (2 Kgs 23:2) after Hilkiah rediscovered the book of the law in the house of the Lord (2 Kgs 22:8–13). And after hearing God's Word, Josiah and the people joined together in a covenant before the Lord, so that they would "follow the LORD" and "keep his commands, statutes, and decrees" (2 Kgs 23:3). Josiah and all the people found God's Word clear enough to be pierced to the heart, brought to repentance, and moved to faith in the Lord (cf. Heb 4:12).

Ezra also assumed the clarity of God's Word when he read it to the people of God. In Nehemiah 8, the people gathered "as one" and Ezra the scribe brought the "Book of the Law of Moses" to be read before the assembly, "men and women and all who were able to understand" (8:2). "All the people listened attentively to the Book of the Law" (8:3). When Ezra stood on the platform and opened the book in the sight of all the people, their response was to bow their heads and worship the Lord with their faces to the ground (8:4–6). Not only did the people hear God's Word read, but it was also explained to them. Several individuals "instructed the people in the Law," and they "read from the Book of the Law of God, making it clear and giving the meaning, so that the people understood what was being read" (8:7–8). This interpretive assistance does not undermine Scripture's clarity, and as we will see, clarity does not guarantee ease in interpretation. To

---

salvation—whom shall I fear?" "This idea anticipates the gospel message of the New Testament that Jesus is indeed the true light (John 1:4–9; 1 John 1:5–7)" (Allan Harman, *Psalms: Volume 1: Psalms 1–72* [Fearn, Ross-shire, Scotland: Christian Focus, 2011], 306). We should also include John 8:12 where Jesus says he is the light of the world.

28. VanGemeren, *Psalms*, 879.

the contrary, the fact that God's Word could be interpreted and then understood supports Scripture's clarity. If it was not clear, then it could not be explained, let alone comprehended and obeyed.[29]

Second, the New Testament's use of the Old assumes the clarity of Scripture. One of the most powerful examples is found in Jesus's wilderness temptation (Matt 4:1–11). Satan kept tempting Jesus, but Jesus each time responded by quoting Old Testament Scriptures. The encounter between Jesus and Satan assumes the clarity of the Old Testament. Satan twists Scripture to deceive, and Jesus correctly quotes Scripture to show that God's Word is clear on how one should live in obedience to God.

Jesus's confidence in the clarity of the Old Testament is obvious in various questions and statements he made to his critics:

- "Haven't you read what David did . . . ? Or haven't you read in the Law . . . ?" (Matt 12:3, 5).
- "Haven't you read . . . ?" (Matt 19:4).
- "Have you never read in the Scriptures . . . ?" (Matt 21:42).
- "Have you not read what God said to you . . . ?" (Matt 22:31).
- "Go and learn what this means: 'I desire mercy, not sacrifice'" (Matt 9:13; cf. Hos 6:6).
- "You are Israel's teacher and do you not understand these things?" (John 3:10).
- "You are in error because you do not know the Scriptures or the power of God" (Matt 22:29).[30]

What should we make of the Pharisees and their confusion (even vehemence!) over Jesus's appeal to the OT? These were men who spent their lives studying the Law, and yet when Jesus came, it was apparent that they were interpreting or applying it incorrectly. In response, we must recognize that their confusion was not because the Old Testament was unclear, but because the Pharisees twisted its true meaning in their own hypocrisy (Matt 23:1–36), or they failed to interpret it

---

29. Other texts to consider include Deut 6:7; Ps 1:2; Acts 17:11; 1 Cor 1:2; 2 Cor 1:13; Gal 1:2; Phil 1:1; Col 4:16. Some have objected to the clarity of Scripture by appealing to Mark 4:10–12; Acts 8:30–31; and 2 Pet 3:14–16. However, see the response and interpretation of these texts by Thompson, *A Clear and Present Word*, 102–8.

30. Though directed toward his disciples instead of his enemies, one might also note Luke 24:25: "How foolish you are, and how slow to believe all that the prophets have spoken!" For these examples and many others, see Wayne Grudem, "The Perspicuity of Scripture," *Themelios* 34, no. 3 (2009): 292.

properly because of their own bias and interpretive agenda (Mark 7:8). Ignorance was not their problem. Where they failed to understand or interpret God's Word correctly, it was because they refused to allow the true meaning of the Old Testament to transform their false conceptions and reorient their behavior.[31]

This is not to say that Jesus did not think there were parts of the OT that would take considerable work to understand. This much is discernible in his exhortation, "Let the reader understand" (Matt 24:15). Jesus does not mean that understanding comes without effort, nor that the text will always appear translucent. At the same time, the only reason Jesus could quote Scripture the way he did was because he assumed it was clear and could be understood by his audience. Otherwise, Jesus would be unjustified when confronting those who believed they knew the Scriptures but refused to respond in faith and repentance to the very one the Scriptures spoke about (John 5:36–47).[32]

Jesus was not alone in his belief in the clarity of Scripture. The New Testament authors were just as confident. We read in Romans 15:4–6 (ESV):

> For whatever was written in former days was written for our instruction, that through endurance and through the encouragement of the Scriptures we might have hope. May the God of endurance and encouragement grant you to live in such harmony with one another, in accord with Christ Jesus, that together you may with one voice glorify the God and Father of our Lord Jesus Christ.

Paul could tell Timothy that all Scripture is breathed out by God and that it is "profitable for teaching, for reproof, for correction, and for training in righteousness, that the man of God may be complete, equipped for every good work" (2 Tim 3:16–17 ESV). Postmodernism's murky waters are absent from these passages. Nor do we find the need for an official interpretation as argued by Rome. Instead, we find Paul's absolute trust in the sufficiency of Scripture because it can be understood. It was written for our instruction.[33] If Scripture is inherently unclear, as some claim, why do the New Testament writers frequently quote and allude to the Old Testament to settle disputes? Indeed, the

---

31. Thompson, *A Clear and Present Word*, 85.
32. Ibid.
33. Ibid., 109.

New Testament authors quote and allude to more than twenty-five hundred verses from the Old Testament![34] The book of Hebrews is a good example. The unity of the canon, exhibited in Scripture being its own interpreter, serves to demonstrate Scripture's clarity.

Third, the clarity of Scripture is confirmed when we examine the audience the biblical authors had in mind. I offer four classes in particular that highlight Scripture's clarity:

1. Scripture was not just for the educated, but for the uneducated (James 2:5–6).
2. Scripture was not just for adults, but for their children (Deut 6:7; Eph 6:1–3).
3. Scripture was not written to scholars, but was actually meant for those in the church (John 20:30–31; 1 Cor 1:2; Gal 1:2; Phil 1:1; Col 4:16; 1 Tim 4:13).[35]
4. Scripture was not just for Jews, but for non-religious gentiles as well (Acts 13:46; 18:6; 22:21).

The last point is extraordinary in the context of the first century. When Jesus's disciples took the gospel to the lost, they shared this message with Jews who knew their Old Testament. They did not have to explain who Abraham, Isaac, and Jacob were. Biblical knowledge could be presumed, though its significance in light of Christ had to be explained. What is amazing is that the disciples took God's Word to gentiles who had no idea who Jesus was and were not even familiar with the Old Testament (e.g., Acts 17:16–34).[36] It is nothing short of amazing that Paul's communication with gentiles is just as filled with Old Testament allusions as is his communication with the Jews.[37] Apparently Paul, as indicated by his missionary journeys in Acts, saw no inherent barrier in explaining the Old Testament to gentiles. Gentiles, not just Jews, heard the good news of the gospel, which was enveloped in Old Testament allusions, and they believed. Of course, this was the work of the Spirit in their hearts. But this is the key point: the Spirit did not have to work in spite of the Old Testament, but actually worked

---

34. Ryken, "Accessible Word," 124.

35. Note how Scripture is to be read publicly in the churches: 2 Cor 1:13; Eph 3:4; Jas 1:1, 22–25; 1 Pet 1:1; 2:2; 2 Pet 1:19; 1 John 5:13. See Grudem, "Perspicuity of Scripture," 293.

36. There no doubt were exceptions to this rule.

37. Thompson, *A Clear and Present Word*, 88.

through it, bringing to light Old Testament texts that spoke of the Savior who was to come into the world.

Clarifying the Clarity of Scripture

The clarity, or perspicuity, of Scripture means that the Bible can be comprehended and understood by all who are aided by the Holy Spirit and by ordinary means.[38] As the Westminster Confession of Faith (WCF) says:

> All things in Scripture are not alike plain in themselves, nor alike clear unto all: yet those things which are necessary to be known, believed, and observed for salvation, are so clearly propounded, and opened in some place of Scripture or other, that not only the learned, but the unlearned, in a due use of the ordinary means, may attain unto a sufficient understanding of them.[39]

Unfortunately, perspicuity is one of the most misunderstood attributes of Scripture. Perhaps we will best understand this attribute by examining what clarity does *not* mean.

First, the clarity of Scripture does not mean that there are no passages in the Bible that are hard to understand. Sometimes it is assumed that for Scripture to be clear, there can be no difficult texts to interpret. There are several problems with such logic:

First, it assumes that clarity is always accompanied by ease of understanding—a passage is clear if it is easy and effortless to understand. Should the hard work of study be necessary to illuminate its meaning, the passage can no longer be considered clear. But this assumption is misguided. As any persistent student will tell you, clarity often comes through labor. The two are not mutually exclusive, and the presence of one does not rule out the other. Often, we must labor and persist in seeking understanding until the concepts are clear to us, but in the end they are clear. Even Peter acknowledged that some of Paul's writings were hard to understand (2 Pet 3:16), and certain individuals twisted

---

38. Many qualifications could be added to this definition. Grudem's are helpful: "Scripture affirms that it is able to be understood but (1) not all at once, (2) not without effort, (3) not without ordinary means, (4) not without the reader's willingness to obey it, (5) not without the help of the Holy Spirit, (6) not without human misunderstanding, and (7) never completely" (Grudem, "Perspicuity of Scripture," 291).

39. "The Westminster Confession of Faith," in *Reformed Confessions of the 16th and 17th Centuries in English Translation, Volume 4, 1600–1693,* ed. James T. Dennison Jr. (Grand Rapids: Reformation Heritage, 2014), 236 (I.VII).

these writings for their own purposes. But Peter does not use this as an excuse to avoid these truths. He gives it as a motivation to be diligent in deciphering a right from a wrong interpretation (3:17–18). He assumes that those who twist Paul's words are ignorant, but those who listen to them are full of knowledge that leads to life.

We should also avoid wrongly assuming that every passage in Scripture must be *equally* clear. Few Protestants have defined clarity in this way. Instead, while they admit that there are hard passages in Scripture, the saving message of Scripture is clear and can be understood and comprehended. As the WCF says, while not all things in Scripture are "alike plain" or "clear unto all," those things necessary to be known for salvation are "clearly propounded."[40]

In addition, we can wrongly assume that clarity is contingent upon the *interpreter*, rather than the text itself. The clarity of Scripture does involve both text and reader. According to David Garner, "A claim to Scripture's clarity becomes an abstraction apart from consideration of the hearer; both speaker and receptor must exist for communication actually to *function* perspicuously."[41] However, with the influence of postmodernism, some have gone too far, making the clarity of Scripture not an attribute of the text but something that is contingent upon the reader and the meaning the reader would assign to the text. It has been argued that Scripture is not clear *by itself*.[42]

Such an argument fails to distinguish between the clarity of Scripture and hermeneutics, and confuses the *nature* of Scripture with its *reception*. These two are not interdependent. We cannot relocate "perspicuity away from the Bible, making scriptural clarity contingent upon the reader's understanding and turning perspicuity into an interpretive matter rather than an essential, textual matter."[43] To do so is to

---

40. Ibid. See also Francis Turretin, *Institutes of Elenctic Theology*, ed. James T. Dennison Jr., trans. George Musgrave Giger (Phillipsburg, NJ: P&R, 1992), 1:144; Herman Bavinck, *Reformed Dogmatics*, vol. 1, *Prolegomena*, ed. John Bolt, trans. John Vriend (Grand Rapids: Baker, 2003), 1:450; "The Chicago Statement on Biblical Hermeneutics," in *Hermeneutics, Inerrancy, and the Bible: Papers from ICBI Summit II*, ed. Earl D. Radmacher and Robert D. Preus (Grand Rapids: Zondervan, 1984), 886 (article 23).

41. David B. Garner, "Did God Really Say?," in *Did God Really Say? Affirming the Truthfulness and Trustworthiness of Scripture*, ed. David B. Garner (Phillipsburg, NJ: P&R, 2013), 143.

42. For example, James Callahan, *The Clarity of Scripture: History, Theology, and Contemporary Literary Studies* (Downers Grove, IL: InterVarsity Press, 2001), 11, 50; Fish, *Is There a Text in This Class?*

43. Garner, "Did God Really Say?," 143.

conflate the "objective and the subjective."[44] Clarity is not the reader's property, but it is a property of Scripture itself.[45] Therefore, as important as the interpretive covenant community is as the recipient of divine revelation, we must not fall prey to a postmodern view that would make the clarity of the text itself an intrinsic attribute dependent upon the listener.[46] To do so would mean God himself is contingent upon his listeners for the clarity of his own speech.

Second, the clarity of Scripture does not mean that everyone will understand the Bible. It goes without saying that many today *misunderstand* the Bible. However, we should not assume fault lies with the biblical text. There are several factors external to the text that can lead to faulty interpretation.

We must start by acknowledging that interpreters are sinful. Sin acts as a blinder over our eyes, keeping us from seeing the truth. When the sinner approaches the biblical text, his sinful prejudices may get in the way, distorting the meaning of the text. This is a reminder that unbelievers do not approach the text neutral, but rather as condemned sinners with sinful biases against God and his Word. Until the light of the gospel shines into their dark souls, their eyes will never see God's Word clearly (John 3:19; 2 Cor 4:3). The Spirit's work of regeneration is essential if the unbeliever is to understand the biblical text in a saving way.

Yet sin is not restricted to unbelievers, as believers remain sinners even though they have a new identity in Christ. Perfection does not immediately follow regeneration. Christians live in between the already and not yet of salvation. We have been born again and justified, but our sanctification is progressive, unfinished until glory. Hence, the Spirit's *illumination* of the biblical text is crucial. The text of Scripture is undeniably clear, yet sin clouds our judgment still. Nevertheless, the illuminating of the text by the Spirit enables us to see the text clearly (Ps 119:18; 1 Cor 2:12–15; Eph 1:17–19).[47] It is not God's Word that is obscure and needs further clarity, as if God needed to somehow do a better job of communicating his message. Rather, it is the reader whose thought is confused, cloudy, and sinful, and until it undergoes a

---

44. Ibid.
45. Grudem, "Perspecuity of Scripture," 295.
46. Garner, "Did God Really Say?," 144–45.
47. See John Owen, *The Causes, Ways, and Means of Understanding the Mind of God in His Word,* in *The Works of John Owen,* ed. William H. Goold (Edinburgh: Banner of Truth, 1967), 4:124–25, 201–6.

paradigm shift produced by the Spirit's illuminating power, it will not see Scripture for what it is (1 Cor 2:13–14).[48] John Webster sifts out the issue: "Interpretation of the clear Word of God is therefore not first of all an act of clarification but the event of being clarified."[49] What this means is that reading the Bible is an exercise in humility. God must break down our stubborn wills, whereby we rebelliously strive to justify our idolatry in the text, suppressing the truth of the text that doesn't fit nicely into the realm of our sinful agenda.[50] This painful process involves the Spirit ripping off the sinful scales from our eyes so that we see the text afresh under his divine light.

To illustrate, it is like a man with mud on his eyes trying to look at the sun. How silly it is for the man to claim (as Roman Catholics and postmoderns do) that the problem is with the sun.[51] If only the sun were a brighter sun, then he would see it. To the contrary, the sun is perfectly bright. The problem is with the man's skewed vision. What he needs is someone to wipe off the mud from his eyes. Only then will he see clearly.

We must also recognize that interpreters are finite. The interpreter, even if extremely educated, cannot know everything. Even years of study tend to humble the best scholars. The search for knowledge often results in an ironic conclusion: we come to realize just how much we don't know. Such a quest exposes our ignorance while manifesting God's omniscience. In that light, whenever we come to the biblical text of Scripture, we must approach it with humility. Should we encounter what appears to be a problem passage, rather than assuming fault lies with the biblical author, we should assume we do not yet know enough information that would enable us to read the text correctly. We are finite individuals, and often what seemed like a contradiction at first is easily resolved later with further study.

We also know that interpreters are influenced by other interpreters and their interpretive traditions. It is embarrassingly naive to think that we come to the biblical text neutral, uninfluenced by others. In reality, we come to the biblical text with a host of conversation partners.

---

48. Such illuminating power can be attributed not only to the Spirit but to Jesus as well: John 9:39; Luke 10:22; 24:27, 31.

49. John Webster, *Confessing God: Essays in Christian Dogmatics*, vol. 2 (London: T&T Clark, 2005), 63–64.

50. Ibid.

51. Martin Luther, *The Bondage of the Will*, in *LW* 33:27.

This is a good thing, for the right conversation partners can assist us in understanding a passage that we would not otherwise understand properly.[52] Usually the best conversation partners are the old ones, which should encourage us to read and interpret Scripture with the history of interpretation in the passenger seat, instructing us how to drive. However, if we are not careful, we may be influenced by an interpreter who is misguided. Should this be the case, we can fall into the proverbial mistake of the blind leading the blind. Once again, we are prodded to the importance of *sola Scriptura*. We look to the help of other voices, but always subject them to Scripture, allowing Scripture to tune those voices that are off key.

No doubt there are other factors we can consider, but these three are sufficient to demonstrate that we should not automatically assume it is Scripture's fault when we cannot understand its meaning.[53] In light of the many external factors that swerve our judgment, we must recognize that the problem lies with us, not with the biblical text.

These qualities of the interpreter (especially sinfulness and finiteness) take us back to the classic debate between Luther and Erasmus.[54] Erasmus sharply disagreed with Luther, who taught, following Augustine, that man is pervasively depraved and his will is enslaved to sin, spiritually unable and unwilling to turn to God. But many don't know that Erasmus also took issue with Luther's approach to theology and the Bible. Erasmus was irritated by Luther's belief, as stated in his *Assertion of All the Articles* (1520), that Scripture is in and of itself "so certain, accessible and clear that Scripture interprets itself and tests, judges and illuminates everything else."[55] Erasmus found Luther's assertion on this point preposterous! How could Luther say

---

52. See J. Todd Billings, *The Word of God for the People of God: An Entryway to the Theological Interpretation of Scripture* (Grand Rapids: Eerdmans, 2010).

53. Another factor would be culture. The culture we are imbedded in can influence the way we interpret Scripture.

54. For an overview of this debate and a treatment of Luther's doctrine of Scripture, see Thompson, *A Clear and Present Word*, 143–50; Mark Thompson, *A Sure Ground on Which to Stand: The Relation of Authority and Interpretive Method in Luther's Approach to Scripture* (Carlisle, UK: Paternoster, 2004). Luther was not the only one who defended perspicuity; see Ulrich Zwingli's *Of the Clarity and Certainty of the Word of God*, in *Zwingli and Bullinger*, ed. G. W. Bromiley, LCC (Louisville: Westminster John Knox, 1953), 95.

55. Martin Luther, *Assertio omnium articulorum M. Lutheri per bullam Leonis X novissiman damnatorum*, repr. in *D. Martin Luthers Werke: Kritische Gesamtausgabe, Schriften*, ed. J. K. F. Knaake et al., vol. 7 (Weimar: Böhlaus Nachfolger, 1883–), 97 [*WA* 7.97]. For Erasmus's treatise against Luther, see *Luther and Erasmus: Free Will and Salvation*, trans. E. Gordon Rupp and A. N. Marlow, LCC 17 (Philadelphia: Westminster, 1969), 35–97.

that Scripture is clear when the divine author is unsearchable and he does not desire for us to penetrate the secret places of his Word? In his treatise against Luther, Erasmus argued that even the things God has given us to contemplate in his Word are meant to lead us into mystic silence. Erasmus pointed out that countless commentators disagree with one another on the meaning of passages and Christian doctrine. Surely such disagreements demonstrate that Scripture is *not* clear on many matters, and God has instead chosen to hide the answers from us.

Luther's response was fatal to Erasmus's entire argument: the Holy Spirit is no skeptic![56] Luther distinguished between *external* and *internal* clarity.[57] External clarity means that the Bible is plain because God has utilized ordinary human language to communicate with us, and not just with us, his children, but with the whole world through the public proclamation of the gospel by the church.[58] Anyone and everyone can read the Scriptures for themselves and see what they say. One does not have to be a Christian to understand and comprehend the words on the pages of the Bible. External clarity keeps us from mistakenly thinking that the Bible can be grasped only by the spiritually elite who possess a secret knowledge of what the text says. Indeed, even the demons understand who Jesus is and no doubt know what Scripture says (James 2:19). Let's not forget that the devil himself is more than capable of exhibiting sound exegesis![59]

But internal clarity is quite different. Because the unbeliever is spiritually blind, he cannot see the truth of Scripture in a saving way unless his eyes are opened by the Holy Spirit.[60] So while a person may read and memorize the Scriptures backward and forward, exegete its words, diagram its sentences in the original languages, and masterfully describe the historical and cultural background of an individual text, this is not to say that the person has truly understood Scripture's message. There is knowing Scripture, and then there is *knowing* Scripture. The latter is the work of the Holy Spirit.

As we've hinted at already, such a distinction can be found in Jesus's interaction with the religious leaders. Certainly they knew the

---

56. Luther, *Bondage of the Will*, in *LW* 33:284.
57. Ibid., 33:28, 89–91.
58. Ibid., 33:28.
59. R. C. Sproul, "Biblical Interpretation and the Analogy of Faith," in *Inerrancy and Common Sense*, ed. Roger R. Nicole and J. Ramsey Michaels (Grand Rapids: Baker, 1980), 132.
60. Luther, *Bondage of the Will*, in *LW* 33:28 (cf. 98–99).

Old Testament, even memorizing it. However, what Jesus pointed out repeatedly was that they had not truly understood its meaning and fulfillment, for if they had, then they would have recognized him as the Son of God (e.g., John 5:1–47; 8:48–59). This is not so for the believer. The same Spirit who carried along the biblical authors in the act of inspiration moves within God's elect to open their eyes to understand, believe, and accept the truths of God's Word.[61] Internal clarity should drive the interpreter to his or her knees in prayer, asking the Spirit for help and assistance to understand not only Scripture's message but how it is to be applied.[62]

Luther's distinction is a helpful admonishment that the clarity of Scripture does not mean that Scripture can be clearly understood using our *reason alone*. Such a belief is a remnant of the Enlightenment. While in one sense the Bible is a book like other books (it has words, syntax, genres, etc.), it must be qualified that it is *not* a book like any other book.[63] It is a book that is inspired by God. While it was written by human authors, these human authors were superintended and carried along by the Holy Spirit, and the Bible is a masterpiece of the Spirit. Inspiration is his work of art. But his work does not end there. He also has a role in the illumination of Scripture. While *inspiration* is the Spirit's work of breathing out God's revelatory word in written form, *illumination* is the Spirit's work of taking that written Word and making its spiritual meaning clear to the individual reader. Illumination is not further revelation, but rather the Spirit's work of opening our eyes to the revelation that is already there.

Word and Spirit, therefore, not only go together in the past historical and objective work of inspiration but also go together in the ongoing work of illumination. The two should not and cannot be separated. While we can have a purely cognitive comprehension of Scripture (knowing facts and dates), we should not assume that this is all there is to interpreting Scripture. This would be to fundamentally misunderstand what kind of book we are dealing with. God has given us a message concerning himself and his redemptive acts, and the

---

61. Thompson, *A Clear and Present Word*, 165.

62. See John Calvin, *Commentary on Isaiah* (Grand Rapids: Baker, 2005), 3:420–21; John Calvin, *Commentary on the Epistles of Paul the Apostle to the Corinthians* (Grand Rapids: Eerdmans, 1948), 1:429–31. See also Puritan works such as Owen, *Causes, Ways, and Means*, 4:121–60.

63. Billings, *Word of God for the People of God*, 36–37.

recipients of that message are sinners whose eyes are blinded (Isa 60:2; Eph 4:17–18; 5:18; Col 1:13; Jas 3:19). If sinners are to understand the significance of God's redemptive acts spoken of in the Bible, they must have the scales of spiritual blindness surgically removed from their eyes, something only the Spirit can do (1 Cor 2:9–13; Eph 1:17–18; cf. John 9:39).[64]

This is not to say that when the Spirit works, he does so apart from the mind. Rather, it is *through* the mind that the Spirit works, restoring and renewing the mind so that while it previously hated the divine author, now it finds his Word its life stream. The proper order is not understanding seeking faith, but faith seeking understanding. Reason is not enough; faith is an essential ingredient to interpreting the text clearly.[65] The Spirit must illuminate the text of Scripture not by discarding our reason but by utilizing it in the way it was meant to be used. John Webster captures the balance we are looking for when he warns against "hermeneutical naturalism," where the mind "claims sufficiency," yet also warns against "hermeneutical immediacy," in which "seizure by the Spirit breaks off the exercise of intelligence and interpretation becomes rapture."[66]

Third, the clarity of Scripture does not mean that everyone will agree on how to interpret the Bible. This is an all-too-common assumption, but it is not what we mean by the clarity of Scripture. Some see disagreement among even the smartest scholars and conclude that Scripture cannot be clear. Sadly, even the most well-meaning Christians have gone the route of postmodernism, concluding that an interpretive pluralism must mean that there is no true meaning in the text, and one interpretation is as true as another. Practically speaking, what results is hermeneutical agnosticism. While we might enjoy reading Scripture, we can never be confident of its meaning due to all of the disagreement.[67] Once again, this is a failure to recognize that the fault does not lie with Scripture, but with the interpreter. The issue is not that Scripture is muddy, but rather that mud covers our eyes so that we cannot see clearly. Blindness on our part does not preclude objectivity and clarity in the text.

---

64. Webster, *Domain of the Word*, 50–64.
65. For example, consider Thompson's definition: "The clarity of Scripture is that quality of the biblical text that, as God's communicative act, ensures its meaning is accessible to all who come to it in faith" (Thompson, *A Clear and Present Word*, 165).
66. Webster, *Domain of the Word*, 61.
67. For example, Smith, *Bible Made Impossible*.

Fourth, the clarity of Scripture does not mean each text is to be isolated on a hermeneutical island. Unfortunately, many readers approach the text demanding that it say everything, and when it doesn't, they declare it "unclear." We do the same with entire books of the Bible. For example, if we cannot understand Hebrews in and of itself, then it must be obscure.

But Scripture is a unitary whole. While there are many human authors, there is one divine author, and his authorship guarantees that the Bible, from beginning to end, is an unbroken unit. Scripture should not be sliced and diced, nor can we isolate a passage or a book from the rest of the canon.[68] As many of the church fathers and Protestant Reformers observed, Scripture is its own interpreter, and Scripture interprets Scripture. This is what the Reformers called the "analogy of Scripture" (*analogia Scripturae*).[69] Since God is the divine author of the *entire* biblical text, all of Scripture must be taken into account whenever we read one portion of it. And should we come to what appears to be a difficult, obscure passage, we turn to other passages that seem transparent and clear to better understand the former. As a rule and principle, the clear passages always serve to interpret the less clear passages.

This is not to suggest that we should make a hard-and-fast division between "clear" and "unclear" passages in Scripture. With time and resources, and the illuminating work of the Spirit, texts whose meaning at first appeared mysterious later become lucid. As Luther argued in his response to Erasmus, such textual or doctrinal difficulties are temporary and short-lived. Therefore, we should be hesitant to say *Scripture* is unclear. It is more accurate to say *our understanding* of Scripture is unclear. Scripture is immutable, but our understanding of Scripture progresses from dark to light, from dim to bright. Again, if there is a problem, it is not with Scripture but with the reader-interpreter.

One implication of this is that we should avoid concluding that one passage or author of Scripture contradicts another. Such a conclusion reveals our hermeneutical hubris. Instead, when we come to an

---

68. For a helpful corrective, note the importance of Richard Lints's three horizons in *The Fabric of Theology: A Prolegomenon to Evangelical Theology* (Grand Rapids: Eerdmans, 1993), 293–311.

69. Heinrich Bullinger, *The Decades of Henry Bullinger*, ed. Thomas Harding, 4 vols. (1849–1852; Grand Rapids: Reformation Heritage, 2004), 1:75–78; Richard A. Muller and John Thompson, eds., *Biblical Interpretation in the Era of the Reformation* (Grand Rapids: Eerdmans, 1996).

apparent contradiction, a tension between two texts or two authors, we should continue to treat the divine author seriously and look further at the whole counsel of God until our eyes are opened to the resolution.[70] If the matter remains inconclusive, we are not to determine that the text is unclear, contradictory, or errant. To do so is to declare ourselves judge over the text. Rather, in light of the divine author, we approach the issue with humility, understanding that there is a reconciliation of the issue even if it escapes us at this time. Prayer for further illumination accompanied by diligent study has shown many scholars that what appeared at first to be irreconcilable later became harmonious and compatible.

A second implication of this principle is that we should pursue the assistance of others, dead and alive. If biblical passages are not exiled to a desert island, neither should the interpreter be exiled. And in light of the barriers internal to the interpreter (sinfulness and finitude), it is not a violation of Scripture's perspicuity to look to the interpretive help of others. In fact, God never meant for us to read and interpret Scripture on our own. This is a caricature of *sola Scriptura* and looks more like the *nuda Scriptura* of the radical reformers. As we will see in chapter 10, while the voices of tradition do not play a magisterial role, they do have a ministerial role. We are to read Scripture in the community of the church, always standing on top of the shoulders of others as opposed to reinventing the wheel each time we approach a passage.[71] Where we are blind, others can see, and it is often necessary to borrow their hermeneutical light.

But Isn't Language a Problem?
Kant, Barth, Brunner, and Bultmann

For most of Christendom over the past two millenia, language has not been an insurmountable problem. In modern theology and philosophy, however, language has become the *big* problem. Today many doubt whether language can actually convey truths about transcendent things. This line of argument was put forth by linguistic philosophers like Ludwig Wittgenstein and Alfred J. Ayer as well as

---

70. Thompson, *A Clear and Present Word*, 137.

71. On the importance of recognizing that Scripture comes to us "within a community of shared faith" and is "mediated by certain theological presuppositions and assumptions," see Billings, *Word of God for the People of God*, 17.

their contemporary disciples.[72] We now find this skepticism within the Christian community as well, as some now doubt whether God has truly spoken in and through the Bible, communicating truths about himself to mankind.[73]

Such skepticism can be traced back to Immanuel Kant. As Packer observes, Kant introduced a "lethal combination of a priori deism and a posteriori agnosticism," persuading others that no serious intellectual could believe in a speaking God. For Kant, religion should be formulated within the bounds of pure reason. "While God might be a necessary postulate, He cannot strictly be *known* in any sense, by any means, at any time, any more than can be the *Ding-an-sich* (thing-in-itself) in the natural order." As a result, Kant "bequeathed to us the now chronic misunderstanding of God's transcendence and incomprehensibility as implying that, in His personal existence, He is both remote and unintelligible."[74]

Kant's view infiltrated not only the ranks of Liberalism, but even Neo-Orthodoxy. One of the ways Barth countered the Liberalism of his day was to recover the transcendence of God. But such transcendence meant that God could not be "clearly revealed to men" or "clearly represented by human words and concepts."[75] For Barth, human language does not reveal God but hides him.

The Kantianism that Barth imbibed did not stop with him. Many of Barth's disciples went further. While Barth sits on the right, Emil Brunner is to his left, and to the far left of Brunner sits Rudolf Bultmann. For Brunner, divine revelation cannot be propositional if it is to remain personal. And for Bultmann, the Word of God "yields no factual information whatever." One must trust God since, "in the strict sense, one knows nothing about Him at all."[76] Brunner presents a false dichotomy, for Scripture presents divine revelation as *both* personal and propositional (see chapters 5–7). As for Bultmann, he robs us of any knowledge of God. But the first and last thing we read when we open the Bible is the simple yet profound truth that God is not silent, but

---

72. J. I. Packer, "The Adequacy of Human Language," in Geisler, *Inerrancy*, 203.
73. Ibid., 204.
74. Ibid., 215.
75. John Frame, "God and Biblical Language," in *God's Inerrant Word: An International Symposium on the Trustworthiness of Scripture*, ed. John Warwick Montgomery (Minneapolis: Bethany Fellowship, 1973), 215.
76. Packer, "Adequacy of Human Language," 205.

speaks with the full intention of being heard, understood, and obeyed (Gen 15:6; Exod 24:3; Rev 1:1–3).

Barth's legacy continues today with a strong emphasis by some on the transcendence of God. However, Barth's perceived strength also proves to be a weakness. In Barth's emphasis on God's transcendence, he refused to equate Scripture and the Word of God, thereby forfeiting divine immanence. Ironically, in an effort to recover God's freedom, Barth restricted God, dismissing the belief that the words of Scripture can be identified as revelation—the very Word of God.[77] He traded one type of theological slavery for another. What Barth failed to perceive is that language itself is a gift from God, and because we are made in his image, God "has made us fit speech partners for himself."[78]

The gospel demonstrates that God's purpose in redemptive history is not to hide himself but to make himself known, and this divine intention will not be hindered by his transcendence.[79] God accommodates himself by using human language to communicate his message, though this never means that his accommodation approves or absorbs errors in his Word. Human language is not a barrier for God—indeed, he created it!—but it is the divinely designed instrument he uses to beautifully and accurately convey his will and purpose.[80] Nor does human language obscure Scripture, but instead it serves to communicate God's message and will to finite creatures (e.g., John 17:3, 6–8).[81] God gave us language as a gift so that we could enter into communion with him. Far from being a barrier, language is the God-orchestrated means through which he speaks to us so that we can know him. As the sovereign Creator, God is the master of language; it poses no threat when he accommodates himself in its utilization.[82] Divine accommodation through human language, then, only buttresses the clarity of Scripture.

One might object that human sin makes it impossible for God to

---

77. For an overview of Barth's view, see chapter 3.

78. Thompson, *A Clear and Present Word*, 68.

79. Ibid.

80. Ibid., 69 (cf. 79–80); Richard Gaffin, "Speech and the Image of God: Biblical Reflections on Language and Its Uses," in *The Pattern of Sound Doctrine* (Phillipsburg, NJ: P&R, 2004), 191; J. I. Packer, "The Adequacy of the Autographa," in Geisler, *Inerrancy*, 197–228.

81. See "The Chicago Statement on Biblical Inerrancy," in Geisler, *Inerrancy*, 494 (article IV).

82. Vern S. Poythress, "God and Language," in Flugher, *Solid Ground*, 96–97. See also Vern S. Poythress, *In the Beginning Was the Word: Language—A God-Centered Approach* (Wheaton, IL: Crossway, 2009).

use human language unconvoluted by human error or ambiguity. Sin, no doubt, makes language more difficult to use. But who is to say God cannot use language in an undefiled manner? Do we really want to restrict God to this degree? God's use of language after the fall is never seen as problematic. For example, after the confusion of the people through language at Babel, God calls Abraham, and he clearly communicates to him his divine purposes. Nothing in the story line indicates that God is now struggling to make himself known, having "confused the language of the whole world" (Gen 11:9).[83] God does not merely put up with language but actually restores it to its redeeming purpose, as exemplified at Pentecost (Acts 2:1–13).[84]

And yet it is still not enough to say that God has "sanctified" language in order to speak to his people through it. The impression some today give is that language itself is inherently and intrinsically problematic, and God must purify it to make himself known via the written text. But language is not *inherently* unclear. There is nothing innately abstruse or ambiguous about language.[85] There is nothing intrinsic to language that would necessitate its being vague or corrupt. Coherence is the norm, not the exception. "Misunderstanding in language," observes Garner, "occurs in the context of essential understanding. Incoherence is flawed coherence; coherence is not flawed incoherence. Miscommunication is flawed communication; communication is not flawed miscommunication."[86]

Language is a divine gift intended to be received and understood by God's image-bearers. Yes, language has been used for ill motives, as the fall demonstrates (Gen 3). However, God need not purify or sanctify language of some intrinsic sinfulness, as if language itself is corrupt. It is not language that is the problem, but those who use it (i.e., corrupt mankind). Therefore, if there is a problem with language, it is with the speaker. Yet God is not only a *holy* speaker, but he is the Creator and architect of language itself; he is the original speaker, and language moves at his command. Language works because he says so. It has value because he created it with significance and purpose.[87] And he uses it as his maidservant to bring about a saving relationship with his people who are made in his image (Gen 1:27), uniquely designed to hear and

---

83. Thompson, *A Clear and Present Word*, 69.
84. Ibid., 69–70.
85. Gaffin, "Speech and the Image of God," 191.
86. Garner, "Did God Really Say?," 150.
87. Thompson, *A Clear and Present Word*, 166.

understand their Creator. He speaks, they listen, and then they respond with words of worship.

In creating Scripture, God used fallen individuals to write down what he intended. However, these human authors were redeemed by God, and their minds were renewed by the power of the Spirit. Furthermore, since God is the ultimate author, the Spirit's superintendence of the human author's words guarded him from any potential abuse or unholy use of language. The ultimate reason for Scripture's clarity is that it has God as its divine author. In his divine speech, God has accommodated himself to us, and in doing so, he does not stammer or stutter.[88]

The most pressing proof that language is not a barrier too hard for God to climb over is the incarnation itself.[89] Listen to how the author of Hebrews opens his letter: "Long ago, at many times and in many ways, God spoke to our fathers by the prophets, but in these last days he has spoken to us by his Son, whom he appointed the heir of all things, through whom also he created the world" (Heb 1:1–2 ESV). God has spoken not only by the prophets but by his own Son, who has dwelt among us (Isa 7:14; Matt 1:23). If the second person of the Trinity can take on human flesh, certainly the triune God can communicate through human language. We would never say that the addition of a human nature somehow distorts the divine nature or makes incarnation impossible. So why would we say the same about God speaking through human language? If God can perform the miracle of the incarnation, then inscripturation is not difficult for God.[90] And if God found the incarnation a fitting means by which to reconcile us with God, why should Scripture not be a fitting means to unite us to Christ?[91]

We must remember that language is a good gift from God. He is the Lord of language, for he is its Creator and Sustainer, and he has chosen to address his people through this human medium. We must not fall prey to hermeneutical Pelagianism.[92] We do not merit knowledge of our Creator and Lord. Rather, it is given to us, which is itself an act of grace

---

88. Garner, "Did God Really Say?," 151. See also Bavinck, *Reformed Dogmatics*, 1:308; John M. Frame, *The Doctrine of the Word of God* (Phillipsburg, NJ: P&R, 2010), 165.

89. Carl F. H. Henry, *God, Revelation, and Authority* (Wheaton, IL: Crossway, 1979), 4:116.

90. Thompson, *A Clear and Present Word*, 111.

91. Packer, "Adequacy of Human Language," 220.

92. John Webster, *Holy Scripture: A Dogmatic Sketch* (Cambridge: Cambridge University Press, 2003), 100.

in light of our fallen condition. We are absolutely dependent upon God and his use of language if we are to know him truly and savingly. We do not approach Scripture laying down our demands, but with humility as those who have been brought out of darkness and into the light because of the saving power (and clarity!) of God's Word (1 Cor 2:9; 2 Cor 4:6; Col 1:13). How we read the Bible is to be hermeneutically Augustinian. Knowledge of God is a gift to be received, not earned.[93]

Rome's Muddy Tiber

Besides postmodernism, the other heavyweight contender to scriptural clarity is Rome. Rome denies the Protestant view of clarity, arguing that Scripture is unclear and dependent upon an infallible interpreter to make it clear, and that infallible interpreter is the Roman Church. We read from Vatican II, the "task of authentically interpreting the word of God, whether written or handed on, has been entrusted exclusively to the living teaching office of the Church."[94] Vatican II asserts that "sacred tradition, sacred Scripture, and the teaching authority of the Church . . . are so linked and joined together that one cannot stand without the others."[95]

We will critique Rome's view of authority and scriptural insufficiency in the next chapter, but here we should observe that Rome is certainly not a bastion of clarity. It portrays itself as the necessary and infallible interpreter that supplements Scripture, but this just isn't so. As a matter of historical fact, it is hard to see how Rome's teachings of the past can compare to Scripture in internal coherence and consistency as well as simple clarity.[96] Today there are libraries filled with Rome's official teaching, even on matters essential for salvation, and few churchgoers dare turn a page lest they be lost in a labyrinth of technicalities.[97] This has served to cultivate Rome's advocacy of *implicit faith*, whereby Christians are told it is sufficient to simply believe whatever the church teaches, regardless of whether one actually understands it.[98]

The situation is only more confusing when the studious Christian

---

93. Thompson, *A Clear and Present Word*, 135 (cf. 165).
94. Walter M. Abbott, ed., *The Documents of Vatican II*, trans. Joseph Gallagher (New York: American, 1966), 117.
95. Ibid., 118.
96. Michael Horton, *The Christian Faith* (Grand Rapids: Zondervan, 2011), 195.
97. Ibid.
98. Ibid.

ciphering through endless volumes of detailed Catholic teaching realizes that some teachings that have been declared official church dogma were previously labeled heretical. Indeed, Luther himself came to this realization, as did other Reformers. As we saw in chapter 1, from 1309 to 1437 several popes vied with one another for supremacy, even anathematizing each other. The Great Western Schism hung like a black cloud over Christendom, reminding all believers that they stood under the condemnation of at least one pope![99] This raised the irritating question: Would the real pope *please* stand up? Uncertainty remained as to which pope was truly justified in his anathemas. How different these papal squabbles are from the inspired and clear text of Scripture we have examined.[100]

There is another reason not to trust Rome's claim to be the infallible interpreter, namely, that Rome has abandoned the true gospel. As John Calvin pointed out in his debate with Sadoleto, since Rome views the Protestant understanding of the gospel as heretical, we cannot believe that Rome is the church's infallible teacher of the Word of God, as she claims.[101] This much was apparent with the Council of Trent (see chapter 1). While progress has certainly been made by contemporary ecumenical conversations, nevertheless, Rome cannot retract her prior *conciliar* statements, including Trent's anathema of the Protestant affirmation of the gospel and justification by faith alone.[102] *Sola Scriptura* is inseparable from *solus Christus, sola gratia*, and *sola fide*.

Rome often points the finger at Protestantism's disarray of denominations to demonstrate what happens when you don't have an infallible interpreter. And Protestants must certainly take responsibility for their lack of unity. But the past shows that Rome's history is just as problematic. While both traditions have muddy waters, Protestants have never claimed that their river (tradition) is infallibly clear. That place of honor belongs only to Scripture. But Rome *has* claimed to be infallibly clear, though all the while its Tiber of tradition is muddy. And if it has a muddy Tiber, what hope does that give us when looking at the biblical

---

99. Ibid.

100. Ibid.

101. *Reply by John Calvin to Letter by Cardinal Sadolet to the Senate and People of Geneva*, in *John Calvin: Tracts and Letters*, ed. and trans. Henry Beveridge (Edinburgh: Banner of Truth, 2009), 1:48–49. See also Horton, *Christian Faith*, 197.

102. This point became abundantly clear to the media when Pope Francis visited the United States in September 2015. The media came to realize that the pope could not change the church's stance on issues like homosexuality; nevertheless, they commended him for changing the rhetoric and tone to sound sympathetic toward those in same-sex relationships.

text *if* the biblical text is not clear in and of itself, as Rome claims, but depends upon an infallible interpreter who turns out to be flawed?

Clarity Clearly Matters

Does the clarity of Scripture matter today? Absolutely. If we take the Bible out of the hands of God's people and limit it to the spiritually and academically elite, then we will end up with biblically illiterate churches. Such a phenomenon is not unprecedented. Reformers like Tyndale gave their lives to make sure God's Word made it into the vernacular, the language of the people. Rome's restriction of God's Word to the Latin mass and to the priest meant that those in the pew suffered a literary drought of the Word of God. Rome taught that God's Word was not clear enough to be put into the hands of the laity, which would surely result in hermeneutical and doctrinal chaos and undermine papal authority. The Christian must simply depend upon the church. So Christians were told for many years.

The Reformers understood that if Christians lost confidence in the clarity of God's Word, few would read their Bibles, especially if political pressure heated up. So with the Protestant Reformation came an assurance that God's Word is indeed clear, which motivated Christians to read their Bibles so that they might hear what God himself had to say. The doctrine of scriptural clarity created within souls the eager expectation that they could now hear God himself. The result was reformation in doctrine and practice. Hearing God's Word proved to be a means to authentic faith and obedience.[103]

But it is not enough simply to put the Word of God into the hands of the people of God. The people of God must also approach Scripture as pupils, rather than as masters. Regrettably, many today who deny Scripture's clarity do the latter, approaching Scripture as a foggy puzzle that only the academically elite can put together via their critical methods.[104] But to deny Scripture's clarity is the highest form of arrogance.[105] Rather than coming to the text to hear and listen, we too often come shouting over it. The prayer of every believer should be that of the psalmist: "Open my eyes that I may see wonderful things in your law" (Ps 119:18; cf. 2 Pet 1:19).

---

103. Thompson, *A Clear and Present Word*, 161.

104. For example, Kenton L. Sparks, *God's Word in Human Words: An Evangelical Appropriation of Critical Biblical Scholarship* (Grand Rapids: Baker Academic, 2008), 70.

105. Garner, "Did God Really Say?," 135.

CHAPTER 10

God's Speech Is Enough: The Sufficiency of Scripture

I defy the pope and all his laws, and if God spare my life, ere many years, I will cause a boy that driveth a plow shall know more of the Scripture than thou doest.

—*William Tyndale*

Scripture is the school of the Holy Spirit. Just as nothing is omitted that is both necessary and useful to know, so nothing is taught except what is expedient to know.

—*John Calvin*

Scripture is the womb from which arises divine truth and the Church. —*Martin Luther*

Some readers may be curious as to why we have waited until the end of this book to address Scripture's sufficiency. After all, isn't the sufficiency of Scripture synonymous with *sola Scriptura*? Perhaps this is a surprise, but the answer is no. Certainly sufficiency is an essential aspect of *sola Scriptura*, but it is not the whole of *sola Scriptura*. Inspiration, inerrancy, and clarity all are related to *sola Scriptura*, and if we do not understand these attributes properly, then sufficiency will make little sense. It is only because Scripture is authoritative, God-breathed, trustworthy, and clear that we can also say it is sufficient for the Christian life.

Assuming that sufficiency is the entirety of *sola Scriptura* presupposes an incorrect definition of *sola Scriptura*. As we have already seen, *sola Scriptura* does not mean Scripture is our only source of authority. Instead, argued the Reformers, *sola Scriptura* means Scripture is our only inspired, inerrant, and sufficient source of divine revelation, in contrast to Rome who elevated tradition as a second and equal source of divine revelation. Scripture alone is our *final* authority, and therefore sufficient for faith and practice.[1] We come full circle, back to our definition of *sola Scriptura* given at the start of this book: *Sola Scriptura* means that *only Scripture, because it is God's inspired Word, is our inerrant, sufficient, and final authority for the church.*

With this in mind, we turn in this final chapter to an explanation and defense of the Bible's sufficiency for the Christian life. We will (1) seek to understand why we need Scripture in the first place if God has provided general revelation, (2) define and explain what sufficiency means and entails, (3) look to Scripture's own witness to its sufficiency, and (4) address several contemporary challenges to the sufficiency of Scripture today, challenges every Christian should be aware of and ready to respond to.

The Necessity of Scripture, or Why Isn't General Revelation Sufficient?

There are several questions that beg to be answered before we can address the specifics of sufficiency. Why do we need Scripture in the first place? Why isn't general revelation sufficient? We must admit, if general revelation was sufficient, then we surely wouldn't need the Bible. This route was embraced by many deists in the eighteenth century, but it is misguided. As important as general revelation is, it is insufficient for a saving faith and practice.

But why? We addressed this question in more detail in chapter 4, so here we'll simply review the main points. Though general revelation in the created order is available to all people, it is limited in its scope. While general revelation may bear witness that there is a Creator who exists (Ps 19:1; Acts 14:16–17) and while some of his attributes may be made manifest (Rom 1:19–21), nevertheless, it does not convey a saving gospel message found in the person and work of Christ. To make matters worse, since we are born sinful, we suppress and distort even the truth that is revealed to us in general revelation (Rom 1:28–31).

Therefore, while general revelation is sufficient to condemn (Rom 1:18–32; we are "without excuse"), it is insufficient to save. Saving

---

1. For example, consider the definitions of *sola Scriptura* in Keith Mathison, *The Shape of Sola Scriptura* (Moscow, ID: Canon, 2001), 259; K. Scott Oliphint, "Because It Is the Word of God," in *Did God Really Say? Affirming the Truthfulness and Trustworthiness of Scripture*, ed. David B. Garner (Phillipsburg, NJ: P&R, 2013), 7.

knowledge comes only through special revelation, which is not only far more detailed in its scope but efficacious in its power to save when accompanied by the Holy Spirit. Because we suppress the natural law written on our consciences (e.g., Gal 4:3–9; Col 2:8, 20), we desperately need the special saving revelation that God bestows upon sinners in his Word. Only in Scripture, then, does God extend the gospel to us. In that light, Scripture is not only *necessary* but *sufficient* for faith and practice.

What Is Sufficiency?

The sufficiency of Scripture means that all things necessary for salvation and for living the Christian life in obedience to God and for his glory are given to us in the Scriptures. Not only is the Bible our supreme authority, it is the authority that provides believers with all the truth they need for reconciliation with God and for following after Christ.[2]

Because sufficiency was such an important doctrine to the Reformers in their fight against Rome (who denied Scripture's sufficiency in her elevation of Tradition), some of the most well-articulated expressions of sufficiency can be seen in the sixteenth century. Whether it is the French Confession of 1559, the Belgic Confession of 1561, or the Thirty-Nine Articles of 1563, the sufficiency of Scripture was defended and affirmed in the spirit of the early Reformers.[3] But as helpful as each of these confessions can be, it's in the seventeenth century that we receive (arguably) one of the most brilliant and elaborate definitions and articulations of sufficiency from the Westminster Assembly. In the Shorter Catechism, for example, we see sufficiency affirmed concisely:

> Q. What do the Scriptures principally teach?
> A. The Scriptures principally teach, What man is to believe concerning God, and what duty God requires of man.[4]

---

2. If we were to place this definition in the context of redemptive history, we might say something more specific, such as sufficiency means that at each point in redemptive history, God provided his people with all the divine words and truth they needed. In other words, sufficiency should not be used to undermine the *progressive* nature of divine revelation, nor should the progressive nature of divine revelation be used to deny sufficiency. God's adding further revelation (e.g., the canon of the NT) does not undermine the principle of sufficiency.

3. "The French Confession (1559)," in *Reformed Confessions of the 16th and 17th Centuries in English Translation, Volume 2, 1552–1566*, ed. James T. Dennison Jr. (Grand Rapids: Reformation Heritage, 2010), 142 (article V); "The Belgic Confession (1561)," in ibid., 427 (article VII); "The Thirty-Nine Articles (1562/63)," in ibid., 755 (article VI).

4. "Westminster Shorter Catechism (1647)," in *Reformed Confessions of the 16th and*

In the Westminster Confession of Faith (1646) we receive a much fuller definition of what the catechism entails:

> The whole counsel of God concerning all things necessary for his own glory, man's salvation, faith and life, is either expressly set down in Scripture, or by good and necessary consequence may be deduced from Scripture: unto which nothing at any time is to be added, whether by new revelations of the Spirit, or traditions of men (2 Tim 3:15–17; Gal 1:8–9; 2 Thess 2:2). Nevertheless, we acknowledge the inward illumination of the Spirit of God to be necessary for the saving understanding of such things as are revealed in the Word (John 6:45; 1 Cor 2:9–12) and that there are some circumstances concerning the worship of God, and government of the Church, common to human actions and societies, which are to be ordered by the light of nature, and Christian prudence, according to the general rules of the Word, which are always to be observed (1 Cor 11:13–14; 14:26, 40).[5]

It is hard to find a better definition of sufficiency than this one. Let's briefly reflect on this definition as a guide to understanding what sufficiency means and what it does not mean.

1. *Sufficiency means that all things necessary for God's glory, salvation, and the Christian life are provided for God's people in the Scriptures.* In this sense, sufficiency is comprehensive in its scope. Everything we need to live for God's glory is given to us in his Word. Consider two ways this occurs: (a) Scripture communicates the saving message of the gospel, which is necessary and essential for the conversion of the lost. Therefore, everything the unbeliever needs to know and believe to be saved is found in the Holy Scriptures. (b) Scripture also communicates God's will so that the Christian can live in obedience to God and for his glory. The Bible, as the believer's final authority, provides the Christian with all the truth and divine words needed for following after Christ and living a life of godliness.

17th Centuries in English Translation, Volume 4, 1600–1693, ed. James T. Dennison Jr. (Grand Rapids: Reformation Heritage, 2014), 353 (Q.3.).

5. "The Westminster Confession of Faith (1646)," in *Reformed Confessions, Volume 4*, 235 (I.VI). For a helpful commentary on each aspect of this definition, see J. V. Fesko, *The Theology of the Westminster Standards* (Wheaton, IL: Crossway, 2014), 81–90.

However, the Westminster divines added a very helpful qualification to sufficiency precisely at this point. Notice that while Scripture is sufficient, this does not mean that all things will be explicitly spelled out on the pages of Scripture. The confession says, "The whole counsel of God concerning all things necessary for his own glory, man's salvation, faith and life, is either *expressly set down in Scripture, or by good and necessary consequence may be deduced from Scripture*" (emphasis added).[6] Sufficiency does not mean that Scripture addresses all things in the same way. Some matters are not addressed *directly* by God's Word. We should not assume, however, that Scripture does not speak to those issues. To the contrary, many issues in life and even many doctrines of the faith may be addressed by Scripture *indirectly*. For example, one will be hard-pressed to find a passage of Scripture that explicitly defines and explains the Trinity, the hypostatic union, the intermediate state, or nuanced questions of polity.[7] The same could be said when it comes to practical matters in the Christian life. At times we may need to think through the many implications and applications a particular teaching of Scripture or a specific biblical passage can have not only for our development of doctrine but for living the Christian life.

2. *Sufficiency means that nothing should be added to the Bible.* We should not be seeking out additional divine words from God. As we will see in this chapter, God has given to us in Scripture all the divine words we need. As we discovered in chapter 4, Scripture is the sufficient constitution of the covenant. Hence the Westminster Confession warns against adding to the Word,

---

6.   Fesko, following Warfield before him, rightly qualifies that the authors of the confession are not defaulting here to reason in the spirit of rationalism. Rather, such logic of deduction falls within the broader hermeneutical framework of the Reformed principle of the analogy of Scripture. It also sees our reason as a ministerial instrument through which we understand and properly interpret Scripture, never as a magisterial authority that stands over Scripture. See Fesko, *The Theology of the Westminster Standards*, 89; Benjamin B. Warfield, "The Westminster Doctrine of Holy Scripture," in *The Works of Benjamin B. Warfield*, ed. E. D. Warfield et al., 10 vols. (1931; repr., Grand Rapids: Baker, 1981), 6:226.

7.   This is a crucial point because some Roman Catholics in the 16th and 17th centuries argued that doctrine must be limited to the express statements of Scripture, which certainly meant relying upon infallible Tradition for everything else. Of course, others took this tactic as well, such as the Socinians and certain Arminians. To see how the Reformers and Reformed responded, see Fesko, *Theology of the Westminster Standards*, 587.

either by appealing to new, additional revelations from the Spirit (as was the case with certain radical reformers in the sixteenth century) or by looking to man-made tradition (2 Tim 3:15–17; Gal 1:8–9; 2 Thess 2:2), as if it is an additional revelation that supplements Scripture (as Rome did during the Reformation era and continues to do to this day). In the twenty-first century, this second point is most seriously debased by various sects that add other "divine books" (e.g., Latter-Day Saints' addition of the *Book of Mormon*).

3. *Sufficiency does not preclude the inward illumination of the Holy Spirit.* While we should not be seeking revelation from the Spirit in addition to Scripture, we must not go to the other extreme (as some evangelical rationalists have done) and eliminate the Spirit entirely. Rather, Word and Spirit go together. God gives us his sufficient Word, but he intends the Spirit to come alongside us to help us understand his Word. Therefore, much like Calvin (see chapter 1), the Westminster Confession advocates the *illuminating* work of the Spirit: "The Spirit . . . [is] necessary for the saving understanding of such things as are revealed in the Word (John 6:45; 1 Cor. 2:9–12)."

4. *Sufficiency does not annihilate general revelation.* As we saw previously, general revelation is revelation from God manifested both in nature and in the human conscience. Yet as wonderful as general revelation may be in bearing witness to the character of our Creator, it is limited in its scope and does not provide us as sinners with the saving word of the gospel, which we absolutely must have to be redeemed. While general revelation may serve to condemn us (e.g., Rom 1), it cannot save us. General revelation proves insufficient for salvation and the Christian life.

However, it would be wrong to conclude that since God has given us a more specific and saving revelation in the Scriptures, general revelation is irrelevant. Quite the contrary. General revelation remains *God's* revelation. We should not elevate it to a status of sufficiency and deny our need for the Scriptures, relying completely on general revelation (remember, this was the tendency of many during the Enlightenment period). Yet nor should we think that special revelation and general revelation are enemies, opposed to each other. As we will explore further in our discussion of science, general revelation is a magnificent means through which our reason explores the natural order, makes discoveries, and, if done right, leads us to worship our Creator (Ps 19:1–6). General revelation should always serve to complement what we know from special revelation, specifically the Scriptures.[8] General revelation does not function autonomously. As a testimony and witness to the Creator and his glory in the created order, general revelation is supportive and consistent with that special revelation which alone is all-sufficient, namely, the Bible.

In that light, the Westminster Confession can state that there may be "circumstances" in which "the light of nature" (or natural revelation) serves to assist us, even inform, guide, and instruct us. As mentioned already, how we are to go about such "circumstances" may not be prescribed in Scripture. Nevertheless, we may receive assistance from the light of nature. And yet, the Westminster Confession qualifies, even here the light of nature is always to be used "according to the general rules of the Word, which are always to be observed (1 Cor 11:13–14; 14:26, 40)." Even the light of nature, therefore, falls under the authority of Scripture, so that while it may inform us, it should never be used to contradict God's Word.

Consider two concrete illustrations of this that relate to the Confession's mention of worship. Scripture never tells us what time to have our Sunday morning worship service. Shall we meet at 2:00 a.m., 4:00 a.m., or 10:00 a.m.? Scripture is silent on this question. However, the "light of nature" helps us here, providing us with the common sense we need to discern that in most circumstances, barring persecution or the need to meet secretly for worship, the 10:00 a.m. option is best. Or consider the discipline of hermeneutics. A knowledge of the world via general revelation serves to benefit our approach to hermeneutics, for it presumes an understanding of the human languages of Hebrew, Greek, and Aramaic; the geography of ancient Near Eastern and Mediterranean worlds; the history of ancient cultures; and countless other things. Such factors demonstrate the

---

8. For more on this point, see John M. Frame, *The Doctrine of the Word of God* (Phillipsburg, NJ: P&R, 2010), 356–57.

high importance of general revelation, even guarding us against certain biblicist caricatures of *sola Scriptura*.[9]

One implication of this is that we should not approach the Bible as if it addresses all information in the world. One cannot look up 2 + 2 in the Bible and discover that the answer is 4. The Bible is not an encyclopedia, a dictionary, or a textbook. Nor did God mean for it to be treated in this way. Yet while the Bible does not address all information or all fields of practice (hence the "light of nature"), this does not mean that the Bible fails to provide God's people with general biblical principles applicable regardless of one's vocation. Indeed, the Bible provides us with a theological and moral framework and worldview that extends to all of life.

Practically, this means that the Bible does not demand the exclusion of extrabiblical data (a point we will return to later). Human knowledge and thought in all disciplines always involves and requires extrabiblical data. It must, for God has situated us in his world where we are always surrounded by extrabiblical data. Therefore, every discipline (e.g., astrophysics, nuclear physics, medicine) must interact with, engage, and respond to information in this world beyond what the Bible addresses.[10] Our explanation of *sola Scriptura* up to this point assumes this much, for it does not intend to say that the Bible provides us with all information on every subject. Rather, it conveys that the Bible alone is our supreme and final authority in all of life and therefore sufficient, providing God's people with all the truth they need for salvation and godliness.

Far more could be said about the ins and outs of sufficiency (and we will explore some of these toward the end of this chapter). However, we must first turn to Scripture's own witness.

The Sufficiency of Scripture: A Biblical Doctrine

The first thing we must understand about the sufficiency of Scripture is that it is a doctrine that Scripture itself teaches. First, consider God's

---

9.   I owe both of these illustrations to David VanDrunen, whose insight on this section I very much appreciate.

10.   John M. Frame, *Apologetics to the Glory of God* (Phillipsburg, NJ: P&R, 1994), 19; Frame, *Doctrine of the Word of God*, 220–24.

dealings with Israel in the Old Testament. Deuteronomy 1–3 recounts how Israel had disobeyed the Lord, refusing to enter into the Promised Land (1:19–24), and as a consequence of their rebellion the Lord sent them back into the wilderness (1:34–46). While God's promises were sufficient for Caleb and Joshua (1:36, 38), the people grumbled against the Lord, which led to further wandering and eventually death. Since Moses was forbidden to enter the promised land, Joshua was God's chosen one to lead the next generation into the land beyond the Jordan (3:23–29). Then, in Deuteronomy 4, Moses spoke to Israel, instructing them to listen and obey the Lord, so that they might "live and may go in and take possession of the land" that God had promised. The word from God given to Moses for the people was considered sufficient. Moses warned, "Do not add to what I command you and do not subtract from it, but keep the commands of the LORD your God that I give you" (4:2; cf. 12:32; Prov 30:5–6). Moses told the people to make the Lord's commands and his covenant at Sinai known to their children and to their children's children (4:9). The "commands" taught to Israel by the Lord through Moses were sufficient for them and their children. To add to them, neglect them, or take away from them was to deny not only the sufficiency and authority of the commands but the Lord as well, for they were his commands.

Deuteronomy 8:3 also testifies to the sufficiency of God's commands. Sounding a note similar to Deuteronomy 4:1–2, Israel was again commanded to do all that the Lord had commanded that they might possess the land. Israel was reminded how the Lord humbled her by letting her hunger in the wilderness, making her entirely dependent upon the Lord for food. The Lord provided Israel with manna from heaven so that it would become clear that "man does not live on bread alone but on every word that comes from the mouth of the LORD" (8:3). Here again we witness the sufficiency of God's commands. The Lord knew that if Israel had plenty, she would forget the Lord, his long history of deliverance and provision, and his covenant, and go after foreign false gods—a problem that would apply to Israel once she was in the land (8:11–20). Israel was to stick to the commands of the Lord and remember them always, for these commands were all she needed. They were the spiritual food that was to satisfy and sustain her soul. She was to mark every word from God's mouth.

It was no accident that Jesus quoted from Deuteronomy 8:3 in

Matthew 4:4. Jesus was in the wilderness just as Israel was, symbolically indicated by his forty days and forty nights of fasting.[11] Like Israel, he was hungry. So the devil came to him, as he did to Israel, tempting him to break his fast by feasting on stones the devil said Jesus could turn into bread. Jesus saw through Satan's schemes, something Israel could not do, and quoted from Deuteronomy 8:3 to show that the words of God were his food, sufficient even in his time of testing. Israel failed to live by God's all-sufficient words, but Jesus, in his exodus, did not fail but found them to be enough, making good on their promises.[12]

In the book of Acts, the Bereans were characterized as believing in the sufficiency of Scripture. Paul and Silas traveled to Berea and taught the Jews there in the synagogue. We read, "Now the Berean Jews were of more noble character than those in Thessalonica, for they received the message with great eagerness and examined the Scriptures every day to see if what Paul said was true" (Acts 17:11). What is assumed in the Berean response to Paul? First, their actions assume that Scripture is the final authority. The validity and veracity of Paul's message is tested against the Scriptures. Second, their actions assume that Scripture is enough; it is enough to verify or disprove Paul's message. What was the result of taking Scripture seriously? Faith. "Many of them believed" (17:12).

Or consider Paul's letter to the Romans. Paul writes in 15:4, "For everything that was written in the past was written to teach us, so that through the endurance taught in the Scriptures and the encouragement they provide we might have hope." Paul is referring to the Old Testament, and not only does he assume the inspiration of the Old Testament but he also assumes its sufficiency. The Old Testament was written for the instruction of the new covenant believer in Jesus Christ (cf. 1 Pet 1:10–12). Here is evidence that Scripture transcends its original time and place of impact. The Old Testament not only instructed Old Testament saints but New Testament saints as well. Paul even goes so far as to say that this was one of its purposes and goals. Paul seems to have in mind the christological nature of the Old Testament, for in Romans 15:3 (ESV) he applies Psalm 69:9 to Christ, who "did not please himself" but suffered the reproach of others. The Old Testament, then, pointed forward to Christ, which is one of the major

---

11. Grant R. Osborne, *Matthew*, ZECNT (Grand Rapids: Zondervan, 2010), 133.
12. Compare Luke 16:17, 24–29; 24:25–27; John 4:34; 6:35; Acts 2:14–40.

ways it instructs us still today, even when it comes to the practicality of living in harmony with one another.

Paul also appeals to the Old Testament to warn New Testament believers, in 1 Corinthians 10:1–12, against idolatry. Paul draws his Corinthian readers to "our fathers" who "ate the same spiritual food" and "drank the same spiritual drink," for they "drank from the spiritual Rock that followed them, and the Rock was Christ" (10:1, 3–4 ESV). Tragically, "God was not pleased with most of them; their bodies were scattered in the wilderness" (10:5). Why did all of these things take place? Paul says, "These things occurred as examples to keep us from setting our hearts on evil things as they did" (10:6). Paul reiterates his point in verse 11, "These things happened to them as examples and were written down as warnings for us, on whom the culmination of the ages has come." Once again, Paul appeals to the written Scriptures, the Old Testament, to show that they were written to instruct not only Israel but those living at the end of the ages as well.

Perhaps the most important passage supporting sufficiency is 2 Timothy 3:14–17. Paul instructs Timothy to continue in the "Holy Scriptures" that he has known since childhood for they "are able to make you wise for salvation" (v. 15 ESV). Then Paul says, "All Scripture is God-breathed and is useful for teaching, rebuking, correcting and training in righteousness, so that the servant of God may be thoroughly equipped for every good work" (3:16–17). Scripture is not merely helpful but is *the* source we turn to for all of life as a Christian. Anything God would call us to do in obedience to his will as his children can be found in Scripture. Scripture teaches, reproves, corrects, and even trains us in righteousness. Those who follow God follow Scripture and find that Scripture will instruct them in living a godly life.

Paul says the same in regard to the preaching of God's Word. "Preach the word; be prepared in season and out of season; correct, rebuke and encourage—with great patience and careful instruction" (2 Tim 4:2). The belief is that God's Word is competent to do all that is necessary to lead God's people in the way they should go.

Peter also teaches Scripture's sufficiency. He starts off his second epistle saying that God's "divine power has granted to us all things that pertain to life and godliness, through the knowledge of him who called us to his own glory and excellence" (2 Pet 1:3 ESV). Then Peter not only affirms the inspiration of the prophets (1:20–21) but tells his readers to pay attention to "the prophetic message as something completely reliable" (v. 19). Why? Because it is like a "light shining in a dark place, until the day dawns and the morning star rises in your hearts" (v. 19; cf. Ps 119:105). That day, which refers to Christ's second coming, has not yet arrived. In the meantime, we need this light if we are going to see and not stumble in darkness. As Calvin noted, without the light of the Word, there is nothing left but darkness.[13]

Finally, we see the sufficiency of Scripture in the last book of the Bible. We read in Revelation 22:18–19, "I warn everyone who hears the words of the prophecy of this scroll: If anyone adds anything to them, God will add to that person the plagues described in this scroll. And if anyone takes words away from this scroll of prophecy, God will take away from that person any share in the tree of life and in the Holy City, which are described in this scroll." John's warning implies that the book of Revelation is inspired by God and is just as authoritative and canonical as the Old Testament. John's warning concerns the book of Revelation in particular, not all Scripture. However, it is not improper to apply his words here to all Scripture, for the principle stands. After all, John is reiterating what the Old Testament said, as seen in Deuteronomy 4:2; 12:32; Proverbs 30:5–6. Moreover, in God's providence, Revelation is the last word to his church. Because of its place in the canon, it speaks to the whole canon and warns against taking away or adding to what God has inspired.[14]

Sufficiency isn't a doctrine Protestants invented as they parted ways with Rome. It is biblically rooted and supported, having enormous implications for how the believer lives the Christian life.

What about Extrabiblical Sources?

If Scripture is sufficient, is it wrong for the believer to look to or utilize extrabiblical sources? No. Remember, *sola Scriptura* is not arguing that Scripture is the only authority or the only source from which we can draw (i.e., *nuda Scriptura*).[15] It is arguing that while there may be

---

13. John Calvin, *Commentaries on the Catholic Epistles*, trans. and ed. John Owen (repr., Grand Rapids: Baker, 2005), 388 (commentary on 1 Pet 1:19).

14. Other texts to consider on sufficiency include Matt 5:43–44; 15:2–9; Mark 7:5–13; Luke 16:31; Acts 17:11; 1 Cor 4:6.

15. For a very helpful treatment of this point, see Anthony N. S. Lane, "*Sola Scriptura?* Making Sense of a Post-Reformation Slogan," in *A Pathway into Holy Scripture*, ed. P. E. Satterthwaite and D. F. Wright (Grand Rapids: Eerdmans, 1994), 297–328.

other good sources, these are always fallible and inferior to Scripture, which alone is infallible and supreme, and unlike other sources it alone is divine revelation. When the Reformed confessions say Scripture is our "sole" authority, they do not mean that there are no other authorities we should listen to or even submit to (creeds, councils, etc.), but rather that these authorities and sources are always subordinate to Scripture. Therefore, it is not a violation of *sola Scriptura* to recognize that extrabiblical sources, though never to be put on par with Scripture, can be helpful and advantageous.[16]

That said, two steps must be taken whenever we utilize extrabiblical sources. First, from the start we must acknowledge that no matter how impressive the source, it is always a *fallible, imperfect source*, unlike Scripture, which, as we have seen, is our only inerrant authority. As long as we are dealing with an uninspired, fallible source, it cannot be fully sufficient for faith and practice. Contrary to Rome, this means that we do not look to the church to give us a supplemental revelation, one that goes above and beyond the Bible. Rather, the church serves to come beside us, directing our attention to the definitive, final, and sufficient Word of Scripture.[17]

We also can't seek a revelation from the Holy Spirit that will supplement the Bible or improve upon it. Since Scripture is sufficient for all people at all times, the Spirit's role is to assist us in understanding and applying God's definitive Word. Scripture reassures us that should we come to God's Word with the Spirit as our counselor, the Lord will reward our hungry soul with sweet and satisfying food (1 John 2:20, 26–27).[18]

Second, our use of extrabiblical sources can never be done *independently* of Scripture. Doing so can quickly lead to the subordination of Scripture to an extrabiblical resource. Since Scripture is the supreme and final standard, then all other sources must be subservient to Scripture. Archaeology, mathematics, psychology, literature, philosophy, and, yes, even science are maidservants to the only inspired and inerrant source, Scripture.[19] These other sources are not to function as

---

16. Frame, *Apologetics to the Glory of God*, 19.
17. Scott R. Swain, *Trinity, Revelation, and Reading: A Theological Introduction to the Bible and Its Interpretation* (New York: T&T Clark, 2011), 86.
18. Ibid.
19. Vern Poythress, *Inerrancy and Worldview* (Wheaton, IL: Crossway, 2012), 209.

interpretive lords, but as interpretive assistants.[20] So where the methods, presuppositions, and conclusions of these disciplines (and many others) contradict those of Scripture, they must be abandoned.[21]

Contemporary Challenges to Sufficiency

Unfortunately, today there are several ways in which sufficiency is challenged and undermined. Three deserve our attention.

1. Traditionalism

As seen in chapter 1, the role of tradition is at the core of the Protestant-Catholic divide. However, before we dive into those shark-infested waters, we must first wade through a preliminary issue, namely, the discomfort evangelicals have with tradition.

Evangelicalism's Allergy to Tradition

I wish I could say that all evangelicals have a crisp, accurate grasp of *sola Scriptura*. I am hopeful that many understand how a Protestant view of Scripture and tradition differs from Rome's position. However, I am less confident that evangelicals understand the difference between *sola* and *nuda Scriptura*, for all too often the latter is assumed to be the identity of the former.[22]

Some evangelicals, intentionally or unintentionally, have followed in the footsteps of Alexander Campbell (1788–1866), who said, "I have endeavored to read the Scriptures as though no one had read them before me, and I am as much on my guard against reading them today, through the medium of my own views yesterday, or a week ago, as I am against being influenced by any foreign name, authority, or system

---

20. Swain, *Trinity, Revelation, and Reading*, 85–87.
21. Frame, *Apologetics to the Glory of God*, 21.
22. Unfortunately, evangelicals who have converted to Rome have only made the situation worse. They all too often confuse and equate *nuda Scriptura* with *sola Scriptura*, assuming the former to be the Protestant position. For example, Francis Beckwith, "Part 2: Catholicism," in *Journeys of Faith: Evangelicalism, Eastern Orthodoxy, Catholicism, and Anglicanism*, ed. Robert L. Plummer (Grand Rapids: Zondervan, 2012), 81–136; Christian Smith, *The Bible Made Impossible: Why Biblicism Is Not a Truly Evangelical Reading of Scripture* (Grand Rapids: Brazos, 2011), 4–5, 181; Christian Smith, *How to Go from Being a Good Evangelical to a Committed Catholic in Ninety-Five Difficult Steps* (Eugene, OR: Cascade, 2011), 29–32, 83–91 (esp. 89–90). With both Beckwith and Smith, one can see that in swimming the Tiber, they sometimes had a mistaken understanding of what *sola Scriptura* means and entails. This same misunderstanding of *sola Scriptura* can be found in Stanley Hauerwas, *Unleashing the Scripture: Freeing the Bible from Captivity to America* (Nashville: Abingdon, 1993), 155.

whatever."[23] Ironically, such a view cannot preserve *sola Scriptura*. While tradition is not being elevated to the level of Scripture, the individual is! In this approach, our individual opinion of what we think is or is not biblical becomes the supreme judge and final arbitrator.[24] To be sure, such a view lends itself more in the direction of Enlightenment individual autonomy than Reformational and scriptural accountability. When such a view takes off in the context of a community, what results is anti-traditional traditionalism of the worst kind.[25] As a Baptist, I will be the first to admit that my own heritage has at times contributed to this form of ecclesiastical cancer.

So how do we correct such a mistake? First, we must guard against taking on an individualistic mind-set that prides itself on what "I think" rather than listening to the past. To do that we must acknowledge that "Scripture alone" doesn't mean "me alone."[26]

Second, tradition is not a second infallible source of divine revelation alongside Scripture; nevertheless, where it is consistent with Scripture, it can and should act as a *ministerial* authority. The historic creeds and confessions are examples. While the Nicene Creed and the Chalcedonian Creed are not to be considered infallible sources of divine revelation, their consistency with Scripture means that the church spoke authoritatively against heresy. Therefore, it should trouble us, to say the least, to find ourselves disagreeing with orthodox creeds that have stood the test of time. Innovation is often the first indication of heresy. This is why the Reformers sought to tie their exegesis all the way back to the patristic tradition, countering Rome's accusations that the Reformers were inventing new doctrines. Of course, the Reformers ultimately appealed not to the fathers but to Scripture itself, a method the fathers themselves would have approved.[27]

In that light, abandoning *nuda Scriptura* does not require us to go to the other extreme, namely, elevating tradition to the level of

---

23. *The Christian Baptist*, April 3, 1826, 229, cited in Nathan O. Hatch, *The Democratization of American Christianity* (New Haven: Yale University Press, 1989), 179. See also Nathan O. Hatch, "*Sola Scriptura* and *Novus Ordo Seclorum*," in *The Bible in America*, ed. Nathan O. Hatch and Mark A. Noll (Oxford: Oxford University Press, 1982), 59–78.

24. Mathison, *Shape of Sola Scriptura*, 252.

25. Richard Lints, *The Fabric of Theology: A Prologomenon to Evangelical Theology* (Grand Rapids: Eerdmans, 1993), 91.

26. Mathison, *Shape of Sola Scriptura*, 252.

27. Timothy George, *Reading Scripture with the Reformers* (Downers Grove, IL: IVP Academic, 2011), 81.

Scripture. But it does require the humility to realize that we are always standing on the shoulders of those who came before us (Gal 1:8; 2 Thess 2:15; 2 Tim 3:14–15). Indeed, the very concept of tradition—from the Latin *traditio*, meaning "handing over, handing down, or handing on"—is inherently biblical (e.g., Luke 1:2; 16:4; 1 Cor 11:23; 15:1–4; 2 Thess 2:15; 2 Tim 1:14; Jude 3).[28] The Reformers were standout models in this regard. The fathers, they insisted, were valuable (though not infallible) guides in biblical interpretation, and yet Scripture stands above them. We would be wise to listen to Luther: "Now if anyone of the saintly fathers can show that his interpretation is based on Scripture, and if Scripture proves that this is the way it should be interpreted, then the interpretation is right. If this is not the case, I must not believe him."[29]

Rome's Elevation of Tradition

While strands of evangelicalism may suffer from a malnourished dose of tradition, Rome's view, for the evangelical, is tradition on steroids. But before we can see why, we must review what Rome believes.[30]

As we discussed in chapter 1, Rome affirms Tradition 2, meaning that both Scripture and unwritten oral tradition are sources of divine, infallible revelation. While there were some theologians in the medieval period who believed tradition was subservient and ministerial to Scripture, the canon lawyers saw both Scripture and tradition as equal sources of authority.[31] In the sixteenth century, the Council of

---

28. Alister E. McGrath, "Faith and Tradition," in *The Oxford Handbook of Evangelical Theology*, ed. Gerald R. McDermott (New York: Oxford University Press, 2010), 84–85.

29. *LW* 30:166.

30. Space constrains us, but time would be well spent to also survey the view of Eastern Orthodoxy, which differs from Rome in certain ways. See Timothy Ware, *The Orthodox Church* (London: Penguin, 1997); Hierodeacon Gregory, *The Church, Tradition, Scripture, Truth, and Christian Life: Some Heresies of Evangelicalism and an Orthodox Response* (Etna, CA: Center for Traditionalist Orthodox Studies, 1995); Georges Florovsky, *Bible, Church, Tradition: An Eastern Orthodox View*, ed. Richard S. Haugh, The Collected Works 1 (Vaduz: Büchervertriebsanstalt, 1987); Archimandrite Chrysostomos and Archimandrite Auxentios, *Scripture and Tradition* (Etna, CA: Center for Traditionalist Orthodox Studies, 1994); Daniel B. Clendenin, ed. *Eastern Orthodox Theology* (Grand Rapids: Baker, 1995); James Stamoolis, ed., *Three Views on Eastern Orthodoxy and Evangelicalism* (Grand Rapids: Zondervan, 2004). For a critique, see Mathison, *Shape of Sola Scriptura*, 225–35; Michael Horton, "Are Eastern Orthodoxy and Evangelicalism Compatible? No," in Stamoolis, *Three Views on Eastern Orthodoxy and Evangelicalism*, 126–28.

31. For the former theologians, see, e.g., Duns Scotus, Pierre D'Ailly. See Michael Horton, *The Christian Faith* (Grand Rapids: Zondervan, 2011), 187; Richard A. Muller, *PRRD*, 1:41. My discussion of Rome is indebted at points to Horton.

Trent (1545–1563) rejected the Reformers' doctrine of *sola Scriptura*, arguing that God's Word consists of both Scripture and tradition. The latter, Rome argued, has been passed down from Peter to his successors, a belief that assumes Peter's office continues to this day with the pope and magisterium. Therefore, Rome affirms a three-legged stool in terms of authority: Scripture, tradition, and the magisterium (the official teaching office of Rome, consisting of the pope, bishops, and councils).

In 1870 the First Vatican Council officially declared papal infallibility dogma, meaning that when the pope speaks "from the chair" (*ex cathedra*) he does so infallibly.[32] The Second Vatican Council (1962–65) also affirmed the succession of Peter's office in the pope and continued to uphold tradition as an equal authority. Tradition and Scripture were said to flow "from the same divine wellspring" and "merge into a unity."[33] "Consequently, it is *not* from sacred Scripture *alone* that the Church draws her certainty about everything that has been revealed. So, both sacred tradition and sacred Scripture are to be accepted and venerated with the *same* sense of devotion and reverence."[34] This last sentence strongly echoes the Council of Trent. Like Trent, Vatican II rejects *sola Scriptura*, elevating tradition to an equal platform as Scripture, both said to be flowing from the same source as divine revelation. "Sacred tradition and sacred Scripture," says Vatican II, "form one sacred deposit of the word of God, which is committed to the Church."[35]

Therefore, Vatican II asserts, the "task of authentically interpreting the word of God, whether written or handed on, has been entrusted exclusively to the living teaching office of the Church." While the document goes on to say that "this teaching office is not above the word of God, but serves it," Vatican II cannot mean this in the way that the Reformers did, for it then says this teaching office "draws from this one deposit of faith everything which it presents for belief as divinely revealed."[36] So while this teaching office may serve the Word of God,

32. Session 3 of the "First Vatican Council," in *Creeds and Confessions of Faith in Christian Tradition*, vol. 3, *Part Five: Statements of Faith in Modern Christianity*, ed. Jaroslav Pelikan and Valerie Hotchkiss (New Haven: Yale University Press, 2003), 346.

33. Walter M. Abbott, ed., *The Documents of Vatican II*, trans. Joseph Gallagher (New York: American, 1966), 115–16.

34. Ibid., 117, emphasis added.

35. Ibid.

36. Ibid.

it originates from the one holy deposit along with Scripture and must be equally revered as God's Word. Vatican II then concludes, "It is clear, therefore, that sacred tradition, sacred Scripture, and the teaching authority of the Church, in accord with God's most wise design, are so linked and joined together that one cannot stand without the others, and that all together and each in its own way under the action of the one Holy Spirit contribute effectively to the salvation of souls."[37] Scripture, therefore, is absolutely dependent upon tradition and the authority of the church so that, apart from it, Scripture cannot stand. Here we see the abandonment of Scripture's sufficiency.

Some contemporary, progressive Roman Catholics, such as Karl Rahner, Hans Küng, Yves Congar, George Tavard, and J. R. Geiselmann have sought to promote a view which says Scripture, in some sense, is uniquely normative.[38] Geiselmann, for instance, kicks against the traditional interpretation of Trent, what we called Tradition 2 (T2) or the two-source view in chapter 1. This is the view that revelation is contained partly in Scripture and partly in Tradition. However, Geiselmann argues that Trent left the issue undecided. We should not believe, he insists, that there are two taps, Scripture and Tradition, but rather one. Revelation has one source, though expressed in two modes, Scripture and tradition.[39] Most ecumenically minded, progressive Catholics today take this line of argument.[40]

---

37. Ibid., 118.

38. For example, J. R. Geiselmann, "Scripture, Tradition, and the Church: An Ecumenical Problem," in *Christianity Divided*, ed. D. J. Callahan, H. A. Obermann, and D. J. O'Hanlon (London: Sheed and Ward, 1962), 39–72; Karl Rahner, *Theological Investigations*, vol. 6 (London: Darton, Longman & Todd, 1974), 107–12; Thomas G. Guarino, "Catholic Reflections on Discerning the Truth of Sacred Scripture," in *Your Word Is Truth: A Project of Evangelicals and Catholics Together*, ed. Charles Colson and Richard John Neuhaus (Grand Rapids: Eerdmans, 2002), 79–101.

39. Here the distinction between formal and material sufficiency is clarifying. Strimple explains that all Catholics agree, whether progressive or conservative, that Scripture is *formally* insufficient. This means that "the Bible is not sufficient in itself to give anyone a knowledge of God's will because that cannot be understood apart from the authoritative understanding and interpretation of the Scripture." Where the debate lies, however, concerns the material sufficiency/insufficiency. Is Tradition merely explicative or does it actually have a "constitutive value"? Progressives try in some way to affirm material sufficiency while rejecting its formal sufficiency. Robert Strimple, "The Relationship between Scripture and Tradition in Contemporary Roman Catholic Theology," *Westminster Theological Journal* 40, no. 1 (1977): 24–25.

40. For this reason, certain Protestants have been ecumenically optimistic. E.g., G. C. Berkouwer, *The Second Vatican Council and the New Catholicism*, trans. L. B. Smedes (Grand Rapids: Eerdmans, 1965). However, this is a mistake. As Strimple points out, such Protestants fail to realize that proposals like Geiselmann's are grounded in a post-Kantian

However, the response of Cardinal Ratzinger (Pope Benedict XVI) speaks volumes as to where Rome has stood and still does stand on this issue. Since those like Geiselmann are Catholic theologians, Ratzinger argues, they must "hold fast to Catholic dogmas as such, but none of them is to be had *sola scriptura,* neither the great dogmas of Christian antiquity, of what was once the *consensus quinquesaecularis,* nor, even less, the new ones of 1854 and 1950."[41] By "new ones" Ratzinger has in mind the 1854 bull *Ineffabilis Deus,* which promulgated the Immaculate Conception of the Virgin Mary (i.e., Rome's belief in her perpetual sinlessness), as well as the 1950 Apostolic Constitution *Munificentissimus Deus,* which declared the Bodily Assumption of the Virgin Mary into heaven official church dogma.[42] With *extrascriptural* dogmas like these in mind, dogmas *every* Catholic theologian must subscribe to as official church teaching, "what sense is there," asks Ratzinger, "in talking about the sufficiency of Scripture?" In the spirit of Trent's opposition to the Reformers, Ratzinger then concludes: "Scripture is *not* revelation but at most only a *part* of the latter's greater reality."[43] In other words, room within the category of revelation must be made for Tradition, for it too is said to be an infallible source of divine revelation.

Notice, Ratzinger is very honest here: there are doctrines of the Catholic faith not found in Scripture. Instead, they are found in Tradition.[44] But from a Protestant vantage point, not only are these

---

and post-Bultmannian view of revelation. "On Geiselmann's view, the contemporary Roman Catholic view, *neither* Scripture *nor* tradition is truly authoritative. That is why the theological situation in the Roman Catholic Church today is *worse,* if anything, than it was at the time of the dispute with the Reformers" (ibid., 31).

41. Karl Rahner and Joseph Ratzinger, *Revelation and Tradition,* trans. W. J. O'Hara (Freiburg: Herder, 1966), 33. *Consensus quinquesaecularis* is a reference to Rome's belief that the church was characterized by ecclesiastical unity and doctrinal purity until AD 500.

42. Pope Pius IX, *Ineffabilis Deus* (December 8, 1854), Papal Encyclicals, http://www. papalencyclicals.net/Pius09/p9ineff.htm; Pope Pius XII, *Munificentissimus Deus* (November 1, 1950); Vatican, http://www.vatican.va/holy_father/pius_xii/apost_constitutions/documents/hf_p-xii_apc_19501101_munificentissimus-deus_en.html.

43. Rahner and Ratzinger, *Revelation and Tradition,* 29, 36–37, 44.

44. For this reason, those who hold a traditional interpretation of Trent argue that the burden of proof is on individuals like Geiselmann and his new interpretation. As Strimple insightfully observes, "To show that the Roman Catholic Church has been wrong for four hundred years requires extremely persuasive proof, these theologians insist. They view Geiselmann's 'one-source' theory of revelation as an ecumenical device. To say that all Roman Catholic doctrines are found in the Bible, they argue, is patently false. Consider for example ... the doctrine of the bodily assumption of the blessed virgin Mary. Where in the Bible is the doctrine of the assumption of Mary to be found? The fact that there are seven sacraments:

doctrines *in addition to* Scripture (i.e., extrabiblical), but these doctrines (e.g., bodily assumption of Mary, immaculate conception of Mary) are *in contradiction to* Scripture (i.e., contra-biblical).[45] In the end, it seems that Ratzinger and Rome have conflated inspiration and illumination. "Eliminating any qualitative distinction between apostolic and postapostolic offices and traditions," laments Michael Horton, "Rome denies the sufficiency of Scripture as the sole rule for faith and practice. Just as the New Testament supplements the Old Testament, Ratzinger argues, the church's ongoing interpretation supplements both."[46] This is nothing less than a rejection of *sola Scriptura*.

That said, we must do justice to the diversity that exists among Catholics on the relationship between Church and canon. Some have argued that the Church simply recognized the canon but did not create it. Michael Kruger points out that they still argue that the Church is the "sole and fundamental means by which we infallibly *know* which books belong in the canon."[47] In this sense, then, the canon depends upon the Church. Representatives argue that this is the position taken by Vatican I.[48]

But many others disagree. It is not enough to see the Church as the "sole and fundamental means by which we infallibly *know* which books belong in the canon." Scripture is actually *derivative* from the Church, so that the Church creates and causes the canon, investing it with authority. Variations of this view can be seen in the writings of Karl Rahner, Peter Kreeft, Hans Küng, and many others. As Küng claims,

---

where, the conservatives argue, is that doctrine found in the Bible? If Geiselmann or others should answer that there is a 'hint' of it in the Scripture, they reply that this is hardly sufficient to satisfy the statement that all revelation is contained in the Scripture. No, they insist, tradition goes beyond Scripture in both clarity and content" (Strimple, "Relationship between Scripture and Tradition," 27–28).

45. Sinclair B. Ferguson, "Scripture and Tradition," in *Sola Scriptura: The Protestant Position on the Bible*, ed. Don Kistler (Orlando, FL: Reformation Trust, 2009), 107. Also see Anthony N. S. Lane, "Roman Catholic Views of Biblical Authority from the Late Nineteenth Century to the Present," in *The Enduring Authority of the Christian Scriptures*, ed. D. A. Carson (Grand Rapids: Eerdmans, 2016), 306–7.

46. Horton, *Christian Faith*, 189.

47. Michael J. Kruger, *Canon Revisited: Establishing the Origins and Authority of the New Testament Books* (Wheaton, IL: Crossway, 2012), 41. For my points above, I am indebted to Kruger.

48. Joseph T. Lienhard, *The Bible, the Church, and Authority* (Collegeville, MN: Liturgical, 1995), 72; George H. Tavard, *Holy Writ or Holy Church: The Crisis of the Protestant Reformation* (New York: Harper, 1959), 66. On Vatican I, see Norman P. Tanner, ed., *Decrees of the Ecumenical Councils*, 2 vols. (Washington, DC: Georgetown University Press, 1990), 2:806.

"Without the Church there would be no New Testament."[49] This view sounds similar to that expressed by Cardinal Stanislaus Hosius, papal legate to the Council of Trent, when he boldly declared, "The Scriptures have only as much force as the fables of Aesop, if destitute of the authority of the Church."[50]

In the end, both views compromise *sola Scriptura* and a biblical understanding of the canon, which brings us to our next point under discussion.

Sufficiency, Canon, and Authority

How are we to respond to Rome's elevation of tradition? To begin with, evangelicals can learn something from Rome. Sadly, some evangelical circles have emptied their churches of historical awareness and appreciation, and few laypeople today know anything about the seven ecumenical councils or the church fathers. When confronted with information about them, they see them as irrelevant to Christian living. Is it any surprise, then, that when a tradition-starved churchgoer stumbles across Rome's veneration of tradition, he decides to cross the Tiber? Indeed, some feel robbed of this rich heritage. So our first response to Rome should not be to rid our churches of tradition, for this will only leave evangelical churches theologically shallow.

While we should reintroduce a healthy dose of tradition back into our evangelical churches, we cannot go in the direction of Rome for several reasons.

First, Rome reverses the biblical order between the Word of God and the people of God. As seen already, Rome functionally elevates Tradition to the level of Scripture. But behind this elevation is an assumption, namely, that the Church created and brought into existence the Scriptures (the canon). Apart from the Church declaring the books of the Bible to be Scripture, these books would not be authoritative or canonical. In short, the Church not only decides but actually invests authority into the books we now call canonical.[51] Therefore, the

---

49. Hans Küng, *The Council in Action: Theological Reflections on the Second Vatican Council*, trans. C. Hastings (New York: Sheed and Ward, 1963), 187. See also Peter Kreeft, *Catholic Christianity* (San Francisco: Ignatius, 2001), 20; Karl Rahner, *Foundations of Christian Faith: An Introduction to the Idea of Christianity* (New York: Crossroad, 1997), 362; Karl Keating, *Catholicism and Fundamentalism* (San Francisco: Ignatius, 1988), 127.

50. Quoted in Kruger, *Canon Revisited*, 39–40.

51. *Canon* means rule, measure, or list. When applied to Scripture, we are referring to the books of the OT and NT that are fixed and final.

authority of the Church precedes the authority of the canon.[52] As a result, Scripture in and of itself is insufficient. The Church is needed from the start as Scripture's originating cause and birth mother. Such a view impacts not only Scripture's sufficiency but also its *necessity*. The Bible may be crucial for the Church's *well-being* (*bene esse*). However, when it comes to the Church's *being* (*esse*), its very existence, the Bible is unnecessary. If the Bible were to be erased from history tomorrow, the Church would continue, thanks to its second authoritative and infallible source of divine revelation: Tradition. Since the Church produced Scripture, it can survive even if Scripture vanishes.[53]

The Reformers, and Protestants ever since, protested such a view.[54] The people of God did not create the Word of God, but the Word of God created the people of God. Scripture itself bears witness to this proper relation between Word and people. From the beginning of creation, God spoke and brought not only the cosmos into existence but Adam and Eve whom he made in his own image and likeness (Gen 1:27). God called Abraham out of his country to a land that God would give him, promising that he would make a great nation out of him (Gen 12:1–3) and create a people for his own glory (Isa 43:1, 7). "I AM" then spoke to Moses from the burning bush, instructing him to go to Pharaoh, for God would set his people free (Exod 3:4). When Israel was delivered from Pharaoh through plagues and the parting of the Red Sea, and entered the wilderness, it was the Lord who spoke once more, entering into a covenant with his people. With his own finger Yahweh wrote down his Law, and Israel was to follow it out of obedience to the God who had made them his chosen people (Exod 20:1–21). God handed Israel his written Law; Israel received it and recognized it for what it was: the Word of God.

God then promised to cut a new covenant, God being the one who would give his people a new heart and a new spirit (Ezek 36:26), causing them to walk in his statutes, putting his Sprit within (36:27). God would open their graves and raise up their dead, dry bones (37:12). As promised, the dead bones rattled at the word of the Lord, and with flesh on them they became a great army (37:4–10).

---

52. Oliphint, "Because It Is the Word of God," 13.

53. Bavinck critiques Rome on this point repeatedly. Herman Bavinck, *Reformed Dogmatics*, vol. 1, *Prolegomena*, ed. John Bolt, trans. John Vriend (Grand Rapids: Baker, 2003), 1:450.

54. Muller, *PRRD*, 2:172–79.

When the new covenant came, it was inaugurated through the blood of Christ. But who is Christ? He is the eternal Word (John 1:1). And what does the Word do? He grants grace (John 1:16) and bestows eternal life (John 3:16–17), and by giving eternal life he creates a people who are spiritually alive. How does the Word do this? The eternal Word who created the cosmos (1:1) creates a new covenant people through his blood, the blood of the covenant (Matt 26:28). He is the shepherd and we are his called-out sheep (John 10:1–5).

At Pentecost, it was the Helper, the Spirit whom Jesus promised, who took the word of the gospel and fashioned a global people (Acts 2). As the word of the gospel was preached, the Spirit drew God's elect to the Son, and the church came together around the Son, being called Christians (Acts 11:26). The apostles were the recipients of the Spirit Jesus had promised would bring to their remembrance all that Jesus had taught them (John 14:26). As seen throughout Acts, not only did the apostles proclaim this good news, but they put this gospel into writing. The churches who received the Word did not function as lords over it, but as servants. They did not claim authority over the message, but submitted to it as God-breathed and authoritative. They did not create it, but merely recognized it for what it was, the Word of God. The church, therefore, was and is an assembly of the Word and an assembly under the Word.[55]

We do not want to deny the obvious fact that chronologically speaking, the written Scriptures came after the establishment of God's people (e.g., Israel was called out of Egypt before they received the Ten Commandments, and the church assembled in Acts prior to receiving the letters of the apostles, or at least the entire New Testament canon).[56] True as this may be, it does not follow that the authority of Scripture is derived from the church. Such logic fails to recognize, as the Reformers rightly did, both the unwritten and written word—*verbum agraphon et engraphon.*[57] It was God himself who established his people, and he did this by speaking words to them, words that brought them into existence

---

55. On the Word as the foundation of the church, see Deut 4:1; Isa 8:20; Ezek 20:19; Luke 16:29; John 5:39; Eph 2:20; 2 Tim 3:14; 2 Pet 1:23. Bavinck, *Reformed Dogmatics,* 1:458.

56. Ibid., 1:469–72.

57. See Muller, *DLGTT,* s.v. *verbum Dei,* 324; Heinrich Bullinger, *The Decades of Henry Bullinger,* ed. Thomas Harding, 4 vols. (1849–52; repr., Grand Rapids: Reformation Heritage, 2004), serm. 1, 1:54.

in the first place and were eventually written down. As chapter 5 notes, God's speech was not only powerful but creative, effecting exactly what he intended. God's people did not invest God's words with authority. Quite the opposite. It was God who breathed out his own words, words that called his elect to himself and gathered them together, only to then give them a written Word that would have permanent value. Therefore, when it comes to the books of the Bible, it was God, not his people, who invested Scripture with authority (more on this in a moment). As Luther said so vividly, "Scripture is the womb from which arises divine truth and the Church."[58]

What does this mean for the canon? It means that a canon exists the minute the books of the New Testament are written. For the canon is comprised of only those books that God has inspired and given to his bride, the church.[59] The church did not give us the canon, but God gave the canon to the church, which leads us to our next point.

Second, Rome has misunderstood the role of the church. In light of the previous discussion, the question naturally arises: What role, then, do the people of God have if it is not an inspired one on par with Scripture? Contrary to Rome, the church does not have an originating role, but rather its role is *derivative* and *instrumental*. Rather than creating the canon, as if the church itself imputes authority into the biblical books, the church simply *recognizes* the Bible for what it is, the Word of God. No more has the church given us the canon than Sir Isaac Newton gave us the power of gravity.[60]

Let's consider some illustrations of this. For example, what happens when a Christian confesses that "Jesus is Lord"?[61] When a Christian says these words, he is not *making* Jesus Lord, as if Jesus was not Lord until the individual spoke these words. Rather, Jesus's lordship is inherent in who he is and what he has done. Our words simply recognize what is already true. Consider another analogy. We can compare the church to a thermometer, but it should never be a thermostat. Both devices can tell us how hot or cold it is in a room, yet the thermometer merely reflects the temperature while the thermostat actually determines the temperature.[62] Or consider several illustrations from Calvin

---

58. Martin Luther, *First Lectures on the Psalms 1*, in *LW* 10:397.
59. Kruger, *Canon Revisited*, 38 (cf. 58).
60. J. I. Packer, *God Has Spoken: Revelation and the Bible* (Grand Rapids: Baker, 1993), 109.
61. This illustration is from R. C. Sproul, who has used it in various lectures.
62. Illustration from Michael J. Kruger, "Recent Challenges to the New Testament

in his response to Rome's objection: "How can we be assured that this [the Bible] has sprung from God unless we have recourse to the decree of the church?" Calvin answers, "It is as if someone asked: Whence will we learn to distinguish light from darkness, white from black, sweet from bitter? Indeed, Scripture exhibits fully as clear evidence of its own truth as white and black things do of their color, or sweet and bitter things do of their taste."[63]

Calvin's illustrations remind us of the *self-authenticating* nature of God's Word (see the end of chapter 3). Scripture does not depend upon a higher authority for its verification. The pope, reason, experience, culture, and science do not sit above Scripture. Rather, Scripture possesses its own infallible authority "by virtue" of what it inherently is (the Word of God). While everything else is vulnerable to error, Scripture is not and serves as its own witness.[64] Scripture is not waiting around for some other authority to authenticate, confirm, or justify what it says. Scripture is not longing for someone or something else for its validation. Scripture's authority finally rests upon the God of truth. We are to receive his Word precisely because it is *his* Word, not ours. We don't accept it because we have in some clever way proven it to be his Word or because we have authoritatively and decisively declared it to be his Word.[65] Rather, we accept it because of what it inherently is, namely, the Word of the living God. Or to state the point philosophically, "Self-attestation is embedded authority."[66]

Many will balk at this point, saying that we believe Scripture is the Word of God because Scripture says it is the Word of God. But Christians are not merely saying that the Bible is God's Word because the Bible says so, but because God himself says so. Oliphint writes, "The point is that Scripture is the Word of God because God, who is truth itself, is its author."[67]

Unfortunately, Roman Catholics are not the only ones who have

---

Writings," in Garner, *Did God Really Say?*, 69.

63. John Calvin, *Institutes of the Christian Religion*, ed. John T. McNeill, trans. Ford Lewis Battles, 2 vols. (Philadelphia: Westminster, 1975), 1.7.2. Also note Johannes Wollebius's illustration of how it is foolish to think a candle receives light from the candlestick. See John W. Beardslee, *Reformed Dogmatics* (New York: Oxford University Press, 1965), 5–9.

64. Oliphint, "Because It Is the Word of God," 16.

65. Ibid., 15. See also Richard A. Muller, *PRRD*, 1:436–37.

66. Oliphint, "Because It Is the Word of God," 15.

67. Ibid.

rejected the self-authenticating nature of Scripture. Today, some Protestants do as well, emphasizing that the Bible is a human creation at its core.[68] However, such a view fails to recognize that the church is the *creatura verbi*—creation of the Word. The church did not elect a canon; the canon selected itself.[69] Or we can say that God selected his canon and then guided the church in its recognition of it. It's incorrect to state that without the church there can be no canon. What we should say is that if there is no canon, there can be no church.[70]

Third, Rome has misunderstood the foundational role of the apostles and the nature of authority thereafter. Scripture does not teach, as Rome claims, that there is a succession of apostles who make up an infallible stream of tradition and provide the infallible interpretation of Scripture, adding to Scripture their own infallible dogmas and traditions as they develop.[71] After the apostolic era, it is the written Word

---

68. For example, Craig D. Allert, *A High View of Scripture? The Authority of the Bible and the Formation of the New Testament Canon* (Grand Rapids: Baker Academic, 2007).

69. Kruger, "Recent Challenges to the New Testament Writings," 69. And as Barth said, "The Bible constitutes itself the Canon. It is the Canon because it imposed itself upon the Church" (Karl Barth, *Church Dogmatics*, 2nd ed., 14 vols., trans. G. W. Bromiley and T. F. Torrance [Edinburgh: T&T Clark, 1975], 1.1.107).

70. See Kruger, "Recent Challenges to the New Testament Writings," 69–70.

71. As addressed via Luther in chapter 1, Rome appeals to Matthew 16:18 as textual proof for the papacy, papal supremacy, and apostolic succession. However, there are several problems with Rome's exegesis: (1) It is rigorously debated whether it is upon Peter or his confession that Christ says he will build his church. Even if it is the former, this is a far cry from papal succession and supremacy. Jesus still makes such a promise to Peter *in light of Peter's confession*. In other words, Peter functions as the "rock" *in his act of confessing* Jesus as Messiah. Therefore, Jesus is not teaching that he will build a church with Peter as its supreme head. While Peter may be the genesis of such an ecclesiastical process (see Acts), Peter (via his confession) remains merely a witness to Christ, who alone is head of the church. Moreover, the other disciples would equally confess Christ and therefore be the foundation upon which the church was built (see Eph 2:20; Rev 21:14). (2) Yes, Jesus gives the keys of the kingdom to Peter, but Jesus does the same with the rest of the apostles as well (e.g., Matt 18:18; John 20:23). See Martin Luther, *On the Papacy in Rome against the Most Celebrated Romanist in Leipzig*, in *LW* 39:86–87. (3) Matthew 16:22–23 only undermines Petrine and papal infallibility and supremacy since Jesus rebukes Peter, even calling him Satan. Indeed, at times he is even made inferior to the other apostles, as evident in Paul's rebuke of Peter (Gal 2:6–11). At other times, the other disciples are placed on equal footing with Peter (Acts 8:14; 1 Cor 12:28; Gal 2:6, 9; Eph 4:11; Rev 21:14). Peter saw himself as merely a fellow elder to the other disciples (1 Pet 5:1–3), even one who must give an account to the other apostles (Acts 11:1–18). At the Jerusalem council, Peter's voice is no greater than that of anyone else, and James (not Peter) appears to have the leading voice in the matter (Acts 15:7–11). We also cannot forget that while Peter plays an instrumental role at the start of Acts, he is dropped from the narrative in Acts 15 as Paul becomes the focus of the early church and the NT canon. When Matthew 16:18 is interpreted in light of the rest of the NT, the rest of the apostles are just as foundational to the church as Peter (e.g., Matt 16:15–16; Eph 2:20). The NT, therefore, does not elevate Peter above the other disciples in authority. (4) Nowhere in this

alone that is apostolic. And those who pass on this apostolic tradition are never labeled apostles in Scripture, but preachers and teachers of the faith "once for all entrusted" to the saints (Jude 3). As Robert Saucy writes, "The apostolic word thus continues in the church through the authoritative Scriptures and not in an authoritative teaching office of the church."[72]

Such a point is clarified in Scripture. In Ephesians 2:19–20, for example, Paul says that the "household of God" is "built on the foundation of the apostles and prophets," and Jesus himself is the "cornerstone" (ESV; cf. 1 Pet 2:6–8). Calvin comments, "If the teaching of the prophets and apostles is the foundation, this must have had authority before the church began to exist."[73] To teach an apostolic succession is to stack layers of foundations upon the original foundation.[74] It is giving authority to ordinary ministers to lay the foundation all over again. But that undermines Paul's (and Peter's) metaphor entirely. There is one foundation, the apostles and prophets. The spiritual house that is then built on top is made up of the living stones (i.e., believers, not more apostles); in this house, every believer is a priest (1 Pet 2:4–5). In short, pouring the foundation is not the role or responsibility of the "living stones" that make up the "spiritual house" (1 Pet 2:5). We must distinguish between the apostles who laid the groundwork and all non-apostolic ministers who came after to add to the structure. Paul appears to assume such a metaphor when he says, "Like a skilled master builder I laid a foundation, and someone else is building upon it. For no one can lay a foundation other than that which is laid, which is Jesus Christ" (1 Cor 3:10–11 ESV). In the next chapter Paul warns the Corinthians: "Do not go beyond what is written" (4:6). Michael Horton says Paul "invoked the principle of *sola Scriptura* in forbidding the saints from going beyond the written texts." The Corinthians were to stay away from those "superapostles" who "led many Corinthians astray by

---

text is there even a hint of papal succession, and absent is any notion of an ongoing, perpetual, and infallible office. This notion has to be read back into the text. Similar arguments could be given in response to Rome's appeal to John 21:15–23.

72. Robert Saucy, *Scripture: Its Power, Authority, and Relevance* (Nashville: Nelson, 2001), 236, emphasis added.

73. Calvin, *Institutes*, 1.7.2. Also revisit our discussion of this passage and issue in chapter 1.

74. Herman Bavinck, *Reformed Dogmatics*, vol. 4, *Holy Spirit, Church, and New Creation*, ed. John Bolt, trans. John Vriend (Grand Rapids: Baker, 2008), 362.

their claim to extraordinary revelation that circumvented the apostolic circle."[75] Indeed, one will look in vain to find either apostolic succession or an infallible, extrabiblical postapostolic tradition that invests the canon with authority in these verses or any others. What one does find, however, are warnings not to add to Scripture, which is already sufficient.

But what about passages like 1 Corinthians 11:2, 2 Thessalonians 2:15 and 3:6, and 2 Timothy 2:2 where a "tradition" is affirmed and commanded to be passed down? Isn't it true that this tradition came prior to the established canon?[76] To begin with, the traditions Paul speaks of are those teachings of the apostles to the churches. Unlike the centuries to follow, the first century was unique, not paradigmatic. The Old Testament was in place, but the New Testament was still in the process of being committed to writing as inspired Scripture. Therefore, it should not surprise us that during this in-between time, apostles such as Paul taught the churches to maintain the *oral* teachings or traditions of the apostles. However, once those oral traditions were committed to *writing* as inspired Scripture, the situation changed. Note that the oral tradition and the written Scriptures did not contain dissimilar revelatory material, nor were they intended to indefinitely supplement one another. Rather, the gospel orally communicated was simply put into writing, becoming the New Testament Scriptures. The early church father Irenaeus (c. 130–200), bishop of Lyon, makes this very point: "We have learned from none others the plan of our salvation, than from those through whom the gospel has come down to us, which they did at one time proclaim in public, and, at a later period, by the will of God, handed down to us in the Scriptures, to be the ground and pillar of our faith."[77]

The Reformers, following the example of the early church fathers, did not hesitate to acknowledge that very early on in the apostolic era, oral tradition and written Scripture were two avenues of God's unified revelation. However, they rejected the notion that the postapostolic

---

75. Horton, *Christian Faith*, 193–94.
76. For a more in-depth treatment of biblical tradition and canon than can be provided here, see Herman N. Ridderbos, *Redemptive History and the New Testament Scriptures*, trans. H. De Jongste (Phillipsburg, NJ: P&R, 1963), 15–47.
77. Irenaeus, *Against Heresies* 3.1.1 (*ANF* 1:414).

era perpetuated these unique circumstances.[78] Nor did they assent to
the idea that in the postapostolic era an oral tradition, *different* in
revelatory material from written Scripture, continued as an infallible
supplement to Scripture. Postapostolic noninspired traditions, originating from ordinary pastors, were not to be equated or confused with
the inspired, revelatory, and infallible tradition originating from the
extraordinary ministry of the apostles.[79] Precluded, in other words, is
Rome's idea that postapostolic tradition continues as a *living voice*, one
that is supplemental to written Scripture and in possession of extrabiblical material necessary for church beliefs.

This explains why Jesus can condemn noninspired traditions that
the Pharisees illegitimately elevated to the level of inspired Scripture
(Matt 15:6; Mark 7:8), and Paul can tell the churches to uphold the
apostolic inspired traditions he has taught them (1 Cor 11:2; 2 Thess
2:15; 3:6). As Horton explains:

> Jesus recognized a qualitative difference between the inspired
> Scriptures (the Law and the Prophets) and the noninspired tradi-
> tion of the elders. However, Jesus commissioned officers of the
> new covenant who stood on a par with the prophets. After the
> apostles, the church is served by ministers who are called not to lay
> the foundation but to build on it. When the traditions of the elders
> (in either covenant) are faithful interpretations of Scripture, they
> are valid, but when they raise themselves to the level of Scripture
> itself, they are invalid.[80]

Therefore, while apostolic teaching (oral and then written) had
magisterial authority, postapostolic teaching (oral and written) had
ministerial authority. Or to use the metaphor of our judicial system:
"The court is not the author of its own constitution."[81]

To get this magisterial-ministerial distinction right is simply to
recognize the difference between *inspiration* and *illumination*. In
Scripture, the latter is not synonymous with the former. Postapostolic
tradition that is biblical isn't the Spirit's work of inspiration, but the

---

78. For example, see Calvin, *Institutes*, 4.8.14. See also Horton, *Christian Faith*, 191.
Additionally, consult our discussion of this issue in our treatment of Calvin and his response
to Sadoleto in chapter 1.

79. Horton, *Christian Faith*, 191.

80. Ibid.

81. Ibid., 192.

result of the Spirit's work of illumination. Rome, unfortunately, conflates the two, teaching that Christians must believe all things taught by the Church (i.e., *fides implicita*), and they must do so based on the authority of the Church. Protestants, on the other hand, are obligated to believe all that is taught in the Scriptures. Even if an angel suddenly appeared in our presence and was to teach a different gospel, says Paul in Galatians 1:6–9, the Christian must stick to the Scriptures.[82] Certainly the church is subordinate to the Scriptures if Paul can tell the Galatians to not listen to an angelic being!

Fourth, Rome falls prey to a similar elevation of tradition that Jesus condemned. Consider Mark 7:5–13:

> And the Pharisees and the scribes asked him, "Why do your disciples not walk according to the tradition of the elders, but eat with defiled hands?" And he said to them, "Well did Isaiah prophesy of you hypocrites, as it is written,
>
> > 'This people honors me with their lips,
> >   but their heart is far from me;
> > in vain do they worship me,
> >   teaching as doctrines the commandments of men.'
>
> You leave the commandment of God and hold to the tradition of men."
>
> And he said to them, "You have a fine way of rejecting the commandment of God in order to establish your tradition! For Moses said, 'Honor your father and your mother'; and, 'Whoever reviles father or mother must surely die.' But you say, 'If a man tells his father or his mother, "Whatever you would have gained from me is Corban"' (that is, given to God)—then you no longer permit him to do anything for his father or mother, thus making void the word of God by your tradition that you have handed down. And many such things you do." (ESV)

Phrases like the "tradition of the elders," the "tradition of men" (Mark 7:8; Col 2:8), and "your tradition" (Matt 15:3, 6; Mark 7:9, 13) all make reference to the oral instruction which served as a commentary on the Law.[83] But it went beyond mere commentary, telling

---

82. Ibid.

83. D. A. Carson, "Matthew," in *Matthew, Mark, Luke*, ed. Frank E. Gaebelein, EBC 8 (Grand Rapids: Zondervan, 1984), 348.

the Israelites what rules should be followed to obey the Law appropriately. This oral tradition would have acknowledged different rabbinical interpretations. When Jesus arrives, however, the Pharisees saw this oral tradition as authoritative and binding, even elevating its authority to the level of the Old Testament itself.[84] In doing so, they rightly receive Jesus's stern rebuke.

Interestingly, the Pharisees' elevation of their oral traditions to the same level as the canon shares many similarities with what Rome has done. But notice, Jesus condemns such a view, plain and simple. Not only does it elevate uninspired tradition but it does so at the expense of inspired Scripture, making void the "word of God" by tradition. The Reformers saw Rome embracing unbiblical doctrines in this noninspired tradition that contradicted Scripture (e.g., purgatory, transubstantiation, the immaculate conception of Mary, the bodily assumption of Mary, indulgences). Such a move by Rome is problematic because it undermines the sufficiency of Scripture. After the writings of the New Testament, the church no longer receives apostles and revelation. The Bible is enough. Furthermore, why did the early church acknowledge only those books of apostolic origin, refusing to broaden its criteria for canonization, if the "postapostolic tradition" was indeed a recognized continuation of the "apostolic tradition"?[85] Criteria were in place for recognizing which books were canonical, and such criteria concerned the "nature of the texts" rather than "the authority of the church."[86] The fathers did not consider the traditions subsequent to the apostles to be inspired revelation. If they did, then it makes no sense why someone like Irenaeus could write against the Gnostics and their belief in ongoing revelation.[87]

To conclude our response to Rome, Augustine's dictum is often quoted in support of Rome: "I should not believe the gospel except as moved by the authority of the Catholic Church."[88] Read properly, Augustine is merely relaying how he came to Christ. He is not explaining where the authority of his faith rests, nor its ultimate source.[89] In other words, Augustine recalls how the church was a *motive* for faith,

---

84. Ibid.
85. Horton, *Christian Faith*, 192.
86. Ibid., 195.
87. Ibid., 192.
88. Augustine, *Against the Epistle of Manichaeus* 5 (NPNF[1] 4:131).
89. Calvin, *Institutes*, 1.7.3; Francis Turretin, *Institutes of Elenctic Theology*, vol. 1, First through Tenth Topics, ed. James T. Dennison Jr., trans. George M. Giger (Phillipsburg, NJ: P&R, 1992), 2.6; Horton, *Christian Faith*, 190.

but he is not saying that the church was the *final ground* of faith.[90]
Belief comes *"through* the church," not *"because* of the church."[91]
Or as Heiko Oberman puts it, for Augustine the church possesses an
"instrumental authority, the door which leads to the fullness of the
Word itself."[92] The church may be the *rule* of faith (*regula fidei*), but it
is not the *foundation* of faith (*fundamentum fidei*). That role belongs
only to Scripture.[93]

Can a Protestant affirm Vatican II, which says that "both sacred
tradition and sacred Scripture are to be accepted and venerated with the
same sense of loyalty and reverence"? Not without becoming a Roman
Catholic.[94] While we can stand behind the "coinherence" of Scripture
and tradition (each complementing the other), we cannot affirm their
"coequality."[95]

2. Science and Reason

Just as tradition can be abused and turned into traditionalism, the
same problem can be applied to science. Science is a magnificent means
through which our reason explores the natural order, makes discoveries, and, if done correctly, leads us to worship our Creator (Ps 19:1–6).
Therefore, *sola Scriptura*, as J. I. Packer warns, should *not* entail a
"Bible-without-science" mentality as sometimes is evident in the worst
forms of the Fundamentalist movement.[96]

---

90. Bavinck, *Reformed Dogmatics*, 1:457; cf. Calvin, *Institutes*, 1.7.3; Richard A.
Muller, *PRRD*, 2:351–52.

91. Horton, *Christian Faith*, 193; Kruger, *Canon Revisited*, 42–48.

92. Oberman notes how it is at the end of the Middle Ages that the Church interpreted Augustine's statement on the "practical authority of the Church as though it implied
a metaphysical priority" (Heiko A. Oberman, *The Dawn of the Reformation* [Grand Rapids:
Eerdmans, 1996], 278).

93. Bavinck, *Reformed Dogmatics*, 1:453.

94. At the end of our defense of *sola Scriptura* against Rome, one might throw out
a final objection: Scripture itself never teaches *sola Scriptura*! For example, Peter Kreeft,
Catholic Christianity (San Francisco, Ignatius, 2001), 20. But this objection is strange
indeed. If followed logically, can we really say that other (even orthodox) doctrines are taught
in Scripture? Where do we find a proof-text, for example, on the Trinity, the deity of Christ,
creation *ex nihilo*, etc.? But this is a simplistic approach to the Bible. Instead, we are to put all
Scripture together, utilizing good biblical and systematic theology. When we do, as we have
sought to do here, we see an overwhelming affirmation of Scripture's inspiration, inerrancy,
necessity, clarity, sufficiency, and authority.

95. Timothy George, "An Evangelical Reflection on Scripture and Tradition," in
Colson and Neuhaus, *Your Word Is Truth*, 34.

96. J. I. Packer, "The Bible in Use: Evangelicals Seeking Truth from Holy Scripture,"
in Colson and Neuhaus, *Your Word Is Truth*, 78.

However, today there is the tendency among some Christians to elevate science above Scripture, or at least to a place of equal authority.[97] Science, they would argue, is just as authoritative as Scripture and should be followed in its findings, even if those findings conflict with Scripture. In such a view, Scripture is to be interpreted through the grid of science, not vice versa. Should science and Scripture meet an impasse, Scripture, not science, must be either rejected or reconfigured.

This is not the place to rehearse the long and ongoing debate over evolution since Darwin.[98] However, we should draw attention to the many ways in which the Bible's authority can be compromised at the expense of adopting evolutionary claims. The twentieth century has proven that like-minded Christians have disagreed over evolution. Some evangelicals reject evolution entirely as incompatible with who God is and how the Bible says he created the universe, while others seek to retain theism and reconcile it with an evolutionary view of origins, though one initiated and guided by God (i.e., theistic evolution).

Today, however, this debate has escalated into questioning whether Adam was a historical person, though in reality this tussle is an old one.[99] Some have gone so far as to conclude that, in light of evolution, the biblical authors were wrong in assuming or affirming a historical Adam. For example, Peter Enns thinks it's a fool's errand to try to reconcile evolution with what the biblical authors say about Adam. These two are incompatible and at odds. We must realize, says Enns, that Paul was mistaken when he referred to Adam as a historical person in texts like Romans 5 and 1 Corinthians 15. As a first-century man with a primitive view of the cosmos, Paul naturally thought Adam was a historical person. But we know now, in light of centuries of scientific inquiry (i.e., evolution), that this cannot be the case.[100] Enns's we-

97. I would place John Polkinghorne in this category. See John Polkinghorne, *Reason and Reality: The Relationship between Science and Theology* (London: SPCK, 1991); idem, *Science and Creation: The Search for Understanding* (London: SPCK, 1988); idem, *Science and the Trinity: The Christian Encounter with Reality* (London: SPCK, 2004). For a helpful critique, see Kirsten Birkett, "Science and Scripture," in Carson, *Enduring Authority of the Christian Scriptures*, 966–86.

98. Alister E. McGrath, *Science and Religion: An Introduction* (Oxford: Blackwell, 1999), 21–26, 187–93.

99. For the various views in this debate, see Matthew Barrett and Ardel B. Caneday, eds., *Four Views on the Historical Adam* (Grand Rapids: Zondervan, 2013).

100. Peter Enns, *The Evolution of Adam: What the Bible Does and Doesn't Say about Human Origins* (Grand Rapids: Brazos, 2012), especially chapters 5–7 and the nine theses in the conclusion.

now-know-better approach, itself a remnant of the Enlightenment, has led him to give up the doctrine of inerrancy and to reject something as important as the historicity of Adam.[101]

Others approach the Bible with a similar hermeneutic. For example, Kenton L. Sparks believes there is a *trajectory* in Scripture whereby more recent revelation (New Testament) corrects older revelation (Old Testament) that is in error.[102] Sparks believes evangelicals are wrong to assume that the Bible has a unified theology. Instead, he says there is a diversity of theologies at play, and many of these theologies are at odds with one another. Our job, he argues, is to move beyond the Bible and be open to other authorities, including scientific voices, even if they contradict what we read in Scripture.[103] For Sparks, the Bible is full of errors, and not just factual ones, but ethical and doctrinal ones, some even misrepresenting God himself. We must look outside of the Bible, he says, to fields like science to correct Scripture's primitive anthropology.[104] We must come to grips with the reality that science even "trumps" the Bible's teaching.[105]

Enns and Sparks are just two examples of those who have rejected total inerrancy and Scripture's sufficiency. They are honest in their critique, concluding that the Bible just gets it wrong, it cannot be followed, and the Scriptures alone are not enough. They say that something more is needed, in this case science. When the Bible collides with science, it is the Bible that must give way. As a consequence, *sola Scriptura* is undermined and with it the authority and sufficiency of God's Word. Where, exactly, the Christian should follow what the Bible says ends up becoming a game of "pick and choose." For one person, the Bible's affirmation of a historical Adam must go; for another, it is

---

101. Peter Enns, "Inerrancy, However Defined, Does Not Describe What the Bible Does," in *Five Views on Biblical Inerrancy*, ed. J. Merrick and Stephen M. Garrett (Grand Rapids: Zondervan, 2013), 83–141; Peter Enns, *The Bible Tells Me So: Why Defending Scripture Has Made Us Unable to Read It* (New York: HarperCollins, 2014).

102. Kenton L. Sparks, *Sacred Word, Broken Word: Biblical Authority and the Dark Side of Scripture* (Grand Rapids: Eerdmans, 2012), 114–17. See also idem, *God's Word in Human Words: An Evangelical Appropriation of Critical Biblical Scholarship* (Grand Rapids: Baker Academic, 2008). For a response, see Albert Mohler Jr., "When the Bible Speaks, God Speaks: The Classic Doctrine of Biblical Inerrancy," in Merrick and Garrett, *Five Views on Biblical Inerrancy*, especially 55; Robert W. Yarbrough, "The Embattled Bible: Four More Books," *Themelios* 34, no. 1 (2009): 6–25.

103. Sparks, *Sacred Word, Broken Word*, 33–39, 91.

104. Ibid., 92.

105. Ibid., 116, 135.

the Bible's stance against homosexuality; yet for another it is Christ's deity or resurrection. As we saw in chapter 2, this approach is not new. It has a long history, and it's hard to see how it avoids postmodern subjectivism, making each individual his own hermeneutical lord.

In the end, science, when done rightly, will always conform to the truths of Scripture. Science in and of itself is not an enemy of Scripture. Indeed, science serves to brilliantly support Christianity. Science becomes problematic only when we misuse it and draw false conclusions, conclusions that are incompatible with the truths of God's Word. As with tradition, we must understand science's role as ministerial rather than magisterial.[106]

3. Experience and Culture

It is naive to think that we can approach the Bible as if we were a blank slate, free from cultural presuppositions. Such an Enlightenment mentality was rightly critiqued and shown wanting by postmodernism, which demonstrated that we are always products of the culture we live in. This is not necessarily a bad thing. Cultures and experiences grounded in truth can have a positive and formative impact upon those within them. It is a good thing, for example, when a child is born into a Christian home; that child, not even realizing it, will naturally imbibe biblical values and teaching (e.g., 2 Tim 1:5; 3:14–15). Sadly, the opposite can also be the case when all someone knows is a culture that is corrupt and idolatrous. Personal experience and cultural influences are both critical in the development of any individual's worldview and play either a positive or negative role in one's development.

As we saw with tradition, reason, and science, when our experience and culture are elevated above the Bible, then *sola Scriptura* is compromised. This temptation is not limited to those in the world but often can be seen within Christian communities as well. In fact, it is safe to say that many Christians today do elevate their own spiritual experience above the Bible. Scripture may serve an important role, but "my experience" is just as important. "Experience" may even be the governing grid through which Scripture is interpreted. For such individuals, as Dietrich Bonhoeffer insightfully observed, Scripture's message is sifted "through the sieve of one's own experience, despising and shaking

---

106. For an example of such an approach, see Vern S. Poythress, *Redeeming Science: A God-Centered Approach* (Wheaton, IL: Crossway, 2006).

out what will not pass through; and one prunes and clips the biblical message until it will fit in a given space, until the eagle can no longer fly in his true element but with clipped wings is exhibited as a special showpiece among the usual domesticated animals."[107] Experience sits as judge in all matters, even over those addressed by Scripture itself. As far as Scripture is in agreement with one's own experience, it is accepted. But as soon as Scripture contradicts one's experience, Scripture must be either reinterpreted or rejected.

The same problem occurs where the worldview of the Bible meets the wider culture. As informative as the culture may be for contextualizing theology, many go much further, taking their cue from the culture rather than from the biblical text. *Sola Scriptura* is replaced with *sola cultura*.[108] Bonhoeffer's observation of his own day is relevant in ours. We seek a fixed point in the culture, all the while viewing Scripture as "movable, *questionable*, uncertain."[109] This was one of the major problems conservatives had with liberals in the twentieth century, namely, seeking a Christianity that takes its marching orders from the culture. As Carl Henry noted, the culture gets to set the agenda for the Bible.[110]

Consider just two examples where experience and culture can rival Scripture's authority. In our day a multitude of church leaders and denominations have rejected the Bible's authority and placed their stamp of approval on homosexuality. "I stand ready to reject the Bible," says Episcopal Bishop John Shelby Spong in his book *Living in Sin: A Bishop Rethinks Human Sexuality*, "in favour of something that is more human, more humane, more life-giving, and, dare I say, more godlike."[111] Today Spong's words resonate with many who have abandoned biblical authority in light of its teaching on homosexuality.[112]

---

107. Dietrich Bonhoeffer, *Vergegenwärtigung neutestamentlicher Texte*, in *Gesammelte Schriften*, ed. Eberhard Bethge (Munich: Chr. Kaiser Verlag, 1960), 3:304–5.

108. David F. Wells, *God in the Whirlwind: How the Holy-Love of God Reorients Our World* (Wheaton, IL: Crossway, 2014), 17.

109. Bonhoeffer, *Vergegenwärtigung neutestamentlicher Texte*, 3:304–5, emphasis added.

110. See Carl F. H. Henry, *God, Revelation, and Authority* (Wheaton, IL: Crossway, 1979), 4:54–55.

111. John Shelby Spong, *Living in Sin: A Bishop Rethinks Human Sexuality* (San Francisco: Harper & Row, 1988), 133.

112. Spong's views are adopted by the General Convention of the Episcopal Church USA, and many other denominations are considering doing the same. Terry L. Johnson, *The Case for Traditional Protestantism: The Solas of the Reformation* (Carlisle, PA: Banner of Truth, 2004), 20.

Their message is often blunt: the Bible teaches that homosexuality is wrong, so the Bible, on this point, must be rejected.[113] Various reasons are given for why the Bible is wrong on sexuality. Some argue that Scripture was written in a primitive era by authors who were blinded by their chauvinistic bias. Underneath this argument is a denial of Scripture's inspiration and inerrancy. No longer can the biblical authors be trusted. Here, ultimately, is an example of how the culture trumps Scripture.[114] Whether they realize it or not, these individuals have sided with the cultural consensus over the biblical one.[115]

Or take into account the role of experience for the ordinary church-goer. While many Christians would pay lip service to the Bible as their authority, *functionally* it is experience that steers the ship. Their spiritual or religious feelings become the grid through which Scripture must be interpreted, rather than the other way around. Rarely do such individuals say they are doing so, but when they live out the Christian life, the way they make decisions or discern the will of God proves that it is a *mystical experience* or a *spiritual feeling* that takes priority over the Bible and serves as the controlling grid by which the Bible is interpreted.

Shouldn't it be the other way around? Shouldn't Scripture be interpreting (and judging) our experience? The proper role of experience begins to be identified only when we honestly recognize just how culturally conditioned our experience can be. Its contingency should guard us from elevating our experience as an infallible or fixed standard for how we view and interpret God's Word.[116] We are not meant to sift through the Bible to find that nugget passage that somehow justifies our immovable experiential grid, as if the Bible is the servant who answers to experience. The gospel announced in and through the Bible

---

113. For example, Lev 18:22; Rom 1:18–32; 1 Cor 6:9–10; 1 Tim 1:8–11.

114. For fuller treatments of this issue, see Robert A. J. Gagnon, *The Bible and Homosexual Practice: Texts and Hermeneutics* (Nashville: Abingdon, 2001); Wesley Hill, *Washed and Waiting: Reflections on Christian Faithfulness and Homosexuality* (Grand Rapids: Zondervan, 2010).

115. To qualify, others (e.g., Matthew Vines, Ken Wilson) claim to uphold a high view of biblical authority since they argue that the Bible doesn't teach that all same-sex relations are wrong. However, Keller demonstrates that these authors have decisively shifted "ultimate authority to define right and wrong onto the individual Christian and away from the biblical text," and therefore they are guilty of undermining biblical authority (Tim Keller, "The Bible and Same-Sex Relationships: A Review Article," Redeemer Presbyterian Church, http://www.redeemer.com/redeemer-report/article/the_bible_and_same_sex_relationships_a_review_article).

116. J. Todd Billings, *The Word of God for the People of God* (Grand Rapids: Eerdmans, 2010), 130.

is not our experience incarnated. Instead, the inscripturated gospel comes down on us to judge and condemn, redeem and recalibrate our experience, particularly around the person and work of Jesus Christ. Our experience, in other words, does not set the terms; the Bible alone sets the agenda, interpreting our experience for us. Contrary to Liberalism, warns Todd Billings, the "Christian message accessed through Scripture should not be seen as an expression of our experience but a reorientation of our experience, such that we learn 'the story of Jesus and Israel well enough to interpret and experience [ourselves] and [our] world in its terms.'"[117] How then should we approach Scripture and experience? Experience doesn't get to bark orders, telling us how to interpret God's Word. Instead, Scripture redesigns and refashions how we experience the world we live in.[118]

The elevation of individual experience is often masked in the name of the "Spirit." As we saw in chapter 1, such was the case with some of the radical reformers who believed the Spirit even trumped the Bible. The internal, personal word or revelation from the Spirit *they* received took priority over what the Bible said. Today this heritage continues in some Pentecostal circles.[119] While the Bible is appreciated, even revered, what is of ultimate significance and authority is a *new, additional* revelation from the Spirit, one that goes above and beyond the Bible.[120]

Again, such views butt heads with the sufficiency of Scripture. Protestants have argued that the canon of Scripture is closed, especially in light of the finished work of Christ, who is the final revelation of God. While in the Old Testament era God spoke by his prophets, in "these last days" he has "spoken to us by his Son" (Heb 1:2). The Son gave his revelatory word to his apostles, who not only proclaimed it but put it into writing via the Holy Spirit. Therefore, with the coming of Christ and the Spirit at Pentecost, redemptive history has met its pinnacle moment. The saving work of Jesus was, as Hebrews says repeatedly, once for all. It is safe to conclude that the word Christ gave to his apostles was once for all.[121] Hence, with the advent of Christ and

---

117. Ibid.

118. Ibid.

119. Of course, many charismatic groups do not necessarily go this far, but instead affirm *sola Scriptura* and argue that their view of the gifts is not to be set over or against Scripture.

120. At a very popular level, we might add the ongoing claims by individuals that they have "gone to heaven and back" and lived to tell about it. See the multitude of books (and movies!) on the market making this claim in the last ten years.

121. Frame, *Doctrine of the Word of God*, 139.

subsequently his gift of a written Word to the church by his apostles, we have the definitive, once and for all, totally sufficient Word from God. To now seek new revelation is to add another foundation on top of the one God has already laid. New revelation, therefore, serves only to undercut, challenge, and weaken the Bible's sufficiency.[122]

With the church's reception of the inspired New Testament books, everything the church needs for faith and practice is now found in the Bible. We need not look for new revelation, as if we are present-day prophets or apostles, but to Scripture alone as our all-sufficient Word from God. The Holy Spirit does not work against the Word or above and beyond the Word, but in and through the Word. While the Spirit's work of illumination continues (illumination *of the Word*!), his special work of inspiration was reserved for the Old and New Testaments.[123] In short, the Bible is enough; we need not look for a new, additional, or better revelation. We have God's *best* Word already, and nothing needs to be added to it.

Sufficiency Meets Real Life

To conclude, few attributes of Scripture have such warm, practical implications for real life as sufficiency. Consider just a few.

First, sufficiency is a fountain of comfort for the minister and the layperson in evangelical ministry. Everything the minister needs to train their church in righteousness and to equip their people for every good work is in Scripture (2 Tim 3:16).[124] What a relief it is to the pastor counseling a couple having marriage problems, a teenager facing suicidal thoughts, or a widow who has just lost her husband of fifty years to cancer. God's Word is enough. It will help the Christian not merely survive but thrive.

Second, sufficiency moves the believer from mere head knowledge to action, from knowing to doing. "The sufficiency of Scripture for the life of faith," observes Scott Swain, "awakens in the reader a desire to search the Scripture's vast plains, to savor its numerous delicacies, and to follow its wise paths. If the narrow way that leads to life has indeed been found, there is nothing else to do but to set our feet to traveling."[125]

---

122. Sinclair Ferguson, *The Holy Spirit* (Downers Grove, IL: InterVarsity Press, 1996), 231.

123. Space does not permit me to enter into the charismatic debate, but see Wayne Grudem, ed., *Are Miraculous Gifts for Today: Four Views* (Grand Rapids: Zondervan, 1996).

124. Swain, *Trinity, Revelation, and Reading*, 85–87.

125. Ibid.

Third, sufficiency reminds us that God's Word is to take center stage in the church. The evangelical church has in many ways absorbed the consumeristic mentality that is so prevalent in the culture. Churches approach worship as if they are selling a product and the attendee is the consumer. Since the product is up for sale, churches must show that their product is more entertaining than anything else the world has to offer. Churchy gimmicks are the name of the game. Whatever keeps people coming back for more takes first priority and becomes the controlling principle for all things church related. The preaching must be relevant, the music must entertain, and church events must keep people on the edge of their seats. If the church doesn't sell itself, then it will be out of business.[126] F CCC

However, the sufficiency of Scripture, when applied in ministry, is like pouring an ice-cold bucket of water in the face of the church. No longer can we turn to the culture to decide what the church should be and do. God, his gospel, and his bride are not products to be sold. And those who walk through the church doors on Sunday morning are not customers to entertain.[127] Such an approach makes man the center and treats the church like a business, something that is utterly foreign to the New Testament.[128]

In contrast, we must draw churchgoers and church leaders back to Scripture, which is our final authority and sufficient rule for worship. In doing so, we must recover the ordinary means of grace (the preached Word, baptism, the Lord's Supper) that God uses to equip the saints and transform us into the image of Christ. At its most basic level, this means the Word of God must take first place among the people of God. Sunday mornings are focused not around flashy guitar solos, funny anecdotes, or feel-good messages, but around the proclamation of the Word. Only then can we sincerely and genuinely repeat after the psalmist: "I will never forget your precepts, for by them you have preserved my life. . . . Your word is a lamp for my feet, a light on my path" (Ps 119:93, 105).[129]

126. Lints, *Fabric of Theology*, 45–47; Billings, *Word of God for the People of God*, 126–27; Philip D. Kenneson and James L. Street, *Selling Out the Church: The Dangers of Church Marketing* (Nashville: Abingdon, 1997).

127. For a treatment of this problem, see the issue of *Credo Magazine* entitled *Churchy Gimmicks: Has the Church Sold Its Soul to Consumerism?* (4.2 [2014]).

128. See John Piper, *Brothers, We Are Not Professionals*, 2nd ed. (Wheaton, IL: Crossway, 2013).

129. There is an important connection between sufficiency and the fear of the Lord, which involves humility rather than pride (Prov 2:6, 22, 29; 3:5, 7; 4:25). See John Webster, *The Domain of the Word: Scripture and Theological Reason* (London: T&T Clark, 2012), 18.

Conclusion

Always Reforming according to the Word of God

> We ought surely to seek from Scripture a rule for
> thinking and speaking. To this yardstick all thoughts
> of the mind and all words of the mouth must be
> conformed. —*John Calvin*

> There is nothing which can give greater joy or
> assurance or comfort to the soul than the Word of its
> creator and maker. —*Huldrych Zwingli*

> It is blessed to eat into the very soul of the Bible until,
> at last, you come to talk in scriptural language, and
> your spirit is flavoured with the words of the Lord, so
> that your blood is *Bibline* and the very essence of the
> Bible flows from you. —*Charles Spurgeon*

My mother gave me a Bible when I was a boy and told me to read it. So I did. And God saved me.

Looking back, I never cease to be amazed at the simplicity of my conversion. By God's sovereign grace, I read the Bible, believed the Bible, and was united to the Christ of the Bible. Some would call this elementary. But I think it shows just how powerful God's Word is. God said it, I believed it. Martin Luther's well-known words proved true in my life: "The Word comes first, and with the Word the Spirit breathes upon my heart so that I believe."[1]

While some hiss at biblical authority, I cherish it. If God did not speak with authority in his written Word, I would be lost in my sins to

---

1. *LW* 54:63.

this day, and so would you. So it is with much confidence that I can say that if the authority of Scripture is abandoned, our faith will be too. It is only a matter of time. To quote Augustine: "Faith will start tottering if the authority of scripture is undermined."[2]

I cannot prove that the Bible is true. Only the Spirit can do that. And until he does, you will never see Scripture as God's Word. We must remember this in the midst of today's battle over the Bible. Those who reject the Bible as God's authoritative, inspired, inerrant, clear, necessary, and sufficient Word ultimately reveal more about themselves than about the Bible. They show the world that where the problem really lies is not with the Bible but with the human heart. As Herman Bavinck said, "The battle against the Bible is, in the first place, a revelation of the hostility of the human heart."[3]

In light of the darkness of the human heart, we must approach people and the Bible differently. The first step is to take people to the Bible itself. The Bible testifies to its own identity. But this isn't enough. We must then pray that the Spirit would irresistibly persuade sinners that the Bible is what it says it is. "Without this ministry," says Sinclair Ferguson, "sin-blinded eyes cannot see that Scripture is the word of God, sin-darkened hearts cannot respond to it as the Word of God, and sin-deafened ears cannot hear the voice of the Father addressing them in it."[4]

The remarkable thing is that when the Spirit works, we become silent. Our mouths are shut. We become like Isaiah and must say, "Woe is me! For I am lost; for I am a man of unclean lips" (Isa 6:5 ESV). And when the Spirit opens our mouth once again, we cannot help but cry out, "This God—his way is perfect; the word of the LORD proves true; he is a shield for all those who take refuge in him" (Ps 18:30 ESV).

2. Augustine, *Teaching Christianity (De Doctrina Christiana)*, ed. John E. Rotelle, trans. Edmund Hill, The Works of Saint Augustine (New York: New City, 1996), 1.41.

3. Herman Bavinck, *Reformed Dogmatics*, vol. 1, *Prolegomena*, ed. John Bolt, trans. John Vriend (Grand Rapids: Baker, 2003), 1:440.

4. Sinclair B. Ferguson, *From the Mouth of God: Trusting, Reading, and Applying the Bible* (Carlisle, PA: Banner of Truth, 2014), 56.

Select Bibliography

Abbott, Walter M., ed. *The Documents of Vatican II*. Translated by Joseph Gallagher. New York: American, 1966.

Abraham, William J. *The Divine Inspiration of Holy Scripture*. Oxford: Oxford University Press, 1981.

———. *Divine Revelation and the Limits of Historical Criticism*. Oxford: Oxford University Press, 1983.

Achtemeier, Paul J. *Inspiration and Authority: Nature and Function of Christian Scripture*. 2nd ed. Grand Rapids: Baker Academic, 1998.

Alexander, T. Desmond. *From Eden to the New Jerusalem: An Introduction to Biblical Theology*. Grand Rapids: Kregel, 2008.

Allen, Michael, and Scott R. Swain. *Reformed Catholicity: The Promise of Retrieval for Theology and Biblical Interpretation*. Grand Rapids: Baker Academic, 2015.

Allert, Craig D. *A High View of Scripture? The Authority of the Bible and the Formation of the New Testament Canon*. Grand Rapids: Baker Academic, 2007.

Althaus, Paul. *The Theology of Martin Luther*. Translated by Robert C. Schultz. Philadelphia: Fortress, 1966.

Armstrong, John H., ed. *The Coming Evangelical Crisis: Current Challenges to the Authority of Scripture and the Gospel*. Chicago: Moody, 1996.

Avis, Paul. *Beyond the Reformation? Authority, Primacy, and Unity in the Conciliar Tradition*. New York: T&T Clark, 2006.

———. *In Search of Authority: Anglican Theological Method from the Reformation to the Enlightenment*. London: Bloomsbury, 2014.

Bacote, Vincent, Laura C. Miguélez, and Dennis L. Okholm, eds. *Evangelicals and Scripture: Tradition, Authority, and Hermeneutics*. Downers Grove, IL: InterVarsity Press, 2004.

Bainton, Roland H. *Here I Stand: A Life of Martin Luther*. Peabody, MA: Hendrickson, 1950.

Barr, James. *Fundamentalism*. London: SCM, 1977.

———. *Holy Scripture: Canon, Authority, Criticism*. Oxford: Oxford University Press, 1983.

———. *The Scope and Authority of the Bible*. London: SCM, 1980; Philadelphia: Westminster, 1981.

Barth, Karl. *Church Dogmatics* 1.1. Edinburgh: T&T Clark, 1975. Reprint, Peabody, MA: Hendrickson, 2010.

———. *Church Dogmatics* 1.2. Edinburgh: T&T Clark, 1975. Reprint, Peabody, MA: Hendrickson, 2010.

———. *The Epistle to the Romans.* Translated by Edwyn C. Hoskyns. London: Oxford University Press, 1933.

Barton, John. *The Nature of Biblical Criticism.* Louisville: Westminster John Knox, 2007.

Bauckham, Richard, and Benjamin Drewery, eds. *Scripture, Tradition, and Reason: A Study in the Criteria of Christian Doctrine.* New York: T&T Clark, 2004.

Bavinck, Herman. *Prolegomena.* Vol. 1 of *Reformed Dogmatics.* Edited by John Bolt. Translated by John Vriend. Grand Rapids: Baker Academic, 2003.

Bayer, Oswald. *Martin Luther's Theology: A Contemporary Interpretation.* Translated by Thomas Trapp. Grand Rapids: Eerdmans, 2008.

Beale, G. K. *The Erosion of Inerrancy in Evangelicalism: Responding to New Challenges to Biblical Authority.* Wheaton, IL: Crossway, 2008.

Beegle, Dewey M. *The Inspiration of Scripture.* Grand Rapids: Eerdmans, 1963.

———. *Scripture, Tradition, and Infallibility.* Grand Rapids: Eerdmans, 1973.

Berkouwer, G. C. *The Second Vatican Council and the New Catholicism.* Translated by Lewis B. Smedes. Grand Rapids: Eerdmans, 1965.

———. *Studies in Dogmatics: Holy Scripture.* Grand Rapids: Eerdmans, 1975.

Billings, J. Todd. *The Word of God for the People of God: An Entryway to the Theological Interpretation of Scripture.* Grand Rapids: Eerdmans, 2010.

Bloesch, Donald. *The Ground of Certainty: Toward an Evangelical Theology of Revelation.* Grand Rapids: Eerdmans, 1971.

———. *Holy Scripture: Revelation, Inspiration, and Interpretation.* Downers Grove, IL: IVP Academic, 1994.

———. *A Theology of Word and Spirit: Authority and Method in Theology.* Downers Grove, IL: InterVarsity Press, 1982.

Blomberg, Craig L. *Can We Still Believe the Bible? An Evangelical Engagement with Contemporary Questions.* Grand Rapids: Brazos, 2014.

Boice, James Montgomery. *Does Inerrancy Matter?* Oakland, CA: International Council on Biblical Inerrancy, 1979.

———, ed. *The Foundation of Biblical Authority.* Grand Rapids: Zondervan, 1978.

———, ed. *God's Inerrant Word: An International Symposium on the Trustworthiness of Scripture.* Minneapolis: Bethany Fellowship, 1974.

———. *Standing on the Rock: Upholding Biblical Authority in a Secular Age.* Grand Rapids: Baker, 1984.

Boice, James Montgomery, and Benjamin E. Sasse, eds. *Here We Stand: A Call from Confessing Evangelicals.* Grand Rapids: Baker, 1996.

Bray, Gerald. *Biblical Interpretation: Past and Present.* Downers Grove, IL: IVP Academic, 1996.

Brecht, Martin. *Martin Luther: His Road to Reformation, 1483–1521.* Minneapolis: Fortress, 1985.

Brettler, Marc Zvi, Peter Enns, and Daniel J. Harrington, S. J. *The Bible and the Believer: How to Read the Bible Critically and Religiously.* Oxford: Oxford University Press, 2012.

Briggs, Charles A. *Whither?* New York: Charles Scribner's Sons, 1889.

Bromiley, G. W., ed. *Zwingli and Bullinger.* The Library of Christian Classics. Louisville: Westminster John Knox, 1953.

Brown, Colin. *Christianity and Western Thought: A History of Philosophers, Ideas, and Movements.* Vol. 1, *Ancient World to the Age of Enlightenment.* Downers Grove, IL: IVP Academic, 1990.

Brown, William P., ed. *Engaging Biblical Authority: Perspectives on the Bible as Scripture.* Grand Rapids: Eerdmans, 2007.

Brueggemann, Walter. *The Book That Breathes New Life: Scriptural Authority and Biblical Theology.* Minneapolis: Augsburg Fortress, 2011.

Bush, L. Russ, and Tom J. Nettles. *Baptists and the Bible.* 2nd ed. Nashville: B&H Academic, 1999.

Callihan, James. *The Clarity of Scripture: History, Theology, and Contemporary Literary Studies.* Downers Grove, IL: InterVarsity Press, 2001.

Calvin, John. *Institutes of the Christian Religion.* Edited by John T. McNeill. Translated by Ford Lewis Battles. Philadelphia: Westminster, 1960.

———. *John Calvin: Tracts and Letters.* Edited and translated by Henry Beveridge. 7 vols. Edinburgh: Banner of Truth, 2009.

Carson, D. A. *Collected Writings on Scripture.* Wheaton, IL: Crossway, 2010.

———. *The Gagging of God: Christianity Confronts Pluralism.* Grand Rapids: Zondervan, 1996.

———, ed. *The Enduring Authority of the Christian Scriptures.* Grand Rapids: Eerdmans, 2016.

Carson, D. A., and John D. Woodbridge, eds. *Hermeneutics, Authority, and Canon.* Grand Rapids: Zondervan, 1986. Reprint, Eugene, OR: Wipf & Stock, 2005.

———, eds. *Scripture and Truth.* Grand Rapids: Baker, 1983.

Colson, Charles, and Richard John Neuhaus, eds. *Your Word Is Truth: A Project of Evangelicals and Catholics Together.* Grand Rapids: Eerdmans, 2002.

Conn, Harvie M., ed. *Inerrancy and Hermeneutic.* Grand Rapids: Baker, 1988.

Cowan, Steven B., and Terry L. Wilder, eds. *In Defense of the Bible: A Comprehensive Apologetic for the Authority of Scripture.* Nashville: B&H Academic, 2013.

Croy, N. Clayton. *Prima Scriptura: An Introduction to New Testament Interpretation.* Grand Rapids: Baker Academic, 2011.

Crump, David. *Encountering Jesus, Encountering Scripture: Reading the Bible Critically in Faith.* Grand Rapids: Eerdmans, 2013.

Daniell, David. *William Tyndale: A Biography.* New Haven: Yale University Press, 1994.

Demarest, Bruce A. *General Revelation: Historical Views and Contemporary Issues.* Grand Rapids: Zondervan, 1982.

Dempster, Stephen G. *Dominion and Dynasty: A Biblical Theology of the Hebrew Bible.* Downers Grove, IL: InterVarsity Press, 2003.

Dennison, James T., Jr., ed. *Reformed Confessions of the 16th and 17th Centuries in English Translation.* 4 vols. Grand Rapids: Reformation Heritage, 2008–2014.

Descartes, René. *Discourse on the Method*. Part 4. Translated by Laurence J. Lafleur. Indianapolis: Bobbs-Merrill, 1960.

DeYoung, Kevin. *Taking God at His Word: Why the Bible Is Knowable, Necessary, and Enough, and What That Means for You and Me*. Wheaton, IL: Crossway, 2014.

Dockery, David S. *Christian Scripture: An Evangelical Perspective on Inspiration, Authority, and Interpretation*. Eugene, OR: Wipf & Stock, 1995.

Dorrien, Gary. *The Making of American Liberal Theology*. 3 vols. Louisville: Westminster John Knox, 2001-3.

Dules, Avery. *Models of Revelation*. New York: Doubleday, 1983.

Dumbrell, William J. *Covenant and Creation: A Theology of the Old Testament Covenants*. Carlisle, UK: Paternoster, 1984.

Dunn, James D. G. *The Living Word*. 2nd ed. Minneapolis: Fortress, 2009.

Ebeling, Gerhard. *The Word of God and Tradition: Historical Studies Interpreting the Divisions of Christianity*. Translated by S. H. Hooke. Philadelphia: Fortress, 1968.

Edwards, Brian. *Nothing But the Truth: The Inspiration, Authority, and History of the Bible Explained*. Darlington, England: Evangelical Press, 2006.

Enns, Peter. *The Bible Tells Me So: Why Defending Scripture Has Made Us Unable to Read It*. New York: HarperCollins, 2014.

———. *The Evolution of Adam: What the Bible Does and Doesn't Say about Human Origins*. Grand Rapids: Brazos, 2012.

———. *Inspiration and Incarnation: Evangelicals and the Problem of the Old Testament*. Grand Rapids: Baker Academic, 2005.

Erickson, Millard J., Paul Kjoss Helseth, and Justin Taylor, eds. *Reclaiming the Center: Confronting Evangelical Accommodation in Postmodern Times*. Wheaton, IL: Crossway, 2004.

Evans, G. R. *The Language and Logic of the Bible: The Road to Reformation*. Cambridge: Cambridge University Press, 1985.

Ferguson, Sinclair B. *From the Mouth of God: Trusting, Reading, and Applying the Bible*. Edinburgh: Banner of Truth, 2014.

Fish, Stanley. *Is There a Text in This Class? The Authority of Interpretive Communities*. London and Cambridge: Harvard University Press, 1980.

Fluhrer, Gabriel N. E., ed. *Solid Ground: The Inerrant Word of God in an Errant World*. Phillipsburg, NJ: P&R, 2012.

Fosdick, Harry Emerson. *The Modern Use of the Bible*. New York: Macmillan, 1924.

———. "Shall the Fundamentalists Win?" In *American Sermons: The Pilgrims to Martin Luther King Jr.* Edited by Michael Warner. New York: Library of America, 1999.

Frame, John M. *The Doctrine of the Word of God*. Phillipsburg, NJ: P&R, 2010.

———. *A History of Western Philosophy*. Phillipsburg, NJ: P&R, 2015.

———. "Inerrancy: A Place to Live." *JETS* 57 (2014): 29-39.

———. *Systematic Theology*. Phillipsburg, NJ: P&R, 2013.

Frei, Hans. *The Eclipse of Biblical Narrative*. New Haven: Yale University Press, 1974.

Gaffin, Richard B., Jr. *God's Word in Servant-Form: Abraham Kuyper and Herman Bavinck on the Doctrine of Scripture*. Jackson, MS: Reformed Academic Press, 2008.

Garner, David B., ed. *Did God Really Say? Affirming the Truthfulness and Trustworthiness of Scripture*. Phillipsburg, NJ: P&R, 2012.

Gaussen, Louis. *The Divine Inspiration of Scripture*. Fearn, Ross-shire, Scotland: Christian Focus, 2007.

Gay, Peter, ed. *Deism: An Anthology*. Princeton, NJ: Van Nostrand, 1968.

Geisler, Norman L., ed. *Biblical Errancy: Its Philosophical Roots*. Grand Rapids: Zondervan, 1981.

———, ed. *Inerrancy*. Grand Rapids: Zondervan, 1979.

Geisler, Norman L., and William C. Roach. *Defending Inerrancy: Affirming the Accuracy of Scripture for a New Generation*. Grand Rapids: Baker, 2011.

Gentry, Peter J., and Stephen J. Wellum. *Kingdom through Covenant: A Biblical-Theological Understanding of the Covenants*. Wheaton, IL: Crossway, 2012.

George, Timothy. *Reading Scripture with the Reformers*. Downers Grove, IL: IVP Academic, 2011.

———. *Theology of the Reformers*. Rev. ed. Nashville: B&H Academic, 2013.

Gerstner, John H. *An Inerrancy Primer*. Grand Rapids: Baker, 1965.

Gignilliat, Mark S. *Old Testament Criticism: From Benedict Spinoza to Brevard Childs*. Grand Rapids: Zondervan, 2012.

Goldingay, John. *Models for Scripture*. Grand Rapids: Eerdmans; Carlisle, UK: Paternoster, 1994.

Goldsworthy, Graeme. *According to Plan: The Unfolding Revelation of God in the Bible*. Downers Grove, IL: IVP Academic, 1991.

Gordon, Bruce. *The Swiss Reformation*. New York: Manchester University Press, 2002.

Graves, Michael. *The Inspiration and Interpretation of Scripture: What the Early Church Can Teach Us*. Grand Rapids: Eerdmans, 2014.

Grenz, Stanley J. *A Primer on Postmodernism*. Grand Rapids: Eerdmans, 1996.

Grenz, Stanley J., and John R. Franke. *Beyond Foundationalism: Shaping Theology in a Postmodern Context*. Louisville: Westminster John Knox, 2001.

Hannah, John D., ed. *Inerrancy and the Church*. Chicago: Moody Press, 1984.

Harrisville, Roy A. *Pandora's Box Opened: An Examination and Defense of Historical-Critical Method and Its Master Practitioners*. Grand Rapids: Eerdmans, 2014.

Harrisville, Roy A., and Walter Sundberg. *The Bible in Modern Culture: Baruch Spinoza to Brevard Childs*. 2nd ed. Grand Rapids: Eerdmans, 2002.

Harvey, A. E. *Is Scripture Still Holy? Coming of Age with the New Testament*. Grand Rapids: Eerdmans, 2012.

Hatch. Nathan O., and Mark A. Noll, eds. *The Bible in America*. Oxford: Oxford University Press, 1982.

Hauerwas, Stanley. *Unleashing the Scripture: Freeing the Bible from Captivity to America*. Nashville: Abingdon, 1993.

Hays, Christopher M., and Christopher B. Ansberry, eds. *Evangelical Faith and the Challenge of Historical Criticism*. Grand Rapids: Baker Academic, 2013.

Helm, Paul, and Carl R. Trueman, eds. *The Trustworthiness of God: Perspectives on the Nature of Scripture*. Grand Rapids: Eerdmans, 2002.

Hendrix, Scott H. *Luther and the Papacy: Stages in a Reformation Conflict*. Philadelphia: Fortress, 1981.

———. *Martin Luther: Visionary Reformer*. New Haven: Yale University Press, 2015.

Henry, Carl F. H. *Evangelicals in Search of Identity*. Waco, TX: Word, 1976.

———. *God Who Speaks and Shows: Fifteen Theses, Part Three*. Vol. 4 of *God, Revelation, and Authority*. 6 vols. Reprint, Wheaton, IL: Crossway, 1999.

———, ed. *Revelation and the Bible: Contemporary Evangelical Thought*. Grand Rapids: Baker, 1974.

Hermann, Wilhelm. *The Communion of the Christian with God: Described on the Basis of Luther's Statements*. Edited by Robert T. Voelkel. Philadelphia: Fortress, 1971.

———. *Faith and Morals*. Translated by Donald Matheson and Robert W. Stewart. New York: Putnam, 1904.

———. *Systematic Theology*. Translated by Nathaniel Micklem and Kenneth A. Saunders. New York: Macmillan, 1927.

Hillerbrand, Hans J., ed. *The Protestant Reformation*. Rev. ed. New York: Harper Perennial, 2009.

Hodge, Archibald A., and Benjamin B. Warfield. *Inspiration*. Grand Rapids: Baker, 1979.

———. "Inspiration." *Presbyterian Review* 2, no. 6 (1881): 225–60.

Hodge, Charles. *Systematic Theology*. Vol. 1. Reprint, Grand Rapids: Eerdmans, 1986.

Hoffmeier, James K., and Dennis R. Magary, eds. *Do Historical Matters Matter to Faith? A Critical Appraisal of Modern and Postmodern Approaches to Scripture*. Wheaton, IL: Crossway, 2012.

Horton, Michael. *The Christian Faith*. Grand Rapids: Zondervan, 2011.

House, Paul. *Old Testament Theology*. Downers Grove, IL: IVP Academic, 2008.

Hughes, Philip E. *Theology of the English Reformers*. London: Hodder and Stoughton, 1965.

Huijgen, Arnold. *Divine Accommodation in John Calvin's Theology: Analysis and Assessment*. Edited by Herman J. Selderhuis. Reformed Historical Theology 16. Göttingen: Vandenhoeck & Ruprecht, 2011.

Hunsinger, George. *Thy Word Is Truth: Barth on Scripture*. Grand Rapids: Eerdmans, 2011.

Hyland, Paul, ed. *The Enlightenment: A Sourcebook and Reader.* London: Routledge, 2003.

Israel, Jonathan I. *Radical Enlightenment: Philosophy and the Making of Modernity 1650–1750.* New York: Oxford University Press, 2001.

Jensen, Peter. *The Revelation of God.* Downers Grove, IL: InterVarsity Press, 2002.

Johnson, Terry L. *The Case for Traditional Protestantism: The Solas of the Reformation.* Edinburgh: Banner of Truth Trust, 2004.

Kistler, Don, ed. *Sola Scriptura! The Protestant Position on the Bible.* Orlando, FL: Reformation Trust, 2009.

Kline, Meredith G. *The Structure of Biblical Authority.* 2nd ed. Eugene, OR: Wipf & Stock, 1997.

Kolb, Robert, and Charles P. Arand. *The Genius of Luther's Theology: A Wittenberg Way of Thinking for the Contemporary Church.* Grand Rapids: Baker Academic, 2008.

Kruger, Michael J. *Canon Revisited: Establishing the Origins and Authority of the New Testament Books.* Wheaton, IL: Crossway, 2012.

———. *The Question of Canon: Challenging the Status Quo in the New Testament Debate.* Downers Grove, IL: IVP Academic, 2013.

Küng, Hans. *Infallible? An Enquiry.* Translated by Eric Mosbacher. London: Collins, 1971.

La Due, William J. *The Chair of Saint Peter: A History of the Papacy.* Maryknoll, NY: Orbis, 1999.

Legaspi, Michael C. *The Death of Scripture and the Rise of Biblical Studies.* Oxford Studies in Historical Theology. New York: Oxford University Press, 2010.

Lessing, Gotthold. *Lessing's Theological Writings.* Translated by Henry Chadwick. A Library of Modern Religious Thought. Stanford, CA: Stanford University Press, 1956.

Levering, Matthew. *Engaging the Doctrine of Revelation: The Mediation of the Gospel through Church and Scripture.* Grand Rapids: Baker Academic, 2014.

Lewis, Gordon, and Bruce Demarest, eds. *Challenges to Inerrancy: A Theological Response.* Chicago: Moody, 1984.

Lightner, Robert. *A Biblical Case for Total Inerrancy: How Jesus Viewed the Old Testament.* Grand Rapids: Kregel, 1978.

Lindbeck, George. *The Nature of Doctrine: Religion and Theology in a Postliberal Age.* Louisville: Westminster John Knox, 1984.

Lindsell, Harold. *The Battle for the Bible.* Grand Rapids: Zondervan, 1976.

———. *The Bible in the Balance.* Grand Rapids: Zondervan, 1979.

Linnemann, Eta. *Biblical Criticism on Trial: How Scientific Is Scientific Theology?* Grand Rapids: Kregel, 2001.

———. *Historical Criticism of the Bible: Methodology or Ideology? Reflections of a Bultmannian Turned Evangelical.* Translated by Robert Yarbrough. Grand Rapids: Eerdmans, 1990.

Lints, Richard. *The Fabric of Theology: A Prolegomenon to Evangelical Theology.* Grand Rapids: Eerdmans, 1993.

Lohse, Bernhard. *Martin Luther's Theology.* Translated by Roy Harrisville. Minneapolis: Fortress, 1999.

Longfield, Bradley J. *The Presbyterian Controversy: Fundamentalists, Modernists, and Moderates.* New York: Oxford University Press, 1991.

Luhse, Bernhard. *Martin Luther: An Introduction to His Life and Work.* Minneapolis: Fortress, 1986.

Luther, Martin. *The Works of Martin Luther.* Edited by Jaroslav Pelikan and Helmut T. Lehmann. 55 vols. Philadelphia: Fortress, 1958–75.

MacArthur, John, ed. *The Inerrant Word: Biblical, Historical, Theological, and Pastoral Perspectives.* Wheaton, IL: Crossway, 2016.

———, ed. *The Scripture Cannot Be Broken: Twentieth Century Writings on the Doctrine of Inerrancy.* Wheaton, IL: Crossway, 2016.

———. *Why Believe the Bible?* Grand Rapids: Baker, 1980.

Machen, J. Gresham. *Christianity and Liberalism.* Grand Rapids: Eerdmans, 1923.

———. *J. Gresham Machen: Selected Shorter Writings.* Edited by D. G. Hart. Phillipsburg, NJ: P&R, 2004.

Maier, Gerhard. *The End of the Historical-Critical Method.* Translated by Edwin W. Leverenz and Rudolph F. Norden. St. Louis: Concordia, 1977.

Manly, Basil. *The Bible Doctrine of Inspiration.* Harrisonburg, VA: Gano, 1985.

Marsden, George M. *Fundamentalism and American Culture.* New York: Oxford University Press, 2006.

———. *Reforming Fundamentalism: Fuller Seminary and the New Evangelicalism.* Grand Rapids: Eerdmans, 1987.

Marshall, I. Howard. *Biblical Inspiration.* Grand Rapids: Eerdmans, 1982.

Mathison, Keith A. *The Shape of Sola Scriptura.* Moscow, ID: Canon, 2001.

McDonald, H. D. *Theories of Revelation: An Historical Study 1700–1960.* Grand Rapids: Baker, 1979.

McGowan, A. T. B. *The Divine Authenticity of Scripture: Retrieving an Evangelical Heritage.* Downers Grove, IL: IVP Academic, 2007.

McGrath, Alister E. *The Intellectual Origins of the European Reformation.* Oxford: Basil Blackwell, 1987.

———. *Reformation Thought.* 4th ed. Oxford: Wiley-Blackwell, 2012.

———. *Science and Religion: An Introduction.* Oxford: Blackwell, 1999.

McGuiness, Philip, et al., eds. *John Toland's Christianity Not Mysterious: Text, Associated Works, and Critical Essays.* Dublin: Lilliput, 1997.

Meadors, Gary T., ed. *Four Views on Moving beyond the Bible to Theology.* Grand Rapids: Zondervan, 2009.

Meadowcroft, Tim. *The Message of the Word of God.* The Bible Speaks Today. Downers Grove, IL: InterVarsity Press, 2011.

Merrick, J., and Stephen M. Garrett, eds. *Five Views on Biblical Inerrancy.* Grand Rapids: Zondervan, 2013.

Montgomery, John Warwick. *God's Inerrant Word: An International Symposium on the Trustworthiness of Scripture.* Minneapolis: Bethany Fellowship, 1973.

Morrison, John Douglas. *Has God Said? Scripture, the Word of God, and the Crisis of Theological Authority.* Evangelical Theological Society Monograph. Eugene, OR: Wipf & Stock, 2006.

Muller, Richard. *Post-Reformation Reformed Dogmatics.* Vol. 2, *Holy Scripture: The Cognitive Foundation of Theology.* Grand Rapids: Baker, 1993.

Muller, Richard A., and John Thompson, eds. *Biblical Interpretation in the Era of the Reformation.* Grand Rapids: Eerdmans, 1996.

Nash, Ronald. *The Word of God and the Mind of Man.* Grand Rapids: Zondervan, 1983.

Newman, John Henry. *An Essay on the Development of Christian Doctrine.* Notre Dame, IN: University of Notre Dame Press, 1989.

Nichols, Stephen J., and Eric T. Brandt. *Ancient Word, Changing Worlds: The Doctrine of Scripture in a Modern Age.* Wheaton, IL: Crossway, 2009.

Nicole, Roger R. "John Calvin and Inerrancy." *JETS* 25 (1982): 425–42.

Nicole, Roger R., and J. Ramsey Michaels, eds. *Inerrancy and Common Sense.* Grand Rapids: Baker, 1980.

Nietzsche, Friedrich. *The Will to Power.* Translated by Walter Kaufmann. New York: Vintage, 1967.

Noll, Mark A. *Between Faith and Criticism: Evangelicals, Scholarship, and the Bible in America.* 2nd ed. Grand Rapids: Baker, 2004.

Noll, Mark A., and Carolyn Nystrom. *Is the Reformation Over? An Evangelical Assessment of Contemporary Roman Catholicism.* Grand Rapids: Baker Academic, 2005.

Oberman, Heiko. *Forerunners of the Reformation: The Shape of Late Medieval Thought Illustrated by Key Documents.* Philadelphia: Fortress, 1981.

———. *The Harvest of Medieval Theology: Gabriel Biel and Late Medieval Nominalism.* Rev. ed. Cambridge: Harvard University Press, 1963.

———. *Luther: Man between God and the Devil.* New Haven: Yale University Press, 2006.

Olson, Roger E. *The Journey of Modern Theology: From Reconstruction to Deconstruction.* Downers Grove, IL: IVP Academic, 2013.

Owen, John. *The Causes, Ways, and Means of Understanding the Mind of God in His Word.* Vol. 4 of *The Works of John Owen.* Edited by William H. Goold. Edinburgh: Banner of Truth, 1967.

———. *Divine Original.* Vol. 16 of *The Works of John Owen.* Edited by William H. Goold. Edinburgh: Banner of Truth, 1967.

Ozment, Steven. *The Age of Reform, 1250–1550.* New Haven: Yale University Press, 1980.

Packer, J. I. *Beyond the Battle for the Bible.* Wheaton, IL: Crossway, 1980.

———. *"Fundamentalism" and the Word of God: Some Evangelical Principles*. Grand Rapids: Eerdmans, 1998.

———. *God Has Spoken: Revelation and the Bible*. 3rd ed. Grand Rapids: Baker, 1979.

———. *Truth and Power: The Place of Scripture in the Christian Life*. Downers Grove, IL: InterVarsity Press, 1999.

Padgett, Alan G., and Steve Wilkens. *Faith and Reason in the 19th Century*. Vol. 2 of *Christianity and Western Thought: A History of Philosophers, Ideas, and Movements*. Downers Grove, IL: IVP Academic, 2000.

———. *Journey to Postmodernity in the 20th Century*. Vol. 3 of *Christianity and Western Thought: A History of Philosophers, Ideas, and Movements*. Downers Grove, IL: IVP Academic, 2009.

Pearse, Meic. *The Great Restoration: The Religious Radicals of the 16th and 17th Centuries*. Carlisle, UK: Paternoster, 1998.

Peckham, John C. "Sola Scriptura: Reductio Ad Absurdum?" *Trinity Journal* 35 (2014): 195–223.

Pelikan, Jaroslav. *Obedient Rebels*. London: SCM, 1964.

Pelikan, Jaroslav, and Valerie Hotchkiss, eds. *Creeds and Confessions of Faith in Christian Tradition*. 3 vols. New Haven: Yale University Press, 2003.

Pinnock, Clark H. *Biblical Revelation: The Foundation of Christian Theology*. Chicago: Moody, 1971.

———. *A Defense of Biblical Infallibility*. Philadelphia: P&R, 1967.

———. *The Scripture Principle*. San Francisco: Harper & Row, 1984.

Piper, John. *A Peculiar Glory: How the Christian Scriptures Reveal Their Complete Truthfulness*. Wheaton, IL: Crossway, 2016.

Plummer, Robert L. *40 Questions about Interpreting the Bible*. Grand Rapids: Kregel, 2010.

Pope Pius IX. *Ineffabilis Deus*, "The Immaculate Conception" (December 8, 1854). Papal Encyclicals Online. http://www.papalencyclicals.net/Pius09/p9ineff.htm.

Pope Pius XII. *Munificentissimus Deus*, "Defining the Dogma of the Assumption" (November 1, 1950). Papal Encyclicals Online. http://www.vatican.va/holy_father/pius_xii/apost_constitutions/documents/hf_p-xii_apc_19501101_munificentissimus-deus_en.html.

Popkin, Richard. *The History of Scepticism: From Savonarola to Bayle*. New York: Oxford University Press, 2003.

Potter, G. R. *Zwingli*. New York: Cambridge University Press, 1976.

Poythress, Vern Sheridan. *Inerrancy and the Gospels: A God-Centered Approach to the Challenges of Harmonization*. Wheaton, IL: Crossway, 2012.

———. *Inerrancy and Worldview: Answering Modern Challenges to the Bible*. Wheaton, IL: Crossway, 2012.

Preus, J. Samuel. *Spinoza and the Irrelevance of Biblical Authority*. New York: Cambridge University Press, 2001.

Preus, Robert. *The Inspiration of Scripture: A Study of the Theology of the Seventeenth Century Lutheran Dogmaticians.* Concordia Heritage Series. Edinburgh: Oliver & Boyd, 1957.

Radmacher, Earl D., and Robert D. Preus, eds. *Hermeneutics, Inerrancy, and the Bible.* Grand Rapids: Zondervan, 1984.

Rahner, Karl, and Joseph Ratzinger. *Revelation and Tradition.* Translated by W. J. O'Hara. Freiburg: Herder, 1966.

Ridderbos, Herman. *Redemptive History and the New Testament Scriptures.* Translated by H. De Jongste. Biblical and Theological Studies. Phillipsburg, NJ: P&R, 1963.

Ritschl, Albrecht. *The Christian Doctrine of Justification and Reconciliation.* Translated by H. R. Mackintosh and A. B. Macaulay. Edinburgh: T&T Clark, 1902.

Rogers, Jack B., and Donald K. McKim. *The Authority and Interpretation of the Bible: An Historical Approach.* San Francisco: Harper & Row, 1979.

Rupp, E. Gordon. *Luther's Progress to the Diet of Worms.* New York: Harper & Row, 1964.

Rupp, E. Gordon, and Philip S. Watson, eds. *Luther and Erasmus: Free Will and Salvation.* Philadelphia: Westminster, 1969.

Satta, Ronald F. *The Sacred Text: Biblical Authority in Nineteenth-Century America.* Princeton Theological Monograph Series. Eugene, OR: Pickwick, 2007.

Satterthwaite, Philip E., and David F. Wright. *A Pathway into the Holy Scripture.* Grand Rapids: Eerdmans, 1994.

Saucy, Robert. *Scripture: Its Power, Authority, and Relevance.* Nashville: Thomas Nelson, 2001.

Schaeffer, Francis. *No Final Conflict: The Bible without Error in All That It Affirms.* Downers Grove, IL: InterVarsity Press, 1975.

Schleiermacher, Friedrich. *The Christian Faith.* Translated by H. R. Mackintosh and J. S. Stewart. 2 vols. New York: Harper & Row, 1963.

———. *On Religion: Addresses in Response to Its Cultured Critics (Research in Theology).* Translated by Terrence N. Tice. Richmond, VA: John Knox, 1969.

Schreiner, Susan E. *Are You Alone Wise? The Search for Certainty in the Modern Era.* Oxford Studies in Historical Theology. New York: Oxford University Press, 2011.

Schreiner, Thomas R. *The King in His Beauty: A Biblical Theology of the Old and New Testaments.* Grand Rapids: Baker Academic, 2013.

Schweitzer, Albert. *The Quest of the Historical Jesus.* Translated by W. Montgomery. London: A. & C. Black, 1922.

Sexton, Jason S. "How Far beyond Chicago? Assessing Recent Attempts to Reframe the Inerrancy Debate." *Themelios* 34, no. 1 (2009): 26–49.

Shead, Andrew G. *A Mouth Full of Fire: The Word of God in the Words of Jeremiah.* New Studies in Biblical Theology 29. Downers Grove, IL: InterVarsity Press, 2012.

Smith, Christian. *The Bible Made Impossible: Why Biblicism Is Not a Truly Evangelical Reading of Scripture*. Grand Rapids: Brazos, 2011.

Sparks, Kenton L. *God's Word in Human Words: An Evangelical Appropriation of Critical Biblical Scholarship*. Grand Rapids: Baker Academic, 2008.

———. *Sacred Word, Broken Word: Biblical Authority and the Dark Side of Scripture*. Grand Rapids: Eerdmans, 2012.

Spinoza, Baruch. *Tractatus Theologico-Politicus*. Translated by Samuel Shirley. Leiden: Brill, 1989.

Sproul, R. C. *Are We Together?* Orlando, FL: Reformation Trust, 2012.

———. *Scripture Alone: The Evangelical Doctrine*. Phillipsburg, NJ: P&R, 2005.

Stark, Thom. *The Human Faces of God: What Scripture Reveals When It Gets God Wrong (and Why Inerrancy Tries to Hide It)*. Eugene, OR: Wipf & Stock, 2011.

Steinmetz, David C. *The Bible in the Sixteenth Century*. Durham, NC: Duke University Press, 1990.

———. *Luther in Context*. 2nd ed. Grand Rapids: Baker Academic, 2002.

Stonehouse, N. B., and Paul Woolley, eds. *The Infallible Word: A Symposium by the Members of the Faculty of Westminster Theological Seminary*. 2nd ed. Phillipsburg, NJ: P&R, 2002.

Strange, Daniel, and Michael Ovey. *Confident: Why We Can Trust the Bible*. Fearn, Ross-shire, Scotland: Christian Focus, 2015.

Straus, David. *The Life of Jesus Critically Examined*. 4th ed. Edited by Peter C. Hodgson. Translated by George Eliot. Philadelphia: Fortress, 1972.

Strimple, Robert. "The Relationship between Scripture and Tradition in Contemporary Roman Catholic Theology." *Westminster Theological Journal* 40, no. 1 (1977): 22–38.

Swain, Scott R. *Trinity, Revelation, and Reading: A Theological Introduction to the Bible and Its Interpretation*. New York: T&T Clark, 2011.

Thompson, Mark D. *A Clear and Present Word: The Clarity of Scripture*. Downers Grove, IL: InterVarsity Press, 2006.

———. *A Sure Ground on Which to Stand: The Relation of Authority and Interpretive Method in Luther's Approach to Scripture*. Eugene, OR: Wipf & Stock, 2004.

Tierney, Brian. *The Crisis of Church and State, 1050–1300*. Englewood Cliffs, NJ: Prentice Hall, 1964.

———. *Origins of Papal Infallibility 1150–1350*. Leiden: Brill, 1988.

Tindal, Matthew. *Christianity as Old as the Creation*. London: Routledge, 1995.

Treier, Daniel J., and David Lauber, eds. *Trinitarian Theology for the Church: Scripture, Community, Worship*. Downers Grove, IL: IVP Academic, 2009.

Turretin, Francis. *Institutes of Elenctic Theology*. Vol. 1. Edited by James T. Dennison Jr. Translated by George Musgrave Giger. Phillipsburg, NJ: P&R, 1992.

van den Belt, Henk. *The Authority of Scripture in Reformed Theology*. Studies in Reformed Theology 17. Leiden: Brill, 2008.

Vanhoozer, Kevin J. *The Drama of Doctrine: A Canonical Linguistic Approach to Christian Theology*. Louisville: Westminster John Knox, 2005.

———. *First Theology: God, Scripture, and Hermeneutics*. Downers Grove, IL: InterVarsity Press, 2002.

———. *Is There a Meaning in This Text? The Bible, the Reader, and the Morality of Literary Knowledge*. Grand Rapids: Zondervan, 1998.

Vawter, Bruce. *Biblical Inspiration*. Theological Resources. Philadelphia: Westminster, 1972.

Volf, Miroslav. *Captive to the Word of God: Engaging the Scriptures for Contemporary Theological Reflection*. Grand Rapids: Eerdmans, 2010.

von Harnack, Adolf. *History of Dogma*. Translated by Neil Buchanan. 7 vols. 3rd ed. New York: Dover, 1961.

———. *The Origin of the New Testament*. Translated by J. R. Wilkinson. New York: Macmillan, 1925.

———. *Outlines of the History of Dogma*. Translated by Edwin Knox Mitchell. Boston: Beacon, 1957.

———. *What Is Christianity?* Translated by Thomas Bailey Saunders. Philadelphia: Fortress, 1986.

Vos, Geerhardus. *Biblical Theology*. Grand Rapids: Eerdmans, 1948.

Wallace, Daniel B. *Revisiting the Corruption of the New Testament: Manuscript, Patristic, and Apocryphal Evidence*. Grand Rapids: Kregel, 2011.

Walton, John H., and D. Brent Sandy. *The Lost World of Scripture: Ancient Literary Culture and Biblical Authority*. Downers Grove, IL: InterVarsity Press, 2013.

Walvoord, John F., ed. *Inspiration and Interpretation*. Grand Rapids: Eerdmans, 1957.

Ward, Timothy. *Word and Supplement: Speech Acts, Biblical Texts, and the Sufficiency of Scripture*. Oxford: Oxford University Press, 2002.

———. *Words of Life: Scripture as the Living and Active Word of God*. Downers Grove, IL: IVP Academic, 2009.

Warfield, Benjamin Breckinridge. *Revelation and Inspiration*. Vol. 1 of *The Works of Benjamin B. Warfield*. Grand Rapids: Baker, 2003.

———. *Selected Shorter Writings*. Edited by John Meeter. 2 vols. Nutley, NJ: Presbyterian and Reformed, 1973.

Webster, John. *The Domain of the Word: Scripture and Theological Reason*. T&T Clark Theology. London: T&T Clark, 2012.

———. *Holy Scripture: A Dogmatic Sketch*. Cambridge: Cambridge University Press, 2003.

Wellhausen, Julius. *Prolegomena to the History of Israel*. Edinburgh: A. & C. Black, 1885.

Wenham, John. *Christ and the Bible*. 3rd ed. Grand Rapids: Baker, 1994.

Whitaker, William. *Disputations on Holy Scripture*. Morgan, PA: Soli Deo Gloria, 2000.

White, James R. *Scripture Alone: Exploring the Bible's Accuracy, Authority, and Authenticity*. Minneapolis: Bethany, 2004.

Williams, D. H. *Evangelicals and Tradition: The Formative Influence of the Early Church*. Grand Rapids: Baker Academic, 2005.

———. *Retrieving the Tradition and Renewing Evangelicalism: A Primer for Suspicious Protestants*. Grand Rapids: Eerdmans, 1999.

Williams, George Huntston. *The Radical Reformation*. Philadelphia: Westminster, 1962.

Williams, George H., and Angel Mergal, eds. *Spiritual and Anabaptist Writers*. Philadelphia: Westminster, 1957.

Williamson, Paul R. *Sealed with an Oath: Covenant in God's Unfolding Purpose*. Downers Grove, IL: InterVarsity Press, 2007.

Wolterstorff, Nicholas. *Divine Discourse: Philosophical Reflections on the Claim That God Speaks*. Cambridge: Cambridge University Press, 1995.

Woodbridge, John D. *Biblical Authority: A Critique of the Rogers/McKim Proposal*. Grand Rapids: Zondervan, 1982.

———. "Evangelical Self-Identity and the Doctrine of Biblical Inerrancy." Pages 104–40 in *Understanding the Times: New Testament Studies in the 21st Century*. Edited by Andreas J. Köstenberger and Robert W. Yarbrough. Wheaton, IL: Crossway, 2011.

Work, Telford. *Living and Active: Scripture in the Economy of Salvation*. Sacra Doctrina. Grand Rapids: Eerdmans, 2002.

Worthen, Molly. *Apostles of Reason: The Crisis of Authority in American Evangelicalism*. Oxford: Oxford University Press, 2014.

Wright, N. T. *The Last Word: Beyond the Bible Wars to a New Understanding of the Authority of Scripture*. San Francisco: HarperSanFrancisco, 2005.

———. *Surprised by Scripture: Engaging Contemporary Issues*. New York: HarperOne, 2014.

Yarbrough, Robert W. "Bye-Bye Bible? Progress Report on the Death of Scripture." *Themelios* 39, no. 3 (2014): 415–27.

———. "The Future of Cognitive Reverence for the Bible." *JETS* 57, no. 1 (2014): 5–18.

———. "Should Evangelicals Embrace Historical Criticism? The Hays-Ansberry Proposal." *Themelios* 39, no. 1 (2014): 37–52.

Young, E. J. *Thy Word Is Truth: Some Thoughts on the Biblical Doctrine of Inspiration*. Edinburgh: Banner of Truth, 1957. Reprint, 1997.

Zwingli, Ulrich. *Ulrich Zwingli (1484–1531): Selected Works*. Translated by Lawrence A. McLouth. Reprint, Philadelphia: University of Pennsylvania Press, 1972.

Scripture Index

Subject Index

Faith Alone—The Doctrine of Justification

What the Reformers Taught ... and Why It Still Matters

Thomas Schreiner; Matthew Barrett, Series Editor

Historians and theologians have long recognized that at the heart of the sixteenth-century Protestant Reformation were five declarations, often referred to as the five "solas": *sola Scriptura*, *solus Christus*, *sola gratia*, *sola fide*, and *soli Deo gloria*. These five statements summarize much of what the Reformation was about, and they distinguish Protestantism from other expressions of the Christian faith. Protestants place ultimate and final authority in the Scriptures, acknowledge the work of Christ alone as sufficient for redemption, recognize that salvation is by grace alone through faith alone, and seek to do all things for God's glory.

In *Faith Alone—The Doctrine of Justification*, renowned biblical scholar Thomas Schreiner looks at the historical and biblical roots of the doctrine of justification. He summarizes the history of the doctrine, looking at the early church and the writings of several of the Reformers. Then he turns his attention to the Scriptures and walks readers through an examination of the key texts in the Old and New Testament. He discusses whether justification is transformative or forensic and introduces readers to some of the contemporary challenges to the Reformation teaching of *sola fide*, with particular attention to the new perspective on Paul.

Five hundred years after the Reformation, the doctrine of justification by faith alone still needs to be understood and proclaimed. In *Faith Alone* you will learn how the rallying cry of "sola fide" is rooted in the Scriptures and how to apply this *sola* in a fresh way in light of many contemporary challenges.

God's Glory Alone—
The Majestic Heart of
Christian Faith and Life

What the Reformers Taught
... and Why It Still Matters

*David VanDrunen; Matthew Barrett,
Series Editor*

Historians and theologians have long recognized that at the heart of the sixteenth-century Protestant Reformation were five declarations, often referred to as the "solas": *sola Scriptura, solus Christus, sola gratia, sola fide,* and *soli Deo gloria.* These five statements summarize much of what the Reformation was about, and they distinguish Protestantism from other expressions of the Christian faith. Protestants place ultimate and final authority in the Scriptures, acknowledge the work of Christ alone as sufficient for redemption, recognize that salvation is by grace alone through faith alone, and seek to do all things for God's glory.

In *God's Glory Alone—The Majestic Heart of Christian Faith and Life,* renowned scholar David VanDrunen looks at the historical and biblical roots of the idea that all glory belongs to God alone. He examines the development of this theme in the Reformation, in subsequent Reformed theology and confessions, and in contemporary theologians who continue to be inspired by the conviction that all glory belongs to God. Then he turns to the biblical story of God's glory, beginning with the pillar of cloud and fire revealed to Israel, continuing through the incarnation, death, and exaltation of the Lord Jesus Christ, and culminating in Christ's second coming and the glorification of his people. In light of these stunning biblical themes he concludes by addressing several of today's great cultural challenges and temptations—such as distraction and narcissism—and reflecting on how commitment to God's glory alone fortifies us to live godly lives in this present evil age.

Christ Alone– The Uniqueness of Jesus as Savior

What the Reformers Taught . . . and Why It Still Matters

Stephen Wellum; Matthew Barrett, Series Editor

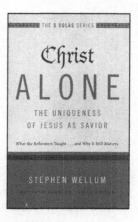

Historians and theologians alike have long recognized that at the heart of the sixteenth-century Protestant Reformation were five declarations (or "*solas*") that distinguished the movement from other expressions of the Christian faith.

Five-hundred years later, we live in a different time with fresh challenges to our faith. Yet these rallying cries of the Reformation continue to speak to us, addressing a wide range of contemporary issues. The Five Solas series will help you understand the historical and biblical context of the five *solas* and how to live out the relevance of Reformation theology today.

In *Christ Alone–The Uniqueness of Jesus as Savior*, Stephen Wellum considers Christ's singular uniqueness and significance biblically, historically, and today in our pluralistic and postmodern age. He examines the historical roots of the doctrine, especially in the Reformation era, and then shows how the uniqueness of Christ has come under specific attack today. Then he walks us through the storyline of Scripture from Christ's unique identity and work as prophet, priest, and king to the application of his work to believers and our covenantal union with him to show that apart from Christ there is no salvation. Wellum shows that we must recover a robust biblical and theological doctrine of Christ's person and work in the face of today's challenges and explains why a fresh appraisal of the Reformation understanding of Christ alone is needed today.

Grace Alone—Salvation as a Gift of God

What the Reformers Taught ... and Why It Still Matters

Carl Trueman; Matthew Barrett, Series Editor

Historians and theologians alike have long rec-
ognized that at the heart of the sixteenth-century Protestant Reformation
were the five "*solas*": *sola Scriptura, solus Christus, sola gratia, sola fide,*
and *soli Deo gloria*. These five *solas* do not merely summarize what the
Reformation was all about but have served to distinguish Protestantism
ever since. They set Protestants apart in a unique way as those who place
ultimate and final authority in the Scriptures, acknowledge the work of
Christ alone as sufficient for redemption, recognize that salvation is by
grace alone through faith alone, and seek to not only give God all the
glory but to do all things vocationally for his glory.

The year 2017 will mark the 500th anniversary of the Reformation. And
yet, even in the twenty-first century we need the Reformation more than
ever. As James Montgomery Boice said not long ago, while the Puritans
sought to carry on the Reformation, today "we barely have one to carry
on, and many have even forgotten what that great spiritual revolution
was all about." Therefore we "need to go back and start again at the very
beginning. We need another Reformation."* In short, it is crucial not only
to remember what the *solas* of the Reformation were all about but also to
apply these *solas* in a fresh way in light of many contemporary challenges.

* James Montgomery Boice, "Preface," in *Here We Stand: A Call from Confessing
Evangelicals* (Grand Rapids: Baker, 1996), 12.